MISSOURI UNDER RADICAL RULE
1865–1870

Missouri Under Radical Rule

1865-1870

by

WILLIAM E. PARRISH

UNIVERSITY OF MISSOURI PRESS

Columbia · Missouri

PUBLICATION OF THIS BOOK

HAS BEEN AIDED BY THE FORD FOUNDATION PROGRAM

TO SUPPORT PUBLICATION,

THROUGH UNIVERSITY PRESSES, OF WORK IN THE

HUMANITIES AND SOCIAL SCIENCES

To MY PARENTS

PREFACE

THE FIVE YEARS following the Civil War were a critical period in Missouri's history. The state had suffered physically and emotionally during the conflict, and the bitter political and military struggles of the war years had left Missourians divided and wary. The conservative groups that had long dominated the politics and economics of the state found themselves split over a variety of issues. Into the power vacuum thus created stepped a group of opportunists who had coalesced their various interests in the Radical Union party. Few of these men had enjoyed any measure of prestige or power before the war. Now they found themselves linked by their desire to rid Missouri of slavery, which, while it did not dominate the state's economy, did symbolize the vaunted power of conservative rule. Generally progressive in their outlook, the Radicals anticipated a large-scale influx of population and capital into the state if Missouri could change its image from a state beridden with guerrilla warfare to one offering opportunity and advancement to all newcomers. Although somewhat divergent in their views of how to accomplish this, Radical leadership under Charles D. Drake secured the adoption of a rather thorough and generally forward-looking revision of the state's constitution. In the immediate postwar era the General Assembly, under Radical domination, passed a variety of laws reflecting much progressive wisdom. The state advanced economically and socially, and the foundations of a modern educational system were laid. Having freed the slaves from bondage, the Radical leadership did not abandon the Negro to fend for himself; rather, they sponsored a comprehensive package of civil rights and education for the freedmen while trying to move the white population toward a gradual acceptance of the idea of Negro suffrage.

Yet, for all the progress made by Missouri during this period, the shadow of proscription loomed heavily over the scene. The methods used by the Radicals to maintain themselves in power heightened political bitterness and paved the way for the breakup of their coalition and the eventual downfall of the party. In view of their vindictiveness, the positive contributions of the Radicals to Missouri's development have frequently been overlooked. It is the hope of the author that this work will help to restore a balanced picture of Missouri under Radical rule.

This study has benefited from the assistance of numerous individuals and institutions. The author wishes to thank especially the staffs of the Manuscripts Division of the Library of Congress, the National Archives, the Huntington Library, and the Reeves Library at Westminster College; Mrs. Ernst A. Stadler, archivist of the Missouri Historical Society at St. Louis; Dr. Richard S. Brownlee, Mr. James E. Moss, Mr. Kenneth Holmes, Mrs. Elizabeth Comfort, and their assistants at the State Historical Society of Missouri; Dr. Lorenzo Greene of Lincoln University; and my Westminster colleagues, Professors John H. Keiser and Robert G. Hoerber. The American Association for State and Local History provided a research grant that made possible the exploration of materials in Washington and St. Louis, and a sabbatical leave granted by Westminster College enabled me to complete the writing of this manuscript.

To my wife, Kaye, a special place of mention must be given in appreciation of her valuable aid as chief editor and critic; this book owes much to her understanding and inspiration.

W.E.P.

Fulton, Missouri
April, 1965

CONTENTS

CHAPTER I

THE RISE OF RADICALISM

F ROM ITS high perch above the chairman's desk the American Eagle towered over the assembling delegates on that Saturday, January 7, 1865. The small hall of the St. Louis Mercantile Library had been "tastefully fitted up" with American flags, which had been draped around the chandeliers and along the wall beneath the King of Birds, while "starry bunting hung in graceful folds about the iron pillars supporting the ceiling." The seats that ordinarily filled the room had been replaced by tables and chairs more adapted to the comfort and convenience of those who were to occupy these precincts for the next three months. All stood in readiness for the Missouri State Convention of 1865. The committee in charge of arrangements, appointed at the opening session the previous afternoon, had done its work quite efficiently.[1]

The men who gathered that morning at the Mercantile Library had come at the direction of a large majority of Missouri voters to plan the future course of their state. Missouri,

here at the close of the Civil War, was emerging from four
long, terrible years of internecine strife. Bushwhackers and
guerrillas still roamed many areas of the state and continued
to terrorize the populace.[2] Neighbor distrusted neighbor, as
many of the ex-Confederates began to drift back home in the
wake of disaster and defeat. Some counties with dominant
Unionist sentiments made it abundantly clear that the returning "rebels" were not welcome.[3] In an effort to secure peace
the same voters who had approved the meeting of this convention had also swept a new political party into power. Missourians had temporarily turned their backs on the well-tried
conservative leadership of a dead era; they now faced the
future riding on a high wave of Radicalism.

Missouri's Unionist element had kept the state in the Union
in 1861 by a great effort and under exceedingly adverse circumstances.[4] This group, however, embraced a wide range of
political tenets. The more conservative Unionists, under the
leadership of Provisional Governor Hamilton R. Gamble, desired to preserve the *status quo* as much as possible while
still asserting Missouri's sovereignty over its own internal
affairs against federal encroachment. They represented the
vested-property interests of the state and had long held both
political and economic domination. When the Lincoln administration began to push the issue of emancipating the slaves
in the border states in the spring of 1862, the conservatives
resisted any such move. As their brethren in the other border
states, they failed to see the inevitable outcome of the civil
conflict and clung to the vain hope that the future would be
as ordered as the past.[5] By their continued intransigence the
conservatives forced the more liberal, progressive Unionists
into increasingly open opposition. This liberal group included
a variety of elements: the Germans, who first began coming
into Missouri in large numbers during the 1850's, with their
strong antislavery bent; the small farmers and the poor whites
of the Ozark area, who had no interest in slavery but who

saw their region continually torn by guerrilla warfare because of it; the St. Louis merchants and would-be capitalists, who feared that the presence of slavery would stifle the state's potential for economic growth after the war; and a few ardent abolitionists, who sincerely desired the betterment of the Negro's lot.[6]

In the legislative election of 1862 the question of emancipation was the major issue. The old party labels had long since disappeared. Since many of the state's citizens had been barred from the polls because of their refusal to take the loyalty oath prescribed by the Provisional Government, only the Unionists were able to vote. Yet, within the Unionists' ranks three rather distinct factions had begun to emerge: the Charcoals, who favored some form of speedy emancipation; the middle-of-the-road Claybanks, who were slowly facing up to the inevitability of emancipation, but who hoped that the process would take place gradually and that a definite plan of compensation would be offered to the slaveowner; and the Snowflakes, who still refused to give an inch on the slavery question. Although the results of the election were mixed, they did reveal that most of the Missourians who voted favored some form of emancipation. Because the vote was divided rather evenly between the Charcoals and the Claybanks, no concrete plan for emancipation emerged in the legislative session that followed.[7]

Pressure for decisive action continued to mount. In June, 1863, Governor Gamble, who by this time had adopted a more moderate position, called the state convention of 1861 into session for the fifth time since its inception. This body had originally been called in March of 1861 to consider the question of secession; however, after Union military forces had driven the regular state government into exile, it had established the Provisional Government in July of that same year. Since that time the convention had served as a quasi-legislative arm of the Provisional Government. This particular session of the convention, dominated by the Claybank faction, produced, after long and sometimes vitriolic debate, an emancipation ordinance that provided for the extinction of slavery in Missouri on July 4, 1870. This ordinance also contained a provision stipulating that varying periods of apprenticeship of the slaves under their former owners would follow their liberation, with the length of apprenticeship being determined by the age of the slave at the time of emancipation.[8]

Such a slow-paced program proved too much for the Charcoals. They launched a full-scale campaign against the Gamble administration over the question of emancipation and other issues. Many of them had long felt that the Provisional Government was too lenient in its dealings with Southern sympathizers. They attributed the continuance of guerrilla warfare in Missouri to the insistence of Gamble that only the state militia was to be used to preserve internal order. These troops had proved inadequate in the eyes of the Charcoals, and they wanted greater federal protection. The Union military commander at St. Louis, Major General John M. Schofield, had favored the Gamble policy because it meant the release of regular troops for badly needed service elsewhere, and President Lincoln had sustained this program for the same reason. The Charcoals, however, saw only the turmoil around them. They strongly feared that the continuation of the unsettled conditions in Missouri, which had been enhanced by the unrealistic emancipation policy just enacted, would seriously handicap their hopes for Missouri's economic development after the war. To remedy this situation, they called for the removal of the conservative Provisional Government and urged that federal intervention be increased.

In the late summer of 1863 the Radical Union party of Missouri began to coalesce around the various liberal elements. Leading the movement was Charles Daniel Drake, a St. Louis attorney whose political views had almost undergone a complete metamorphosis since the beginning of the war. Drake, who was a skilled demagogue and opportunist, had once studied law under Governor Gamble. In the 1850's he had been successively a Whig, a Know-Nothing, and a Democrat. In the election of 1860 he supported Stephen A. Douglas and Claiborne Jackson, and as late as July, 1861, he still spoke out strongly against antislavery agitation. During the following winter, however, Drake experienced a profound conversion; he came to see slavery as the root of all the state's difficulties. By the spring of 1862 he had become an ardent advocate of emancipation.[9]

Drake assumed command of the Radical cause at the state convention of 1863. After being defeated there in his attempt to secure more immediate emancipation, he carried the fight to the people. During July and August he toured central and western Missouri, speaking almost daily to those who shared his sympathies. Others joined him in spreading the message: George R. Smith, who had suffered financial reverses as a town builder in the war-torn area in the western part of the state; Henry T. Blow, Drake's brother-in-law, who was a St. Louis merchant and a would-be entrepreneur in lead mining; J. T. K. Hayward, president of the Hannibal and St. Joseph Railroad, who had already begun an active campaign to lure emigrants to settle along his right of way; Emil Pretorius, the able editor of the German-language newspaper *Westliche Post* in St. Louis. Radical papers sprang into existence to help propagate the gospel of immediate emancipation. Their articles also denounced the "Gamble regime" and conservative rule as roadblocks on the highway to progress. With each passing month the tempo quickened, the language became more vituperative, and the mood assumed more bitter and vindictive characteristics. At the end of July, 1863, a call went out for a mass Radical convention to be held at Jefferson City on September 1. Drake and his coworkers did their best to drum up enthusiasm for this meeting. In the midst of their exhortations guerrilla warfare reached a climax when Quan-

trill and his men raided Lawrence, Kansas, on August 21. The
Missouri-Kansas border was aflame. It appeared for a few
days that Kansans would make a retaliatory strike into Missouri. Although General Schofield went quickly to the border
and took personal charge of matters, the Radicals on both
sides of the state line cried out against Gamble's supposed
laxness and demanded more positive federal action.[10]

When the Radical mass convention met in September, it
attracted about seven hundred delegates from approximately
three-fourths of the counties in Missouri. This meeting officially launched the new party on the road of political opportunity. With Drake setting the tone in his address as keynote
speaker, the group called for the resignation of the Provisional
Government, the removal of General Schofield, the appointment of a committee of seventy to carry the grievances of the
Radicals to President Lincoln, and the establishment of a committee of public safety to supervise the protection of the loyal
citizenry. The convention also nominated candidates for the
special election of justices to the Supreme Court of Missouri,
which was scheduled for November. This election would mark
the first real political test of the newly organized Radical
Union party.[11]

At the end of September Drake led the committee of seventy to Washington. They secured an interview with President Lincoln but received little help from him. He refused
to consider the removal of General Schofield. With the need
for troops so great in Tennessee and elsewhere, he hesitated
to give serious consideration to their demand for the replace-
ment of Missouri militia by federal forces. He did agree, however, that there should be strict observation at the polls in
order to guarantee that only those who had taken the loyalty
oath voted.[12]

The campaign for the election of the Supreme Court justices revealed a Radical strategy that was to become increasingly familiar. In rally after rally across the state, Radical

speakers denounced their Conservative opponents as "copperheads" who were not true Union men. Some urged the election of judges who would unseat the Provisional Government on constitutional grounds. Soon there emerged among the Radicals an unrelenting attitude of vindictiveness toward anyone who disagreed with their political party and its platform.[13] Coupled with and underlying this vituperativeness was a Radical appeal to the business interests to support them as the party of progress, which could ensure an atmosphere in the state conducive to the attraction of immigrants and commercial investment. The Radicals urged the laboring man to join them in the battle of democracy versus aristocracy and to avoid the Conservative circles, which looked upon him merely as "poor white trash." They admonished the eligible soldier electorate to vote as they shot—that is, to support the "loyal men" in their efforts to secure protection at home for all "true" Unionists.[14] Such appeals as these were to be issued again and again by Radical orators in subsequent campaigns.

Since the Conservatives were the political group in power and therefore had control of most of the state offices and the patronage that went with them, they did not consider it necessary to establish an official party organization. Furthermore, they enjoyed the favor of the national administration and its military commander at St. Louis, which strengthened their cause. They supported the incumbent judges, who had been appointed by Governor Gamble in 1862, and replied to the Radicals' charges mainly through their own press. Appealing to the basic conservative natures of Missourians, they attacked their Radical opponents as opportunists who were more concerned with securing office than working for the welfare of the state. They often placed their foes on the defensive by directing public attention to their incendiary statements. They pictured the Radicals as desperate men ready to undertake revolution, if necessary, to accomplish their ends. In this last charge they could point to General

Schofield's obvious concern over the matter, as evinced by his
directive, issued in the middle of September, that promised
fines and punishment for those endeavoring to promote dis-
affection among the militia or trying to incite violence among
the people.[15]

The results of the election proved to be close, and the final
outcome was in doubt for some weeks. Considerable dispute
arose over the vote of the soldiers; the Conservatives charged
fraud in some returns, and the Radicals claimed that the legal
ballots of many soldiers went uncounted. The official returns,
when finally announced, showed the Conservative ticket victorious by a vote of 43,180 to 40,744. General Schofield reported to the President that it had been a quiet election. This
was confirmed by most of the outstate press.[16] An analysis
of this initial test of strength of the Radicals reveals that the
party received its strongest support in the southwest, where
guerrilla warfare had worked its greatest havoc; in the extreme northern parts of the state; and in St. Louis and its
immediate vicinity, where the German vote was the determining factor in the majorities. The Conservatives dominated
the central and southeastern areas along the rivers, where
the large landowners concerned with the security of their
slaves and other tangible property resided.[17]

Although temporarily sobered by their setback in the judicial contest, the Radicals moved forward by consolidating
their strength in the Missouri General Assembly, which convened in December. They secured the election of B. Gratz
Brown to the United States Senate, and they supported the
moderately conservative John B. Henderson, who had been
serving by appointment since 1862, for the other Senate seat.
Brown, who had a long antislavery record stretching back to
the 1850's when he was editor of the St. Louis *Missouri
Democrat,* had been an ardent Radical from the outset of the
movement. Henderson had been among the small Conservative minority that realized at an early date that Missouri

must face up to the ultimate emancipation of its slaves. He had worked toward this end both in Washington and at home. From this time forward he was to move progressively into the ranks of the Radicals in order to protect his political future.[18]

By February, 1864, the Radicals had become strong enough to push through a bill calling for a referendum at the fall election on the question of holding a new state convention to consider emancipation, suffrage, and revision of Missouri's constitution. Apparently confident of the outcome of such a referendum, the Radicals included in the bill a provision stipulating that members of the convention would be chosen in the same election.[19]

Internally, the Radicals faced a crisis in 1864 over the problem of whom to support for the Presidency. Many of the more fervent spirits within the Missouri party, as well as many within the Radical movement nationally, considered Lincoln's policies too conservative. Condemning him for not having gone beyond the Emancipation Proclamation of January 1, 1863, they ardently demanded further action in the border states. This extreme group also feared that Lincoln's amnesty proclamation of December, 1863, heralding his future program of reconstruction, was too conciliatory to former rebels, and they particularly dreaded its political consequences. They not only deplored Lincoln's retention of the conservative Edward Bates, who was Gamble's brother-in-law, and the moderate Montgomery Blair in the Cabinet but also bitterly resented his continued support of the Provisional Government. One indication of the reluctance of many Radicals to support Lincoln for a second term, in view of their realization of the inevitability of his renomination, can be seen in the vote on a resolution introduced in the Missouri General Assembly in January, 1864, to endorse his candidacy. The motion was tabled by a vote of 46 to 37 with 39 legislators absent or not voting. Only three Radicals supported the resolution, and most of the absentees, who obviously de-

sired to avoid the issue so early in the race, came from that
camp. A subsequent motion to endorse the administration
generally also failed, the vote being 46 to 33 with 44 absent.[20]
Ultimately, the responsible Radical leadership realized that
it had no choice but to co-operate with the national Republican party regardless of the outcome of the national convention.
Although some Missouri Radicals, led by B. Gratz Brown,
joined their compatriots from fifteen other states in the abor-
tive nomination of General John C. Frémont at Cleveland in
May, the regular party leadership controlled the state convention and sent an uncommitted delegation to the Republican national convention at Baltimore.[21]

The Conservatives, meanwhile, had been organizing Lincoln
clubs throughout Missouri and loudly proclaiming their support of the President. They held a state convention in May
and also nominated delegates to go to Baltimore. These men
were pledged to vote for Lincoln for a second term.[22] It consequently became a question, and a quite vital one, as to
which delegation from Missouri would secure official party
recognition. A series of intricate political maneuvers at Baltimore resulted in the seating of the Radicals. This group
promptly embarrassed those who supported its admission to
the convention by casting the only votes on the first ballot
against the nomination of Lincoln for the Presidency. The
Missourians supported General Ulysses S. Grant, but to no
avail; they then graciously moved to give the President the
unanimous support of the convention. Important to Missouri
in the proceedings at Baltimore was the official stamp of acceptance given the Radicals by the national party. The withdrawal of Frémont from the presidential race later that fall
made full unity of the Missouri Radicals possible.

The rejection of the Missouri Conservatives at the convention left that group in an untenable position politically unless
it wished to divide the Union vote. Some Conservatives
quietly supported the Lincoln ticket but refrained from any

action on the state level. The rest drifted into the ranks of the Democratic party, which the remainder of Missouri's "old guard" had resuscitated in June.[23]

The state-wide election contest in 1864 thus revolved around the Radical Republican and the Democratic tickets. The Radicals nominated Colonel Thomas C. Fletcher for governor. Because Fletcher had been serving as a brigade commander with Sherman's Army of the Tennessee, he had not been active in recent state politics and therefore made an ideal compromise candidate. Drake and other Radical leaders had tended to alienate one group or another by their stands on various questions, but Fletcher had not offended anyone. Indeed, his military record, which was to be further enhanced before the election, could be cited with considerable commendation by the party that sought "to secure the peace for which the men were fighting."[24] General Thomas L. Price headed the Democratic ticket. A wealthy merchant and landowner, Price had earned his commission with state troops during the Mexican War. Having been a staunch Benton Democrat in the 1850's, he had a long political career, which included a term as mayor of Jefferson City and brief service in both the Missouri General Assembly and the national House of Representatives.[25]

General Sterling Price's invasion of the state interrupted the electoral campaign. The marauding Confederates reached the Missouri River and traveled almost the entire width of the state before meeting defeat at the Battle of Westport, after which they were driven back into Arkansas. The Price raid took place during most of October and made any extensive canvass virtually impossible, which undoubtedly aided the Radical cause. Colonel Fletcher had returned home in time to participate actively in the drive against the Price raiders. Although his gubernatorial opponent held no relationship to the Confederate general, the similarity of their names did not help Thomas Price.[26]

When the ballots had been counted, the Radicals had triumphed decisively. Fletcher led the ticket with a 40,000-vote
majority, and the state went for Lincoln by about the same
margin. This victory gave the Radicals control of both houses
of the new General Assembly by strong majorities. They
swept every congressional race except the one in the First
District, where a Radical split between pro- and anti-Lincoln
factions made it possible for Democrat John Hogan to be
elected. The Radical proposal for a new state convention met
with strong approval, and approximately three-fourths of the
men selected to sit therein belonged to the Radical camp.[27]
A comparison of the election map of 1864 with that of 1863
gives an even clearer picture of the Radical sweep. Only
fifteen counties produced Democratic majorities in this presidential election year. These consisted of a block along the
Missouri River on the western border of the state, the area
of "Little Dixie" in central Missouri, and four scattered counties in the southeast. With one exception, these counties were
to be consistently in the conservative Democratic camp
throughout the postwar era. For the most part their faithful-
ness to the party of the "right" can be attributed to either a
relatively large Negro population or a high per-capita value
of real and personal property, or in some cases to both.[28]

Many factors helped secure this Radical victory. Because
of the decision of the Baltimore convention, the Radicals became linked with the Lincoln administration, which certainly
strengthened their appeal to the uncommitted portion of the
electorate. General Sherman's campaign in Georgia and General Grant's relentlessness in Virginia, which seemed to bring
the end of war within sight, aided the administration ticket
in Missouri, as elsewhere. The Price raid, coming after a
renewal of guerrilla warfare, contributed to general dissatisfaction over the Conservatives' seeming ineptness. Many now
accepted the Radicals' promises that they could bring peace
and tranquillity to the state. The death of Governor Gamble

early in 1864 had removed the Conservatives' strongest political figure, and they had no one who could adequately fill the void. The comparative military records of the respective gubernatorial candidates further benefited the Radical cause. In addition, the disfranchisement of many Missourians under the test oath of 1861 eliminated a bloc of votes that undoubtedly would have fallen to the Democratic side. Nearly 52,000 fewer Missourians went to the polls in 1864 than in the previous presidential election.

Undergirding all these factors was the apparent feeling of most Missourians that new times demanded new leadership. As they faced a future fraught with many problems, social and economic, Missourians handed the Radicals the reins of power in a decisive fashion. Governor Fletcher, in his inaugural address on January 2, 1865, presented the challenge to the Twenty-third General Assembly: "Being victorious everywhere, let magnanimity now distinguish our action; and, having nothing more to ask for party, let us, forgetful of past differences, seek only to promote the general good of the people of the whole commonwealth."[29]

Yet, it was not so much the General Assembly as the forthcoming state convention that was to set the pattern of reconstruction and progress for the next five years. It remained to the delegates gathering under the American Eagle in the Mercantile Library to map out Missouri's future.

CHAPTER II

THE MISSOURI STATE
CONVENTION OF 1865

N EARLY THREE-FOURTHS of the sixty-six delegates to the 1865 state convention were Radical Unionists. Few of them had had much political experience. Only thirteen lawyers could be found in their ranks. Fourteen of the delegates followed agricultural pursuits, twelve were merchants, and another fourteen practiced medicine. Of the remainder, no two could be found to be of the same occupation. A local minister, who viewed the dominant philosophy of the group with favor, thought that "taken as a whole, they were in capacity mediocre, and most of them by their occupations had not been fitted to grapple with questions that pertained to the fundamental law of the State."[1] Charles D. Drake considered the delegates "almost without exception . . . sensible, upright, and worthy men," but he hastened to add that "only a very small number of them had ever had experience in lawmaking." Considering himself one of the most experienced, as he reported in his highly egotistical autobiography, Drake immediately began to scrutinize every part of the existing state constitution. He also explored the basic documents of other states for improved features that Missouri might profitably borrow. By the middle of December, 1864, he had made much progress toward drafting a substantially new constitution. Drake denied any ulterior motive in this; he saw it, so he said, simply as the duty of every conscientious delegate.[2]

Whatever the reason for his labors, there can be little doubt that Drake dominated the proceedings that followed. He worked actively at his job within the convention as well as in preparation for it. Since 1862 he had been the most ardent and effective speaker of the party in carrying the doctrine of Radicalism to rural outstate Missouri. This area soon became the source of Drake's political strength. At the convention the Radical delegates from rural Missouri followed his lead on nearly every crucial vote. They were to continue to give "Mr. Radical" their support until a new and more dominant figure arose in 1868 in the person of Carl Schurz, who was able to woo some of them away from him.[3]

Drake called the first session of the convention to order and nominated Arnold Krekel of St. Charles as temporary chairman. The following day the group ensconced Krekel permanently in the chair and chose Drake as vice-president. During the three months that followed Drake also served as chairman of the committee on the legislative department, chairman of the revising and enrolling committee, a member of the special committees on emancipation and elective franchise, and a member of the committee on boundaries. Yet, most of his work was accomplished on the convention floor and in the committee of the whole. His name dominates the pages of the convention journal and the proceedings. Although in ill health much of the time, he was absent only two of the seventy-eight days the convention actually met. There can be no doubt that he was the driving force that pushed the group to the completion of its work in the form he wanted. As Drake had made clear almost from the outset, he wished nothing less than a completely new constitution.[4]

Since most of the delegates were of one mind in their basic philosophy, the convention had little difficulty in organizing into a workable group. They were directed by the legislative act calling them into existence to "proceed to consider, first, such amendments . . . as may be by them deemed necessary for the emancipation of slaves; second, such amendments . . . as may be by them deemed necessary to preserve in purity the elective franchise to loyal citizens, and such other amendments as may be by them deemed essential to the promotion of the public good." A resolution by Drake that established eleven standing committees and outlined their duties passed without dissent. It directed each of them to examine carefully those parts of the constitution referred to them and to report what amendments, if any, were needed.[5]

One rather amusing incident marked the proceedings. William F. Switzler of Columbia, a member of the Conservative minority, raised the question of the delegates' taking an oath before entering upon the performance of their duties. Drake replied that he assumed everyone had taken a loyalty oath much more stringent than the one prescribed by the state constitution when he became a candidate for the convention and now he could see no need to repeat the performance. If Switzler knew of anyone who had not complied with this requirement, he should mention it now. The Columbian, amid laughter from the crowd, accepted Drake's contention and said that it mattered little to him if the delegates did not wish to require another oath. When the convention reconvened after the weekend adjournment, it prepared to swear in its newly elected officers. But before such action could be carried out, a motion to administer the oath to all the members was made and passed. In the debate over the question Switzler had his own laugh as he chid the delegates: "Why, sir, Sunday's reflection, perhaps, has brought members to believe that I was right on Saturday." The whole incident seemed somewhat at variance with what was to evolve as Drake became increasingly concerned with oath-taking and Switzler stood firmly against him.[6]

After the initial organization of the convention had been completed, the delegates got down to the first business at hand—the matter uppermost in everyone's mind—emancipation. Because so many ordinances were introduced, a special committee was appointed to sift the proposals and to bring back an acceptable formula. Under the chairmanship of George P. Strong, a St. Louis attorney, this group reported after only twenty-four hours of consideration. In agreement with an opinion expressed early during floor debate, the committee presented a brief ordinance that provided for the instant and unconditional freeing of all slaves in Missouri. In a forceful presentation Strong urged quick action and hoped that "before the genial heat of the sun shall dispel the covering of snow which now hides the soil of Missouri, the action of this assembly, will reveal to us that soil purified from the stain of slavery." Drake, who had been prevented from attending the special committee's one meeting because of illness, feared that the slaves, once freed, might be cast adrift with little protection. He therefore proposed an amendment that guaranteed the freedmen certain fundamental rights. The flurry of debate that followed revealed an inner conflict that was to come increasingly to the fore when the convention considered the question of civil rights in later sessions. Now the majority was in no mood to waste time on such matters. Strong commented that his committee had deliberately avoided including these questions in its report because of the controversy it might arouse. The convention could consider them later, he said, as parts of a bill of rights. In view of this consideration the Drake amendment was voted down. A proposal by Switzler to provide an apprenticeship system for the

freedmen between the ages of twelve and twenty-one received similar treatment.

After this brief interruption the members of the convention
hurried on to the ordinance itself and passed it with only
four negative votes being given. These came from Switzler,
Thomas B. Harris of Callaway County, Samuel A. Gilbert of
Platte County, and William A. Morton of Clay County, all
of whom represented strongly conservative counties with com-
paratively large slave populations. These men were not voting
against emancipation but rather against the enactment of the
proposed ordinance, which did not make adequate provisions
for the guidance of the Negroes and for the protection of
their white owners. Gilbert probably summed up quite accurately the feeling of many of his constituents when he cried
out during the debate, "In the name of God, if you are going
to free negroes, send them from us."[7]

Missouri's slaves had really been freed in everything but
name for over a year. Given the chaotic situation within the
state, the existence of the federal Confiscation Act, and the
active recruitment of Negro troops since the previous summer, there were few Negroes who still remained with their
masters under the old arrangement at the time the convention
cut the last legal cord. The announcement of the final vote
brought loud applause, accompanied "with the waving of
handkerchiefs and swinging of hats," from the audience assembled to watch the proceedings. It was some time before
the sergeant at arms could quell the enthusiasm so that the
Reverend Dr. William G. Eliot, president of Washington University, could offer a prayer of thanksgiving.[8]

When word reached Jefferson City that Wednesday afternoon, January 11, both houses of the legislature promptly
adjourned and reassembled in the House chamber for a celebration with the private citizenry. A committee waited upon
the Governor to invite him to join in the jubilee. Speech
followed speech as the exultant Radicals rejoiced, and the

meeting closed with a rousing chorus of "John Brown's Body." Everyone then hastened home to prepare for a more formal celebration at seven o'clock that same evening. In the interim Governor Fletcher returned to his office and issued a formal proclamation announcing the end of slavery in Missouri.[9] Other communities celebrated similarly when the word reached them. After much unofficial rejoicing, St. Louis held its official observance on Saturday, January 14. Large crowds of both races in festive mood moved through the streets, where flags bedecked every building. In the middle of the afternoon, at the request of the mayor, General Grenville M. Dodge ordered the firing of a sixty-gun salute. George K. Budd, one of the local members of the convention, read the Governor's proclamation as the shouts of the throng almost equalled the roar of the guns. That evening the city was aglow—artificial lights gleamed from every window, while fireworks burst in the skies.[10]

Not content with the accomplishment of emancipation only in their own state, the convention dispatched a resolution to Missouri's congressional delegation and urged them to vote for the proposed constitutional amendment, which would abolish slavery nationally. Even Switzler favored this action. He wrote to his friend, Congressman James S. Rollins: "No difference how many or how few governments we may have, slavery is dead. And since it is wiped out in Missouri, you had as well wipe it out elsewhere. . . . Let us now that we are rid of it, make a clean sweep."[11] When the Thirteenth Amendment, which Missouri's Senator John B. Henderson had helped to draft, was sent to the states for ratification the following month, the General Assembly promptly approved it by a concurrent resolution. Missouri thereby gave its firm assent to thoroughgoing emancipation.[12]

The convention remained in session to complete its business. By early February it had accomplished little by way of concrete measures beyond the emancipation ordinance. Those

who had hoped for a speedy consummation of its duties
began to complain quite vocally. On February 2 the State
Senate passed a resolution condemning the group for its
endless wrangling and authorized the establishment of a
committee to consider the propriety of calling another convention.[13]

For over a month the convention had had various articles
under consideration that had been proposed by Drake and
his lieutenants in an effort to push forward their program
of thorough revision of the constitution. As the debate over
the issues was prolonged, opposition to Drake and his tactics slowly built up within the convention. Much of this
came from the large delegation of Germans, who had distrusted Drake since his Know-Nothing days in the General
Assembly a decade earlier. They were ably aided and abetted
by moderates and Conservatives, who had their own motives
for wanting to slow Drake down. The Germans found new
grounds for suspecting Drake's prejudice against them in
two areas of the proposed revisions: the narrow definition,
as they saw it, of religious freedom, together with a variety
of restrictions placed upon churches;[14] and the exclusion of
aliens from the suffrage. Moderates and Conservatives, on
the other hand, were becoming increasingly alarmed at attempts to secure civil and other rights for the Negro.[15] A
large part of Drake's difficulty lay not merely in the stands
that he took on various issues but in the exceedingly egotistical attitude he displayed in taking them. His great faith in
his own infallibility alienated him from his friends on many
occasions. He became so imbued with a sense of his own
importance as the mastermind of the convention that he
frequently insisted upon the adoption of his own specific
and peculiar phraseology.[16]

On February 3 debate on the proposed article on elections
reached a fever pitch in the committee of the whole. When
Abner L. Gilstrap of Macon threatened to introduce a dis-

franchising ordinance as a substitute for this article in the hope that the convention would adopt it and adjourn, Drake replied in bitter tones. He denounced Gilstrap and the legislature for their attempts to interfere with the business of the convention: Let those who wished only to pass ordinances and nothing more go home if they so desired; let the legislature stay within its own sphere of operations and leave the convention alone. As for himself, Drake declared, he only "desired to make a glorious Constitution, worthy of the Convention and the constituents" who had sent them there.[17] In view of this acid challenge to Gilstrap, a number of delegates began holding meetings to determine a more effective course of opposition. Their ultimate move. as they saw it, would be to resign and persuade enough of the other delegates to do the same to prevent a quorum. Circulating an agreement to this effect, this group began soliciting signatures, and nearly a score had signed before the matter came to Drake's attention.

The actual existence of this circular first became known to Drake in debate on February 14 when Isidor Bush, a German Radical from St. Louis, accused Drake of trying to force his own views down the throat of the convention. If his overbearing manner continued, Bush cautioned, the convention might dissolve. Drake ridiculed this remark and tried to make it appear that it was Bush who was demanding conformity. "I do not wish the gentleman to misrepresent me," the German cried loudly. "I say if there is a deviation from sound principles, I and others will resign. Have you any objection to that? Can you prevent twenty-five members from resigning?" Drake dismissed Bush's threat with a shrug, refusing to believe that enough delegates would resign to break up a quorum. He warned Bush that if he did resign, he "had better look out for the wrath of the people."

Later that same day one of the dissidents made the mistake of approaching Chauncey I. Filley of St. Louis in an effort to solicit his signature to the agreement. Filley refused and reported the matter to Drake. That evening the Drake forces held a caucus at Filley's home. Some rural delegates who had signed the circular without fully realizing its intent also attended. Drake warned them that the course advocated in the agreement would be disastrous for the state and would strengthen the forces of the disloyalists. Agreeing with Drake, the entire group plotted its strategy and decided to force the issue on the convention floor.[18] The next morning Drake flung down the gauntlet by introducing resolutions declaring that the popular referendum of the previous fall constituted a demand by the people for a thorough revision of the constitution. His proposals went on to bind the convention to this task, "trusting that our work, when completed, will vindicate itself before them."[19] Drake then contended that all the complaints and clamor about the slow pace of the convention were unjustified. Although little work had been completed, a great deal had been begun and promised to bear fruit in time. He compared each of the dissidents to a man going into a machine shop who, without knowing anything about what he saw there, quickly demanded that the workmen account for the apparent confusion of the place. In view of what he had learned of the threats to resign and break up the convention, he wanted that body to go on record once and for all.

Led by Bush and Emory S. Foster of Warrensburg, the anti-Drake men struck back with a resolution of their own. It simply stated that the convention should do that for which it had been called and should "refrain from all amendments about which this Convention is almost equally divided, and for which this time of war is by no means propitious." An attempt by Bush to table both sets of resolutions failed by only two votes. The convention then struck down the dissidents' substitute by a vote of 34 to 14 and adopted Drake's resolution, 29 to 19. The Germans and the Conservatives made up most of the opposition. Bush later declared that it was a day "upon which barn-yard fowls pair off. A *Drake* set up the *quack* that there was an attempt to break off the Convention. Several *geese,* mistaking this drake for the real *gander,* followed him."[20]

On the evening of the following Saturday, February 18, the Germans held a mass meeting at Turners' Hall to protest the convention's action. About two hundred persons heard two of the delegates, James W. Owens of Franklin County and Gustavus St. Gem of Ste. Genevieve, condemn the convention for exceeding its authority. St. Gem depicted the convention as another "Long Parliament" and called for "a spirit that will have the force of a Cromwell, and walk up in those halls and dissolve" it. The assemblage passed several resolutions of protest that the delegates were to present to the convention, but these were hardly designed to have the effect of a Cromwellian blast. Indeed, St. Gem found himself under strong attack in the convention the following week and escaped censure only by backtracking and stating that he meant no offense by his remarks.[21]

Having failed in their attempts to limit the work of the convention by the threat of resignation, the dissidents now pursued a variety of parliamentary tactics, such as introducing a motion to recess and reconvene in Jefferson City or one to adjourn sine die by a certain date. The Drake men defeated these, and the debates droned on. It often seemed as if the opposition simply thought they could talk the convention to death. Finally, the Drake forces found it necessary to amend the rules of procedure by shortening the time for individual debate on any particular motion to ten minutes. The rule that required a two-thirds vote of those present to sustain a call for the previous question and thus to shut off debate was changed to require only a simple majority.[22]

Throughout these turbulent days a voice of moderation and conciliation constantly heard was that of Arnold Krekel, the presiding officer. Although Krekel was a native of Prussia and therefore usually in sympathy with his fellow Germans, he nevertheless kept his equanimity most of the time. He had opposed Drake's motion for a thorough revision of the constitution; when the majority decided differently, however, he accepted their verdict and did his best to steer the convention through the rough seas to its final goal. On one occasion, when Drake vehemently protested the procrastination by the dissidents, Krekel sought to pour oil on the troubled waters. He subtly tried to flatter Drake's ego by telling the convention leader that he "would remember him and his valuable services here as long as life lasted." At the same time he assured Drake that "when he differed with him he did so honestly and earnestly," and he disclaimed "opposition to any measure because Mr. Drake introduced it."[23] Several days later Isidor Bush became so angry at Drake that he asked to be relieved from further duty on the committee on revision. He felt that "the great pertinacity of his colleague in claiming precedence for his own peculiar views" rendered it unnecessary for anyone else to sit in the group. Krekel again stepped in and asked the German leader to continue as a personal favor to him. Bush simmered down and agreed.[24]

During one of the minority attempts to force adjournment to Jefferson City, Krekel stated that he feared the convention was arriving at a point where it might break up if a readiness to compromise was not displayed by both sides. He insisted that he did not wish to revive old party issues, but instead sought to "draw attention to the importance of uniting in the work for which we are called." Although he might not agree with the method decided upon by the convention to accomplish that work, Krekel reiterated his willingness to accept the majority rule and urged the other delegates to do likewise: "Let members stop criticizing each other's work and go to work themselves."[25]

As the tense situation continued, absenteeism became an

increasingly serious problem. Roll calls regularly showed from one to two dozen members absent with or without excuses. Because the convention rules required a majority of the total membership to approve any amendment, the high number of vacant seats enabled a minority to thwart, if it so desired, any positive action by the majority. As the convention's work entered its final stages, the Drake men forced a change in these rules, which provided that approval by a majority of those present and voting was adequate to pass an amendment. In the days that followed, when the number of absentees consistently hit thirty, as few as one-third of the total number of delegates were casting affirmative votes and carrying the motions of the day.[26] Apparently, many took to heart the angry retort of George Husmann from Gasconade County: Since the minority now had little voice in the proceedings, they might as well go home. The "Drake's bitters," as one delegate phrased it, were simply being administered in too large a dose.[27]

In view of the turmoil among the delegates, the question naturally arises as to why Drake and his followers were so intent on writing a new constitution. There can be little doubt that many of these men, in their own fanatical way, sincerely believed that postwar Missouri needed a new organic law to guide it. Drake bolstered them with continual assurances that the popular vote in 1864 had given them a mandate to produce a new constitution. Many of the Radicals, including Drake, had a basic distrust of the General Assembly; they were afraid that if the day should come when the conservative Democrats would regain control of the legislature, much ground would be lost in advancing the social and economic development of both races in Missouri. Drake declared, "We intend to erect a wall and a barrier in the shape of a constitution that shall be as high as the eternal heavens, deep down as the very center of the earth, so that they [the Democrats in the legislature] shall neither climb over it nor dig under it, and as thick as the whole territory of Missouri so that they shall never batter it down nor pierce through it."[28]

In an effort to accomplish this aim, the convention placed numerous restrictions on the general legislative process. Many of these restrictions, such as the requirement that bills could only be passed by an absolute majority of both houses and that the yeas and nays had to be entered upon the record, were procedural in nature.[29] Others limited the power of the General Assembly to make laws and amend the constitution. The legislature could not make special laws in regard to thirteen classes of cases and, more specifically, could not create special legislation when a general law could be made applicable.[30] This restriction was included because there had been great abuse of power in this area in the past. Although the General Assembly could propose amendments, these had to be submitted to the voters for ratification and published four months before the election. The General Assembly could call a new constitutional convention only with the approval of a popular referendum, and the work of that body had to be submitted to the people for their approval before going into effect.[31]

The work of the convention went forward even though the debate over the extent of its powers continued to rage intermittently. Probably the greatest amount of time and energy was consumed in the discussion of suffrage qualifications. Of prime importance was the specific admonition of the convention's call to "preserve in purity the elective franchise to loyal citizens." There was little disagreement as to the necessity for this, but the matter of how to accomplish it evoked considerable disagreement. Many delegates wished simply to enact some kind of disfranchising ordinance, following the pattern used for the emancipation decree, and then to quickly adjourn. To offset this faction, Drake rapidly pushed through the committee on elective franchise an article concerning elections and voter qualifications. Reported out on January 16, this article went to extreme lengths in providing for "rebel" disfranchisement. It required an individual to swear under oath that he had never committed any one of eighty-six different acts of supposed disloyalty against the state and the Union. These included taking up arms in rebellion; giving aid, comfort, countenance, or support to anyone engaged in such contumacious activity; contributing money, goods, letters, or information to the enemy; advising any person to enter enemy service; expressing sympathy for the enemy cause or for any specific foe; engaging in guerrilla warfare or aiding and abetting those who did. Not only would such an oath be prescribed for voters, but it would also be required of all candidates for public office, jurors, lawyers, corporation officials and trustees, teachers, and ministers. The General Assembly, by an absolute majority in each house, might revoke the test oath as a requirement for voting after January 1, 1871; it would have to wait an additional four years, however, to rescind the oath in the other instances.[32]

Such stringent restrictions met opposition from the Conservatives and from some of the Germans and moderates. This group, led by William F. Switzler, proposed that the article should not be retroactive beyond December 17, 1861. In the first few turbulent months of the war many Missourians had taken stands and made statements that they soon regretted. Their actions were understandable in view of the circumstances under which war had come to Missouri. Consequently, the state convention of 1861, acting in accord with an earlier proclamation by Governor Gamble, had provided a general amnesty for all those who took an oath of allegiance to the state and the Union by December 17, 1861, regardless of their previous activity. In this matter the Provisional Government had the backing of the Lincoln administration and the military commander at St. Louis. Many who had supported Claiborne Jackson and Sterling Price in the initial enthusiasm of asserting states' rights took advantage of the offer. Because of these events Switzler believed that the 1865 convention, in drawing up a new oath, had no right to ignore or repudiate the pledge of its predecessor. Drake, in answer to Switzler, denied that any breach of faith was involved. The action of the earlier convention had guaranteed the repentants security "in their persons, in their property, in their lives" —nothing more. Certainly, Drake held, disfranchisement did not interfere with any of these.

Isidor Bush and Dr. Moses L. Linton, two of the three present delegates who had served in the convention of 1861, condemned Drake's interpretation. They maintained that the suffrage had indeed been encompassed by the earlier action, as evinced by the simplified test oath for voting enacted by the former convention in June, 1862. They contended that that oath should be sufficient for the present situation. As the debate waxed hotter, Dr. Linton deplored Drake's incessant demand for acceptance of the so-called iron-clad oath and remarked, "He suggests to me in his violent speech the Code of Draco."[33] Thereby, the term "Draconian Code" first appeared. This expression was to gain general acceptance among Drake's opponents in the months that followed as a fit approbation for the entire constitution. James W. Owens voiced the complaint of a number of delegates when he surmised that no one except Drake understood precisely what the iron-clad oath meant. He suggested that it might be well "to have it read every Sunday morning at church, so that everybody would get to know what was in it, at some time or other." Drake retorted that he had copied it, for the most part, from the Maryland constitution and assured Owens that people there knew what it meant.

In spite of the efforts of those opposed to Drake's severe restrictions, the Switzler proposal was defeated.[34] Debate continued. Meanwhile, the Radicals held meetings in county after county across the state, urging disfranchisement. The more ardent extremists at the convention, particularly those from the strife-torn western border, introduced atrocity stories of guerrilla cruelty to support their demands for even sterner measures. Others called for the confiscation of all "rebel" property and expressed regret that every disloyal person could not be hanged. William H. Folmsbee of Gallatin summed up the feelings of these men and himself when he proclaimed that he had come to the convention "to protect the interests of the loyal men who had been ground to powder." It was he who introduced an amendment that made it illegal for ministers to teach or preach without first taking the iron-clad oath. The original article had only prevented ministers from performing the marriage ceremony, which Drake considered a civil contract, if they had not taken the oath. Aside from this alteration, the disfranchisement article was adopted with relatively little change.[35]

To further protect the suffrage, the convention required the General Assembly to establish machinery for a systematic biennial registration of all voters. Since the Radicals contended that anyone guilty of the high crimes of treason and disloyalty would probably have few scruples about committing perjury, such a registration system would offer a means of uncovering those who would take an oath under false pretenses. Under this plan the registering officers would be the final judges of loyalty. They alone could hear and pass on the validity of each oath and determine the fulfillment of the qualifications of each prospective voter.[36]

Two other aspects of the suffrage question received considerable attention in debate. The first concerned the possible enfranchisement of the new freedmen, which will be discussed in a later chapter.[37] The other dealt with the question of suffrage for aliens who had declared their intentions of becoming citizens. The staunch support given the Union cause by the Germans had created considerable sentiment for favorable action on this matter. Since Missourians were actively encouraging immigration into their state, the Germans argued that a liberal suffrage policy would attract more settlers. Drake opposed suffrage for noncitizens; yet, he could give no compelling reasons for his views, except that he saw it as another artful scheme of his opponents to defeat the constitution. Isidor Bush retorted quickly, "Who would defeat it because of this amendment? The Know-Nothings?" Drake replied, "I thought that party was dead and buried." "You are living proof that it is not," shouted Bush.[38] In the parliamentary scuffle that followed, Drake failed in his attempt to table a compromise amendment introduced by Bush that gave the alien the right to vote if he had declared his intention of seeking citizenship one year before exercising the suffrage. This proposal became a part of the constitution by a vote of 24 to 14.[39]

Other proposals by Drake also incurred the enmity of the Germans. One required counties with more than one representative or senator in the General Assembly to elect their legislators through single-member districts. The division of each county into these units would be done by the county court in a convenient, compact, and equitable manner. Such a proposal would considerably reduce the German influence in St. Louis County, the principal area to be affected. As long as the St. Louis legislators were elected at large, the Germans could wield substantial power over all of them. However, if they were elected strictly by districts, the German strength would be confined to the one or two areas of the city where the bulk of their population resided.

The *Westliche Post*, St. Louis' principal German-language paper, attacked Drake's plan as part of a scheme to edge B. Gratz Brown out of the United States Senate and to promote Drake's own ambitions by curtailing the German influence in the election of the legislators. Drake denied any desire for a Senate seat or any other public office and insisted that he had proposed the change because he believed it to be more democratic.[40] In this Drake showed his progressive tendencies.

At the same time Drake urged the rural delegates to agree to a change in the apportionment of the General Assembly. He contended that a majority of the House had been chosen by only one-fifth of the total vote cast. To correct this situation, Drake proposed the establishment of one hundred House districts based on population without regard to county equality. This time he was asking too much of his outstate supporters, and they refused to comply. Instead, the convention re-established the old system by which each county was entitled to at least one representative. The convention, however, did change the divisor by which the ratio for additional seats was determined from 140 to 200. Although this modification did not end the old discrimination, it did help to distribute representation more equally among the larger counties.[41]

Early in the session Moses P. Green of Hannibal had offered a resolution calling for a reorganization of the judicial system. He wanted to declare all judicial offices "from the Supreme bench down" vacant and to give the Governor power to fill them by appointment. In routine fashion his proposal went to the judiciary committee for consideration.[42] Meanwhile, pressure quickly built up in support of such a move. The *Missouri Democrat,* the Radicals' chief organ in St. Louis, urged the action so that the party could sweep clean the last vestiges of Conservative control over the state government. Many Radicals contended that they had lost the judicial election of 1863 fraudulently. Here was a chance to correct the books and more besides: Who could tell what interpretation a Conservative judiciary might put on the work of the convention? Petitions demanding action began to flow into St. Louis from across the state; they complained of almost daily mistreatment of loyal men by Conservative judges.[43]

On February 20 the judiciary committee reported. Since the state was undergoing social and political revolution, it was deemed urgent to bring the judicial arm of the government into harmony with the executive and legislative branches. If such an adjustment was not made, the functioning of the social system would be "harsh, discordant and incapable of efficient result." The committee recommended an ordinance that vacated, as of May 1, 1865, the offices of all judges and clerks of the Supreme Court of Missouri, the circuit courts, the county courts, and the special courts of record and of all county recorders and circuit attorneys. The Governor would fill all vacancies until the next election.[44] Coming as it did in the immediate aftermath of the Turners' Hall meeting, which had protested the decision for a new constitution,[45] the Ouster Ordinance, as it became known, aroused the opposition of Drake as well as the Conservatives and moderates. Drake regarded it as another attempt to distract the convention from the main business at hand. Despite the clamor for action from outstate, he could see no pressing demand for a special ordinance. Because he preferred to incorporate similar provisions directly into the constitution, he moved that consideration of the question be postponed until March 15. His motion passed.[46]

Petitions continued to come in demanding action on the judiciary problem. Governor Fletcher provided further stimulus for discontent when he declared in a proclamation, issued March 7, that no organized enemy force existed in Missouri. He hoped that military authority could now be gradually relinquished and civil power re-established. The Governor's action had been taken somewhat reluctantly under pressure from President Lincoln and his military authorities at St. Louis, who wished to completely disengage federal forces in the state now that the war was coming to an end. General John Pope, the new department commander, wrote Lincoln that Missouri had a loyal state administration and therefore should be able to solve most of its own problems. Consequently, he would suspend martial law by private instruction in areas where civil courts were operating.[47] Such a course of events made a "loyal" judiciary even more imperative, in the minds of most Radicals.

By the middle of March, Drake could no longer avoid the judiciary issue. Since the accomplishment of his ultimate goal was in sight, he felt that he could now be more congenial. He actively joined in the fight to defeat an amendment by Isidor Bush that would give the Governor power to remove only disloyal officials rather than all of them and one by William A. Morton that would exempt those officials elected in November, 1864, on the ground that the state was then in loyal hands. Another motion by Bush that prohibited any member of the convention from filling a vacated office also failed to win approval by a large margin. The delegates added the office of sheriff to those being vacated just before final passage of the Ouster Ordinance, which went sailing through by a vote of 43 to 5. All told, about 800 offices were to become vacant on May 1.[48] This action caused Dr. Moses L. Linton, one of the convention's sparkling wits, to produce one of the barbed epigrams with which he occasionally enlivened the proceedings:

> Disloyal judges, all agree
>   Should be decapitated;
> So just is this that such a point
>   Should not have been debated.
> And those who are good Union men,
>   Unfaltering, firm, and hearty,
> Should be turned out, that *Radicals*
>   *May harmonize their party!*[49]

In late March and early April the convention engaged in the routine business of revision and enrollment. The vote on the final document came on the afternoon of April 8, at which time each delegate had the opportunity to explain his stand. The constitution carried by a vote of 38 to 13, but this count did not indicate that all those who voted in the affirmative approved it. Some delegates, such as Ethan A. Holcomb of

Chariton County, cast affirmative votes merely to bring the convention to an end, and they announced that they would go home and fight against ratification. Others viewed the constitution as the best that they could get under the circumstances and agreed with Ellis G. Evans of Crawford County that the people would "promptly demand some amendments." The negative votes, on the other hand, came from the ranks of the Conservatives and the Germans, who deplored the convention's going beyond what they considered to be its original purpose. Some attacked various sections of the constitution that seemed unwise to them. William F. Switzler spoke for many when he said: "The Constitution was not conceived in statesmanship, but in a spirit of malice and revenge—a spirit at war with the wise policy of the times, and unworthy of a victorious and magnanimous people."[50]

At the time of the final voting thirteen members were absent. Drake contended in his autobiography that nearly all of the absentees opposed the constitution, and a scanning of the list would tend to verify this. Some had absented themselves from the convention for a week or more in view of the inevitable outcome. They doubtless saw little need to return to officially register a protest they had already made on many previous occasions. After the announcement of the official vote the delegates were called by roll to come forward and sign the two enrolled copies of the constitution, thereby authenticating it as an official act of the convention. Only four of the thirteen who voted against it would join the others in this formality. To Drake it was "plain that war was ahead," and he made ready for the battle to secure ratification.[51]

Its work completed, the convention met one last time on Monday morning, April 10, to wind up miscellaneous business. In the midst of these proceedings word arrived of the surrender of General Robert E. Lee at Appomattox Court House. Drake seized an American flag, sprang upon a chair, and called for nine cheers. For this auspicious occasion Dr. Linton contributed another one of his epigrams:

> Richmond is ours, Rebellion's crushed,
>   And Treason now must yield;
> Yea, yield it must altho' there were
>   "Three Richmonds in the field."
> The victor power, the glorious power
>   Will then its scourgings cease,
> And welcome back her erring sons
>   With Godlike smiles of peace.[52]

The last two lines seemed to be empty mockery in view of the constitution just completed. A majority of the convention delegates displayed their true temperament, once again, when they voted down the second of two resolutions proposed by Moses P. Green. The first, which was sustained by a unanimous vote, thanked God, the President, and the military forces for the victory. But the second proclaimed: "We are ready to sustain our noble President, in the hour of victory, in whatever terms of amnesty he, with his constitutional advisers, may think best to offer to those who have been in arms against the Government; except that we will not be willing to sanction any terms of peace which will admit of the perpetuation of slavery in any part of the Republic." This was something else again. On a motion by Drake this proposal was defeated by a vote of 31 to 10.[53]

CHAPTER III

THE RATIFICATION CAMPAIGN

T HE QUESTION of a popular referendum on the work of the convention had first been raised by the dissident press during the heated February debates. Although Drake did not feel it necessary to submit the constitution for the voters' approval, he realized that this represented the popular course. He probably hoped that his support of such a proposal might help to mollify some of the opposition. Consequently, when Abner L. Gilstrap of Macon proposed an amendment to this effect on March 22, Drake quickly acquiesced. He secured, without a dissenting vote, a resolution instructing the committee on the legislative department, of which he was chairman, to make provisions for the referendum.[1] Some of the opponents of the constitution pushed for a vote in the late summer or early autumn in order to give them more time to organize their campaign. The Radical majority, however, fixed June 6 as the day of the election in the hope of selling their document after a brief, hard-hitting effort. They controlled the electoral machinery in most counties and already had a comprehensive organization, which the opposition lacked.[2]

Although Drake apparently never doubted that he would receive the voters' approval of his constitution, he nevertheless took two precautions. Through his supervision, Section 6 of Article XIII of the new constitution provided that "no person shall be allowed to vote who would not be a qualified voter according to the terms of this Constitution, if the second Article thereof were then in force." This meant that the iron-clad oath would determine the electorate.[3] Without this requirement ratification would have proved impossible. Drake also secured passage of a special ordinance that required the Governor to send messengers with poll books to the several army posts outside Missouri in order that the state's soldiers could help decide its future. To give these men "a proper understanding of the Constitution," the state would also provide copies for the messengers to circulate among the soldiers before collecting their ballots. The Secretary of State ordered 10,000 ballots printed for this purpose and appointed Drake to superintend the process.[4]

Drake lost no time in carrying his fight for the constitution to the people. The first of seven letters, entitled "Charles D. Drake to the Radical Union Men," appeared in the *Missouri Democrat* on April 10, the same day the convention finished its work. Other Radical papers throughout the state reproduced the letter. In it Drake presented the constitution as the only means of "fixing Missouri firmly on a foundation of Loyalty" and warned that if the referendum was defeated, the Radicals had little or no future in the state. He left no doubt that he considered support of the constitution a matter of party loyalty when he called the Radicals "to harness immediately for the conflict," by the issue of which "the truly loyal people of Missouri must stand or fall."[5]

That not all Radicals agreed with Drake quickly became evident. Prominent in the ranks of the opposition was Gover-

nor Fletcher. In a letter to former Congressman Sempronius
H. Boyd on April 14, the Governor wrote that he found many
provisions of the constitution distasteful and consequently
would vote against it. Specifically, Fletcher considered the
document too proscriptive in its limitations on the franchise
and thought that other sections, "though suited perhaps to
our present condition, will soon be wholly inapplicable to the
condition of a progressive people." It would have been better
to let the legislature decide many of its provisions so that
they could "be more easily altered or repealed as experience
may show to be our best interest." The Governor also hinted,
in rather broad terms, that the failure to provide for Negro
suffrage disappointed him.[6]

Although Governor Fletcher had given no indication in his
letter that he intended to lead an active fight against the
constitution, the German and Conservative press quickly rallied to his support. The *Westliche Post* praised the Governor's
stand and sought to raise him to the position of an alternative
leader to Drake within the Radical ranks. Now, the *Anzeiger
des Westens* gloated, "this crazy fabric of Drake will be
damned and defeated." Rumors began circulating that other
prominent Radicals, including Senator B. Gratz Brown and
Secretary of State Francis Rodman, would join the opposition.[7] The *Missouri Democrat* vigorously denied these reports.
On April 28 it published a letter written by Senator Brown,
who gave the constitution a lukewarm endorsement. "While I
may have heretofore expressed antagonism to the New Constitution on some points," he wrote candidly, "yet a more mature
consideration convinces me that the facility of amendment
through the Legislature, which it provides, holds out infinitely
more hope . . . than the intricate and almost impracticable
processes of the old Constitution." On May 3 Brown sent a
similar letter to the editor of the *St. Joseph Morning Herald.*[8]
Throughout the rest of the campaign, however, he said little
else.

By the first of May the *Democrat* reported endorsements from both of Missouri's senators and eight of the nine representatives. The *Westliche Post* commented that several of these congressmen had attended a meeting with Governor Fletcher at its office and there had indicated that their only reason for endorsing the constitution was that they saw no alternative if the "loyal men" were to control the state. In fact, most of the congressmen had reservations regarding various parts of the constitution, particularly Senator John B. Henderson, who criticized it severely.[9] Few of them actively aided the campaign; instead, most merely issued a perfunctory letter of support in its closing stages and let it go at that. For instance, Senator Henderson waited until May 27 before he gave a written endorsement; this he sent to a St. Joseph friend who saw that it found its way to the press a few days later.[10]

Following Drake's lead, the *Democrat* sought to make the adoption of the constitution a party question. However, in view of the obvious division within their ranks, only a few Radicals cared to go that far. The attitude of Emory S. Foster, publisher of the *Missouri State Times* at Jefferson City, was typical. Having been one of the thirteen delegates at the convention who voted against the constitution, he now supported it simply because it was the only means of accomplishing disfranchisement. "The attempt to make the vote upon this question a test of Unionism or of Radicalism is simply absurd," he wrote in his newspaper. "The Constitution is a disgrace to the body that framed it."[11] Governor Fletcher remained hostile to the constitution, but his opposition was an inactive dissent. A week before the election he wrote James W. Owens that his only reason for voicing his objections was to show that some Radical opposition did exist, but he did not feel justified in doing any more. Apparently, he felt that the people would approve the constitution; if this happened, he would see to its enforcement.[12]

As a result of this lethargy on the part of many of the
leading Radicals, the brunt of the ratification campaign fell
to Drake's lot. He traveled widely making speeches, organizing committees, and holding conferences. He thereby continued to be the center of controversy as he had been in the
convention. In one of his letters to the *Missouri Democrat,*
Drake contended that many of the sections of the constitution causing opposition were minor and provided no reason
for voting against the entire document, which was "easily
amendable." Indeed, Drake even admitted that there were
several items that he, too, would like to see removed by the
amendment process.[13] Dr. Moses L. Linton, one of the most
able critics of the constitution, held Drake's contention up
to ridicule:

> His reason for adopting the Constitution is, that it is so
> easy to pull to pieces. The chief merit of this Constitu-
> tion seems now, even in the eyes of its friends, that it
> can be mended in so many ways—that it is a Constitu-
> tion of "shreds and patches"; and you may tear off a
> "patch" any time, and put on some other sort of a "patch"
> —as if "constitutions were intended for nothing else but
> to be mended." Do vote for Drake's Constitution. He
> don't like it himself in many particulars—wouldn't vote
> for it himself I suspect, but that he will have so nice a
> job mending it. Doubtless he is already gloating over his
> darning needles and pack thread and "patches." . . . But
> stop. Let us not be unjust. The friends say it will do a
> heap of good in the meantime. It will do harm in some
> ways, but an overbalancing good in others. It may stick
> its finger nails into your eyes with one hand, but it will
> rub you on the back and cure you of the rheumatism
> with the other; or if it kicks you in the shins it will at
> the same time use Mr. King's fine tooth-comb on your
> head. "All in all," it's a great Constitution![14]

One article in the constitution stipulated that only government property and that used for public schools would be
exempted from taxation. Linton, the convention's most promi-

nent Catholic member, considered this a "novel" provision in that it implied that church property, cemeteries, and charitable institutions, among other things, would be taxed. He had sniped constantly at this article during the convention debates: "Are you going to tax graveyards," he asked sarcastically, "and take the tombs for paving stone if the tax is not paid? There are thousands of dollars in monuments of one kind or another." In the same vein: "But worse than all, will you tax the orphan asylums where hundreds of otherwise unprotected children are cared for? Would you tax charity itself?" As for those who favored taxing churches, Linton held that they did not believe much in these institutions "whatever their high professions to the contrary." However, if such taxation had to be, the doctor felt:

> The State should go to no expense
> For railroads, bridges, domes,
> When to get money it must rob
> Graveyards and Orphans' Homes.[15]

When an article similar in meaning to this epigram appeared in the *St. Louis Dispatch* under pseudonymous authorship, Drake assumed that Linton was the author and consequently launched a vigorous attack on the doctor and the Roman Catholic Church in general. Drake had a decidedly anti-Catholic bias, which accounted for some of his Know-Nothingism in the 1850's. From the tone of his criticism it is not unreasonable to infer that he and some of the other convention members had the Catholic Church specifically in mind when they pushed for the adoption of the sections on taxation. Yet, Drake declared that the reason religious and charitable holdings had not been made tax-exempt was because the state was nearly bankrupt and needed all the money it could get. He insinuated, however, that Linton and his church, in taking the stand they did, must favor repudiation of the large state debt. Not only did he accuse the Catholics

of running a "money-getting and money-making machine"
that had never paid its share of taxes, but he also charged
them with being generally disloyal during the war, which
might account for their reluctance to help pay the debt accumulated by the state during that conflict.[16] In this kind of
demagoguery Drake was obviously playing to a larger audience—rural outstate Missouri, where strong anti-Catholic sentiment prevailed.[17]

Dr. Linton lost little time in making a formal reply. Denying authorship of the pseudonymous article, he assured Drake
that he would not hesitate to sign anything he wrote. As for
his opposition to the taxing features of the constitution, he
refused to acknowledge that his stand reflected Catholic
prejudice. He noted that he was the only Catholic in the convention who voted against this section and pointed out that
his church had always paid taxes on nonchurch building
property. In regard to Drake's diatribe in general, Linton
commented sardonically:

> Mr. Drake's letter is very long, but there is very little in
> it. His friends, however, are, or pretend to be, delighted
> with it. There is no accounting for tastes. The great
> dramatist [Shakespeare] represents even the FAIRY
> QUEEN as falling in love with BULLY BOTTOM THE
> WEAVER, though the mischevious Puck had planted a
> pair of asses' ears on Bottom's head. Nevertheless, under
> some strange delusion, she looked on him as a heavenly
> creature.[18] . . . These gentlemen may, therefore, really
> think that Mr. Drake's long and empty letter is a piece of
> perfection.[19]

St. Louis served as the focal point for the organized opposition to the constitution as the bulk of the German Radicals
joined with Conservatives and moderates in seeking to thwart
ratification. Toward the end of April, thirteen delegates issued a long letter in which they reiterated their charges that
the convention had exceeded its powers and asked the people

to vote against its brain child. On May 1 many of these same delegates joined a number of German leaders at Turners' Hall and there, before a large crowd, denounced the iron-clad oath and other features of the constitution as wrong in principle and possibly dangerous in practice.[20]

One of the most influential leaders of the opposition was Edward Bates, the staunch Conservative who had served as Lincoln's attorney general throughout the war. Although his feeble health did not permit him to participate actively as a speaker, Bates wrote a series of effective letters to the *Missouri Democrat*. In these he took as his general theme: "The Convention was revolutionary, in its origins, in its character and in its acts." He accused the Radicals of riding roughshod over every obstacle to accomplish their ends.[21] In the interior of the state William F. Switzler of Columbia carried the attack into many homes through his *Missouri Statesman*. Former Congressman James S. Rollins of Columbia and former Governor Austin A. King of Ray County also labored tirelessly in behalf of the Conservative opposition. They emphasized the idea that since the war had ended and Missouri had had enough of vindictiveness, all her people should now unite in working for her future in a spirit of co-operation, not hatred. They attacked the narrow partisanship embodied in both the iron-clad oath and the registration system for voting.[22] Some unknown Conservative even took to verse and summarized the opposition's argument:

> All sorts of folks met on a time,
>   And came to the conclusion
> That they were just the sort of men
>   To make a Constitution.
> The time set for their vengeful work
>   Was in a Revolution,
> When they might vent their spite and put
>   It in a Constitution.
> They then mixed up a mighty oath
>   Of very strong solution,

> To be gulped down with other things
> In this strange Constitution.[23]

One of the chief problems confronting the opponents of the constitution concerned the stand they should take when actually faced with the necessity of subscribing to the iron-clad oath before voting. In some respects the vague language of the oath could be interpreted as meaning that anyone who had taken a stand against Claiborne Jackson's pro-Confederate administration before its deposition as Missouri's legal government could be barred from the polls. Technically, it could also be contended that the Radicals, in denouncing the Provisional Government and the Lincoln administration during the war, "had given aid and comfort to the enemy" and therefore ought to be disfranchised. In view of these loopholes, some of the opposition advanced the theory that the oath was really invalid and, consequently, anyone could take it with a clear conscience. Others feared, however, that to subscribe to the oath would be to acknowledge its validity and would indirectly be a recognition of the convention's authority to require it.[24]

Because of all this confusion appeals went to Edward Bates, whom most recognized as one of the state's top legal authorities, to settle the question. He gave his opinion in a letter to Dr. Linton a few days before the election. Bates believed that the convention had no right to require the oath, since the new constitution would not go into effect until after its ratification; yet, he knew that election officials would bar anyone from the polls who did not conform. Thus, the prospective voter must take the oath or be "robbed of his vote by a dishonest trick." To circumscribe this problem, Bates outlined a policy that the *Missouri Democrat* described as "pious perjury": Any man should feel free to take the oath if he "has never borne arms against the Government and knows in his own heart that he bears true and faithful allegiance to the nation and the State."[25]

It would be erroneous to leave the impression that suffrage restriction, or the question of loyalty versus disloyalty, was the only issue discussed during the ratification campaign. Although this subject dominated the speeches and writings of Drake and his opponents, the Radical press stressed a secondary theme: Rejection of the constitution would imply retrogression by the people of Missouri. The newspapers argued that the document symbolized educational, moral, and economic progress to many prospective German, Irish, and Scottish immigrants as well as to investors and potential residents from the East. The *Missouri State Times* at Jefferson City summed up the issue:

> The world is attentively and anxiously observing our progress. With a free State Constitution, and the adoption of a policy that will speedily and effectively eradicate the disloyal element from amongst us, Missouri will be regarded as the emigrant's haven of rest. Reject the proposed Constitution and our State will be flooded with rebels, and those seeking homes in the West will shun us as a community of semi-barbarians.[26]

The assassination of President Lincoln, which occurred at this time, probably aided Drake's contention that generosity to ex-rebels was risky. As Drake saw it, the President's murder "opened the eyes of the nation to the dangers into which its big-souled magnanimity was about to plunge it."[27] There are strong indications that Drake and other Radicals hoped that the new President, Andrew Johnson, would be in greater agreement with their outlook for the future than Lincoln. While lamenting the assassination, B. Gratz Brown wrote Johnson that he rejoiced "that God in His providence has called you to complete the work of rebuilding this nation that it might be stamped with the idea of radical democracy in all its parts." He assured the new chief executive "that the loyal men of Missouri feel that today they have one at the head of this government who can sympathize in their struggles and privations and wants."[28] President Johnson's vindictive pronouncements during the early weeks of his administration particularly pleased Drake. "They come to Missouri Radicals as a new life to the almost dying," he informed the President on April 24. Three days later Drake sent Johnson a copy of the new constitution and sought the President's endorsement.[29] However, such was not forthcoming. As Johnson changed his course to more closely parallel Lincoln's in the months that followed, the Missouri Radicals became dismayed, and by winter they had joined in active opposition to his program.

The results of the referendum remained in doubt for three weeks after the polls had closed. The early returns indicated that the constitution would be defeated. "We have carried St. Louis and St. Charles by good majorities," Edward Bates exulted in his diary, "and to all appearance, the nuisance will be abated."[30] The worst fears of the Radicals indeed became true in St. Louis where the opposition obtained a majority of 5,926 votes out of a total of 16,570 cast. To the Radicals' dismay, much of southeastern Missouri turned against ratification. There the German influence in combination with the Conservative strength simply proved too much for the rest of the Radical vote to overcome. The Missouri River counties, dominated by the same elements, also came out strongly in opposition.[31] The *Missouri Democrat* raised an immediate cry of fraud. "We hear of no one who undertakes to defend the fairness of the election in this city on last Tuesday," it contended. It soon began printing letters received from the interior that claimed many had practiced "pious perjury" or, as in staunchly Conservative pro-Southern Callaway County, had not even bothered to take the oath before voting.[32]

The Radicals had to wait some time before they had favorable indications of the outcome. As the results trickled in from the border areas where they enjoyed their greatest strength, the votes revealed that the counties of northern and southwestern Missouri were returning a sweeping victory for the constitution. Because these areas had suffered most heavily from guerrilla warfare, the residents accepted Drake's thesis readily. Furthermore, these were the regions that hoped to benefit the most from immigration and increased capital investment, which the adoption of the constitution would seemingly encourage.[33] Slowly the ratification forces gained ground. Now it was the Conservatives who complained that violence and intimidation, particularly in ardent Radical territory, had kept many of their number from the polls.[34] Undoubtedly, there were varying degrees of enforcement of the iron-clad oath as a criterion for voter eligibility. In all probability, its rigid requirement in highly partisan Radical areas was equalized by a laxity elsewhere. In some of the counties dominated by extreme Radicalism grand juries brought indictments the following winter against those who had committed "pious perjury" and had managed to fool the election judges. Those found guilty received two-year sentences in the state penitentiary.[35]

Fourteen counties, mostly along the southern border of the state where the population was small and scattered, reported no returns whatever. Conditions there still remained somewhat turbulent. Governor Fletcher's failure to make appointments to fill the offices vacated in this area under the Ousting Ordinance may have had some effect on the situation.[36] By the middle of June the margin against the constitution stood at 2,167, but the *Missouri Statesman* feared that the soldiers' vote might overturn this. Ballots had been particularly slow in coming in from the widely scattered locations of Missouri troops. The early returns of the soldiers who were stationed within the state indicated strong majorities for the constitution; as the military ballots from points outside Missouri were counted, this trend continued.[37]

The St. Louis opponents to the constitution became worried that Secretary of State Francis Rodman, a Radical, would not conduct a fair canvass of the votes. At a mass meeting they appointed Robert E. Rombauer and George B. Kellogg to go to Jefferson City and inspect the election returns. The *Missouri State Times* labeled the two men as "a smelling committee" and rejoiced when Rodman indignantly refused them admittance into his office. The paper also reported that Rodman had turned down a bribe of $150,000 to throw the election. Shortly after this news had been printed, someone broke into the Secretary's office and rifled the drawers; because Rodman had safely deposited the returns in the State Treasurer's vault, the intruders found nothing.[38]

On the morning of July 1 the Secretary of State officially canvassed the votes in his office behind locked doors in the presence of the Governor and the State Auditor, as required by law. Anxiously, Charles Drake waited with several friends across the hall in the Register of Lands' office for the results. When Rodman emerged after three or four hours, he announced that ratification had been secured. The tension broke, and Drake and his company let go with rousing cheers and the waving of hats.[39] The official count revealed that ratification had been won by a bare majority of 1,862 votes out of a total of 85,478 cast. The constitution had, in reality, been carried by the soldiers' vote, which gave it a majority of 2,827; the civilian population, on the other hand, turned it down by the scant margin of 965. The Governor quickly issued a proclamation stating that the constitution would be in force as of July 4, 1865.[40]

The acceptance of the constitution did not end the controversy over it by any means. Much of the opposition continued to feel that the document had been ratified by a minority interest using irregular methods. In the months that followed, both the Radical and Conservative camps issued numerous proposals recommending that a new convention be called or that amendments be submitted to the people to rid the constitution of its more objectionable features.[41] These petitions did not bear full fruit, however, until the election of 1870. In the meantime, not content to wait for these slow-moving processes, the Conservatives sought to test various parts of the constitution, particularly those involving the iron-clad oath, in the courts.

CHAPTER IV

RADICAL VINDICTIVENESS

IN THE MIDST of the ratification campaign the date on which the Ousting Ordinance, passed by the state convention, was to become effective arrived—May 1, 1865. By its terms, 842 officials found themselves automatically suspended from office, and Governor Fletcher faced the problem of appointing their replacements. Even if he had been a more thorough-going Radical than he was, the mere mechanical process of finding enough competent and zealous members of the ruling party to fill these places would have been backbreaking. As it was, he seemed content to retain in office those men whose loyalty could be proven, especially if they had been elected on the Radical ticket the previous November. In other instances he acted on the recommendations of county Radical committees.[1]

Most of the men removed from office submitted without much protest. In Lafayette County, however, the incumbent Conservatives refused to vacate their offices and rallied their supporters to defend them. The Governor quickly called out a company of colored militia to enforce the ordinance. They seized two of the county judges who were thought to be the ringleaders of the conspiracy and locked them up in a building formerly used as a Negro jail. When the attorneys of the two victims petitioned the local circuit judge, who had recently been reappointed, for a writ of habeas corpus, the magistrate deemed it advisable to learn Governor Fletcher's intentions before proceeding further. The Governor quickly informed him that he intended to carry out the Ousting Ordinance regardless of the judge's decision, whereupon the Conservatives grudgingly capitulated and turned the county records over to Fletcher's appointees.[2]

In St. Louis County, Alfred C. Bernoudy, recorder of deeds, refused to vacate his office. The circuit attorney promptly instituted quo warranto ouster proceedings in the circuit court. Bernoudy demurred on the ground that the Ousting Ordinance had been illegally instituted and was therefore inoperative and void. Circuit Judge James C. Moodey, who had just taken the bench under appointment by Governor Fletcher, heard the arguments. To the amazement of many Radicals, he sustained Bernoudy on the broad ground that the ordinance lacked legality because it had not been passed as an amendment to the constitution. Judge Moodey's decision should not have been too surprising; he had been active among the German Radicals in opposing the ratification of the constitution, contending that the convention had exceeded its authority. Julius Conrad, Fletcher's appointee as recorder, immediately appealed Moodey's ruling to the Supreme Court of Missouri, which overturned it in October. For the moment, however, Judge Moodey was lionized by his fellow German Radicals and by the Conservative press.[3]

These proceedings were but a preliminary skirmish, in view of the major battle that was soon to follow. From the outset the Supreme Court of Missouri had been the principal target of the Radicals in their campaign to get rid of the Conservatives. Many Radicals felt that the incumbent judges had been elected under highly questionable circumstances in 1863. Furthermore, they feared that the Conservative judges might be a major obstacle to the implementation of any Radical program. Judge Barton Bates had resigned from the Court in February, 1865, to return to private law practice. Therefore only Judges John D. S. Dryden and William V. N. Bay, both of whom had been elected for six-year terms in the 1863 contest, remained on the high bench when the May 1 deadline arrived.[4]

The high tribunal stood in recess at the time of the scheduled change-over. Dryden and Bay had held court until April 29, at which time they had adjourned the session until May 5. However, before adjournment the Court had accepted Governor Fletcher's certificate of reappointment for Andrew W. Mead, a long-time clerk. When Dryden and Bay did not appear on May 5 or on any of the three succeeding judicial days, most Radicals and other Missourians assumed that they had no intention of contesting their removal.[5] Governor Fletcher proceeded to appoint David Wagner, Walter L. Lovelace, and Nathaniel Holmes to the Supreme Court. Wagner and Lovelace promptly called a special session of court for June 12. Working in secret conjunction with Andrew Mead, the two Conservative judges shortly thereafter issued a similar call for the same day, which the clerk published, though omitting the judges' names. The court sessions ordinarily started at ten o'clock, but on June 12 Dryden and Bay arrived an hour early, took the bench, and began to hear cases. When Wagner and Lovelace appeared at the regularly appointed time, they found themselves without a courtroom. Undaunted, they retired to a nearby room, appointed their own clerk, and issued an order against Mead for the Court's records. Mead refused to comply and secured a counterorder from the "old Court" to back him up. Confusion reigned. In this seeming impasse between the two conflicting jurisdictions Mead appealed to Circuit Judge Moodey for a restraining order against Wagner and Lovelace, which the German Radical promptly granted.

Governor Fletcher was in Louisville on business; when word reached him of the situation, he quickly returned to St. Louis. Arriving on the evening of June 13, he asked Dryden and Bay to vacate their posts and issued an order upholding his new appointees, which he delivered to General David C. Coleman of the militia to enforce. Coleman appeared before the "old Court" the following morning and tried to persuade the two judges to step down. When they refused on the ground of the questionable constitutionality of the Ousting Ordinance, he produced the Governor's order authorizing him to take possession of the court records and install the new judges in their rightful places. Dryden and Bay nevertheless maintained their positions, whereupon Coleman called a police squad, which forcibly removed them from the bench. The two protesting judges were then dragged before a local police magistrate and arraigned on the ludicrous charge of disturbing the peace. After being released on two hundred dollars' bond, they never reappeared. The authorities eventually dropped the matter. While these events were taking place, a new tribunal was ensconced in power, with troops guarding the court house. After the records were forcibly seized from the protesting Mead, the administration of justice was resumed.[6]

Partisanship ran rampant in the days that followed. The Conservatives called a meeting for Saturday evening, June 17, at the St. Louis courthouse. Several of their leading lawyers attacked the Governor for his actions both in St. Louis and in Lafayette County. They contended that the convention had exceeded its authority in passing the Ousting Ordinance, especially in the form it had taken, and that this group had no power other than to amend the constitution.

The ordinance could in no sense be construed as an amendment, and it had never been referred to the people. Furthermore, it arbitrarily removed officials from their posts without
any charge or trial. Although the Provisional Government had
done this same thing earlier, it had acted under the extenuating circumstances of civil war. No such crisis existed
now. The audience listened patiently to the detailed legal
arguments before passing a series of resolutions that denounced the action and called for the impeachment of
Fletcher.[7] The Radicals countered with a meeting of their
own ten days later and there sustained the Governor. Their
speakers used the same arguments that had been advanced
for the passage of the ordinance. They contended that the
present times were indeed extenuating and that the convention of 1861–1863 had passed a wide variety of ordinances
with even less pretense of strict legality.[8]

Beginning with the term of September, 1865, the Supreme
Court of Missouri sought to quiet the dissension through a
series of decisions that upheld the ordinance. The new judges
had deliberately disregarded the earlier injunction of Judge
Moodey against their taking the court records. When Moodey
called certain lesser officials who had been involved in that
action before his court to answer contempt charges, they
immediately appealed to the high tribunal for a writ of prohibition, which the Court quickly granted. Justice Nathaniel
Holmes, who had not been involved in the original imbroglio,
rendered the Court's opinion: The Ousting Ordinance had
been passed by the convention, whose delegates were the
duly constituted representatives of the people, and it had been
legally carried out by the Governor. Therefore, Holmes ruled,
it became the duty of all courts to recognize and abide by
that measure. The Court called any challenge to its own
authority "an unparalleled affront" and asserted, in a strong
fashion, its claim as the official high tribunal of the state.[9]
When Julius Conrad's appeal for a quo warranto against the

recalcitrant Alfred Bernoudy came before the Court a short time later, the judges again recognized the full validity of the ordinance. They ruled that the office of the St. Louis County recorder was vacated and ordered the sheriff to promptly establish the new appointee in that position.[10] The following year a majority of the Supreme Court justices, in an advisory opinion, informed the Governor that the ordinance was organic in nature. It would consequently take more than an act of the legislature to alter, repeal, or impair the document.[11] Subsequent decisions over the next few years strengthened this contention.[12]

Dryden and Bay continued to assert their personal claims. In July, 1865, Dryden filed suit against Governor Fletcher and his officers for $50,000 in damages. By fall, however, both he and Bay announced their official resignations from the bench, for they felt that any further attempt to resume office in the face of military force would be futile. When the Dryden case came before the court of common pleas the following April, the judge, in his charge to the jury, upheld the Ousting Ordinance. Consequently, the verdict was against Dryden, which put an official end to the whole matter.[13]

Having been successful in placing their partisans in most of the state and local offices, the Radicals moved to secure control over federal patronage within Missouri. They had begun efforts in this direction almost immediately after their victory in November, 1864. Because the Lincoln administration was content with retaining its previous appointees, these initial ventures came to naught. Most of the holdovers were Conservatives; as such, they worked against the adoption of the constitution, which led the *Missouri Democrat* to complain bitterly of their opposition to progress.[14]

Even before ratification of the new constitution Missouri's Radical congressmen and others began besieging President Johnson to remove the Conservative postmasters and to replace them with "progressive" men. The Conservatives, in turn, acted with dispatch in defending their own interests. James S. Rollins urged the President to uphold "the original & steady friends of Mr. Lincoln" and warned against "those who wield a temporary local power and who are at best *doubtful friends.*"[15] To their bitter dismay, the Radicals found Johnson increasingly swayed by Rollins and other prominent Conservatives, who made it quite evident that they supported the reconstruction policies the President sought to implement. Johnson's liberal amnesty policy and his obvious desire to restore the South to full partnership in the Union as quickly as possible coincided directly with the Missouri Conservatives' desire to accomplish a similar program in their state.

Rollins and his fellow Conservatives found a ready ally in Frank Blair, who was probably as responsible as any one man for keeping Missouri in the Union in 1861. A member of a highly prominent family in national politics, Blair had served both in the Missouri General Assembly and in Congress before the war. A meteoric military career brought him the command of one of General Sherman's corps during the final campaign through Georgia and the Carolinas, and he returned to St. Louis in triumph in June of 1865. At a banquet in his honor at the Lindell House about three hundred prominent Missourians heard Blair express his doubts about the new constitution and about those who had made and ordained it. He preferred the milder views of his good friend, the late President Lincoln, that retaliation against the mass of Southern people should be held to a minimum.[16] Almost immediately Blair returned to Washington to lead his troops in the Grand Review down Pennsylvania Avenue. In the following months he, his father, and his brother came to have increasing influence with President Johnson, which undoubtedly worked to the advantage of Missouri's Conservatives.[17] On June 7 Rollins urged Blair's appointment as Secretary of War if Stanton resigned from that post as rumored. A number of prominent St. Louis Conservatives endorsed this idea and warned the President of a Radical plot "to take away suffrage from the conquered white and bestow it on the ignorant inexperienced black."[18] The Radicals, on the other hand, fully aware of the dangers of Blair's influence, punctuated their letters to the President with warnings against Blairism and assured him that the General's influence in Missouri was definitely on the wane.[19]

Blair returned to Missouri early in October to take active charge of a Conservative campaign to unite those who supported President Johnson's reconstruction program and those who opposed the vindictive features of the new state constitution. A letter signed by Blair and a large number of other Conservative Unionists was issued, calling for a mass convention at Verandah Hall in St. Louis on October 26. Each county was asked to elect delegates, and Conservatives throughout the state quickly responded with local meetings to accomplish this and to pass preliminary resolutions.[20] In the interim, Blair carried his drive into outstate Missouri. In a blistering speech at Rolla, he denounced the new constitution as "begotten of malice and concocted by a clique who were destitute alike of heart, head, or conscience." He praised President Johnson for his magnanimous policy and linked him with his martyred predecessor as being among the noblest of men. The Conservatives of central Missouri accorded Blair a thunderous response and adopted resolutions endorsing the line he had laid down.[21]

Nearly one thousand delegates gathered at Verandah Hall on October 26 and remained in session for three days. Samuel T. Glover, a prominent St. Louis attorney and a friend of Lincoln who currently stood under indictment for refusing to take the iron-clad oath, presided. Blair, Rollins, and other Conservative leaders from all corners of the state harangued the enthusiastic crowd with their now-quite-familiar denunciations of Charles D. Drake, the Fletcher administration, and the state constitution. Praise for Johnson's policies was heard less frequently, though no less earnest in effort. On the final day of the meeting the group adopted a wide range of resolutions and appointed two committees: one to visit Washington and present the convention's proceedings to President Johnson; the other, made up of one member from each congressional district and six members at large, "to organize the people of the State in opposition to the new Constitution."[22] Frank Blair informed his father a few days later: "Our political prospects in this state are looking very bright." This remark proved to be somewhat optimistic, yet the convention at Verandah Hall had established a foundation on which the Conservatives could build. After their return home, many of the delegates called county meetings to ratify the St. Louis proceedings and thereby help to keep the fires alive for the 1866 electoral campaign.[23]

Continuing his work of organizing the opposition, Blair accompanied James O. Broadhead to Hannibal, where he reiterated his charges to a large, responsive rally. En route, he wrote his brother Montgomery that he intended to test the validity of the iron-clad oath at an upcoming local election in St. Louis the following week. He planned to present himself at the polls with his own oath, which simply declared his allegiance to the state and nation. If the election official refused his ballot and demanded that he take the iron-clad oath, he would declare his ineligibility to do so on the ground that he had taken up arms against Claiborne Jackson in 1861. Certainly with his staunch Union record he could not be accused of disloyalty. Should the election judges persist in their refusal, Blair intended to bring suit against them. He would carry his case all the way to the United States Supreme Court, if necessary, on the ground that the iron-clad oath constituted an ex post facto measure and thereby violated the federal constitution.[24] True to form, Frank Blair appeared at the polls. The judges rejected his ballot, and he brought suit in the St. Louis circuit court. He asked $10,000 in damages

from the two election officials for their refusal to accept his
vote. Of far more significance, however, was his intention
to overthrow the iron-clad oath through the judicial process
and thereby re-enfranchise those who could aid the Conservatives in their struggle against the Radicals.[25]

The case came to trial in the late spring of 1866. Samuel
T. Glover represented Blair and argued that the oath represented ex post facto legislation and therefore made acts
criminal that had not been so considered when done. He
further contended that his client had been penalized by disfranchisement without having been convicted of any crime
by a judicial trial. So crucial did the Radicals consider the
case that Charles D. Drake himself undertook the defense of
the two election officials. He maintained that Missouri's citizens, acting through their sovereign convention, had the in-
disputable power to establish suffrage qualifications and fix
rules for carrying them out without any interference from
"any tribunal or authority in the wide world."[26] Drake had
strong grounds, for the matter of voting procedures had been
historically a state rather than a federal concern. It was not
until June, 1866, that the circuit court issued its decision; by
a divided vote, with Judge Moodey dissenting, it ruled in favor
of the defendants. Blair immediately appealed to the Supreme
Court of Missouri.[27]

During the winter of 1865-1866 the Missouri courts also
became the storm center of other controversies concerning
the validity of the iron-clad oath, particularly as it affected
lawyers and preachers. Under the constitution the members
of various professions were required to subscribe their loyalty
and had sixty days from the day of the Governor's official
proclamation of ratification to do so. During the two months
following the Governor's announcement a great deal of heated
discussion arose over the legality of the oath and its enforcement. In early August several leading St. Louis attorneys
met and declared the requirement ex post facto in nature.

Most of them indicated that they would not take the oath. When asked for an opinion, Attorney General Robert F. Wingate made a contrary pronouncement by upholding the oath's constitutionality.[28]

The September 2 deadline for taking the oath passed with most non-Radical attorneys failing to comply with the procedure. At the next sitting of the criminal branch of the St. Louis circuit court several prominent Conservative lawyers presented lengthy arguments against the oath and asked to be excused from taking it. Judge Wilson Primm denied their motions and declared that he would bar any attorney who did not conform from practicing before his court.[29] Samuel T. Glover, with the full approval of the St. Louis bar, immediately notified the circuit attorney that he had no intention of taking the oath, but that he intended to continue practicing law. The grand jury of St. Louis County quickly indicted him, and he was brought before the criminal court. Judge Primm again upheld the oath, found Glover guilty of illegal practice, and fined him five hundred dollars as required by the constitution. The judge did grant a stay of execution, however, pending appeal.[30] A similar case, involving Alexander J. P. Garesche, came before the Supreme Court of Missouri in October. The lower court had refused to allow him to defend Alfred Bernoudy without taking the oath. When the high tribunal upheld the oath, Garesche filed a bill of exceptions to carry his case to the United States Supreme Court.[31]

In view of these decisions, a number of lawyers in the St. Louis area did take the oath, but under protest. When William B. Napton, former justice of the Supreme Court of Missouri, who would later return to that body, subscribed to the oath, he appended the following:

> I take this oath, with the accompanying declaration, that
> I am not to be understood as denying or disavowing any
> opinions or sympathies expressed or entertained, in ref-

erence to the past action of the federal or state governments, which opinions and sympathies I do not regard
as having anything to do with one's allegiance or loyalty,
and I protest against the validity of all that part of the
oath which related to past acts as conflicting with the
Constitution of the US and the fundamental principles
of all our state govts.

The clerk who administered the oath accepted the attached
diatribe. He told Napton that he considered the whole oath-
taking procedure "a humbug," but that he had no choice but
to do his duty.[32]

In outstate Missouri several judges declared the iron-clad
oath for lawyers unconstitutional and refused to require it in
their courts. Judge Walter King of Ray County declared that
President Johnson's amnesty policy superseded any contrary
provisions of the constitution. Judge William Heren of Platte
County relieved two lawyers from taking the oath, on the
ground that they had served in the militia during the war
and thereby had proved their loyalty. Judge John A. S. Tutt
of Jackson County refused to force any attorney to take the
oath, but required each to act on his own responsibility. "If
an offense be committed it is a matter for inquiry by the
grand jury."[33] Thus, enforcement varied; the matter largely
depended upon the individual sympathies of the judge presiding, and, as might be expected, stricter compliance prevailed in ardent Radical areas. The state, however, provided
no general agency to police the problem.

Equally controversial, if not more so, was the question of
whether the clergy of the state should accede to the oath-
taking demand of the constitution. The Reverend M. M.
Modisett of Louisiana expressed a typical attitude when he
complained to James O. Broadhead on August 8, 1865: "I
confess that I am placed in a very unpleasant situation, not
because of the fear of perjury or of doing violence to my
feelings for any act of my life, by taking said oath, but on

account of the seeming unreasonableness of the thing, and, as I now view it, as being an infringe [sic] of religious liberty, as well as a species of tyranny to which I dislike to submit." Modisett saw three alternatives: to take the oath, to give up preaching, or to deliberately ignore the whole matter and thereby be subject to arrest as a violator of the law. "Or," he inquired, "is there any hope of a speedy repeal of the (to me) obnoxious thing?" Caught on the horns of this dilemma, he sought the best legal advice available in order that he could "discharge my duty first to God & then to my country without doing violence to my feelings."[34] Therein lay the problem of many of Missouri's pastors. Although one newspaper suggested that they discontinue all preaching and teaching, shut down their church operations, and await a test decision on the constitutionality of the oath as it applied to the ministry, such action seemed far from practicable.[35]

The first of several "official" pronouncements by various religious bodies came from the pen of the Roman Catholic Archbishop of St. Louis, the Most Reverend Peter Richard Kenrick. In a letter to the pastors of his diocese he deplored the oath and expressed the hope that it would not be enforced among the clergy. If the civil power should insist on exacting its "sacrifice of ecclesiastical liberty," he advised his priests not to succumb and asked them to keep him informed "of the particular circumstances of your position, that I may be able to give you counsel and assistance."[36] Another bishop, the Right Reverend C. O. Hawks of the Protestant Episcopal Church, announced to his clergy that he had taken the oath, although he strongly protested against what he considered to be its retroactive features. He advised his ministers to take it if they could do so in good conscience; if not, they should refrain from subscribing to the oath, but not necessarily from appearing in the pulpit. Bishop Hawks hoped that this aspect of Radicalism would soon be repealed and that in the meantime the civil authority would not seek to enforce it.[37]

The General Association of Baptists of Missouri held its annual meeting at Boonville in the middle of August. It adopted a long address setting forth five reasons for declining to take the oath. In essence, the document declared that the oath was in conflict with the federal constitution; that it was an unjust attempt to punish ministers for crimes not committed; and that it was an encroachment of state upon church, which Baptists had always fought as a matter of principle. In their district associational meetings across the state that summer most local Baptist groups tended to take a similar stand.[38] That fall, however, the Loyal Missouri Baptist Convention organized at Hannibal and upheld the oath as a means of keeping the pulpit free of disharmonious utterances. The *Missouri Democrat* reported that a large crowd attended this meeting. This group, which established a separate existence from the General Association for the next two years, enjoyed considerable support. It affiliated with the American Baptist Home Mission Society and did considerable church extension work in St. Louis, particularly among the Negroes. In 1867, after the test oath controversy died down, it took steps to effect a reconciliation with the General Association, but stipulated that the state group had to be open to all Baptists regardless of race or color. By the end of that year the schism had been completely healed.[39]

Also in August of 1865 the Methodist Episcopal Church, South, met at St. Louis for its annual conference. Although the sermon of Bishop Henry Kavanaugh dwelt at length and in a caustic fashion upon the dangers of placing temporal power above spiritual power, the conference itself declined to consider the question of the oath as a body. It preferred to allow each minister "to exercise his own discretion in the premises."[40] Almost every Methodist clergyman, however, made his personal decision in the negative.[41]

Governor Fletcher soon brought a rude awakening to those

clergymen who had hoped that a nonenforcement policy on the part of the state would allow them to escape their dilemma. In a letter to the *Missouri Democrat* on August 25 he announced, in language too plain for anyone to misunderstand, that he intended to carry out every provision of the constitution through the full power of his office. Since he considered that document the valid law of the state, pending a different interpretation by judicial authority, he saw no other course open to him. Regarding the problem of the clergy, the Governor asserted:

> Religious liberty is a political right, and when these outraged gentlemen go to the Supreme Court of the United States with their complaint, they will be told that there is not a sentence or a word in the Constitution of the United States which gives them the right to preach at all. That it (the test oath) is an infringement of religious liberty secured to any person by the Constitution of the United States, I deny.[42]

The Radical press warmly applauded this firm statement. The *Democrat* particularly noted that all of the colored clergymen, both in the city and outstate, had taken the oath, which contrasted greatly with the "loyalty" of their more recalcitrant white colleagues.[43]

The Governor's declaration brought a protest from the Reverend Henry A. Nelson, pastor of the First Presbyterian Church in St. Louis. In a letter to the chief executive, forwarded through Senator B. Gratz Brown, he informed Fletcher that although he had taken the oath as a curator of the state university, he refused to recognize the right of the state to exact it of him as a minister. He also expressed the hope that an amendment striking out this provision would soon be forthcoming; in fact, he even predicted that if such a proposal was now submitted to the people, they would approve it overwhelmingly. In a cover letter to the Governor, Brown echoed these same sentiments, but assured Fletcher that until changes could be made he had no wish to "raise obstacles to the putting in force the Constitution."[44]

The deadline for taking the oath arrived on Saturday, September 2, with many clergy across the state having refused to subscribe. The following day Missourians attended religious services in their various churches as usual. Probably, the majority of them heard sermons preached illegally.[45] Father John A. Cummings, the young pastor of the Roman Catholic parish at Louisiana, addressed his congregation in his customary manner that morning. In accordance with the admonitions of Archbishop Kenrick, he had declined to take the oath. Because of his refusal he soon found himself the target of Radical vindictiveness. Several other ministers of the area also became victims. The Radicals lost no time in impaneling a grand jury at Bowling Green, the county seat of Pike County, which brought an indictment against Father Cummings on Tuesday. Three days later the sheriff arrested him and brought him to Bowling Green for arraignment before Circuit Judge Thomas J. C. Fagg, a prominent Radical.[46]

The Cummings case gained notoriety, and, largely because of the martyr complex of the young priest, it came to assume primary importance in the struggle over the iron-clad oath. Other ministers similarly arraigned posted bond at their initial appearances and subsequently had their trials postponed until the spring term of court by circuit judges anxious to let someone else hear the first case. In some instances these men continued to preach, pending final disposition of their cases. A leading Methodist journal, urging them to remain in the state, predicted the overthrow of the oath by the judicial process. It reminded the pastors who had been barred from their pulpits that they could still render great service to their congregations through the ministry of personal visitation in the homes of their parishioners.[47]

Since the Pike County courthouse had been destroyed by fire the previous year, Father Cummings was arraigned in the Bowling Green Methodist Church. To the consternation of Judge Fagg and the attorneys present to try other cases, the young priest refused to post bond. He demanded an immediate trial and announced that he would defend himself. Reluctantly, the Judge ordered his clerk to read the indictment. When asked how he pleaded, Father Cummings promptly replied, "Guilty, sir." This threw the court into further confusion. Judge Fagg, quickly regaining his judicial dignity, declared that since this was the case, it remained only for him to pass sentence. Before doing so, he asked the defendant if he cared to make a statement. Father Cummings had been waiting for just such an opportunity. In what one observer later characterized as "a religious stump speech," the young priest implied that the entire proceedings were an attempt to persecute the Roman Catholic Church and its clergy. He compared his trial with that of Jesus and repudiated the state's right to interfere with his divine calling. Although he admitted his guilt in regard to the indictment just read, Father Cummings vehemently denied that he had broken any just or rightful law.

It so happened that Senator John B. Henderson, a longtime attorney of Pike County, was present in the courtroom in the interests of another case. Ultimately, he was to represent Missouri against Father Cummings before the United States Supreme Court. Now he rose and argued that the priest's final admission should be taken by the court as a plea of "not guilty." When Judge Fagg declined to take the responsibility of reversing the original plea, Henderson gave a penetrating dissection of Father Cummings' statement, which lasted forty-five minutes, and then offered to defend the priest as a token of his good will. Father Cummings declined Henderson's offer, but did agree to accept the aid of a young Conservative attorney, Robert A. Campbell, who was also present. With this arrangement completed, Judge Fagg agreed to allow Cummings to change his plea and declared that the

trial would be continued the following day. Because the accused still refused to post bond, he remained in the Pike
County jail overnight. When the proceedings resumed the
next morning, "justice" moved quickly on its appointed course.
Father Cummings admitted that he had preached without
taking the oath. The court found him guilty and fined him
five hundred dollars, the penalty prescribed by the constitution. Displaying his martyr complex once more, the young
priest refused to pay the fine or to allow his friends to do so.
He was therefore returned to the county jail where he remained exactly one week.[48]

The case became an overnight sensation as the press spread
the details throughout the state. Offers of help poured in.
Archbishop Kenrick at first expressed surprise, but then pleasure at the behavior of the young priest whom he himself had
ordained a short two years earlier. Strong pressure was now
brought on Father Cummings from both Protestant and
Catholic sources to allow his case to be made a test before
the Supreme Court of Missouri. He agreed. After some Protestant friends posted his bond and he was released, he went
to St. Louis to report to the Archbishop.[49]

The Radical press immediately launched an offensive
against Father Cummings and the others who had dared to
defy state authority. Meetings were called in counties with
large Radical populations, and resolutions were passed, re-
affirming the faith of the "loyal men" in the need for stringent
restrictions. These Radicals did not see any incompatibility
between religious and civil duty.[50] Various ministerial groups
also rallied in support of the oath. Early in November the first
Missouri Congregational General Conference met at Hannibal and affirmed its adherence to the principles of "true
Unionism." This group, relatively new in the state, represented Northern church opinion to a large extent and found
only a few adherents among native Missourians. At the same
time the Northern Methodist ministers held a conference at

Warrensburg and passed resolutions upholding the oath and Radical rule in general. Most of these men came from the strife-ridden areas along the southern border where Radicalism existed in its more rampant forms. An interdenominational group, called the Convention of Loyal Ministers, gathered at Macon. They issued a letter that denounced those who refused to accept the oath and called upon their people to abide by all the provisions of the law.[51]

While these events were taking place, arrests continued. How many ministers actually suffered for their convictions is difficult to ascertain. The press made frequent mention of specific cases, and one minister of the Methodist Church, South, at Paris purportedly quit preaching and started delivering "speeches" from his pulpit, as there existed no law against public speaking.[52] A leading Methodist minister declared that "hundreds of priests and preachers were indicted, arrested, and tried in the civil courts for preaching the Gospel." However, even as late as March 1, one religious journal contended that 600 to 1,000 clergymen who had not taken the oath were still preaching throughout the state.[53] Professor Thomas S. Barclay, who has made an extensive study of this problem, reports that he can ascertain only thirty-six specific indictments in approximately twenty-eight counties. Apparently, the extent to which clergymen were intimidated into taking the oath or prosecuted for refusing to do so depended upon the political sentiments of their local area.[54] Unlike the oath for lawyers, the enforcement of which depended upon the control each judge levied on those who practiced before his court, no machinery existed to coerce clergymen if the local populace or law enforcement officials did not do so.

The case of Father Cummings came before the Supreme Court of Missouri late in October of 1865. Robert A. Campbell presented the defense on the ground that the oath constituted both ex post facto legislation and a bill of attainder. E. P. Johnson, the counsel for the state, denied both charges.

He contended that the oath intended no punishment per se for past offenses but merely sought to prescribe qualifications for certain professions. The punishment came, quite constitutionally, only if the individual refused to take the oath. At the same time, the oath could not be considered a bill of attainder because it did not convict anyone of anything.[55] Although few people expected the Supreme Court to repudiate the iron-clad oath in view of the previous decision in the Garesche case, some speculated that the judges might look upon the religious aspect of the matter in a different way.[56] The Court ran true to form, however, by sustaining the argument of the state's counsel and upholding the verdict of the lower court. As for the deeper issues, Judge Wagner, in speaking for a unanimous high tribunal, declared, "It is not for the judiciary to inquire whether laws violate the general principles of liberty or natural justice, or whether they are wise and inexpedient or not."[57]

Campbell immediately filed notice of appeal to the United States Supreme Court. A. J. P. Garesche volunteered his services, which were gratefully accepted. When returning to Louisiana aboard the steamboat *Harry Johnson* after the decision, Father Cummings chanced to encounter Frank Blair, who was on his way to Hannibal to address a Conservative rally. Blair had been following Cummings' case with much interest and now offered to write his brother Montgomery and ask him to help with the case before the Supreme Court. He assured the eager priest that he knew his brother would be glad to assist him without any thought of a fee. Father Cummings readily accepted.[58] Montgomery Blair agreed to take the case and persuaded David Dudley Field and Reverdy Johnson to assist in the presentation. These two eminent attorneys had just won the crucial case, ex parte *Milligan*, before the high tribunal, and Blair felt certain that their aid would be invaluable.[59]

When the adjourned session of the General Assembly of

Missouri convened in November, 1865, Governor Fletcher gave a general summary of the situation in his annual address. "The future good of the State," he asserted, "requires that the question of the right of the people to make it [the oath] be now definitely settled by the Supreme Court of the United States." Maintaining a moderate tone throughout his speech, he recommended that the oath be rescinded for all corporation officials and for teachers in private schools and colleges. He also urged that anyone who had served honorably in the Union army or navy be relieved of taking the oath.[60] The temper of the Radicals in the legislature, however, was far from moderate. Dominated by the members from the northern border and the southwest, the Radical caucus showed no inclination to modify any aspect of the party's program. The outnumbered Conservatives tried in vain to secure amendments abrogating the oath for preachers, teachers, and lawyers. The Radicals would have none of it. "No class of people between heaven and earth, or outside of heaven or hell deserve the curse of God more than disloyal ministers and no class deserve sympathy less than this class," ranted one partisan. "If they can not take the oath, they should go and seek a home elsewhere."[61]

Faced with a hopeless situation in the legislature, the Conservatives looked eagerly to the hearings before the Supreme Court, which heard the arguments in the case of *Cummings v. Missouri* in the middle of March, 1866. The distinguished counsel for the Catholic priest presented no new arguments, but developed much more thoroughly the legal aspects surrounding the basic contentions. Governor Fletcher had appointed George P. Strong, prominent St. Louis attorney and convention delegate, and Senator Henderson to represent the state. The Senator thus became a participant in the final as well as the initial proceedings of the case. He and Strong merely reiterated the presentation made before the Supreme Court of Missouri.[62] Rumors soon began to circulate which

made Conservatives believe the Supreme Court would hand
down a favorable decision for Father Cummings. Supposedly,
Justice Robert C. Grier had informed Frank Blair that the
priest would be upheld. At any rate, Blair claimed fore-
knowledge in several speeches. Reverdy Johnson wrote
Democratic Congressman John Hogan that he had a similar
understanding. Former Senator Orville H. Browning of Illinois recorded in his diary that two of the justices had given
him inside information on the probable outcome of the case
less than month after the hearing.[63] Obviously, the justices
of that era were far from discreet.

In reality, the Court stood narrowly divided on this case
and on another closely related one involving a similar test
oath for lawyers. Without putting either case to a formal vote,
the justices adjourned in May. They ordered the Cummings
case held under advisement and continued to the next term.
The Conservatives expressed bitter disappointment. Some of
them believed they saw the sinister hand of Chief Justice
Salmon P. Chase behind this setback. Supposedly, he wished
the decision postponed in order to aid the Radicals in the
election canvass of 1866. In spite of the postponement, Blair
and others continued to assert that the case would be decided
in Cummings' favor and implied that a positive verdict would
affect the question of the oath's validity for voters as well.[64]

A prominent Radical attorney from northwest Missouri who
was greatly concerned about the matter wrote Chief Justice
Chase, whom he had known earlier in Ohio, and informed
him of Blair's charges. While not desiring "to invade the
sanctity or the proper reserve or respect which we should
ever feel for our highest Judiciary," this Radical spokesman
did wish to know if any decision had been reached in the
Cummings case or if any consultation had even been held.
"Of course I do not ask what the decision is," he hastened to
add, "but if proper I would like to know whether any decision had been arrived at, and if proper I would like permis-

sion to use the information in such way as would be of service in our fight here."[65] Whether the Chief Justice replied is not known. His accumulated letters give no indication of it, and there is no evidence from the newspaper with which this attorney was closely connected that it might have received inside information on the matter.[66]

At least two of Chase's fellow jurists had similar concerns. Justice Samuel F. Miller wrote Chase on June 5 from his home at Keokuk, Iowa, which is just over the line from Missouri, about the Cummings case and the election in the neighboring state. He deplored the "violation of judicial propriety" that one of their colleagues had committed in speaking to either Frank Blair or Reverdy Johnson. Obviously sympathetic with the Radicals, Miller had apparently been the main instigator in having the decision postponed. It now seemed to him that "while we may well feel restrained from stating what *did* take place; there is no wrong, but a manifest propriety in contradicting the assertion that the court has decided an important case, or an important principle when it has done no such thing." Should any of the Radicals ask him about the matter, Miller indicated he would "feel bound to contradict" the Conservatives' statements. He reported, however, that he had not been approached, probably because the Radicals feared confirmation of the claims of their enemies if they did so. Miller suggested that perhaps the Chief Justice might hold a private conversation with one of Missouri's senators "as would at least enable them to deny as boldly as Hogan and Johnson assert."[67] The other jurist who wrote to Chase was Justice Stephen J. Field, who was in San Francisco at the time. Since he was the brother of Father Cummings' chief counsel, he undoubtedly feared that he might be considered the "leak." Such was not the case, however.[68]

Quasi-official contradictions to the Conservatives' charges came from two sources. On June 14 the *Missouri Democrat* published a letter from Senator Henderson to certain Hannibal supporters that denied that any decision had been reached. Henderson made a similar denial in another letter a few days later, which appeared in the *St. Louis Evening News*. In reference to the oath for voters, the Senator had "no doubt at all" of its legal validity, regardless of what the judges might decide in the Cummings case and other related ones.[69] On June 27 the *Democrat* brought forth another letter. Addressed to Charles D. Drake, it came from Gustavus Koerner, a prominent Illinois Republican. He had talked a few days earlier with one of the Supreme Court judges, who had emphatically denied that the Cummings case had been decided. Indeed, the justice reported that "*no vote had ever been taken on it.*" He further stated, in a sharp manner, that the question of the oath for voters did not enter into the case at any point.[70] Koerner had undoubtedly visited with Justice David Davis. Justice Miller wrote Davis immediately: "I am rejoiced at the bold and courageous manner in which you have contradicted the falsehood which has been so largely circulated in Missouri for political effect." Miller had previously heard from Chase, who had agreed with him about the unfortunate impropriety of Johnson and Blair. The Chief Justice would inform the attorneys for Missouri that they had as much information on the case as their rival counsel or anyone else.[71]

When the General Assembly met the following January, the Radicals had just emerged highly successful from an election in which they won large majorities in both houses. Most of them felt quite complacent and had little desire to disturb the *status quo*. Yet, Governor Fletcher in his annual message strongly recommended that the Assembly submit a constitutional amendment that would repeal the oath for lawyers, ministers, and teachers. He admitted quite frankly that many men in these professions openly violated the oath requirement with relative freedom. "The example offered by the disregard of unnecessary laws, especially by so intelligent and

influential a class of citizens," he asserted, "begets a general
disposition to exercise individual discretion in obeying or
enforcing laws—a disposition which leads to anarchy and
impunity in crime."[72]

A group of moderates immediately began to implement the
Governor's suggestion, but before they had time to put their
plan into effect, the United States Supreme Court accomplished their task for them. On January 14, 1867, that tribunal
finally handed down its decision in the Cummings case. Justice Field read the elaborate opinion on behalf of a 5-to-4
majority. It declared that the test oath provisions as applied
to professional groups constituted both a bill of attainder
and ex post facto legislation. As such, the oath had denied
Father Cummings the right to pursue his profession on the
basis of an act not punishable at the time it might have been
committed and on a legislative rather than a judicial proceeding. Thus, the Court reversed the judgment of the Missouri tribunal by attesting the unconstitutionality of these
provisions and declaring them null and void.[73] The four dissenting judges entered a vigorous objection. They denied the
majority's allegations and asserted that the test oath might
be a desirable and necessary thing in protecting the nation
and the state against disloyal men.[74]

This important decision also applied to the case, ex parte
Garland, which involved the constitutionality of a national
statute requiring an iron-clad oath for lawyers practicing before the United States Supreme Court. Now the question of
Missouri's test oath for professional classes seemed generally
taken care of. Alexander J. P. Garesche, Samuel T. Glover,
and other attorneys found themselves welcomed once more to
the bar of the St. Louis courts after an absence of a year and
one half.[75] Charles D. Drake raved about the necessity for
continued resistance to prevent disloyal attorneys from practicing, but few heeded his words.[76] "The war is now over,"
declared the *Missouri Democrat,* "and whether such restric-

tions were or were not legal and necessary during its continuance, the demand for them no longer exists, and the
decision as confined to its legitimate scope and effect, will
do but little practical harm."[77]

Several scores of cases were pending on the dockets of Missouri's circuit courts when the Cummings decision was handed
down. They had been continued from time to time, for the
judges were awaiting the outcome of the test case. Many of
the cases were now dismissed outright; in other instances,
the circuit attorneys entered a nolle prosequi, whereupon the
defendants were discharged. The Supreme Court of Missouri
recognized the authoritative force of its national counterpart
in October, 1867, when it reversed a series of decisions by
lower courts involving the test oath for preachers and lawyers. The key cases were the appeals of Father David H.
Murphy from the Cape Girardeau circuit court and of Samuel T. Glover from the circuit court of St. Louis County. In
its decisions in these cases the Court included a sweeping
announcement that the Cummings decision established the
rule in all similar cases.[78] This action put an effective end
to further legal controversy.

And what of Father John Cummings? After his meeting
with Frank Blair on the steamer, he had lost personal in-
volvement with the whole affair. By the time the Pike County
circuit court received and acted on the Supreme Court order
by reversing its judgment and discharging the defendant,
Father Cummings had been serving as pastor of St. Stephen's
Parish at Indian Creek in Monroe County for nearly two
years. He did not even appear personally before the circuit
court that morning of March 4, 1868. As many others before
him, he had moved briefly into the spotlight, served his purpose, and slipped back into obscurity. He continued as pastor
of St. Stephen's until he became ill in September of 1870.
Three years later, on June 11, 1873, he died in a St. Louis
hospital. No obituary appeared in any newspaper, religious
or secular.[79]

CHAPTER V

THE ELECTION OF 1866

T HE TENSIONS that existed over the test oath focused attention on the need for unity among the various elements in Missouri that were opposed to both the state and national policies of the Radicals. When the Radicals in Congress began their moves to take the reconstruction program out of the hands of the President in December of 1865, the larger unification began to develop. The convention at Verandah Hall in St. Louis in November set the stage for this organization of the opposition. It established a state executive committee composed of representative Conservative Unionists who were to begin the process of co-ordination. By the end of the year this group had established its permanent headquarters in St. Louis. They laid the basis for a state-wide movement by setting up district steering committees made up of one representative from each county. Much of this progress was accomplished at the ratification meetings held in the various counties by the delegates after they returned home.[1]

The Radicals, through their control of the General Assembly, sought to forestall their opponents by passing a comprehensive registry bill. Charles D. Drake took personal charge of this matter. He appeared before a special Radical caucus at the beginning of the adjourned session in November with the bill in his hand. With his followers from the rural areas dominating the party majority, he had little difficulty in securing caucus consent for his proposal, which was introduced in the House on November 10. The small Conservative minority made a concerted effort to secure amendments that would allay the highly partisan provisions of the bill, but Radical unity held. The amendments were defeated, and in little more than a month after its opening meeting the Assembly had the bill on the Governor's desk ready for his signature.[2] Under the terms of this bill the Governor would appoint a supervisor of registration in each county to oversee the 1866 election. In subsequent elections the holder of this office would be decided by the voters. The process of registration outlined by the constitution would take place under the general direction of the supervisor. He would appoint "one competent and prudent person" in each election district to handle the details at the local level. These officials had almost unlimited power to ascertain the loyalty of any individual wishing to register. Each county would have a review and appeals board, but since this board would consist of the supervisor and his district assistants, little redress could be had there. The boards also had absolute authority to add or subtract names from the rolls if they found discrepancies in the work of a local official.[3] The Radical press praised the measure and exultantly looked forward to the coming election. Ratification meetings brought resolutions of approval from the Radical faithful in county after county. The applications for the appointment of supervisor quickly flowed into the Governor's office.[4]

As the Conservatives girded themselves for battle, they

firmly believed that even though they were faced with this major obstacle, they could still win the upcoming election if the officials administered the registry law fairly. Many of them agreed with Henry Myers of St. Louis when he wrote President Johnson about the need for a new party. "The sins of our Democratic party makes it to stink in the nostrils of all good men," Myers asserted, "and it is only a question of taste which of the present parties smell the worse."[5] In adopting the label of Conservative Unionists, the opposition sought to steer clear of any association with the discredited "Copperhead" Democracy as an organization, but extended an open welcome to any of its followers who wished to join them. This new party emphasized adherence to the Union and loyalty to the wartime Provisional Government of Missouri. To present a solid front, such former Whigs as James S. Rollins, William F. Switzler, and James O. Broadhead joined with such Benton Democrats as Frank Blair, Samuel Glover, John S. Phelps, and Thomas Gantt. As the campaign picked up tempo, men of a more pro-Southern bent, such as Lewis V. Bogy, began to adhere to the principles of the new party and infiltrate the leadership. Beyond these groups there stood a handful of disenchanted Radicals who wished to join the opposition, even though the Conservatives tended to hold them at arm's length for a while.[6]

A big question for the Conservatives, as this unity began to evolve, was what stand the state central committee of the Democratic party would take in the campaign. The committee had held a rather tenuous position for some time. If it sought to play an independent role in the election, disaster for the party might be automatic. At a meeting of their small remnant in February, 1866, sentiment seemed generally in favor of merger with the Conservative Union party, at least for the coming election.[7] With many of their leaders openly moving to the forefront of the new movement, the rank-and-file Democrats had little choice but to follow. Any attempt at reviving their own organization would split the vote of the opposition and accomplish nothing. Apparently, only one small group of Democrats in Boone County thought otherwise. They called a Democratic meeting in May. Blair considered their action "an attempt of the soreheads to secure the county offices" and informed Rollins that he had "pitched into" them in a speech at Rocheport. Rollins later intervened directly with the persons involved; through a plea for unity he thwarted the movement before it had hardly begun.[8]

With President Johnson's veto of the Freedmen's Bureau bill on February 19, national issues began to take on greater prominence. Letters of congratulations and support poured in upon the President from the Missouri Conservatives. Twenty-four members of the General Assembly assured him of their ardent support in his efforts "to restore the Union of all the States, with all their dignity, equality and right unimpaired." Conservatives gathered in county meetings to endorse the President, and "Johnson Clubs" began to form. A crowd of an estimated ten thousand gathered at a Johnson rally in St. Louis, which had been called by the state central committee of the Conservative Unionists.[9]

Meanwhile, the Radicals quickly lined up behind their counterparts in Congress. Governor Fletcher telegraphed Senator Henderson in Washington that the Missouri legislature had given overwhelming assent to resolutions sustaining the Republicans there. Henry T. Blow, one of the state's Radical congressmen who had hoped throughout the winter that the White House would co-operate, now wrote Johnson in disparaging tones: "I am both grieved and disappointed at the course you have seen fit to pursue." The Radicals of Putnam County expressed their opinions more bluntly when they proclaimed: "Andrew Johnson, having abandoned the party which elected him, and the principles upon which he was elected, we unhesitatingly denounce him as a traitor, to said party, and to the great principles of our government."[10]

As the state and national struggles merged, matters of patronage became increasingly important. The secretary of the
Conservative Union state central committee wrote to Johnson
on February 27 and enclosed a translation of an article from
the *Westliche Post* that violently denounced the administration. This attack represented no new policy for the German
paper. Why, the secretary asked, should the *Westliche Post*
continue to enjoy "very extensive government patronage from
the War Dept."? Such assistance should be given, instead, to
"sound" Conservative journals that supported the administration.[11] The President agreed and forwarded the letter to Secretary of War Stanton with the request that he look into the
matter. Back came a prompt reply from Stanton that he had
ordered the *Westliche Post* to be stricken from the publication list of his department and notice to be given the publishers to that effect.[12]

The Radicals had been trying with little success to make
inroads into the postal and revenue services since the previous summer. One of the key positions was the postmaster-
ship at St. Louis, held since 1864 by Peter S. Foy, a staunch
Conservative Union man. Before Lincoln's assassination strong
efforts had been made to dislodge Foy by the Radicals, who
pushed for the appointment of the merchant Henry McKee,
brother of one of the proprietors of the *Missouri Democrat*.
McKee enlisted the support of both the Missouri senators and
most of the state's congressmen, but to no avail. The Conservatives fought equally hard for Foy. At the beginning of
February, when it became obvious that the Radicals had little
chance of securing the post, McKee withdrew his application.
The following month President Johnson appointed Foy to a
new term of office and designated Frank Blair as collector
of internal revenue for Missouri. However, when Senators
Brown and Henderson withheld their endorsement from both,
the Senate refused to confirm them.[13]

With the appointment of a new postmaster general in July

and the adjournment of Congress that summer, patronage problems began to look brighter for the Missouri Conservatives. One of their papers noted: "The Internal Revenue department has been pretty well cleaned out, while Postmasters are dropping like the leaves of autumn. Let the good work go on." Foy continued in his post at St. Louis, for no successor was appointed. The Conservatives generally agreed on Daniel M. Grissom, the editor of the *St. Louis Dispatch,* when and if a new appointment had to be made, but they preferred waiting until after the November election, "when to say nothing of other reasons a more judicious opinion can be formed."[14] Also, municipal elections held that spring brought the Radicals a number of stunning setbacks in St. Louis, St. Joseph, Kansas City, and elsewhere. The Conservatives began to smile. The registry act had not yet gone into effect, however, and most Radicals confidently expected that it would help improve their position by November.[15]

The Conservatives, seeking to strike while the opportunity was good, sent Frank Blair on an extensive speaking tour into the interior of the state in early May. At the outset Blair assured his father that "affairs in Missouri [looked] promising" and that victory seemed certain. With an eye on the future, Frank confided, "It is almost a conceded thing that I am to be the Senator in case of our success."[16] The colorful and controversial Blair met a mixed reception as he moved from town to town. Large audiences came to hear him satirize and ridicule the Radicals. Trouble frequently erupted. The Radical press showered him with a torrent of abuse. From Boonville he wrote Rollins that he "had a very good time & a large audience." The Radicals had threatened to disrupt the meeting but failed to show up. "I was interrupted once or twice by them," he reported, "but I took Old Bullion's [Thomas Hart Benton's] plane & insulted them in the grossest terms. The people shouted & cheered & they quieted down very quickly."[17]

The threats became more than vocal at Warrensburg. Blair had been warned not to speak there; undaunted, he came anyway. His supporters set up an improvised speaker's stand near the courthouse, which Blair mounted at one o'clock for a speech that was to last about five hours. In the midst of his bitter discourse an old farmer named Bill Stephens became so incensed that he walked forward shouting "liar" and moved as if to attack Frank. Blair, looking coolly in his direction, bitingly remarked, "I'll take care of the ——." An attorney friend quickly grabbed Stephens by the neck and forced him back into his seat. Frank carried a little derringer pistol in his vest pocket and later told his host that he would not have hesitated to use it if Stephens had gotten any further. While this commotion was going on, one of the old farmer's sons attempted to attack Blair from another direction, but was stabbed by one of Frank's supporters who feared for the General's life. The wounded man was dragged some distance away, where he soon died. The man who wielded the fatal knife eluded pursuers and never came to trial. In the excitement, part of the speakers' stand had given away. Blair's supporters propped up the temporary structure, and Frank continued speaking as if nothing had happened.[18]

In all his speeches Blair preached the Conservative line that President Johnson must be upheld and the test oath and the registry act resisted. He assured his hearers that the United States Supreme Court had already decided the unconstitutionality of the test oath and implied that its ruling would throw the oath out as a requirement for voting. All who had not actually borne rebel arms, Blair urged, should attempt to register and should take the oath without hesitation.[19] He wrote his father that he had delivered some thirty speeches and was almost "broken down with the fatigue of speaking and travelling." In spite of the threats and several hostile demonstrations, both Frank and the state central committee expressed satisfaction with the results of his tour.

The impact of his personality and the wide publicity he received had given the Conservative cause quite a boost.[20]

The Conservative leaders realized that the main obstacle in the road to victory lay in the registry act. By early summer they had evolved a seemingly satisfactory plan to surmount this difficulty. Under the law, voters whose loyalty the registrars doubted had nevertheless to be listed on the poll books with a notation of suspicion. They could still vote; their ballots would simply be marked "rejected" and kept separate from the others. In the tallying of the votes these rejects would not be counted. As the Conservatives saw the matter, the anticipated overthrow of the test oath by the Supreme Court would give strong ground for election contests to be brought forth by their candidates who might be defeated. If the courts ruled a recount, rejected votes would have to be included because they had been thrown out by the authority of an unconstitutional oath. Therefore the word went out for every Conservative to attempt to register and vote, even if it meant the official rejection of his ballot.[21]

As the Conservative bandwagon appeared to be making considerable headway, the Radicals hurriedly began strengthening their local organizations across the state. Radical orators seized every opportunity to exhort the faithful to do their duty not only by going to the polls themselves but also by making sure that no questionable Conservative had the opportunity to cast an acceptable ballot. To supplement the usual party machinery, vigilance committees and associations organized in numerous areas and offered free "assistance" to local registration officials.[22]

The Radical campaign got under way officially on May 10 with a gigantic rally in St. Louis to celebrate the fifth anniversary of the capture of Camp Jackson. Chinese lanterns decorated the courthouse, and large transparencies hung suspended between the pillars on the eastern portico. These banners proclaimed: "Loyal men shall rule, not rebels";

"Union and liberty forever"; "All honor to Gen. Lyon and
the patriots of 1861." No one mentioned that prominent
among the latter had been Frank Blair. To emphasize the
significance of the occasion, Governor Richard J. Oglesby
of Illinois came from Springfield to join Governor Fletcher
on the speakers' rostrum. Unfortunately, Governor Oglesby
became indisposed midway through his talk, perhaps because
of elaborate refreshments served earlier at the Tower Grove
estate of Henry Shaw. Shouts went up for Drake to step
forward, but by the time he arrived on the platform Oglesby
had recovered and finished his talk. A few wags were heard
shouting "Andrew Johnson" from the rear of the audience,
a reference to that individual appearing at his vice-presi-
dential inauguration in a tipsy state. The crowd roared in
laughter, and the Governor sat down somewhat nonplused.
In all other respects, however, the rally marked a grand
start for the campaign.[23] The following week the Radical
state executive committee issued its official address and exhorted the party's adherents to zealously perform their duty.
It also announced that Governor William M. Stone of Iowa
would make a ten-day tour of Missouri on behalf of their
cause in early June. The youthful Governor, a vigorous partisan, would hopefully inspire the Radical rank and file.[24]

The Conservatives rose to the invasion by dispatching
James O. Broadhead and James S. Rollins to challenge Governor Stone along the way. When these men appeared at
the same place on the same day to offer debate, the Governor
became irritated. Although dual meetings frequently occurred
and disorder often followed, the Radical partisans turned out
in large numbers. The Governor castigated President Johnson and the Conservatives as unworthy inheritors of Abraham
Lincoln and as betrayers of the trust placed in their hands.
The tour came to a climax at Jefferson City, and Governor
Oglesby again appeared and lent his support to the grand

finale. The state executive committee considered the entire effort quite worth while.[25]

Governor Fletcher, Lieutenant Governor George Smith, Secretary of State Rodman, and other state officials now took to the stump to build upon the groundwork laid by Governor Stone. Fletcher, particularly, performed yeoman's work as he toured southwest Missouri during early July and spent all of October visiting the other corners of the state. Charles D. Drake plunged into the thick of battle in late June with a speech at Hillsboro and kept up an arduous pace the rest of the summer and fall. Some Jefferson County Conservatives sought to press Drake into an open debate with Blair, but the Radical leader declined to get involved in a "rough-and-tumble squabble," and the two continued their separate paths.[26]

Whether he would admit it or not, Drake had more in mind that summer and fall than simply defending "his constitution" and campaigning for the Radicals. Senator B. Gratz Brown had announced on June 27 that he would not seek re-election before the legislature that winter. He had been in ill health for some time and had never been very enthusiastic about Drake's constitution. Although he had been active in the Radical movement from its inception, he found the current trend of the party of "waving the bloody shirt" distasteful. Brown's support of Negro suffrage and a modification of the test oath displeased many Radicals. Whether Drake's claim that Brown did not stand a chance for re-election, even if he had wanted it, is correct cannot be certain. Quite probably, he would have had competition within the Radical caucus. Nevertheless, now that a Senate seat was in the offing, Drake became a logical choice for the position. Nothing was mentioned during the canvass, but immediately after the election his name was brought forward by the Radical press.[27]

One of the most important aspects of Radical strategy that

summer was the cultivation of the veterans' vote. Soldiers'
Leagues and Soldiers' Associations began to appear in county
after county. Although these clubs were not officially connected with the Radical party organization, their instigators,
in most instances, played an active role within the ranks of
that group. The ostensible purpose of these associations was
twofold: to secure the ex-soldiery its full share of benefits in
postwar times and to make certain that the general citizenry
fully appreciated their military services. They also proclaimed
that they would stand between their country and the disloyal
classes if it should become necessary. These organizations
proved an excellent means of re-enlisting the rank-and-file
Germans in the Radical cause. The Germans had formed the
hard core of Missouri's volunteers in the Union military cause.
Now they fell in line behind their old leaders to enlist in a
new campaign.

A call for an organizational meeting in St. Louis appeared
in the *Missouri Democrat* and the German press. It warned
the city's veterans: "The copperheads and rattlesnakes hidden
under Union flowers . . . are endeavoring to swindle us out
of our victories . . . and to destroy this Republic." Frank
Blair, their former hero, was labeled a "false Moses" who
sought to lead the "rebels" back to their old power. He was
also accused of being a fanatic who would not stop short of
perjury at the polls or rebellion, if necessary, to accomplish
his evil purpose. Should the "Copperheads" win in Missouri,
it predicted, disaster would follow for all "loyal men." The
Radicals

> would be persecuted and driven from our homes in the
> North just as it is already done in the South. The graves
> of our comrades, mouldering in the Southern sand,
> would be desecrated; the rebel soldiers would receive
> pensions and bounties out of the Federal treasury; the
> rebel debt would be paid; the Union declared bankrupt;
> our cripples would be outcasts; our families abandoned

to the bitterest misery, and we ourselves would be insulted and ridiculed.[28]

Few hardened veterans could resist this strong plea. A large group came out to hear a number of prominent Radical leaders address them in both English and German. Emil Pretorius, the proprietor of the *Westliche Post,* headed the program and read a letter from Governor Fletcher that expressed his hope that those who had waged the battle would assert their "right to name and control the terms of settlement after the fight was over." In all of the speeches there was an obvious attempt to equate the Radical program with the welfare of the veterans and their families.[29]

The *Missouri Democrat* and other Radical papers constantly encouraged the formation of Soldiers' Leagues throughout the state. They warned that a reign of terror would follow for the "loyal men" if the Conservatives won. The climax of all this activity came on August 10. Delegates from the local leagues gathered at Turners' Hall in St. Louis to celebrate the fifth anniversary of the Battle of Wilson's Creek and to hold a mass convention for the purpose of improving their state organization. Throughout the day the veterans listened to harangue after harangue by Governor Fletcher and other Radicals against President Johnson, Frank Blair, and the Conservatives in general. That evening they moved—ten thousand strong—to Union Park, where four speakers' stands had been set up for simultaneous use. General John A. Logan of Illinois climaxed the proceedings, and in his speech he denounced the opposition as the "Grand Conservative, Copperhead National Union speckled prodigy of the last dispensation." The whole affair proved to be a tremendous success.[30]

Down at the courthouse the Conservatives, under Blair's leadership, held their own veterans' rally. Because it was a hastily arranged counterdemonstration, the meeting apparently was something less than a success, although the *Missouri Republican* announced that a large group attended.

Blair had advertised that Generals Sherman and Hancock had been invited to speak, but neither man made an appearance. Instead, Blair and others attacked the Soldiers' League as being composed of men who had seen little real action during the war.[31] Despite the efforts of the Conservatives the leagues continued to form. It is doubtful if the Conservatives garnered much of the veterans' vote that fall.

The Conservative Union party held its state convention in the hall of the Mercantile Library of St. Louis early in July. As to personnel, it bore a close resemblance to the gathering at Verandah Hall eight months earlier. Edward Bates wrote the President that "for numbers, individual work, popular estimation and general weight of character" he had never seen its equal in Missouri.[32] The *St. Louis Evening News* took a somewhat dimmer view. Although it admitted that the delegates ranked high in "social status," it described them as "a collection of political driftwood, a floating together of all the political debris of the State."[33] Whatever the tenor of their make-up, the delegates promptly settled down to work —listening to the well-worn speeches of their orators and drafting resolutions similar to those adopted at the county meetings they had previously attended. With due recognition for the wide range of forces within their ranks, they chose a delegation to represent Missouri at the National Union Convention in Philadelphia, which had been called as a nationwide demonstration of support for President Johnson. To co-ordinate the campaign at home, they established a steering committee composed of Frank Blair, Lewis Bogy, James O. Broadhead, Thomas T. Gantt, and Samuel T. Glover.[34]

Even as the Conservatives met, the various supervisors of registration began appointing their assistants and preparing for their work, which was to begin officially in September. Reports of the highly partisan nature of many of these appointments began to filter into the Conservative headquarters in St. Louis. Far from being "competent and prudent," as re-

quired by the registry law, many registrars openly boasted
that it would be "their purpose to disfranchise all who are
not 'unmistakeably loyal.'" To the Conservatives this implied
all those who would not vote the Radical ticket.[35]

Conservative leaders became equally alarmed over reports
that Governor Fletcher was gathering the militia into companies for the purpose of controlling the election. Violence
had recently erupted on the western border and threatened
to spread. These initial outbreaks, however, were totally un-
connected with the election campaign. They had been brought
on by overly zealous Radical officials in Jackson County, who
had been appointed the preceding year by Governor Fletcher
under the terms of the Ousting Ordinance. The area of Jackson County had been the scene of intense guerrilla warfare
throughout the Civil War, and many fathers and sons from
the rural homes had helped to fill the ranks of the bushwhackers. After the conflict most of these men had accepted
President Johnson's amnesty terms and had returned to their
homes peacefully under the assumption that the presidential
pardon cleared them of all past crimes. With the coming to
office of a set of highly partisan Radicals and with the ratification of the new state constitution, grand juries began to
meet and render indictments against some of these men for
wartime crimes. Many of them took to the bush once more,
and turmoil ensued.[36]

As the social and economic wreckage of the war years continued to take its toll in 1865 and 1866, morality was at a
low ebb generally. Readjustment after such an upheaval is
never easy. In view of their wartime experiences, loyal Missourians cannot be blamed for their intense desire to be rid
of returning rebeldom or at least to hold it within tight legal-
istic molds. On the other hand, many of the returning Confederates and the ex-guerrillas who had pictured themselves
as partisan Southern rangers became dismayed and disillu-
sioned as rampant Radical partisanship took stronger political

and economic reprisals. The severity of these retaliations and the strength of unchecked Radicalism determined to a large measure the extent of the continued turbulence in any given area. Early in February, 1866, Governor Fletcher called on General John Pope, who commanded the Department of Missouri, to send one or two companies of cavalry to assist certain sheriffs in executing writs against bushwhackers threatening to disturb the peace. The commander replied that because all of his men were out on the plains, he had no troops available. Personally, Pope deplored the idea of having to use federal troops to preserve order in the state, and he wrote Fletcher, "It seems to me far better for the people of Missouri to put all their law abiding population in arms if necessary to protect the peace than to have one single United States soldier thus employed." He concluded that he would redistribute regular army forces in Missouri "with extreme reluctance and only under the pressure of what would seem to me actual necessity."[37]

On February 13 a group of armed robbers held up the Clay County Savings Association at Liberty, killed a boy who had run into the street to give the alarm, and escaped with sixty thousand dollars. Other robberies soon followed; the era of the desperado had been ushered in.[38] The metropolitan area was also plagued by lawlessness. The *Missouri Democrat* noted in November, 1865:

> Never in the memory of the most ancient citizen . . . has rascality stalked so boldly about our streets as at the present time. Houses are entered every night by burglars, and the inmates robbed, while a bolder class of rogues, who disdain the labor of climbing porches, picking locks, and experimenting on window fastenings, attack citizens on the public thoroughfares and cooly [*sic*] relieve them of their watches, jewelry and money. These operations are carried on by sun light and gas light.

To curb this state of affairs, the St. Louis paper urged the establishment of vigilance committees.[39]

As violence continued, voluntary groups of "regulators" began to appear in many of the counties of western Missouri. Usually composed of Radical partisans, they took the law into their own hands and dealt out heavy-handed "justice." The Honest Men's League of Greene County organized in the summer of 1866 and, like many other such groups, frequently acted first and talked later. As the summer wore on, the activities of these vigilantes began to bear heavy political undertones.[40]

With trouble continuing during the spring and summer Governor Fletcher felt that it was necessary to call up the militia. In many instances these were volunteer companies composed of persons subject to emergency militia duty. Made up primarily of Radicals and armed by the state, they would serve as unofficial posses to aid local officials in making arrests. Frequently, they performed their duties in such a highly partisan manner that they stirred up as much unrest as they quelled.[41] The Conservatives forwarded the details of these disturbances and reiterated their fears of political implications to President Johnson through Congressman John Hogan. They charged that the Radicals had deliberately created general chaos in order to justify their demands for stringent militia rule at election time. "Our friends here are of opinion that the whole of the foul scheme can be killed as it were, in the egg, by a few prompt measures of prevention," wrote Thomas T. Gantt for the state central committee. In his letter he specifically asked that General Pope be replaced by General Winfield Scott Hancock as commander of the department and requested that regular troops be stationed at convenient points throughout the state to keep order and to counteract the effect of the militia.[42]

During a conference at the White House the President passed this material along to General Sherman, who commanded the Division of the Mississippi in which the Department of Missouri was contained, and asked him to look into this matter. When Sherman returned to his headquarters in St. Louis, he promptly arranged an interview with Governor Fletcher and invited Gantt and Samuel Glover to attend as representatives of the Conservatives. The meeting took place on the morning of August 9 in Sherman's office. The General later reported to President Johnson that the four men had a long conversation in which all participated freely. Governor Fletcher was quite co-operative and disclaimed any intention of using the militia to interfere with the upcoming election. His only purpose, he assured the others, had been to preserve law and order so that a "free and open election, without violence or threat" would be assured. Glover, who had just returned from a trip to the interior of the state, contested Fletcher's statement by mentioning numerous instances of militia violence. General Sherman seemed to agree with the two Conservatives that Fletcher had not acted wisely in relying strictly on volunteers to form the militia companies. Although the Governor had good motives, his militia men frequently took advantage of their positions and went beyond the work for which they had been assembled.

At this conference Glover and Gantt also expressed their concern over the arming of organized Negro militia and asked the purpose of this. Governor Fletcher replied that he had commissioned and armed two Negro regiments in St. Louis in order to protect the Negroes and their property. He quickly added that he intended to extend this policy throughout the state in areas where the Negroes had been subject to frequent violence with little redress. When he was asked to name specific instances, however, the Governor could give no answer. The Conservative leaders retorted that the Negroes themselves had claimed that their purpose in arming was to "guard the polls" on election day, and they warned that if this proved to be the case, "there will either be no election or there will be a fight beyond all reasonable doubt." Disavowing any desire for violence, the Conservative leaders urged the disbanding of the various militia units. They believed that such action would have "an immense effect in tranquilizing the state." General Sherman agreed, and the conference ended with the understanding that Governor Fletcher would soon issue a proclamation to this effect. Gantt and Glover received additional assurances when they called on the Governor later that same afternoon.[43]

A few days later Missouri's Conservative delegation to the National Union Convention at Philadelphia stopped in Washington for an interview with President Johnson. They discussed, in rather gloomy terms, the general situation in Missouri. After going over much of the same material that had been covered in the meeting at General Sherman's headquarters, they told Johnson quite bluntly that Missouri's republican form of government stood in danger and hinted that active federal intervention might be necessary to preserve it.[44] When word of this meeting reached St. Louis, it brought a strong retort from Charles D. Drake and the Radical press. Drake denounced the Conservatives' move as an attempt to secure the coming election by force through military interference by the United States government. He denied the right of federal action under the provisions of the constitution and assured the people that their republican form of government was in no way threatened by the Radicals.[45]

President Johnson, however, had acted even before the conferences at St. Louis and Washington had taken place. He assigned General Hancock to the command of the Department of Missouri under General Sherman. Upon his arrival at his new post, Hancock went immediately to Jefferson City to confer with Governor Fletcher. The details of their interview on August 14 and 15 were not publicly disclosed, but the *Democrat*'s correspondent at the capital noted that "at its conclusion both seemed in excellent good humor."[46]

General Hancock later informed the Secretary of War that the conference had been quite satisfactory. The Governor had promised to disarm the partisan forces presently organized under his orders and to rely on civil authorities and federal troops in the future. To insure peace on election day, he would also issue an order forbidding all armed men from approaching the polls. "If he carries out his promises as I believe he will do, we will have a quiet election," the General assured his superior.[47]

Governor Fletcher wasted little time in fulfilling these promises. The day after the interview, August 16, he issued a proclamation declaring that the combined power of both the state and federal governments would be used to insure obedience to the law. He pledged a fair registration and a quiet election and reaffirmed that the militia would be reorganized properly on a less partisan basis.[48] On September 6 the state's Adjutant General ordered the disbanding of "all companies or detachments of the Missouri militia . . . not in conformity with the provisions of the Ordinance for the organization of the Missouri militia." All arms that had been issued must be returned to the Quartermaster General.[49]

General Sherman, on a tour of frontier outposts, endorsed the Governor's proclamation as soon as word of it reached him. He expected the Conservative leaders to do the same, but Gantt and Glover had reservations. "The great difficulty in dealing with Gov. Fletcher," Gantt complained, "is the want of correspondence between promise and performance." The Conservative leader maintained that the Governor had taken no direct steps to disband "the illegal organisations of his partisan militia" but rather had only held out promises "to do this at some period in the indefinite future."[50] General Hancock reported to his touring superior that many others also shared the belief that the Governor was not sincere in his statements. They held that he was "encouraging the secret arming of leagues of the Radical party while disbanding par-

tisan troops." In order to dispel such feelings, Hancock urged
Fletcher to call upon him for troops if they were necessary
to maintain order, even though such a policy had its draw-
backs. Army headquarters had promised three companies of
regulars for Missouri duty. When Sherman expressed the fear
that these soldiers might be detailed from troops badly
needed on the frontier, Hancock hastily reassured him that
such would not be the case. Sherman thereupon accepted
the situation, contingent upon no more than three companies
being used.[51]

Governor Fletcher returned from a trip to the East in the
middle of September. He denied vehemently any ulterior
motives or any connection with unofficial and irresponsible
secret organizations. "My reliance, General, is upon you," he
wrote Hancock. "I desire to do nothing more than to enforce
obedience to the laws of the state. I want no armed militia
for the purpose until you inform me that the force at your
disposal is insufficient." The Governor reported finding doz-
ens of letters from sheriffs and other officials awaiting him
on his return that asked for force to aid them in their duties.
"I have endeavored by supplying additional deputy sheriffs
to strengthen the power of the law, and by appeals to the
civil officers and people to urge them to do their duty,"
Fletcher informed the General.[52]

General Hancock had also been receiving urgent requests
for help from over the state. He forwarded these letters to
the Governor and suggested sending a discreet staff officer
to investigate. He would send troops, but only if Fletcher
asked for them. This became the pattern of procedure in the
month and a half remaining until the election. By the middle
of October Hancock found his three companies spreading
thin. As further requests for help came in, he had to report
that no more troops were available. With Sherman unenthu-
siastic about the policy in general, Hancock tried to do his
best, but his men could not be everywhere at once. During

the week before the election Sherman did agree to release
two additional companies at Fort Leavenworth for temporary
service in Missouri. One company was immediately dispatched to Ray County and the other to Platte.[53] There is
every indication that this policy of using federal troops to
help enforce law and order in Missouri, although obviously
distasteful to many Radicals, had a positive effect. Most disturbances were temporary flare-ups. The mere presence of a
military officer or a small troop in an area usually brought
matters under control without the direct use of force. Many
of the later incidents arose as local groups of armed Radicals
sought to "protect" the registration officials in the performance of their duties or as Conservatives became overwrought
at the tactics used in determining voter eligibility. Governor
Fletcher's statement to Hancock on November 15 indicates
the fortunate effect of the co-operation between the federal
and state agencies: "I was happy in the thought that we
had so well managed to keep peace in the exciting time of
election."[54]

In spite of occasional violence, registration proceeded apace
during September and October. Challenges were frequent
from both sides. In Boone County, for instance, the local
Columbia registry officers denied William F. Switzler, the
prominent Conservative who stood as his party's congressional
candidate, the right to register. They gave no reason for their
refusal. Switzler appealed to the county board of revision and
demanded an explanation; he found that he was under suspicion of having supplied funds for rebel groups in 1861.
After he disproved the accusations, the board added his name
to the list of eligible voters.[55] At the other extreme, Daniel
M. Grissom and A. J. P. Garesche challenged the registration
of Charles D. Drake before the St. Louis board of revision
on the ground that the Radical leader had committed disloyal acts in 1861. Their accusations concerned questionable
utterances purportedly made by Drake at the time of the

Camp Jackson affair, although these charges had long since been disproved in another connection. When Drake appeared in person before the board and read a long defense, the two Conservatives quickly dropped the matter. Nevertheless, the *St. Louis Dispatch,* of which Grissom was editor, sought to make much of the situation by printing such headlines as "The Guillotine and its Inventor" or "The Inventor under his own instrument."[56]

Little uniformity existed in the registration process. The procedure employed depended upon the sentiments of the county and the zealousness of the registering officials. In areas where armed Radical groups offered their protection to the registrars, Conservatives usually stayed away from the registry offices despite the importunities of their leaders. In strongly Conservative areas little difficulty was encountered, although some registration officials later cried that they had been intimidated to accept the enrollment of many persons known to them to be ineligible.[57]

The final decision on the eligibility of the voters belonged to the board of revision. Meeting after the work of the local registration officials had been completed, it heard individual complaints and certified the official lists of the voters that were to be sent to the Secretary of State. Many of these boards worked diligently at their task of "cleansing the rolls." Their work is well illustrated in a dispatch from the St. Joseph correspondent of the *Missouri Democrat*:

> The board of appeals and revision completed their labors late last night, having, during the four days' session, labored very hard. A large number of names were stricken from the registered lists, and yet a large number of the names of the disfranchised were passed, owing to the absence of affirmative testimony. So large a number having passed the registration it will render more arduous the duty of the judges of election in ferreting them out and rejecting their votes. The board rejected only those whose want of qualification was positively proven,

yet for rejecting such as they did the most bitter denunciations are visited upon them by the Conservatives.[58]

A serious outbreak of cholera in St. Louis slowed down
the campaign during August, but with the coming of fall
weather both sides unlimbered their "big guns" to vie for
the city's vote. President Johnson visited St. Louis early in
September on his "swing around the circle." The city accorded him a polite reception; he, in turn, made a highly
vituperative speech that left little doubt as to his sympathies
in the Missouri campaign. The following month the Radicals
employed the services of one of Johnson's bitterest enemies,
General Benjamin F. Butler, to urge their faithful to greater
endeavors in the closing weeks. The *Missouri Democrat*, from
its somewhat biased viewpoint, described Butler's reception
as "the largest and most enthusiastic demonstration that has
taken place in St. Louis for years." Regardless of whether
this was so, the thousands who flocked to hear him felt well
rewarded as he criticized the President and the Conservatives
unmercifully.[59]

Each party had its key speakers stumping Missouri during
October. Drake, Fletcher, and other outstanding leaders crisscrossed the state for the Radicals, while Frank Blair led the
Conservative orators. Meetings frequently stirred minor
clashes, but no serious incidents occurred.[60] Missourians finally went to the polls on November 6. When the votes were
counted, they revealed the Radicals triumphant by large
margins in most areas. "There is no use mincing matters,"
declared one Conservative editor. "The registry act has laid
us out cold. We went in lemons and came out squeezed."[61]
The Radicals would control both houses of the new legislature by overwhelming majorities—Senate: 28 to 8; House:
103 to 36. The Radicals also gained seven of the nine congressional seats. Only in the Third and Ninth districts were
the Conservatives able to put their men in office.[62]

The Radicals claimed that their candidate would have won in the Ninth District if it had not been for the large number of illegal votes cast in the rampantly pro-rebel "Kingdom of Callaway." That county had 1,895 registered voters, but the Radicals knew that there could be no more than a few hundred "loyal men" there. These outcries did not bother William F. Switzler, the triumphant Conservative nominee. Yet they should have. When Secretary of State Rodman canvassed the returns early in January, 1867, he arbitrarily refused to accept the Callaway votes. Thereby the Switzler majority of 1,122 votes became a 178-vote deficit in favor of his Radical opponent, incumbent George W. Anderson of Louisiana.[63] Rodman based his refusal to accept the Callaway votes on a certificate that William H. Thomas, the supervisor of registration in that county, had appended to his copy of the registry law. Thomas contended that such a state of intimidation existed throughout Callaway that his officials were not able to enforce the law against the registration of disloyal persons. Consequently, before turning in his registration list to the Secretary of State, the supervisor had written such judgments as "Enrolled disloyal," "Under Bond," or "In Rebel Armies" after various names. In a letter to Switzler, Thomas cried that "the broth" so smelled of treason that he took it to Jefferson City for analysis. Rodman also found the stench too much for his refined nostrils and therefore set it aside.[64]

Switzler and the Conservatives protested vehemently against Rodman's highhandedness, and a long and bitter contest ensued before the Committee on Elections of the national House of Representatives. Switzler contended that every voter's registration had been reviewed at three different stages and that each one had passed all three. Finally, "a Radical county clerk in Callaway County, William R. Wilson, who certified the returns to the Secretary of State, and OUR RADICAL GOVERNOR, THOMAS C. FLETCHER, WHO COMMISSIONED ON THESE RETURNS ALL THE

COUNTY OFFICERS OF CALLAWAY COUNTY, decided
they were votes." Switzler gathered a mass of affidavits to
support his claims. After two separate hearings he secured
a favorable report from the Elections Committee, only to have
it overturned by the House proper. The whole process consumed more than two years.[65]

Thus, by a variety of means the Radicals assured their victory. There was much grumbling among Conservatives. In
Lafayette County a small-scale war broke out between the
two rival groups over control of the courthouse in a closely
contested election. After much turmoil, state militia finally
terminated the struggle and ensconced the Radical officials
in power.[66] Fortunately, most Conservatives did not carry
their grievances as far as those of Lafayette County.

A week after the election twenty-nine prominent Radicals
in all parts of the state received a letter from the "Acting
Secretary of the Radical Union Executive Committee," which
asked them to attend a meeting at the Planters House in St.
Louis on November 20. Included in this group were Governor
Fletcher, Charles D. Drake, Missouri's Radical congressmen
and senators, and other leaders of the party. The guiding spirit
behind the call was retiring Senator B. Gratz Brown, who
wished to confer on the future policy of the Radical party with
regard to possible constitutional amendments and other questions of public and party interest that might come before the
next session of the legislature. All of the men appeared at the
appointed place and time. No sooner had the meeting begun
than Brown presented three resolutions for the group's consideration. Inasmuch as the Radical party had "won an unprecedented victory in the late election, combating avowedly
for the supremacy here of Free Principles," the Senator proposed to amend the constitution to make it "conform more
nearly to the requirements of genuine Freedom." Specifically, he wanted to provide universal suffrage, which would
include both the Negroes and those whites currently disfran-

chised, and to remove the test oath restrictions on the professions. These proposals caught Drake and the more ardent Radicals completely off guard. Ten of them walked out, but Drake remained. A lengthy discussion ensued. Drake wrote many years later that he "saw instantly that they [the resolutions] meant an abandonment of all that the Radicals of the State had gained after an unequalled struggle, and a proffer of pusillanimous and unmasked surrender of the party, its principles, and its achievements to our adversaries." His arguments proved quite in vain, for the group finally adopted the resolutions by a vote of 16 to 3. Journalist John F. Hume of St. Louis and Congressman Robert T. Van Horn of Kansas City joined Drake in the minority. A committee of five was appointed and directed to draw up a memorial to the legislature embodying the resolutions.[67]

To Drake's dismay, one of the men supporting Brown's proposals was William M. Grosvenor, who had become editor of the *Missouri Democrat* during the recent campaign. Grosvenor, destined to play an increasingly significant role in state Radical politics, had come from New England where he had been editor of the *New Haven Morning Journal and Courier*. Desiring to associate with a western paper, he had secured the aid of George W. Curtis and obtained the position with the *Missouri Democrat*. Immediately, Grosvenor had attracted attention with his forceful editorials. He soon acquired the reputation of being a dynamic speaker and an intelligent, energetic party organizer. It is therefore understandable that Drake feared that Grosvenor might wield the power of his important paper in favor of "the scheme of betrayal."[68]

Drake determined to offset Grosvenor's influence and maintain his own position as the leader of the rural outstate membership of the party, which he felt would oppose Brown's schemes. In two stirring articles for the *St. Louis Daily Evening News* he attempted to expose "the malign character of the plot." "Let others do as they will," he cried. "I will not back down or waver. Regarding the Constitution as in the main the very best in the land . . . seeing in it our only sure protection against Rebellion, Copperheadism, and Blairism . . . I say, once for all, stand by your Constitution just as it is." While quite willing to accept the idea of Negro suffrage, Drake considered the remainder of the Planters House program a threat to the very fiber of his party's existence.[69] He sent copies of his articles to every member of the legislature. The Radical outstate press took up the cry. Apparently, the proprietors of the *Missouri Democrat* overruled Grosvenor in regard to policy. On December 1 that paper commented that if certain Radical leaders wished to propose amendments, it was their prerogative to do so, so long as they did not force their views on a party unwilling to accept them. "We are clear in the conviction," it continued editorially, "that the time has not yet come to make rebel enfranchisement a part of the Radical program in Missouri."[70]

As already seen, Governor Fletcher recommended to the legislature the removal of the test oath for professional classes only to have the United States Supreme Court accomplish the task for him a few days later.[71] The movement for Negro suffrage gained considerable strength during this session of the legislature, and the General Assembly sent an amendment to that effect to the voters for their approval. On January 11 Fletcher wrote Grosvenor: "I am now satisfied that I made a great mistake in not taking grounds in the message for a supplementary act to amend the Constitution and include the rank and file of rebels."[72] In the light of later developments and, more particularly, in view of the tone of the senatorial contest then taking place in the legislature, Fletcher probably chose the wisest policy in remaining silent.

One major electoral task remained to the Radicals after the contest of 1866. They had to select a United States senator to replace B. Gratz Brown. Since they had obtained overwhelming control of both houses of the General Assembly, the party's legislators made this important decision in their caucus. The choice quickly narrowed down to Drake or Fletcher. Although Drake had not actively pushed his candidacy during the canvass, he considered his election "a foregone conclusion" once the Radicals asserted their supremacy. Part of his motives in denouncing the Planters House meeting so vehemently must have been the belief that such action would best advance his candidacy.[73] Led by the *Missouri Democrat*, the Radical press across the state began to line up strongly for Drake by late November. They lauded his long list of achievements in the service of his party and his state. No one could deny that Drake had been in the forefront of every battle the Radicals had fought. When noting the phenomenal press support given to Drake, one St. Louis Radical further remarked, "Where I meet one in favour of Fletcher there is ten in favour of Mr. Drake." Although this observer thought highly of the Governor, it was obvious to him that "nothing would be more satisfactory to the Radical party than the election of Drake." Indeed, he believed that it would "end the political career of any union man that opposed his [Drake's] election for the senatorship."[74]

Surprisingly, considerable opposition to Drake's candidacy developed at the initial Radical caucus on January 7, 1867. This hostility came mainly from three interrelated sources: the Germans, who had never liked the man; the Planters House group, composed of men primarily from St. Louis and northeast Missouri who feared for its program; and some of Missouri's congressional delegation. The *Missouri Democrat's* correspondent in Jefferson City particularly condemned those congressmen who absented themselves from Washington and the business for which the people elected them in order to play politics at the state capital.[75] The Conservatives watched the proceedings hopefully. In view of the apparent dissension over the Planters House proposals, a split in their opponents'

ranks might make possible a coalition of moderate Radicals
and Conservatives. Such a union might not only make possible
the election of someone other than Drake to the Senate but
also guarantee the adoption of the Planters House program.[76]

The *Democrat's* reporter learned that at the second Radical
caucus on January 8 the anti-Drake men promised the regulars that they would support anyone else named if Drake
withdrew his candidacy. The Drake men, fully aware that
they had the upper hand, refused to accede. The Conservative *Missouri Statesman* at Columbia claimed that Drake himself had attended the caucus and "cracked his whip like the
tyrant he is known to be."[77] Tempers must have flared with
bitter words exchanged. Governor Fletcher withdrew, obviously embittered and convinced that the party did not fully
recognize and appreciate his services. He complained to
Grosvenor:

> I have sworn and never will recant that there is no of-
> fice in the United States that I would accept under any
> circumstances. Never! Never! Once out of this I will be
> a Free Man and remain free. . . . The Lord knows what
> I would have done if I had not owned a good deal of
> land so as to be able to sell some of it every few months
> to pay the expense of acting as Governor for Radical
> Missouri.[78]

Since the Governor's withdrawal left the Drake opposition
without a candidate, the revolt collapsed. In a subsequent
caucus Drake received 81 of the 119 votes cast and became
the party's nominee. He easily defeated Frank Blair, the Conservative candidate, in the final election by the legislature.
Only ten members of his party refused to support him in that
last showdown.[79] In accepting the coveted position, Drake
made a lengthy plea for party harmony. After assuring his
partisans that he would stand firmly with the President's opponents in Congress, he warned those who were to continue
to carry the Radical banner in Missouri to be ever alert to

thwart any scheme that would betray the state into the hands of "rebels."[80]

Charles Daniel Drake now stood at the pinnacle of his Radical career. He had triumphed over his enemies both without and within his party. His was the dominant philosophy of the Missouri Radicals and seemed destined to remain so.

CHAPTER VI

THE NEGRO IN POSTWAR MISSOURI

W HILE THE Missouri State Convention of 1865 debated the matter of the Negro's rights, the freedmen found them-selves increasingly harassed by those who did not look favorably upon their new status. During the winter and spring of that year guerrilla terrorism showed an alarming increase. Roving bands of bushwhackers, composed of returning Confederates and others claiming to be, wreaked havoc among the populace. Some of these groups, such as the notorious Jim Jackson and his gang, took special delight in persecuting the new freedmen or any white person who sought to hire them. One night during the middle of February, Jackson and his boys visited the home of Dr. John W. Jacobs in eastern Boone County and proceeded to "string up" one of his hired Negroes. They issued threats of similar treatment to other nearby farmers who would hire the freedmen. Warren Martin, another bushwhacker who labeled himself "the young Helli-gan of Callaway County," was reported "shooting up" Negroes along the Missouri River.[1] Writing from Macon on March 25, General Clinton B. Fisk gave this vivid description of the situation:

> Slavery dies hard. I hear its expiring agonies and witness its contortions in death in every quarter of my district. In Boone, Howard, Randolph, and Callaway the emancipation ordinance has caused disruption of society equal to anything I saw in Arkansas or Mississippi in the year 1863. I blush for my race when I discover the wicked barbarity of the late masters and mistresses of the recently freed persons of the counties heretofore named. I have no doubt but that the monster, Jim Jackson, is instigated by the late slave owners to hang or shoot every negro he can find absent from the old plantations. Some few have driven their black people away from them with nothing to eat or scarcely to wear. The consequence is, between Jim Jackson and his colaborers [sic] among the first families, the poor blacks are rapidly concentrating in the towns and especially at garrisoned places. My hands and heart are full. I am finding homes for them in Northwest Missouri, Kansas, Illinois, and Iowa. There is much sickness and suffering among them; many need help. . . . I am retaining all in Missouri that I can get work for in quiet localities. . . . I hope the waters will soon grow still, and Missouri in peace be permitted to pursue her way in the golden path of freedom and empire.[2]

With the war ending in April and with the President's offer of amnesty being issued the following month, bushwhacking ceased for the most part. A majority of the guerrillas were allowed to give themselves up peacefully and to sign the loyalty oath required by the President's program. Supposedly, acceptance of the amnesty terms wiped the slate clean, although, as seen in Chapter V, new difficulties broke out when certain grand juries thought differently the following winter. However, the *Missouri Statesman* was able to report in the middle of June, 1865, "Our military authorities believe

there is not at this time a single bushwhacker in this county
[Boone]."[3]

The Freedmen's Bureau, recently created by Congress,
moved into Missouri in the late spring of 1865. General John
W. Sprague served as assistant commissioner for the Missouri-
Arkansas district and established his headquarters at St.
Louis.[4] This agency aided both the freedmen and refugee
whites, many of whom were pouring into southern Missouri
from Arkansas as a result of the backwash of guerrilla warfare.[5] By early summer Bureau agents had established posts
at Cape Girardeau, Pilot Knob, Rolla, Springfield, and Cass-
ville and by fall had opened schools at most of them. They
saw to it that Negro couples who had not had the formality
of a wedding ceremony in slavery days complied with the
new Missouri law requiring them to legalize their relationship. Frequently, a number of couples would be married in
a mass ceremony. The agents also arranged labor contracts
for their charges with nearby farmers. The reports to Sprague
each consecutive month showed a notable decrease in the
number of Negroes requiring help. The major problem was
to supply enough clothing and rations to see those still destitute through the coming winter.[6]

In late July, one of Sprague's assistants toured the St. Joseph and central Missouri areas. Many of the counties located there had had a large number of slaves, and the white
population had been strongly pro-Southern. Because the
Freedmen's Bureau had no permanent agent in these areas,
the Negroes had "been obliged to depend on themselves more
fully" than in south Missouri. The aide reported "abundant
employment for all who can and are willing to work at remu-
nerative prices." He found many, however, who were "dis-
inclined to labor except for a short time and then they remain
idle until they have expended their earnings." He also noted
that there were many Negro women with children, "some of
them soldiers' families," who would need the aid of the

Bureau to help them through the winter. Although most of the counties he visited were doing something to help these needy freedmen, many restricted their efforts to those who had resided there for more than twelve months. Another situation the agent observed was that many of the Negroes, "afraid to go into the country," were thronging into the towns. He reported: "Prominent citizens think that a little aid this winter will be needed and after that they will scatter through the county and support themselves." Nevertheless, when considering the problem as a whole, Sprague's aide thought "the prospects of the freedmen is good."[7]

The Bureau's composite report for Missouri at the end of September indicated that only 271 freedmen still received direct aid from its stations. A few more than 1,400 refugees continued on the rolls, but most of these were being sent back to their homes in Arkansas or were being assisted in finding employment with farmers in south Missouri. That same month a new agent, whose headquarters were to be at Jefferson City, was appointed to co-ordinate the work in central Missouri. At the end of October, General Sprague announced that because the greatest need for help was in Arkansas, the district headquarters were to be moved from St. Louis to Little Rock. Henceforth, the agent at Jefferson City would be working directly under the Little Rock office.[8]

In spite of the work of the Bureau, there was still much that needed to be done in obtaining the Negro his rights by law. The *Missouri Democrat* reported in late October that the agent at Jefferson City was having some difficulty in helping Negroes redress their grievances against whites. Local law officers seemed reluctant to give them the equal protection guaranteed under the new constitution. In several instances white employers had refused to pay their Negro laborers the wages agreed upon. In one particular case, when a freedman who had accumulated a good deal of rural property died, a white neighbor drove the widow from her home and took over the farm.[9] Doubtless, similar situations existed elsewhere, particularly in regions where Southern sympathies were still strong. Relatively few reached the press, however, and the reports of the Bureau agents are surprisingly free of such incidents. Early in the fall of 1865 the *Missouri Democrat* boasted rather naïvely:

> Whatever may be the embarrassments growing out of the "freedmen question" in the extreme South, it is evident the matter is coming to a speedy and very satisfactory solution in this State. From accounts received from all parts of Missouri, it is certain that our colored people are doing quite as well, if not a great deal better than anticipated. They appear to be perfectly orderly and industrious, and as a consequence are making no mean headway in the advancement of their own interests.

The Radical newspaper particularly commended the Negroes on their enterprise in the work of self-education and cited as references the establishment of numerous schools, booksellers' reports, and other indicators.[10]

By the winter of 1865–1866 many Negroes began drifting back into the countryside. They returned because of economic necessity, for the towns could no longer support all of them. Those without any particular skill to ply had little choice but to return to the only life they had known. Many wandered back to the farms from which they had come, while others arranged labor contracts elsewhere. In many instances, especially when the Negroes did not have the benefit of the advice of the Freedmen's Bureau, they resumed work under conditions that left them hardly better off than they had been before the war. Paid in monthly wages or by a share of the crop, few of them saved much even when they had the opportunity to do so. As late as 1874 freedmen in some areas received wages lower than those paid hired slaves in the pre-war era. The unskilled found themselves at the mercy of the white farmers who hired them. There is good evidence that both parties frequently disregarded labor contracts and that the arrangements in such circumstances became quite haphazard.[11] Some Negroes, however, did manage to save sufficient funds to purchase their own land. Most of these prospered in the same proportion as their immediate environment made it possible for anyone to do so. Others availed themselves of homesteads that Congress, under an act of June 21, 1866, made available without racial distinctions in Missouri and four other states. General O. O. Howard, who headed the Freedmen's Bureau, reported that about four thousand families had been able to take advantage of this opportunity in spite of the lack of teams and farming implements needed to start any considerable operation.[12]

Those who remained in town engaged in various trades or found opportunities for employment as domestic servants. Many of them showed considerable enthusiasm for bettering themselves educationally as a means to economic advancement and often exhibited remarkable individuality. One Negro barber in St. Louis had accumulated $40,000 by 1871, while another had made at least $25,000 in the same trade. A Negro caterer and restaurateur also reported clearing $25,000. At the end of 1871 the total amount of property owned by the Negroes of Missouri was valued at better than $500,000.[13]

The National Freedmen's Savings and Trust Company opened a branch office in St. Louis on June 29, 1868. During its first eighteen months of operation the association averaged a monthly gain in deposits of better than $1,400. By the middle of 1870 it had a balance on deposit of more than $50,000. The cashier reported that the institution had "gradually ingratiated itself into the confidence of the people" and that it was soon to move into a new banking room at "one of the best locations in the city." Although this bank catered exclusively to a Negro clientele, St. Louis' thirty-nine other banks also had a liberal share of colored patronage.[14]

Early in January, 1867, Isaac H. Sturgeon, the president of the North Missouri Railroad, wrote Representative Charles H. Branscomb about the deplorable situation concerning the arrangements for Negroes on the public conveyances in St. Louis. "As it is now," he declared, "the colored people have to stand on the platforms of the car in front of our street railroads or walk. I have seen neatly dressed colored females on cold days stand on the front platform with tender infants in their arms." Sturgeon urged strong state legislation that would take away the charter of any company failing to provide equal treatment for the races. Heavy penalties ought to be prescribed against anyone who would "eject or attempt to enjoin a colored person from riding inside the cars." Give the Negroes protection, Sturgeon declared, "and if they deport themselves well as I am convinced they will, in six months the prejudice will wear away and there will be no further trouble." Some of the St. Louis representatives tried to push a comprehensive rights bill through the legislature that spring but failed.[15]

Considerable agitation continued to secure basic fair treatment for the Negro on public conveyances. By early June the *Missouri Democrat* announced that an agreement had been reached whereby colored persons could now ride inside the cars. It quickly became evident that not all companies would abide by this decision, however, for two cases of ejection came to the attention of the paper within a day after the announcement. On July 21, 1867, Caroline Williams, a pregnant Negro woman carrying a baby, tried to board a car of the Bellefontaine Railway, but the conductor forcibly pushed her back into the street. She and her husband filed suit in the St. Louis circuit court, seeking an injunction against the line and $5,000 in damages. The court handed down its decision in May, 1868; although it awarded the plaintiffs only one cent in damages, it did decree their right to ride inside streetcars. From this time on there appears to have been little difficulty.[16]

The ratification of the Fifteenth Amendment, guaranteeing national Negro suffrage, in 1870 apparently had some favorable side effects. One colored citizen of St. Louis wrote Frederick Douglass' *New Era,* a leading Negro weekly paper in Washington, D. C.: "The fifteenth amendment is working wonders. Streetcar conductors cannot tell whether you are black or white. I take a look in my glass sometimes to see if by some hocus pocus I have turned white, but it gives back the same old face, and tells me I am a citizen and not a chattel now. It used to be Old Pen, but now it is Mr. Pentalpha."[17]

Newspaper accounts indicate that most public meetings, particularly in outstate Missouri, had segregated audiences. Negroes generally sat on one side of the hall and whites on the other. Both races apparently accepted this pattern as a matter of course. Although no mention of this separation is found in reports of St. Louis gatherings, this does not mean it may not have been the custom. This type of seating arrangement had become the custom in many churches with mixed congregations before the Civil War. Few slaveowners had forbidden religious activity among their charges, but they had generally wished to supervise it themselves. Therefore the slaves had attended church services with their masters. In St. Louis and other large towns where large groups of free Negroes lived, separate congregations were established in the 1850's or perhaps earlier. War and its aftermath brought increased separation by mutual consent.

In the Negro churches there existed the opportunity for leadership training which was available in few other situations. Invariably, both before and after the war, it was the Negro ministers who took the first steps toward the education of their race. Most Negro congregations adopted either the Baptist or Methodist denominations from which they had come. They frequently held services in white churches until they could raise sufficient funds for a building of their own. A typical situation existed in Mexico, where Negroes left the Baptist and Methodist churches to form their own congregations in 1865. At first the two Negro groups alternated services on Sunday afternoons in the Presbyterian edifice; then, in 1868 they received permission to use the courthouse. Two years later the Baptists purchased a one-room building, which had formerly been used as a sawmill, and continued to share with their Methodist brethren.[18]

Although readjustment brought many problems to both races, Missouri progressed much more rapidly toward a lasting, harmonious solution than her former slaveholding sister states. Perhaps the relatively small proportion of Negroes in the populace constitutes one reason why Missouri did not experience more difficulty in adjusting. According to the Census of 1870, Negroes composed only 6.9 per cent of the state's population; this percentage ranked her last among the former slaveholding states if Delaware is excluded. Numerically, the 117,995 Negroes represented a slight decrease from the 3,572 free colored and 114,931 slaves of ten years earlier. Many of the Negroes from Missouri had emigrated to Iowa, Illinois, and other nearby states in 1865 to make a new start for themselves in a more friendly atmosphere. The vast majority of those who remained consolidated in the counties along the state's two great rivers, while nearly a quarter of them settled in the St. Louis area. In 1870, twenty counties reported colored populations in excess of 10 per cent. Of these, only two had concentrations above the twentieth percentile level—Howard County in "Little Dixie" with 30 per cent and New Madrid in the extreme southeastern corner with 22 per cent.[19]

A second factor aiding postwar adjustment in Missouri was the farsighted leadership of many of the Radicals who occupied places of responsibility. The state convention did much in laying an adequate groundwork for the progressive advancement of the Negro. The question of the fundamental civil rights of the Negro naturally arose in the discussion of emancipation. Charles D. Drake, fearful lest the Negro would be set free and forgotten, proposed this amendment to the emancipation ordinance:

> That no person can, on account of color, be disqualified as a witness, or be disabled to contract, or be prevented from acquiring, holding, or transmitting property; or be liable to any other punishment, for any offense, than that imposed on others for a like offense; or be restricted in the exercise of religious worship, or be hindered in receiving an education; or be subjected in law to any other restraints, or disqualifications, in regard to any personal rights, than such as are laid upon others under like circumstances.[20]

The flurry of debate that followed indicated the considerable range of differences that existed over such matters. Rather than allow this disagreement to disrupt the all-important emancipation process, the convention voted down Drake's amendment for the present and moved quickly to the legal securing of the Negro's freedom.[21]

Two days later Drake, serving in his capacity as chairman of the committee on the legislative department, reported the identical proposals as Section III of the Declaration of Rights. Debate began anew. Abner L. Gilstrap of Macon moved that the word "civilized" be inserted after the word "no" in the first line. When Drake asked for a definition, Gilstrap reported that the meaning was self-evident. As the debate continued, it became clear that the major objection concerned the right of a Negro to testify against a white. John W. Fletcher of DeSoto, the Governor's brother, took an extreme view when he argued that he had come to the convention "to represent white men, and to legislate for the benefit of the white men of Missouri." He declared emphatically: "I am not here for the purpose of giving any rights to the negro further than the right of freedom. I desired to see every slave in the State freed, and I desire to see every slave in the country free, but when they are free, I am done with them." He was perfectly willing for Negro to testify against Negro, white against white; but, for Negro to testify against white was unthinkable until the Negro had at least been educated. Other delegates advanced the argument that it was not fair to free the Negro and then deny him his fundamental rights. If he was to have the privilege of owning property, he ought to have the right to testify to protect it. Gustavus St. Gem of Ste. Genevieve, who had served as an assistant provost marshal during the war, pointed out that Negro testimony had been taken by military tribunals and that there was no indication at these that the Negroes were incompetent or unqualified. In the end, Gilstrap's amendment and other ones that would have weakened the section were voted down; Section III went into the final constitution virtually intact.[22]

Two other questions concerning Negro rights dominated the meetings of the convention. Most important of these was the matter of suffrage and officeholding. Senator B. Gratz Brown, in a significant way, first raised this question for public debate. He wrote the *Missouri Democrat* on December 22, 1864, that properly qualified Negroes should not be barred from voting by the convention. In regard to those who feared that such a policy would encourage heavy Negro immigration to the detriment of attracting whites to the state, Brown argued that Missouri must stand as a beacon light of freedom for all people. Only by such an act would the state attract all those who could contribute to its economic and political growth.[23]

Within the convention a variety of views were expressed. The German Radicals generally favored immediate Negro suffrage with no disqualifications except those that applied equally to whites. At the other extreme stood the arch-Conservatives who wished to bar the Negro from suffrage and officeholding forever. During the debate in the committee of the whole Arnold Krekel of St. Charles sought to find an acceptable compromise by proposing a limited colored vote after 1870. Krekel, who really had no qualms against immediate Negro suffrage suggested that voting privileges be given only to those who had served in the war, those who could read, and those who possessed a good moral character. He was also willing to exclude all Negroes who were over sixteen years of age at the time of emancipation. Drake opposed such arrangements and argued strongly for the article on elections as originally reported. This measure provided that the voters could decide the question of Negro suffrage in 1870; if rejected then, it could come up again in 1876. Should the people approve the matter on one of these occasions, the Negro would have no restrictions placed on his voting rights beyond those set for whites.

The vast majority of Missourians at this time held reservations about Negro suffrage. Indeed, probably very few outside the ranks of the German Radicals were willing to accept "universal freedom, equality, humanity." Although Drake did not oppose Negro suffrage per se, he feared that its inclusion in the constitution could lead to rejection of that document by the voters. On the convention floor Drake held as fallacious the idea advanced by some that freedom and franchise were inseparable, and he maintained that although women and foreigners could not vote, this did not make them slaves. Some Negroes might be properly qualified at the present time, but most of them had had little opportunity for any education that would enable them to make wise choices. Drake believed that suffrage should be withheld for the time being and should be offered as an inducement to the Negroes "to elevate themselves in the scale of humanity." In the meantime, he added, free-state immigration into Missouri would help mitigate existing prejudices against the race.[24]

As finally passed, the constitution limited voting and office-holding to qualified white males and made no provisions for broadening the franchise or the right to hold office other than by the regular process of amending.[25] Most Radicals wished to move cautiously in this area.

The problem of Negro education was the third major question relative to the freedman and his rights. In accepting Section III of Drake's Declaration of Rights, the delegates had agreed that "no person can, on account of color . . . be hindered in acquiring an education." In its report of March 29 the committee on education urged provision for the schooling of Negro children on a separate basis from that for whites. Earlier debate had revealed that few desired to open the doors of the white public schools to Negroes. Following a suggestion by Drake, the committee left the actual implementation of a system to legislative authority by providing that the General Assembly "may" establish schools "for children of African descent." Should the legislature act positively in this regard, "all funds provided for the support of public schools shall be appropriated in proportion to the number of children, without regard to color." These sections of the education article passed unchanged.[26]

The Negroes had not waited for constitutional authority to begin the systematic education of their fellows, nor had responsible whites shunned their responsibility to help the colored race in this regard. Although an 1847 amendment to Missouri's original constitution forbade the education of Negroes, attempts had been made in this direction before the Civil War. Hiram R. Revels, who was later to become the first Negro to sit in the United States Senate, opened the first school of any importance for colored pupils in St. Louis in 1856. Some 150 free Negro children attended, and they paid one dollar per month for tuition. Apparently, the school lasted only one winter, for it was dissolved when Revels moved east to take another position.[27] Another effort of a more durable nature was the school established at Hannibal by the Reverend Tom Henderson, a free Negro who had become a Methodist minister. Henderson held his classes at the Second Baptist Church, one of the few colored edifices in existence before the war. Old and young alike paid one dollar a month to attend. When war came, Henderson left, and the work was taken up briefly by Blanche K. Bruce, who had been educated with his master's son when he was a slave. Bruce soon left for Oberlin College and from there went to Mississippi. In 1875 the Radicals there sent him to the United States Senate.[28] Apparently, a number of rural slaveowners gave their charges the rudiments of an education before the war when they had compelling reasons for doing so and could accomplish it unobtrusively.[29]

The credit for considerable advancement in the field of Negro education during the war must be given to the Western Sanitary Commission at St. Louis. This organization had been established to carry out much the same work that the American Red Cross was to perform in later conflicts. By 1862 or 1863 it had begun to concern itself with the plight of the large groups of refugee freedmen who flocked into Union army camps and towns under Union military control. During the winter of 1863–1864, General William A. Pile, who was later to become quite active in the Radical ranks and to be rewarded with a seat in Congress, organized three brigades of colored troops at Benton Barracks near St. Louis. In addition to giving them military instruction, he secured three thousand copies of Sargent's Standard Primer from the Sanitary Commission and set his officers to the task of teaching the recruits to read. The Reverend W. H. Bradley of the Commission assisted in the work.[30]

That same winter the Sanitary Commission organized several of the Negro ministers and other responsible leaders within the free Negro community of St. Louis into a board of education for the colored children. In February, 1864,

this group began operations with four hundred pupils registered in four schools, which were located in rented quarters.
A year later enrollment had expanded to six hundred, and
eight teachers were employed. The work was sustained by
private contributions: $800 from the Sanitary Commission,
$400 from a Mr. Jaccard, $500 from Dr. William G. Eliot,
and $1,230.60 from the colored people themselves.[31] The Sanitary Commission also operated a high school for about fifty
or sixty "advanced scholars of the colored people" in the
basement of one of the churches. It was supervised by one
of Dr. Eliot's nieces and a friend of hers from New England
and sustained by contributions "from friends in Massachusetts."[32]

The Commission maintained yet another school for colored
children in conjunction wth its Freedmen's Orphans' Home,
which had been established in 1864 to care for abandoned
youngsters found by its agents throughout the Mississippi
Valley. Several hundred Negro children passed through this
home during the first few years after its establishment. The
Commission sought to make it a temporary way station for
the orphans. Periodically, it announced that "responsible persons, with good reference or recommendation, can obtain
children from among the number to bring up, and have their
service by assuming a proper obligation for care, support,
clothing, tuition for three months each year, and moderate
wages after they reach the age of fourteen years."[33] When
the Commission completed its work and disbanded at the
end of 1865, a new organization of interested local citizens
continued the home. At the end of 1866 it reported that there
were about sixty youngsters still being cared for. The number
had dwindled to thirty-six by the beginning of 1869, and the
home was in desperate financial straits. The annual report of
its directors included a reminder to St. Louisans not to neglect these children as memory faded of the conflict that had

produced their plight. Help was forthcoming from those who had sustained it earlier.[34]

The General Assembly rescinded the old restrictions on Negro education during the 1865 session and urged school trustees to move rapidly forward in establishing schools for both white and colored youngsters. It assigned no appropriations for the work, however, since it preferred to wait until its adjourned session a year hence to see what would be needed.[35] This situation, together with unsettled conditions, prevented much from being done in the way of schools for Negro children in outstate Missouri before fall. A few schools were started by private individuals, white and colored, and by benevolent associations in towns where the Negro population and interest warranted it.[36]

When the General Assembly convened in January, 1866, State Superintendent of Schools James H. Robinson, in his annual report, urged: "The education of the freedman's child deserves the most liberal legislation." He thought it "astonishing to see such prosperous private schools, supported by the colored people, in many portions of our country" and warned, "Ere the State is ready to contribute the means to educate the colored man, many of them will be prepared to take places as teachers to assist in elevating the standard of his race." With great zeal he argued: "Let it be remembered that mind distinguishes man from the brute creation. Would you widen the breach? Then give effect to the cause—as the arm increases, so will the brain grow, the mind expand and the man develop. Then feeding and exercising their minds, let us elevate the divinity within, and learn [sic] them to honor God."[37] The General Assembly responded with a series of comprehensive laws for the public education of the Negro. Each township or city board of education had to establish and maintain one or more separate schools for colored children within their respective jurisdictions where the number of such youngsters exceeded twenty. Each colored school must be kept open for a winter term equivalent to that for white schools. Persons over twenty-one years of age who desired the rudiments of an education could attend under certain circumstances. If the average attendance for any month should drop below twelve, the board could close the school for a period of not more than six months. The school census must include the Negro children regardless of the number in the district. In areas where the number of children was less than twenty, the Negro portion of the subsequent tax money would be appropriated for their education as the board saw fit.[38]

For all the elaborateness and seeming completeness of this legislation, Negro public education ran afoul of apathy and evasion in many places during the early years of the law's operation. As might be expected, the old "Southern Attitude" had a strong deterrent effect.[39] In the areas where it was difficult to get much support for white public schools, any for Negroes was virtually out of the question. Superintendent T. A. Parker in his annual report of 1867 pointed out how easily school laws could be evaded by a hostile community or its officials. He reminded the General Assembly that it had provided no penalty for those who did not comply.

In this same report, as he summarized the progress of the program of educating the Negroes, Parker noted the existence of three types of Negro schools: those supported by private subscriptions (usually undertaken and maintained by the Negroes themselves), those supported by benevolent societies of other states, and the free public schools. Only a few of the latter existed, and they were located in the larger towns. Reports from the county superintendents indicated that thirty counties had fifty-six schools for colored children, most of which fell under the first two categories mentioned above. Typical of a large number of the reports was that from Bates County: "We have not enough colored people in this county to attract any attention to their education yet." The comment of the Superintendent of Callaway County exemplified the

attitude of the rural areas with a relatively large Negro population: "There is but little interest manifested in the education of the colored people. But I hope a little time will endow
our citizens with a more liberal spirit in regard to this unfortunate race."[40]

By fall of 1869 a Freedmen's Bureau agent reported that
there were 114 Negro schools, mostly public, with 6,240
pupils in attendance throughout the state. The Census of 1870
revealed an enrollment of 9,080 Negro students. Most of these
schools were quartered "in churches and cabins with walls
admirably adapted for ventilation and for admission of copi-
ous shower baths of rain." These statistics showed a strong
increase numerically over 1867; nevertheless, fifty-five counties, which had a total enumeration of 2,984 colored children,
still had done nothing to open schools for them. The potential Negro student group of the entire state contained 42,000
children.[41]

Columbia served as a notable example of what could be
accomplished in outstate Missouri. The board of education
there had opened a school for Negro children in the fall of
1866 with Charles E. Cummings, a colored man of some education, as its teacher. Apparently, the school met in rented
property at first. Whether it was impossible to secure tax
money for a building is uncertain. By the summer of 1868 the
colored people of Columbia had been laboring over a year to
raise funds for a combination schoolhouse-church by means
of dinners, festivals, fairs, and picnics. They planned the erec-
tion of a two-story frame building to be named "Cummings
Academy" for its popular teacher. Title to the land was to
be held by the board of education with the property reverting
to the First African Church if it should ever cease to be used
for educational purposes. A contribution of eight hundred
dollars from the Freedmen's Bureau aided the project greatly.
This money had been obtained through the efforts of William F. Switzler during one of his numerous trips to Wash-

ington in his endeavor to secure a congressional seat. The building was up and in operation by the fall of 1869. Albert L. Aubin, the Freedmen's Bureau agent for Missouri, visited the school in November and came away with high praises for both the facilities and the teacher. The eighty-five pupils attending, he remarked, were a fine representation of Columbia's "orderly, industrious, and thriving" colored community.[42]

The story of the hard work by Columbia's colored people to secure their building was repeated many times across the state during the next few years. The *Missouri Democrat* and other papers carried frequent accounts of Negro fairs, picnics, and other fund-raising activities. In the summer of 1868, one of the largest endeavors in the St. Louis area took place. The colored people of Kirkwood and Carondolet sponsored a Freedmen's Fair to raise funds for the building of schools and churches that lasted several days. Each area had one side of a large hall for its booths and displays, which attracted huge crowds. Entertainment was provided by the Woodson family singers—the nine children of the Reverend E. S. Woodson, a former slave of Edward Bates who had bought his freedom in 1848.[43]

In a few instances some local whites found such evidences of colored industry and prosperity difficult to accept. Late in 1866 an attempt was made to burn a colored school that had recently been opened at Linneus in northwest Missouri. The fire was discovered in its early stages and extinguished before major damage had been done. The local paper reported further evidence of animosity in the treatment accorded the white female teacher at the school. Looked down upon by many Conservatives, she found herself the target of frequent insults and rudeness. Doubtless her experience was somewhat typical of those who dared to enter Conservative communities that questioned the expediency of educating the Negroes.[44] In 1867 drunken white rowdies, firing pistol shots through the doors, suddenly interrupted Christmas Eve services at

St. Paul's Church in St. Louis County. A large crowd of Negroes was in attendance; one man was killed and one woman wounded. The following March renegade whites burned both a Negro school and a church at Roanoke in Howard County, and an unknown assailant shot one of the Negro members of the church who tried to extinguish the flames. Even as late as 1870 the colored people of New Madrid County found their school, erected after several years of sacrifice, burned to the ground within two weeks after its opening.[45]

Fortunately, such instances were rare. Superintendent Parker, in his annual report for 1869, apprised the General Assembly:

> The wise and liberal policy heretofore adopted has borne good fruit. Opposition to the education of the colored people is gradually disappearing. Their rapid improvement and good conduct help to disarm prejudice. The question of the capacity of the race is receiving a solution in these schools. . . . I have witnessed recitations in colored schools which were not inferior in enthusiasm, readiness and grasp in thought to any I ever saw in a white school, considering the time the pupils had studied.[46]

Through the prodding of Superintendent Parker and his successors the General Assembly gradually tightened up loopholes in the school laws for Negro children. The legislature of 1868 gave the state superintendent authority to assume the powers of the local school board in establishing and maintaining Negro schools when that group failed to act. Superintendent John Monteith, who served in the early 1870's, became particularly active in carrying out this directive. He reported establishing between fifty and sixty schools in 1872. Two years later he wrote: "I have levied taxes for negro schools in three instances. The medicine is good and effective, and I trust it will be administered in every similar case in the State until the colored people enjoy schools equally good in

every way with the white schools." Perhaps the sharp decline
in the amount of intervention between the two years can be
attributed to the passage of a law by which school officials
found guilty of the persistent neglect of any duty would be
fined fifty to five hundred dollars.[47] The 1868 legislature also
sought to alleviate another one of the major obstacles in the
path of Negro education—the sparsity of colored population—
by amending the law of 1866 so that schools could be established in districts where only fifteen eligible students resided
and by lowering the average attendance requirement from
twelve to ten. The following year the General Assembly
passed legislation permitting two or more sparsely settled
districts to go together and establish a union school if their
combined Negro population warranted it. Such consolidation
became obligatory in 1874.[48]

The scarcity of Negro students continued to be a major
problem. The 1871 reports from county superintendents
showed that thirty-nine counties had no Negro schools because they had no districts with the required number of
Negro children. The other seventy counties reporting had a
total of 395 districts with the required population, yet only
158 schools had been established. In their annual letters for
1872, twenty-one county superintendents called attention to
this situation and its ensuing problems. The superintendent
of Clark County in northeast Missouri advocated that colored
children be admitted to white schools in districts where the
number of Negroes was too small to form separate schools.
Apparently, this practice was followed in some areas where
no objections were raised.[49]

As might be expected, the state's largest city, with its progressive leaders in the field of education and its considerable
Negro population, made marked strides in caring for its colored children. Three public schools for Negroes, two of which
were located in rented quarters, opened in St. Louis in the
fall of 1866. Four hundred and thirty-seven pupils attended,

with 45 of these being over eighteen years of age. In addition, twelve other schools with an enrollment of 200 to 300 students were maintained by the Negroes themselves through a tuition system or by white benevolent societies. The following year the public system added two more schools. Evening classes began operating in buildings used during the day for whites, and there working Negroes could receive special courses in reading, spelling, penmanship, arithmetic, grammar, and geography. The 1867 report of the board of education stated that "at the annual examination there were exhibited some fine specimens of penmanship; and several classes showed satisfactory proficiency in reading and spelling." The main difficulty seemed to be in securing the "degree of punctuality and regularity in attendance that is obtained in other schools." The report expressed the hope that this problem would be corrected "as soon as these schools are established in localities more convenient to the population who patronize them."[50]

By 1875 Missouri had a well-established Negro public school system, with primary schools having been started in most areas. St. Louis even had a high school for Negroes. With the help of strong legislation and sound educational leadership, prejudice against the education of the colored race was dying out. As early as 1869 Superintendent Parker had announced: "The colored schools of Missouri, when compared with those of other Southern states, will be found in the front rank."[51]

Early in the development of Negro education the question of training colored teachers arose. Few white teachers cared to work with Negro children, and trained colored instructors were difficult to find at this time. Ten county superintendents, in their annual letters for 1873, mentioned the difficulties they were having in obtaining good teachers for their Negro schools. Prejudice existed on the part of both races against whites teaching Negro children. In many cases white teach-

ers did not take the interest or have the patience that a
Negro teacher might have in the pupil's training. The pay
differential between white and colored schools further complicated the matter. In 1873 average salaries ranged from
$46.70 monthly for a male teacher in a colored school to
$82.72 monthly in white schools. In comparison, women teach-
ers in both cases were grossly underpaid: $40 monthly av-
erage in colored schools; $46.64 monthly in white schools.[52]

In his annual report for 1869 to the General Assembly,
Superintendent Parker disclosed:

> There is a school—Lincoln Institute—now in the fourth
> year of successful operation, in Jefferson City, and pos-
> sessing an endowment fund of $7,000, which, on a small
> scale and with limited means is doing good work in the
> right direction. It owns no building and is able to main-
> tain but one teacher. . . . A valuable library of several
> hundred volumes has been obtained, and several good
> teachers have already been sent out.

Parker recommended "that this beginning, so auspiciously
made, be encouraged by the State" with an annual appropriation of $5,000.[53]

Lincoln Institute had indeed been doing good work under
tremendous handicaps. Early in 1866 the idea for the school
had developed among the soldiers of the 62nd Colored Infantry, stationed at Fort McIntosh, Texas. Most of these men
had been recruited in Missouri in 1863. Many had benefited
from the educational program conducted by General Pile and
the Western Sanitary Commission at Benton Barracks that
winter. They had come to realize the importance of education for their race in the postwar world of freedom. The key
man in bringing the idea to fruition was Lieutenant Richard B. Foster. When orders came in January, 1866, to muster
out a large part of the 62nd Infantry, Foster began talking
with some of the other officers and men about the continuation, upon discharge, of the educational training the colored

men had received in service. Out of these conversations emerged the plan that the men of the 62nd Infantry pool their resources and start a school for freedmen in Missouri. The purpose of the institution would be to "combine study with labor, so that the old habits of those who have always labored, but never studied, shall not be thereby changed and that the emancipated slaves, who have neither capital to spend nor time to lose, may obtain an education." Foster agreed to superintend the school when established. A committee was appointed to raise the money and see that the idea became a reality. The officers of the 62nd Infantry contributed $1,034.50, and the enlisted men gave $3,966.50. Another Missouri regiment, the 65th Colored Infantry, which was also stationed at Fort McIntosh, endorsed the program and donated $1,379.50. When one considers the small army pay, particularly for men in the ranks, this amount represented a considerable sacrifice on the part of many of these soldiers.[54]

With money in hand, Foster went to St. Louis to enlist the support of interested parties there. Among those who agreed to help was James E. Yeatman, the director of the Western Sanitary Commission. He became treasurer of the incorporating group and held that position for the next four years. On February 20, 1866, a seven-man board of trustees began to plan incorporation, leading to the establishment of the school by fall. In line with the "study and labor" policy set forth in the original resolutions and in the hope that an outstate location might better serve the interests of a larger proportion of Missouri's Negroes, the board chose Jefferson City as the site for the school. Land could be acquired there for a farm on which the students could be profitably employed. By the time the articles of incorporation were filed on June 25, Governor Fletcher, Attorney General Wingate, and Judge Krekel of the United States District Court had been enlisted, among others, to serve as trustees. Foster had gone to the

East to solicit more funds, but except for a contribution of
two thousand dollars by the Freedmen's Bureau, little was
forthcoming.[55] Quite probably, most philanthropists who were
interested in investing in Negro education preferred to do so
further south.

After the initial acts of incorporation were completed, the
board had to secure quarters in which classes might begin
that fall. Jefferson City had two colored churches, Baptist
and Methodist, which had been established the previous
winter. It seemed logical to consult them first. A school had
already been established in the Baptist edifice by one of the
missionary societies. Foster therefore sought out the Method-
ists and offered to recondition their building and pay a
monthly rental for its use. The trustees approved, but the
minister did not. When an appeal to the white Methodist
church met a similar fate, Foster finally turned to the town
council. They agreed to let him use a dilapidated structure
with two rooms, twenty-two feet square.

On September 17, 1866, Lincoln Institute began operations
with two students attending. As word of its operation spread,
enrollment quickly grew, and before the winter ended, an
assistant teacher had been hired to aid with the work. Two
departments emerged, the preparatory and the normal or
college.[56] The immediate success of Lincoln must be attributed to the hard work of its founder, Richard B. Foster. One
of the many New Englanders who contributed so much to
educational progress in Missouri, he was a native of New
Hampshire and had graduated from Dartmouth College. He
had taught in Illinois and Indiana before the war and became
involved with the abolitionist movement in Kansas. Volun-
teering for service in the Union Army in 1862, he applied for
transfer to a Negro outfit when recruitment of colored soldiers began.[57]

Lincoln Institute's first few years were trying ones indeed.
Foster at one time found it necessary to apply for work teach-

ing Negro children in the Jefferson City schools to supplement his income. In 1868 he enlisted the services of Charles A. Beal as a fund-raiser. Beal, an enterprising young Negro from Adrian College, and W. H. Payne, a schoolmate, had written a number of states seeking employment in Negro education. One of their letters came to the attention of Governor Fletcher, who passed it along to Foster. Foster wrote that he could use both of them if they could arrange to have some benevolent group assume responsibility for their salaries. This they did through the American Missionary Association. Payne was employed to teach, and Beal became field agent for the school. Being very successful in his efforts, Beal raised six thousand dollars that helped clear the Institute's outstanding debt and equip the first permanent building in 1871.[58]

In the meantime, agitation for state support had begun. Superintendent Parker's recommendation of 1869 has already been mentioned. In both 1868 and 1869 an effort was made in the legislature to allocate to Lincoln Institute 10 per cent of the income from the agricultural college land grants provided by the federal government. Justification for this action rested on the supposed original purpose of the school's organizers to prepare the Negro for "study and labor." Nothing came of this proposal, as the Assembly could not agree on the distribution of any of the grants.[59] In January, 1870, a number of leading Negro citizens from all parts of the state gathered in Jefferson City to push legislative action. In addition to seeking some of the land grant funds for Lincoln, they endeavored to have the institute declared a state normal school. An agricultural college bill passed, but without the inclusion of Lincoln. Instead, Representative J. B. Harper of Putnam County introduced a resolution granting five thousand dollars annually in state aid to Lincoln if its trustees would consent to convert the school into one designed for the training of Negro teachers for public schools. The trustees would further have to certify that they held in trust buildings and grounds valued at not less than fifteen thousand dollars for such a purpose. Passed by both houses in February, 1870, this act became one of the milestones in the development of higher education for the Negroes in Missouri.[60]

Under this impetus, Lincoln forged ahead. On the evening of March 10 the Radicals placed the Hall of Representatives at the disposal of Foster and his students for an exhibition. A temporary stage with sliding red curtains replaced the desks of the clerks in the front of the chamber. Dialogues, declamations, and recitations were interspersed with songs in chorus and solo renditions and with some "very pleasing tableaux." The *Missouri Democrat's* correspondent at the capital reported: "The examinations in class studies exhibited intelligence, promptness, and a degree of proficiency that compared well with other schools, and was at once evidence of the capacity of the race and of the earnest labors of the teachers of the school." A large crowd of both Negroes and whites packed the hall. Their enthusiasm heightened the effect of the evening in spite of "villainous catcalls, whistling and vocal blowing of a class of rowdy boys of white persuasion" that erupted between some of the acts. At the close of the exhibition Governor McClurg presided over a fund-raising meeting to help make the school eligible for the legislative appropriation. J. Milton Turner, a prominent Negro educator and political figure, informed the group of the school's financial needs, after which the Governor announced that he would start the collection with one hundred dollars. Lieutenant Governor Edwin O. Stanard donated a similar amount. Before the evening was over, better than one thousand dollars had been raised.[61] Within a year sufficient funds became available for Lincoln to erect its first building. Enrollment was over the one hundred mark and continued to increase throughout the decade. Finally, in 1879 the state took over complete operation of the school.[62]

The educated Negroes of Missouri and many white Radicals, particularly those among the German element, had expressed concern at the failure of the constitutional convention to give the freedmen suffrage. Governor Fletcher listed this omission as one of his reasons for opposing ratification. When the constitution secured the electorate's approval, the Governor and others began urging amendments. Fletcher made several tours during the summer and fall of 1865 in support of the doctrines of equal rights and reconciliation.[63] In October of 1865 a colored mass meeting in one of the St. Louis churches organized the Missouri Equal Rights League. White and Negro speakers hailed suffrage for the colored man as the key to full equality before the law. The group adopted resolutions embracing these sentiments and established a state executive committee to launch a state-wide drive.[64]

The committee wasted little time in getting its campaign under way. On October 12 it issued an appeal to the people of Missouri:

> Out of the fierce conflict which has just closed between an advanced civilization and a relic of barbarism, we at length have been released from chains, lashes, bloodhounds, and slave marts, and to us has a "freedom at large" been ordained. For this, in behalf of our long oppressed race, do we thank God and now ask that this liberty shall be secured and consecrated by those guarantees and privileges, which are enjoyed by every other American citizen, and which can only be found in the exercise of the right of suffrage.[65]

To aid their campaign, the committee persuaded John M. Langston, a prominent mulatto attorney from Oberlin, Ohio, to come to Missouri for an extensive tour. One of the most eloquent spokesmen for his race, Langston had graduated from Oberlin College and had been active as a recruiting agent for colored troops during the war. Recently, he had been elected to the Oberlin City Council. Along with Frederick Douglass, whom the committee hoped to bring later,

Langston stood in the front ranks of those seeking to secure for the Negro his full rights under freedom.[66]

Langston launched his tour at Turners' Hall in St. Louis in late November. A large enthusiastic crowd of Negroes and whites heard him temper his plea for suffrage with a reminder to the colored men that they must not forget the sober responsibilities of citizenship. Langston contended: "There is not a colored man in this State, however humble he is, who can afford to be a bad man—not one. . . . If a single negro in the State of Missouri consents to be anything other than an upright, straightforward, reliable man, he is false to himself and false to the negro race on this continent." The Negro must prepare himself to take advantage of his new-found freedom. "You have got a foe to deal with whom you have not understood," he warned. "You have whipped him on the battlefield, and his boast is that he will now whip you on the field of politics, and there you have got to fight another battle." Langston felt confident of their final triumph: "We are to be given the ballot that we may save the Constitution and write under it *este perpetua*—let it stand forever and may God help the right."[67]

During the next six weeks Langston visited Hannibal, Macon, Chillicothe, St. Joseph, Kansas City, and Sedalia. Petitions calling upon the General Assembly to provide suitable schools for Negro children and to remove the word "white" wherever it appeared in the constitution circulated through the local committees. Over three thousand signatures were secured. On January 9, 1866, Langston ended his outstate tour at Jefferson City with an evening speech in the Hall of Representatives. He had a capacity crowd, and the members of the General Assembly attended en masse. The *Missouri Democrat's* reporter informed his readers that Langston made a simple but eloquent plea for the Negro's cause. Even the Conservatives "acknowledged frankly the fairness and justness of his argument." To help defray the expenses of the

campaign, the state committee published the address in
pamphlet form for distribution at twenty-five cents a copy.[68]
Two days later the Equal Rights League held a "Grand
Emancipation Celebration" in St. Louis to commemorate the
first anniversary of Missouri's ordinance. In spite of inclement
weather, the Negro population made a magnificent occasion
of the affair with a long parade of colored troops, societies,
Sunday schools, and other groups, which bore festive banners
and slogans. At the final rally in Washington Hall, Langston
made one of his best speeches; the committee considered the
effort of bringing him to Missouri quite worth while.[69]

The secretary of the League, J. Milton Turner, also toured
that winter on behalf of the cause of equal rights. Another
Oberlin product, Turner had been born into slavery in Missouri. His father had purchased the freedom of himself and
his family in the 1840's when Turner was quite young, whereupon the family had emigrated to Ohio. Turner entered
Oberlin at the age of fourteen and remained there one year
before returning to Missouri. Little is known of his where-
abouts until the war. Legend places him at Camp Jackson as
a body servant to one of the state officers. Shortly thereafter
he transferred his services to one of Frank Blair's staff
members and followed him to Wilson's Creek and Shiloh.
Wounded during the latter battle, Turner carried a permanent hip injury and limp the rest of his life. During his tour
Turner invaded a hostile southeast Missouri. On at least one
occasion he had "to escape for his life at midnight, barefooted
in the snow." In April, 1866, he became the teacher of the
first public school for Negroes in Missouri at Kansas City. He
constantly worked on behalf of his race in the state until
President Grant appointed him American minister to Liberia
in 1871. Turner thereby became the United States' first Negro
diplomat.[70]

On March 7, 1866, Representative Enos Clarke of St. Louis
addressed the House for an hour and one half as he presented

the petition of the Equal Rights League. He called for support of his resolution instructing the committee on constitutional amendments to report in favor of giving the Negroes suffrage. The House, however, remained unmoved.[71] Agitation continued sporadically throughout 1866.

With the meeting of a new General Assembly in 1867 the movement for Negro suffrage picked up considerable momentum. Senator B. Gratz Brown led the way through the Planters House conference mentioned earlier.[72] Radical politicians who favored a more liberal constitution became more vocal and militant. Charles D. Drake came to the support of the movement, although he refused to go along with the other Planters House proposals to remove the test oath restrictions. "If it is right to make the Negro a voter," Drake asserted, "let it be done because it is right, not as a swap with the rebels." In accepting his Senate seat, he told the legislature:

> The Negro must be enfranchised. Without that he cannot be really free, nor can the Nation be calm. As long as he disfranchised the Nation carries within itself a magazine of oppression and wrong, which, as sure as human rights are a reality, will one day explode, and shake it to its center. With the ballot in his hand the Negro can and will quench the spirit of the rebellion to its very last spark; without it he, by his very helplessness, invites aggression and stimulates the greed of tyranny which begot the late rebellion, and would today light the fires of another if it dared.[73]

The Equal Rights League maintained a strong lobby at Jefferson City. On the second anniversary of the emancipation ordinance it held another huge demonstration in St. Louis with a parade and rally, at which Governor Fletcher was the principal speaker. A few days later the executive committee issued a new plea for help. It reviewed the accomplishments of the past year, called for a renewal of petitions and addresses to the legislature, and asked for more funds to carry on the work. The League had had expenses of $2,221.82 to date, but had received donations of only $900.25; the difference had to be made up quickly.[74] The following month the committee secured Frederick Douglass to speak before another St. Louis rally. Douglass stood as the most distinguished Negro of his generation. Having escaped from slavery in Maryland at an early age, he had taken an active role in the abolition and other reform movements for two decades before the Civil War and had secured a reputation as an earnest and able speaker. After the conflict, Douglass continued lecturing on behalf of his people and their efforts to secure completely the fruits of freedom. A militant figure, he minced few words in calling for the Negro's full voice in government. At the rally a large St. Louis audience from both races gave him an enthusiastic reception.[75]

With all this activity, considerable attention now focused on the General Assembly—the crucial battleground for the struggle over Negro voting rights and related issues. The Radicals found themselves far from united on how they should handle the issue of suffrage or, indeed, on how they felt about the question itself. Some wished to tie it to removal of the test oath, which would mean giving voting rights to both Negroes and "rebels." They thought that such a policy would help to allay white opposition and also promote the "spirit of harmony" necessary for the continued progress of the state. As already seen, this met staunch opposition from Drake and the more ardent Radicals of the western border.

A secret Radical caucus proved quite disharmonious until the party leadership was able to hammer out an agreement among the members not to complicate the question of Negro suffrage with any side issues that might detract from its passage. All bills pertaining to any aspect of this subject had to secure caucus consent before they could be introduced in order that a united front would be presented on the floor of the General Assembly. Having forged their policy, the Radicals proceeded to push through both houses a constitutional amendment, to be submitted to the voters in 1868, that eliminated the word "white" as a qualification for the suffrage. It made no mention of changing the provisions for officeholding. The Conservatives bitterly fought the measure, particularly in the House; they sought the enfranchisement of the large body of suffrageless whites if anyone was to receive the vote, but in vain. Recalcitrant Radicals tried not only to amend the measure by striking out the word "white" wherever it appeared in the constitution but also by broadening the resolution into a thoroughgoing civil rights bill. However, strong party leadership, with the help of Governor Fletcher, was able to bring the measure through virtually unscathed.[76] Thus the Radicals were to place the issue of Negro suffrage before the electorate for consideration at a contest still nearly two years distant. Radical unity had prevailed on the surface; it remained to be seen if it could be preserved in the battles ahead.

CHAPTER VII

THE DEVELOPMENT OF
PUBLIC EDUCATION

As a part of their progressive program to build a better Missouri, the Radicals did a great deal to promote public education. A system of free public schools fit perfectly into the Radicals' image of their party as the protector of the Union and the champion of equal opportunity. In January, 1867, an editorial in the *Missouri Democrat* advised former Confederates that they could hasten the removal of the restrictions on them by adopting the Radical policies of "free labor, free schools, free speech, and the free ballot." Radical newspapers so continually advanced the idea that their opponents were unfriendly to public education that many Conservatives, especially those of Southern origins, came to identify the public school movement with the Radical party and its "Yankee ideas." Their resistance increased accordingly.[1]

Although public education in Missouri had been established by the Geyer Act of 1839, it lacked widespread support. Missouri was dominated by what some called the "Southern Attitude" toward education. This reflected the belief that the public schools existed for the children of the poor; their maintenance was a type of state philanthropy, a necessary expense to be held to a minimum. Those who could afford it sent their children to private academies, if they sent them at all. Parental responsibility included the educating of one's own children, at least in the rudimentary elements of reading, writing, and arithmetic. To tax the property of one man too extensively for the benefit of another's children was considered unfair and unjust.[2]

Some 175,800 pupils, out of a potential of 385,600, attended the public schools of Missouri in 1860. An additional 20,000 students were enrolled in 240 private academies and other schools. With 12½ per cent of the white population of Missouri over twenty years of age illiterate, the state ranked ninth nationally in illiteracy.[3] David P. Dyer in his autobiography described a typical prewar rural school in Lincoln County:

> About one mile south of my home was a school-house built of logs. It was about twenty feet square, with a door in one side and a chimney place opposite. This chimney was built of stone gathered from the hill-side, and the fireplace was of sufficient size to take large pieces of wood. On the third side of the room, a log in its entire length had been left out for the purpose of making a window. Beneath this window a writing desk was made of a long plank about eighteen inches wide. It was on this desk—this plank—that the children were taught to write. The seats were made of logs split in half and supported by legs driven into augered holes. The interstices or cracks between the logs in the house were filled by mortar made of earth, lime and straw. In winter, with a blazing fire going, and the door shut, the room was fairly comfortable. . . . Usually the school year lasted for about four months, and the teacher was paid at the rate of $15.00 per month. He furnished his own board and lodging. Those who attended this school

were the children of poor people and knew what it was to live on short rations.[4]

Secondary education was almost entirely the province of private academies before the Civil War. St. Louis had established a public high school in 1853, and it remained the only one in Missouri until St. Joseph began one at the very eve of the war. The turbulent times that soon plagued the state forced the suspension of operations at St. Joseph almost immediately; they were not revived until 1866.[5]

Finances for the public schools in the middle of the nineteenth century came from much the same sources as today: township, county, and state funds. In a law of 1853 the General Assembly had provided that 25 per cent of all general state revenues was to go into the newly established Public School Fund. Yet, the varying amounts appropriated were seldom sufficient to meet the needs of the schools dependent on them. Some 4,000 schools with 4,700 teachers received a little over $800,000 from all sources in 1860. Of this, $116,000 came from taxation and $447,000 from public funds. A state university had been established at Columbia in 1839 as a capstone to the public education system, but it received no state appropriations and had to subsist on student fees and a small income from federal land grants. Several private institutions of higher learning existed, but they possessed limited facilities.[6]

The war years brought almost total neglect to Missouri's schools outside the St. Louis area. The General Assembly suspended state revenues for education in May, 1861, when it transferred all monies in the Public School Fund to the Militia Fund in order to prepare Missouri for an anticipated invasion by federal troops. Although the state convention of 1861 repealed this act, the turbulent conditions of guerrilla warfare made revenues so small that no new apportionment could be made for schools until 1864. At the outset of the war

the state convention also abolished the office of State Superintendent of Common Schools and those of county school
commissioners outside St. Louis County in order to save
money. It temporarily transferred the functions of the State
Superintendent to the Secretary of State.[7] Under these circumstances most of Missouri's public schools ceased operations.

The state convention of 1865 laid the groundwork for the
new educational system that arose out of the ashes of the
war. Considering "a general diffusion of knowledge and intelligence [as] being essential to the preservation of the rights
and liberties of the people," it required the General Assembly
to maintain free public schools for all youths between the ages
of five and twenty-one. It further gave that body authority
to require a minimum attendance of a term equivalent to
sixteen months by all eligible pupils at some time before the
age of eighteen.

To oversee the state's educational structure, the new constitution established a Board of Education consisting of the
Secretary of State, the Attorney General, and the Superintendent of Public Schools. The latter, an old position with a
new title, had most of the authority and carried a four-year
term of office. The constitution also established a new Public
School Fund, which was to be supplied by the usual sources.
In providing for its disbursement, the convention displayed
progressive tendencies by requiring the General Assembly to
"take into consideration the amount of any county or city
funds appropriated for common schools purposes, and make
such distribution as will equalize the amount appropriated
for common schools throughout the State." The original report of the committee on education had recommended that
school monies be appropriated on the basis of the number
of children attending the public schools and the average time
of their attendance, but this proved to be too advanced. Without even a roll-call vote the convention struck out this inno-
vation and thereby retained in effect apportionment according

to the general enumeration of the school population. Eligibility for state aid required local districts to maintain free public schools for a minimum of three months each year. Should the regular Public School Fund be insufficient to provide at least four months of schooling in each district, the General Assembly could pass additional tax measures to raise the needed revenue.[8]

Many of Missouri's schools reopened in the fall of 1864, particularly in the area north of the Missouri River where conditions were becoming more settled. In his first annual report to the General Assembly in November, 1865, the new State Superintendent noted that Missouri had some 300,000 eligible pupils. No figures existed on actual attendance, but it was undoubtedly small. The Superintendent reported:

> The condition of the common schools of the State is difficult to describe. Many of the districts are unorganized. In these, two citizens are often unable to be found who can take the oath and thereby preserve their school organization. The towns and larger villages, for the most part, are enabled to continue the schools; but the country neighborhoods of many counties are wholly without them. The school houses are almost universally in a bad condition.[9]

In St. Louis, schools were being established in rented facilities as quickly as these could be procured. Nevertheless, they had to turn away over two thousand white children for lack of accommodations. The local superintendent of schools, Ira Divoll, summed up the situation quite tersely in his 1865 report to his board: "The people must build school houses or prisons."[10]

Within the general framework of the new constitution the General Assembly passed several laws early in 1866 that established a thorough and detailed public school system. In practice, these laws proved to be complicated and rather confusing, for a considerable overlapping of functions existed among county, township, and local officers and authority. The basic overseer of the educational system was the county superintendent of schools. The establishment of this office marked a definite advance over the old county commissioners of prewar days. The county superintendent had more power, and his duties were more clearly defined. He had broad supervisory authority and was expected to provide real educational leadership at the county level. Among other duties, he must hold two teacher institutes in his county each year and provide guidance in securing uniform textbook adoptions. Unfortunately, the Assembly made this office elective, which meant that political considerations frequently took precedence in selecting its occupant. The superintendent, nevertheless, was required by law to "possess the qualifications of a competent teacher of public schools and be of good moral character."[11]

To teach, one had to be certified by his county superintendent and had to pass a periodic examination in orthography, reading in English, penmanship, arithmetic, English grammar, modern geography, and history of the United States. If a person planned to teach in a high school, he also had to be proficient in the higher mathematics and natural sciences. The primary certificate remained valid for six months to a year, while that for the high school was issued for a two-year period. Both could be used only in the county that issued them.[12]

The Assembly provided that township boards composed of three trustees could be established in any congressional township when a majority of the people voted to organize themselves into a school district with full corporate powers. These boards had authority to provide as many primary schools in their districts as necessary to accommodate those children wishing to attend. The township could also be divided into local or subdistricts, each of which would have its own board. Each subdistrict clerk held a seat on the township board to

help improve co-ordination between the two groups, but
many local school districts resented the power of the township board to select textbooks and to establish and change
the subdistrict boundary lines. State Superintendent T. A.
Parker, after trying to make this system work for four years,
reported to the General Assembly in 1870 that it had been
almost a complete failure, largely because Missouri did not
have the township form of local government. He described
the provisions of this law as "a strange commingling of the
duties of local and township boards," which often left everyone thoroughly confused as to where real jurisdiction lay.[13]
The General Assembly took no action until 1874, when it enacted legislation that eliminated the local districts.[14]

The legislation of 1866 established the most adequate basis
for local tax support seen up to that time. Local boards could
build schools and tax their districts to cover the costs without having to submit the levy to the voters for approval.[15]
This policy greatly facilitated badly needed school construction, especially in areas that might have proved recalcitrant
because of the old "Southern Attitude." School taxes increased
rapidly between 1865 and 1870. Where possible, old buildings
were repaired or rebuilt. The construction of many new
schools went forward. The Missouri State Teachers Association appointed a committee to draw up recommendations
for a model school building. Superintendent Parker's annual
report for 1868 showed an increase of 1,905 school buildings
over the previous year and the hiring of an additional 838
teachers.[16]

In some areas new blackboards, globes, and other instructional apparatus were purchased as well as new school furniture. Much of this equipment came from James B. Merwin's
Western Publishing and School Furnishing Company in St.
Louis. Merwin established the popular *Journal of Education*
in September, 1868, to help disseminate progressive educational ideas to teachers and parents across the state. Much in

demand as a lecturer at institutes and teachers' meetings, he often chose as his topic the need for modern equipment in the up-to-date schoolroom. "Our inventive genius, ingenuity, and skill," he boasted, "backed up by the laws of physiology, are constantly on the alert to devise new patterns, combining, as far as possible, cheapness with comfort and durability."[17] Yet, in spite of these efforts to improve educational facilities, George O. Garnsey noted in mid-1869 that many pupils still attended "old dilapidated dry goods box structures" where they found themselves "cramped by illy constructed seats, stifled by the foul, closely-confined air" or "else shivering for cold if enough of fresh be admitted to temporarily purify the fetid room."[18]

For general revenue purposes, each local board was to submit each year to the county clerk by the third Saturday in April a list of property owners in the district and an estimate of how much would be required to sustain its school for the minimum four-month period. There was also to be attached a list of all white and colored youth between the ages of five and twenty-one in the district. If the board failed to act, it became the duty of the township clerk to hire an enumerator to do this work. After he had received the information, the county clerk then calculated the tax assessment necessary to make up the difference between what was needed and what the state had provided.

To hold more than four months of schooling, the law required the township board to call a meeting of all the voters within its district. On these occasions the majority ruled. If the voters decided for a longer school term, it also became their duty to vote the tax levy necessary to cover the additional cost. Subdistricts possessed this same power if the larger township refused to act. If the township wished to establish a high school, this, too, had to be handled at a special meeting of the eligible voters. Only they could determine cost and location of the schools and the amount of tax levy necessary to sustain the project.[19]

Neither the constitution nor the new school laws placed any limitations on the amount of taxes that could be levied for school purposes. With former Confederates or Southern sympathizers constituting the principal landowners in many districts, this lack of restrictions sometimes produced a situation in which the enfranchised voted high taxes for school purposes at the expense of their disfranchised neighbors. In 1870 Superintendent Parker reported to the General Assembly that school taxes, particularly for building purposes, were bringing so many complaints that they threatened "to entirely subvert the free school system." School levies should never be so high as to cause a burden. He questioned the wisdom of trying to "force any measure upon the people, however beneficial it might be," if its support would cause financial embarrassment.[20]

The "Southern Attitude," which had been somewhat dormant, began to manifest itself again among the Conservatives. When they regained political power after 1870, many stood ready to oppose further expansion and high tax levies for the "Yankee schools," which they believed had been an unfair imposition. Although never strong enough to destroy the public school system, they frequently wielded enough influence to curtail support at both the local and state levels. Indifferent and careless administration of schools and school funds sometimes resulted. Those seeking to boost public education often had to fight a rear-guard action against destructive legislation at a time when they would rather have pushed for more progressive measures.[21]

Another legislative act of 1866 permitted any incorporated town or city to be organized as a separate school district with its own board of education composed of six directors. Each board could establish the necessary primary and high schools it thought adequate for its town. In such cases the public schools had to be open at least thirty but not more than forty-five weeks each year. Admission had to be free, but the board had the authority to determine the amount of local taxes necessary to the system's maintenance. The law for the urban areas differed from the one affecting rural townships in that the former were required to call a special meeting of voters to approve the purchase or construction of new buildings and the necessary tax levy to cover them. Town school boards could issue bonds to construct or repair buildings, provided they did not exceed a term of twenty years or bear more than 2 per cent interest. Again, no limitations were set on the amount of taxes the board could levy for general support of the schools or on the total sum that could be voted for building purposes.[22]

All of these measures tended to stimulate the rapid development of the public school system throughout the state. The statistics in Superintendent Parker's annual report for 1870 reveal that the number of public schools in Missouri had increased from 4,840 in 1867 to 7,547 by 1870. The number of pupils enrolled jumped from 169,270 to 280,473.[23] Of course, laws do not automatically create a well-organized school system. Some counties and towns built excellent schools; others did practically nothing. The better schools usually existed in areas where the partisans of public education placed heavy emphasis on the relationship between an educated citizenry and community prosperity.

Kansas City was a fast-growing community of 15,000 by early 1867. At this time a group of public-minded citizens became determined to establish a uniform system of graded public schools. At an open meeting called to discuss the situation, the city's common council asserted: "Well attested experience has shown that a system of graded schools, supported by the community, and open to all children free of charge, is the most effective and enduring producer of security, peace, and prosperity in any community, and should have the hearty and united support of all good citizens."[24] The meeting brought the desired results, for the local paper announced that the Kansas City public schools would "open for the reception of pupils on Tuesday, October 1." Not only would there be primary schools but also a high school department with one teacher, which would occupy "the lower room of Mr. Stark's building." Sixteen teachers began work that fall in rented quarters that had been hastily arranged and scantily furnished. The energetic board of education pushed ahead; within a year two new buildings had been opened and others were being contemplated. By 1870 the high school had several teachers and a new building of its own, with provision for four years' work.[25]

St. Joseph served as another example of what could be accomplished by an aroused citizenry. Plans were drawn up as early as 1864 for a vigorous campaign to improve public education. The school board secured the services of Edward B. Neely, an experienced educator, who brought in good teachers, pushed the construction of new buildings, and employed the latest educational techniques. Whereas St. Joseph had previously been "infested with private schools, by 1867 there was scarcely one in the city," the public schools having, like Aaron's rod, "swallowed up all the rest."[26]

At the other end of the state, St. Louis had begun its public school system in 1838 and established a high school fifteen years later. It had been fortunate in finding good leadership over the years, with many of its teachers being imported from New England under the aegis of William Greenleaf Eliot. Much of the credit for the system's excellent status at the end of the war must go to Ira Divoll, who had become superintendent in 1858. Divoll almost killed himself through overexertion as he tried to keep the schools operating during the war with only a minimum of financial resources while at the same time looking ahead to postwar expansion.[27] Faced with the complexity of problems confronting education after the war, Divoll forged ahead to find solutions. When it became necessary for him to take a leave of absence for reasons of health in the fall of 1867, the *Missouri Democrat* pridefully paid tribute: "Since the close of the war probably no other city in the Union has made such rapid progress in the cause of popular education as St. Louis." The article pointed out that at least twelve new schools had been opened in the last two years and five new buildings had been completed. In all, the system had thirty-three schools staffed by 250 teachers. Most of this faculty had received its training from the St. Louis normal school, then celebrating its tenth anniversary. The public school library, started by Divoll less than two years earlier, now had 11,000 volumes and 2,000 outside subscribers.[28]

With Divoll's retirement in May, 1868, the superintendency passed to his assistant, William Torrey Harris, one of the most forward-looking educators of his day. In the next decade he organized the St. Louis public school system into one of the most advanced in the United States. The influence of Harris, who was a firm believer in universal education, was widespread over Missouri through his addresses at teachers' institutes and his articles in Merwin's *Journal of Education*.[29] He shared the Radical philosophy that the public schools were one of the agencies that would help break down caste distinctions and prevent the growth of aristocracy. This viewpoint contrasted decidedly with the attitude of many Conservatives who looked upon the private academies as the most feasible way to produce an educated elite. Writing in the *Journal of Education* in September, 1869, Harris declared that the American educational system must be different than that of a nation possessing a stratified society and asserted that it was the public schools that offered the means for promoting social mobility through equality of opportunity.[30]

Shortly after Harris began his tenure as superintendent, the St. Louis school board acquired O'Fallon Polytechnic Institute from Washington University. On Harris' suggestion the board incorporated this school into the local system as a more advanced institution for practical education than the evening schools established under Divoll's leadership. At O'Fallon one could acquire knowledge in arithmetic; physics (natural philosophy); line, machine, and architectural drawing; English grammar; geometry; and the Spencerian system of penmanship. When the school opened under its new arrangement in October, 1868, about one hundred students enrolled, which more than doubled what had been its top enrollment under the auspices of Washington University.

St. Louis now possessed a "real people's university." The O'Fallon building, in addition to its various classrooms, contained the public school library, the normal school, and rooms for the Missouri Historical Society and other cultural groups that Harris had helped to organize. It also housed the superintendent's office and board rooms. During Harris' tenure this institute was more than merely a vocational school with apprentice shops. It supplemented rather than supplanted the public schools and made possible the development of a variety of programs, all of which were based on the same broad foundation of basic knowledge. Without the fundamentals, purely vocational training would do little to establish that broad-based electorate of educated people so essential to the preservation of democracy.[31]

At the same time, the St. Louis high school proved increasingly popular. Thirty-eight students graduated in June, 1868, and over the next five years an average of 25 per cent of those who entered stayed to finish their work. Accommodations became so crowded that the hall on the third floor of the building was turned into an art room and the second floor space occupied by that department was divided and used for other classes. The enrollment increased to such an extent the following year that this same hall was redivided into four regular classrooms and space in the basement previously considered unfit for classes was refurbished for use.[32]

During this era the public schools, both in St. Louis and outstate, were looked upon as a means of assimilating and Americanizing the large group of immigrant children who had come to Missouri in the decade before the Civil War and who continued to arrive after that conflict. The lack of familiarity that these people had with free institutions could have a corrupting and discordant influence on the life of a state or community if it was not properly channeled through the education of the young.[33] The most dominant emigrant group in Missouri was the Germans, who began arriving in large numbers after the European revolutions of 1848. With a deep longing for freedom and a firm belief in the rights of the individual, the Germans had amply proved their love for their new-found country during the Civil War. Yet, they were exceedingly clannish and did not assimilate easily into the general community. The older generation was determined to preserve the German customs and language among the young people. Wherever they existed in large numbers, the Germans insisted on the use of their language as well as English in class instruction.

The dual-language system had been practiced in some St. Louis schools for more than a decade. By the eve of the Civil War the city had a German population of sixty thousand. Considerable support for the public schools would have been lost if concessions had not been made to them. In the postwar era Harris justified the practice on the basis that the Germans paid their share of local taxes, but he increasingly steered instruction toward a heavier balance on the English side. Generally, not more than 20 per cent of classroom work was taught in the German language. However, in some rural areas where Germans made up the entire village population, less than an hour's instruction each day was devoted to English.[34] Slowly, through the influence of education, assimilation did take place. As early as 1867, Carl Schurz, after visiting a German community near St. Louis, wrote his wife:

> The little German colony in Augusta certainly gives the impression of prosperity. The old people have preserved the tradition of the German spirit and German training, but they are unable to bequeath this tradition to their children. It is an observation which I have made almost everywhere, that here in America, perhaps with the exception of individual cases in the great cities, the children of educated Germans contrast strikingly with their elders. The German spirit fades away. If the training remains wholly German and all contact with Americanism is avoided, a stupid Pennsylvania Germanism results. Where that is not the case, the waves of Americanism soon overwhelm the second and third generations. "The mission of Germanism" in America, about which some speak so loudly, can consist in nothing other than a modification of the American spirit, through the German, while the nationalities melt into one. In a few years the old patriarchs in pleasant little Augusta will be dead and their successors must be carried away by the universal movement.[35]

With the great stress being placed on the stimulation of individualism and self-development, superintendents and normal school leaders frequently warned teachers against doing too much for their pupils. Rather, they should teach each youngster to achieve self-reliance by learning to do things for himself. Therefore educators in Missouri as elsewhere concerned themselves not only with the establishment of schools but also with the general educational techniques that would best train their charges to be useful citizens in the democracy of the future. Many considered the old traditional methods of little help in accomplishing the citizenship goals of education. As early as 1868, Missouri educators began giving a great deal of attention to the "object teaching" methods developed in the normal school at Oswego, New York, by Edward A. Sheldon. It was a rare teachers' meeting or institute that did not discuss the new approaches of "object teaching" and "oral instruction." Teachers and administrators explained the new ideas in articles in their local newspapers and promised a far greater realization of the over-all educational objectives through their use. The *Journal of Education* gave considerable space to the new system's merits.

Undoubtedly, this Pestalozzian method of instruction, which emphasized sense perception, reasoning, and individual judgment, produced marked benefits upon instructional patterns in Missouri's growing school system. It appealed to the practical nature of many Missourians whose environment was not too far removed from frontier conditions. To these people, rote book-learning often seemed impractical, and this new teaching concept frequently admitted as much.[36] An item in the *Sedalia Times*'s educational column summarized this new method quite vividly:

> Human beings come into the world utterly ignorant and stupid. Words to them, are mere noises. The most eloquent periods are senseless sound. It usually takes a quarter of a century for them to attain anything like an apprehension of thought expressed in words. . . . Object-teaching is the mud-wagon that lumbers into the child's territory before the railroads are built. There is no other way of teaching children so effectively as to present the object to the eye. Use globes, outline maps, charts, blackboards, magnets &c&c. These "helps" are essential to success in every schoolroom.[37]

Seeing the value of this theory, the *Kansas City Daily Journal of Commerce* promoted the introduction of newspapers into the schools for advanced reading classes. It was hoped that this type of material would give a fresh and different approach to the study of government and current affairs and stimulate young minds to a livelier interest in the responsibilities of citizenship.[38]

The new educational concepts from the East that permeated Missourians' thinking after the Civil War included more than "object teaching" and the use of more practical curriculum materials. A different attitude toward the pupil was also stressed; the pupil should now be treated with understanding and love. The new view regarded the use of force as "the lowest form of power" and urged the abandonment of physical punishment except in extreme cases.[39] One teachers' institute at Kansas City in 1867 devoted an entire evening's session to the question, "Is Corporeal Punishment in School Unnecessary?" The local paper reported that a number of parents participated with the teachers in the discussion. Although many of them still would not "spare the rod," they believed it should be "resorted to only when moral suasion" failed. In most instances kind understanding was considered more effective than a heavy hand.[40]

William T. Harris applied "punishment American style" during his tenure as both principal and superintendent of the St. Louis schools. This method sought to impress upon the pupil that he was the cause of his own pain and the teacher merely the unwilling instrument of its infliction. One noted educator delighted in telling the story of his punishment when he misbehaved while attending the school of which Harris had recently become principal. A robust and naturally mischievous lad, he had brought his teacher to the point of exasperation following some misdeed. A threat to call the new principal only evoked the boy's laughter, for no one had been able to handle this youngster before. As suspense hung heavy over the classroom, Harris arrived. Spotting the troublemaker, Harris yanked him by his coat collar and the seat of his pants onto the top of a bookcase before the culprit had time to know what was happening and could defend himself. "There, young man," the principal remarked calmly, "you will sit up there until you know how to behave yourself." According to his own telling, the boy was permanently cured.[41]

Educators continually stressed the need for parental and community support if the educational goals for more effective citizenship were to be achieved. The influence of home environment was emphasized as teachers realized that lack of proper parental guidance could undermine their efforts to produce intelligent, law-abiding citizens. Parents were urged to visit the schools and become better acquainted with the work being done there. One writer in the *Journal of Education* stated that such visitation would have the double value of stimulating the children to greater endeavors and encouraging the teacher in his efforts. Another author called for an "educational revivalism" to arouse the dormant interests of parents and the community at large in the ongoing importance of the school program. Teachers should encourage parental and public awareness of their school activities through open houses and periodic special programs.[42]

Underlying the question of new educational objectives and methods was the more vital and far-reaching matter of teachers' training. Without teachers properly instructed to appreciate and use these ideas, little could be accomplished in their implementation. Many Missourians concerned with the adoption of the new techniques felt that their state lagged behind the more progressive commonwealths in the development of trained teachers. Educators worked hard to overcome the prevalent attitude of many that "if I can't do anything else in Missouri, I can teach." While little skill was needed to enforce discipline by the rod and listen to rote recitation, the good teacher had to go far beyond this. It took little preparation to "keep school," as the saying went, but skill and special training were needed to "teach school." Too many Missouri teachers were "*keeping* school," according to an article in the *Journal of Education* of November, 1869. "Let those be read out of the profession who have not prepared for the work and are not professional teachers."[43]

For the average teacher who barely met the meager standards for certification the teachers' institutes furnished the best means of learning about the new methods and ideas of the educators. The school law of 1866 required each county superintendent to hold these meetings at least twice a year if he had sufficient teachers to make it worth while. The law also enjoined each teacher to attend all regular sessions, once his county established such an institute.[44] At the end of 1867 Superintendent Parker reported to the General Assembly that about four thousand teachers had attended ninety institutes held throughout Missouri that year. These were usually of one week's duration, although in areas where they were held more frequently, two or three days would suffice. Parker felt that great progress had been made in establishing these meetings over the past eighteen months. In describing their purpose, he said:

> The institute is a temporary training school for teachers. . . . It is the most effective means of vitalizing and popularizing the teacher's special work. At the session particular instruction is given in the various methods of teaching; of discipline; discussion of theories and their application; history of education, and such other subjects as tend to practical advancement; carefully excluding any mere displays in debate and harangues. The institute is a means of popular culture not only from the facts just stated, but also from the lectures which should be designed for that purpose.[45]

The institutes received popular support, as evinced by newspaper comments in various localities. The *Sedalia Times* urged the attendance of Pettis County's teachers at a meeting to be held there in May, 1869. "We would advise directors not to employ teachers who refuse to attend this Institute," it admonished. "No one can be fit to teach who is so lacking in the spirit of progress."[46] The teachers of Iron County registered their approval in a resolution, typical of those passed by similar groups, that proclaimed institutes were "an absolute necessity inasmuch as they promote training and culture."[47] With the success of the local institutes, Superintendent Parker inaugurated in the fall of 1867 a series of district institutes to bring together the teachers from each congressional district for a broader sharing of ideas. These gatherings proved fruitful and made possible superior instruction that could not be given at the county level.[48]

During the previous year the energetic State Superintendent had called a meeting at St. Louis to reorganize the Missouri State Teachers Association. The two-day convention attracted wide attendance. All of Missouri's railroads except the Hannibal and St. Joseph agreed to transport teachers to St. Louis free of charge. Parker had several pet schemes that he wished to push at this meeting besides the mere reorganization of the association. In his letter of invitation he listed these as topics for discussion: the expediency of publishing a state educational journal, the promotion of the county teachers' institutes, and, above all, the establishment of a state normal school. To emphasize the importance of the state normal school, he invited Richard Edwards, president of Illinois Normal University, to speak.

Inspired by the program Parker had arranged, the teachers passed resolutions endorsing all of his proposals. Specifically, they appointed a committee to draft an extensive memorial to the General Assembly that called attention to the need for teachers' training and asked for a state normal school to serve the outstate area. Up to this time the only normal school in Missouri was the one established by the St. Louis board of education in 1857. It had been doing an excellent job, but most of its graduates went into the city's local system. The State Superintendent closed the meeting with a stirring address on "Republican Education," in which he emphasized several of the themes discussed earlier.[49]

That winter Parker included the teachers' memorial for a normal school in his annual report to the General Assembly. Largely the work of William T. Harris, it made a strong case for teachers' education on an advanced level. The legislature responded in a somewhat different fashion than the educators had expected. The new constitution provided that the state university should contain a normal department. The university's board of curators had authorized such an arrangement at its meeting in July, 1865. It had been impossible, however, to put the department into operation because of the lack of appropriations. Now the General Assembly voted to establish the normal department within the framework at Columbia and to grant sufficient funds for one teacher. It obviously considered this project a less expensive alternative.[50] The president of the university immediately went to work to find a well-qualified man to begin the department's operation. After much correspondence and several interviews he hired Professor E. Z. Ripley from the Michigan Normal School. Twenty-three students began the normal course that fall. Within two years its enrollment had grown to eighty-two, nearly double that of the rest of the university.[51]

Meanwhile, Parker continued to work for a separate normal school system. In his 1867 annual report he presented his program for the establishment of a normal school in each congressional district. The state would undertake the cost of instruction on a tuition-free basis. The counties and local communities where the schools would be located would provide land, buildings, and equipment, or their monetary equivalent. The schools would stand academically below the university whose normal college would offer a higher degree of instruction. Graduates of these institutions would be expected to teach two years in Missouri upon completion of their work.[52] The General Assembly, however, failed to act. The movement languished there until the winter of 1869–1870, when sufficient public opinion had developed to secure legislation.

In view of the obvious need for normal schools and in the hope that the General Assembly would eventually establish a state system, several private institutions sprang up in various parts of Missouri. The first and most substantial of these was the North Missouri Normal School and Commercial College, which began operations at Kirksville on September 2, 1867. Its founder, Joseph Baldwin, was to play a major role in helping to bring about the state system that finally emerged. He had taught in Missouri before the war, had been active in the State Teachers Association, and consequently had considerable familiarity with the state's educational problems. For some ten years after 1856 he had been connected with normal schools in Pennsylvania and Indiana. Early in 1867 he had returned to Missouri at the instigation of James B. Merwin, who considered the time ripe for the establishment of an outstate normal school. Baldwin inspected several sites. Apparently, he preferred St. Joseph. For some reason, however, Merwin thought Kirksville, although it was little more than a village, a better location. Baldwin had no desire to make another investigation. He had somehow lost fifty dollars while traveling and needed money to return to Indiana. Merwin agreed to lend it to him if he would go out to Kirksville first; if Baldwin did not like the place, he need not refund the money. Baldwin went, liked what he saw, and made arrangements for the opening of his normal school there that fall. With a great deal of faith, he agreed to pay one hundred dollars annually for a ten-year lease on an unfinished building originally intended to be an academy.[53] That summer Baldwin, with his team and buggy, canvassed northeast Missouri, recruiting students, holding institutes, and delivering lectures on the importance of teachers' training. He sent large printed posters ahead of him to announce his coming, and he always got a large crowd. Having a remarkable personality, he exhibited great powers of persuasion.

At the opening of the school's first term in September, 140 students appeared. With a faculty of six teachers, recruited from Indiana and from Kirksville's vicinity, Baldwin organized his "Science of Teaching" into three major areas: methods of culture, methods of instruction, and school management. He also established a "model school" for the practical instruction of his future teachers, to which he attracted some 114 youngsters from the surrounding area.[54] From 1867 until it became an official state institution, the North Missouri Normal School and Commercial College was owned and managed by Baldwin himself. He collected all tuition and from it paid expenses, improvements, salaries, rent, and other debts. The difference constituted his salary. The first year's operation showed a deficit of $326, but the second resulted in a surplus of more than $1,000 as enrollment climbed. No deficit existed thereafter. As his college proved eminently successful, Baldwin became an increasingly ardent agitator for a state system. He toured northern Missouri extensively, arguing the need for teachers' training; he thereby influenced popular opinion to help drive the General Assembly off dead center.[55]

In the summer of 1868 the Lawrence County teachers' institute incorporated the Missouri Normal University at Marionville. It acquired an eighty-acre tract and laid the foundation for a large building. Enrollment, however, was less than expected; funds came in slowly, and the continued operation proved to be a constant struggle. Failing to secure state recognition, the school passed to the Methodist Church in 1871 and attained considerable prosperity in the closing years of the century as Marionville College Institute.[56] Still another attempt at private normal education was the Fruitland Normal Institute. It began operations in the Pleasant Hill Academy building near Jackson in Cape Girardeau County in September, 1869. Professor J. H. Kerr, a graduate of Yale College and county superintendent of Cape Girardeau County, served as principal. This experiment was apparently short-lived, and little is known about it.[57]

George P. Beard, who had served as superintendent at Chillicothe and later taught in the St. Louis normal school, came through western Missouri early in the summer of 1869, canvassing for a location for his six-week "Teachers Normal

Institute." He finally settled on Sedalia when its board of education offered him the use of its buildings. As a special feature he announced a four-week "model school" in connection with his institute. Establishing good relations with the area press, he attracted over forty teachers from ten central and western Missouri counties, on rather short notice, for a term beginning July 19.[58] From the outset Beard played heavily on the idea that Sedalia would be a good location for a permanent normal school that could eventually become part of a state system. After one of his evening lectures on the importance of teachers' training the local *Times* applauded his program enthusiastically. It hoped that Beard's remarks would awaken an interest in the hearts of his auditors, "that shall neither slumber nor sleep till we secure to Sedalia a State Normal school." At the close of the summer institute a committee undertook to push for the location of a normal school there at the next session of the legislature.[59] Apparently pleased with the early success of his venture, the professor, as Beard liked to be called, announced that he would permanently establish his Central Normal School at Sedalia. The first twelve-week winter term would begin October 4, and two others would follow. Beard also planned an evening school for those who wanted special courses, if an enrollment of twenty could be obtained. Reporting that he had many unfilled applications for normal-trained teachers, the energetic educator demanded: "When will candidates realize the importance of professional training? Your services in the future will be valued in proportion to your prepaaration."[60]

Under the impetus of these private normal schools and the continuing build-up of public opinion in support of a statewide system by Parker, Baldwin, Beard, and others, the General Assembly finally passed an act in March, 1870, that established two normal school districts to be divided by the Missouri River (St. Louis County excluded). A single board of seven regents would locate a school in each district "in the counties offering the greatest inducements in buildings and lands" and would supervise their operation. The regents would consist of the State Superintendent, the Secretary of State, the Attorney General, and two men from each district appointed by the Governor.[61]

The first board met at Jefferson City on December 1 to make its decisions. As required by law, it had issued notices for the submission of bids six weeks earlier. The amount of these bids had to be sums that two-thirds of the qualified voters of any county would approve at a special election. They could be paid for by issuing twenty-year bonds at not more than 10 per cent. Although rumors had been flying that various counties would advance offers, particularly in the southern district, there appeared to be little competition. Kirksville seemed the obvious choice north of the river, and Joseph Baldwin's appointment as one of the first regents clinched the matter. Adair County promised $67,000 in the form of bonds, land, and buildings, including the one Baldwin had been renting for his college, as its contribution to the enterprise. South of the river the regents made the award to Sedalia and Pettis County, whose bid had been presented by the town's founder, George R. Smith, who was also one of the regents. Here again no competition seemingly existed. A Pettis County bond election held earlier in the fall had secured $75,000 to which a promise of $50,000 cash and ten acres of land had been added.[62]

The issue, however, was not to be resolved so easily. After the adjournment that evening three other tentative offers arrived by telegraph; if the regents would grant an extension of time, formal bids would be forthcoming. The new entrants were Chillicothe township north of the river and Johnson and Franklin counties in the south. Whether the outgoing Attorney General and the State Superintendent, both of whom had been defeated at the recent election in November, actually began conniving on behalf of Johnson County at this point, as the *Sedalia Democrat* later charged, cannot be known. But at a meeting specially called by Chairman T. A. Parker the following morning the regents voted to rescind their action of the previous day, to the great disgust of Baldwin and Smith.[63] It was further decided that bids would be kept open until December 27. In the interim the regents would tour the prospective sites to enable them to make a better evaluation.

The three areas that had issued tentative bids proceeded to hold hastily called bond elections. Chillicothe offered $60,000 and several tracts of land that could be converted into cash; Franklin County $100,000; and Johnson County $150,000 with an additional pledge of twenty acres for the campus site and $110,000 raised by private subscription.[64] In spite of these efforts the regents upheld their original decision when they next met to consider the matter. Rejecting the Chillicothe offer because the law made no provision for accepting a municipal bid, they announced that Baldwin's North Missouri Normal School would become the state institution in the northern district on January 1 and that its former owner would be principal. The bid of Franklin County in the south had not matched that of Pettis County. Although the offer of Johnson County topped the one from Pettis, there was some doubt as to the legality of the election there. Consequently, the regents appointed a subcommittee to procure a building in Sedalia for temporary use and make it ready for a summer term.[65]

The people of Chillicothe and of Johnson County immediately objected. Representative Robert S. Moore of Chillicothe inaugurated an investigation in the General Assembly, but this yielded no new evidence. However, further investigation by a new board of regents at the instigation of Johnson County finally brought a reversal of the decision regarding the normal school in the southern district. Announcement of the board's action on April 26, 1871, caught

Sedalians completely off guard. To their dismay, who should be appointed principal of the new Johnson County normal school at Warrensburg but Professor George P. Beard. An immediate outcry of treachery filled the air. Beard had refused to allow his name to come before a mass meeting at Sedalia called earlier to recommend a faculty for their new school. Now it appeared that he had been secretly in league with the Johnson County group for some time. At the regents' meeting he had testified that the atmosphere of Sedalia was not a good one for the normal school. Further investigation by the regents revealed that Sedalia's election, not that of Johnson County, had been held illegally inasmuch as no registration had taken place. And so the reversal.[66] Having made their final decision, the regents lost no time in implementing it. They secured temporary quarters for the summer session and opened the school at Warrensburg on May 10 with thirty pupils attending.[67] Missouri's normal school system, after much sound and fury, had become a reality.

The same 1870 session of the legislature that saw the climax of the struggle for a state normal school system brought to a culmination a five-year battle over the future of the University of Missouri. Although established in 1839, the university had received no appropriations from the state's revenues in the prewar era and had had to rely on student fees and a small income from federal grants for its resources. The institution had suffered greatly during the war with decreased enrollment, considerable faculty turnover, and periodic occupation of its buildings by military forces, which caused damages estimated at more than $3,000. Only sixty-nine students attended during the winter of 1864–1865. Although the figure climbed to ninety-nine at the first postwar session, half of these students were enrolled in the preparatory department. Four teachers made up the faculty of the university, and there was one vacancy. Encumbered with a $20,000 debt, the school's warrants sold at a 40 per cent discount. To climax the distress, the president's home burned in November, 1865, which resulted in a complete loss; many records were destroyed.[68]

As it faced the postwar future, the university found itself further handicapped by its location at Columbia. The Boone County seat was twenty-two miles from any railroad and thus somewhat isolated. This drawback, however, could be and was overcome. While serving in the prewar legislature, William F. Switzler had secured a charter for a railroad spur to link the town to the North Missouri Railroad at Centralia. This document remained valid, and in 1865 Switzler undertook a campaign to underwrite construction of the road. A mass meeting in October, 1865, endorsed the proposal, and the following February the Boone County court agreed to a bond issue of $200,000 if the company selected to build the line could raise the additional amount needed to complete the road. The response proved strong, and the line was finished in the fall of 1867.[69]

Another problem could not be put to rest as easily. Boone County stood in the heart of "Little Dixie," and its people were deep-dyed Conservatives. Indeed, many residents had shown considerable sympathy for the Southern cause. The Radicals believed that the region was basically disloyal and did not offer an atmosphere appropriate to the education of the state's future leaders.[70] The constitution of 1865 provided for a state university with a science department, a normal school, and an agricultural college; but the convention turned down an amendment by Switzler to designate the Columbia institution as "the state university" by a large majority.[71] At the same time strong Radical efforts were being made in Jefferson City to re-establish the university there "where the State officers can at all times look after its interests," which meant political supervision of the faculty and curriculum.[72] Nothing came of this endeavor, but at the 1865 session of the legislature a resolution in the House to give all university endowments and funds to an agricultural college, to be located elsewhere in the state with the help of federal land grants, failed by only the vote of the speaker.[73]

The controversy continued over the next few years, while the university struggled to maintain itself. By January, 1867, the Columbia institution had gained an important adherent in the person of Governor Fletcher. He devoted several paragraphs of his annual message to the legislature to the needs of the university and stressed that it must be made "worthy of our state and a source of usefulness and pride to our citizens."[74] Two other eloquent advocates bore the major part of the struggle that followed. One was James S. Rollins, former congressman and a staunch Union man during four years of wartime service at Washington. One of the ablest leaders in the ranks of the Conservatives, Rollins probably had a greater degree of respect among the Radicals than any other Conservative spokesman. He had helped establish the university initially and held a long-standing interest in the educational development of Missouri's young people. Of the state's wartime congressmen, he alone had supported the Morrill Land Grant Act of 1862. Elected to the state House of Representatives from Boone County in 1866, he immediately set to work to advance the cause of the university. In the House and the Senate, to which he was "promoted" in 1868, he became the university's most tireless supporter and during the next three years carried the brunt of the legislative struggle to win for it full recognition. Not unworthily is he remembered as the Father of the University of Missouri.[75]

Almost as important was Daniel Read, the university's president-elect. He had been chosen to succeed President John H. Lathrop, who died suddenly in August, 1866, after exhausting himself with the school's wartime and postwar problems. Read had been professor of mental and moral philosophy at the University of Wisconsin for the preceding ten years and had been close to Lathrop during the latter's presidency there. Since the two men had seen most educational matters from a similar viewpoint, Read's selection seemed a logical one. The new president also enjoyed an excellent reputation nationally, so that few could argue with his appointment. He agreed to take the new post only if the legislature presented unmistakable evidence of its willingness to give the university financial support.[76]

During the winter of 1866–1867 Read came to Jefferson City and appeared with Rollins on behalf of the university before a joint evening session of the two houses. One of those present described Read as "a man . . . six feet three or four inches in height, [who] looked for all the world like a strong, rugged and determined western farmer." Fully cognizant of the latent ill-feeling toward Boone County and the university because of the political situation arising out of the war, Read deliberately adopted a tactic designed to win personal approval for himself and thereby for the institution he would soon head. In simple rhetoric he announced:

> I stand before you this evening, a branchless trunk, without a sprig or green leaf to adorn it. I had a son, upon whom I expected to lean in my old age for support and comfort, but I gave him with all my heart to the service of the country to assist in keeping in the sky the flag of our fathers. He was a gallant boy and rode with Sheridan through the valleys and over the mountains of Virginia until he lost his life while fighting before Richmond. I have a *right* to speak to you, you his friends and comrades, and I beg your attention while I raise my voice in behalf of liberal education in the State that suffered as much as any other during the war.

Read then proceeded to present a vigorous, straightforward, and somewhat blunt appraisal of the university's plight. He contrasted the situation in Missouri with that of other states, particularly New York and Michigan, where the legislatures had responded readily. The observer mentioned earlier reported that Read's words electrified the audience and "won the fight for the University." This individual himself became one of those converted that evening, for he had previously sponsored the 1865 measure that would have stripped the university of its endowments.[77]

In the days that followed, the General Assembly appropriated $10,000 to rebuild the president's home and repair the other university buildings. Far more important than this, it designated to the university 1.75 per cent of the state's general revenues after 25 per cent had been paid to the common schools. This action secured an initial increase in the institution's funds of about $16,000—triple that of its other previous sources—and made possible the establishment of the normal department.[78]

Certainly, the legislation of 1867 all but stamped the General Assembly's approval on the institution at Columbia as "the state university." There remained only the question of where to locate the agricultural college. Congress, in July, 1862, had passed the Morrill Act, which granted every state 30,000 acres of United States public lands for each senator and representative under the 1860 apportionment if it would establish a college for instruction in the agricultural and mechanical arts. Missouri was to be allotted 330,000 acres, which could be sold or held. In case the state decided to sell, the monies or land scrip received therefrom had to be invested in "safe stocks" yielding not less than 5 per cent. The lands for this purpose had to be chosen in tracts of not less than 160 acres within the state's boundaries so long as public lands remained available there. Those states without enough public land remaining within their own borders could receive land scrip exchangeable for public domain elsewhere up to a total limit of one million acres in any one state.[79] Missouri's General Assembly accepted this benefice by joint resolution on March 17, 1863, but took no further action until March, 1866, when it empowered the Governor to select three agents to designate lands for this purpose.[80]

In the meantime a struggle had begun over the location of the college and the control of this anticipated endowment. The university's board of curators, at its meeting in July, 1865, had gone on record as favoring the college's location on its campus. Under the leadership of Rollins and Switzler, Boone County held a mass meeting the following November to pledge the necessary land for experimental farms and buildings. Switzler argued editorially in the columns of the *Missouri Statesman* that efficiency and economy should dictate that one major institution should house all branches of learning for the state.[81] Other localities, however, were also eager to have the agricultural college; they, too, held mass meetings and pledged large sums. Springfield, Jefferson City, and Kansas City particularly vied for the honor. After 1867 many people were content to let the university remain at Columbia as a liberal arts institution, but wanted to establish a separate agricultural college elsewhere as several other states had done. This viewpoint, as much as anything, accounts for the continuing struggle over this issue after other matters had been resolved.

For a time it seemed that one of the more serious obstacles to the Columbia effort was the attitude of Missouri farmers. Both the State Horticultural Society and the State Board of Agriculture, which served as the official voices of agricultural opinion, strongly opposed the Columbia location from the outset. Although dominated by Radicals, both groups apparently based their opposition on a genuine fear that an agricultural college at Columbia would be merely a minor appendage of the university and that training in scientific agriculture would be held to a minimum. In other words, the university would get the Morrill endowment, which it badly needed, but the farmers of Missouri would receive little in return. The heart of the opposition came from the Radical small farmers of the Ozark area of southwestern Missouri. They leaned toward a policy of splitting the Morrill endow-

ment among several small colleges conveniently located as
service centers for various regions of the state. This policy,
however, had the obvious disadvantage of slicing the melon
too thin.

The university found several spokesmen within these farm
organizations to plead its case. Rollins, Professor George C.
Swallow, and Norman J. Colman, the noted agricultural journalist, wielded strong influence and gradually began to lead
these groups to a grudging realization that it might take years
to secure the full amount of money from the endowment. If
the agricultural college were established in conjunction with
the university, it could operate temporarily within that framework while waiting for full receipt of its monies. To scatter
the college's functions over the state would lead to waste
and duplication when funds were limited and would hold up
real progress for several years.[82]

While the struggle over the college's location continued, the
state's agents began selecting the lands that would support
it. By the summer of 1867 they had taken up some 244,000
acres for the state's use. All of this land lay in the Ozark
region near the southern border where land values were relatively low. Norman J. Colman predicted that not more than
fifty cents an acre, or $150,000, would be realized for the
college from these tracts and lamented that the better lands
had already been taken. The agents should not be criticized
too hastily, however; by the time they entered the market
only a few small scattered tracts remained north of the Missouri River.[83] More than 98,000 acres of Missouri land had
been appropriated by other states for their use before the
General Assembly concerned itself with acquiring any. When
the homestead claims against the public domain in Missouri,
the railroad land grants, and other miscellaneous demands
are also included as unavailable land, the competition for the
best tracts becomes readily apparent. By June 30, 1867, only
1,835,892 of Missouri's original 41,824,000 acres of public

land remained unclaimed.[84] Thus, given the limited choice
they had, the agents did a good job.

Rollins, meanwhile, continued to work forcefully and effectively to promote the union of the agricultural college with
the university. Indeed, some of his Conservative friends
feared he was neglecting other aspects of their political cause
in his efforts to conciliate Radical support in the legislature
for his educational projects. As wartime animosities died
down, Rollins began to pick up editorial backing from some
of the Radical papers, including the highly influential *Missouri Democrat*.[85] President Read also continued to play an
important role. Ever alert to the possibilities of sharpening
the university's image as an institution for the education of
the state's future leaders, Read molded its program into the
liberal tradition demanded by a progressive Missouri. He participated actively in the Missouri State Teachers Association
and served as its president for 1868–1869. Through this and
other forums he broadened his influence still further and established much grass-roots support. The editor of the *Missouri
Democrat* highly praised his administration in July, 1869,
and asserted that people of Missouri could "feel a just pride"
in their university.[86]

Frustration followed frustration in the legislature, however,
as the 1868 and 1869 sessions brought failure for the effort
at Columbia in the House after approval by the Senate had
been given. Kansas City and Springfield continued their bids
for the location of the agricultural college. Yet, Rollins refused to give up. In his fight he was ably aided by F. T.
Russell, a member of the university's board of curators and
the man who replaced Rollins in the House when he went
to the Senate. To achieve his purpose, Rollins made judicious
concessions here and there, which finally carried the day during the legislative session of 1870. Foremost among these was
a proviso establishing a separate school of mining and metal-
lurgy in southeast Missouri. Representative William N. Nalle

of Fredericktown, who led a large bloc from that mining area, argued that technical schools should be located close to the natural resources they would need. Because he and his followers still supported Rollins' contention that the university should have complete control over administration and funds, the Boone County legislator agreed to the branch when Nalle proposed amendments to this effect. Under this arrangement the university's curators could locate the school of mines in any county within the designated area that offered $20,000 and twenty acres of land for its use. One-fourth of the federal land grant would be set aside for the school's endowment. If no county complied with these terms within three years, several counties could combine to effect the location. Should the curators receive no acceptable bids within seven years, the entire Morrill grant would revert to the university at Columbia.[87]

Word that Governor McClurg had signed the college bill reached Columbia around midnight on the evening of February 24, 1870. President Read ordered the immediate ringing of the university bell, and rockets soared into the sky as students took up the celebration. In spite of the late hour a large body of citizens soon swarmed into the streets as if they had been awaiting the signal. They marched with much jubilation to the residences of Read, Rollins, and Russell, each of whom readily responded to the calls for speeches. In the midst of the general rejoicing, the three men reminded everyone that Boone County still had the responsibility, under the new act, of providing $30,000 and 640 acres of land for the agricultural college. The people had earlier demonstrated their willingness to make such sacrifices, and the Boone County court promptly took care of the raising of the monies through bond issues.[88] Thus, the University of Missouri won its battle; it now faced the future as the state's premier institution.

The same act that finally united the university and the

agricultural college also provided for the disposal of the public lands to furnish the endowment prize. Fortunately, only a few restrictions were placed on the curators. The basic policy had apparently been suggested by one of the members of the university faculty, Professor J. W. Matthias. The curators were to appoint a land commissioner to oversee the appraisal and sale of existing lands and the selection of additional acreage. No land could be sold for less than $1.25 an acre, which helped greatly to alleviate Colman's fears. A deferred payment or lease plan could be instituted whereby a prospective purchaser could select land, live on it, and improve it while making interest payments of no less than 8 per cent of the original appraised price. All such leases had to be terminated by the end of 1881 to prevent the sales from dragging out ad infinitum.[89] The curators, however, encountered great difficulty in disposing of the lands. Various factors contributed to this: lack of industry on the part of the first land commissioner, failure to make prompt appraisal of the lands, general economic conditions following the panic of 1873, and competition from government homesteads and cheaper lands being offered by railroad agents and others. Ultimately, $538,314 was realized by 1955. The curators had suspended sales several years earlier with 18,323 acres of Morrill lands remaining in their possession.[90]

When viewed from an over-all perspective, Missouri made many significant strides in the area of education during the postwar years. For the most part, the Radicals in the 1865 convention and in the legislatures during these times proved to be farsighted. The wise leadership of such educators as T. A. Parker, Ira Divoll, William T. Harris, Joseph Baldwin, James D. Merwin, and Daniel Read also helped enormously. The Census of 1870 revealed that in addition to its public schools Missouri had 37 private colleges and 45 academies. Washington University had the state's only law school, but there were 6 medical colleges and 3 schools of theology. The census also noted 8 commercial schools and 3 academies of art and music. Day and boarding schools numbered 586, while there were 62 parochial and charity schools. Missouri maintained a school for the deaf and dumb at Fulton and a school for the blind near St. Louis, both of which had their origins in the prewar era. Radical legislatures gave them generous appropriations. From all sources, public and private, elementary and higher education received $4,340,805 in 1870. Of this, 75 per cent came from taxation and public school funds.[91]

There is every indication that most Missourians in the postwar era were eager for every possible cultural advantage that came their way. The growth of schools was supplemented by the development of public libraries and the lyceum circuit to provide educational opportunities for the adult population. Most of the state's larger towns had established some type of subscription library by the early 1870's. Typical was the one at California, which had an initiation fee of two dollars and annual dues of the same amount. The library was housed in one of the vacant rooms of the courthouse, which the county court made available free of charge. All of the St. Louis daily newspapers and a number of other journals were available, some of which were donated by members. Missouri's two senators and the district's congressman were made honorary members, in return for which they sent the library the *Congressional Globe* and other official publications. During the winter a librarian was hired for ten dollars a month, and hours were maintained from three in the afternoon until ten at night.[92] "The importance of the Lyceum as a mode of public education has hardly begun to be realized in our city or state," noted a writer for the St. Louis-based *Journal of Education* in December, 1868. The Public School Library Society of St. Louis was sponsoring its third annual course of lectures that winter with Josh Billings, the noted humorist; Du Chaillu, the African explorer; Henry Vincent, the English orator and political reformer; and the

Reverend J. T. Hecker, the Catholic writer and orator, already engaged. Warrensburg, Sedalia, Kansas City, St. Joseph, Macon, Hannibal, and "several others of our growing young cities" had made arrangements for similar programs.[93]

As the shadows of war cleared and old animosities died down, Missourians of all political beliefs looked to a prosperous future. Education in all its forms was one of the keys to that future.

CHAPTER VIII

IMMIGRATION AND TRANSPORTATION

EARLY IN January, 1865, the editor of the *St. Joseph Morning Herald* wrote:

> Missouri now lacks men. She has mines which await labor to develop. She has the finest agricultural breadth that the sun ever shone upon, only awaiting the ploughshare of the husbandman. . . . We want mechanics to improve our waterfalls. . . . A shrewd Yankee would compel every stream to strike a water wheel, and the hum of ten thousand spindles, and the merry shout of thousands of operatives would gladden, illumine, and make happy miles of the valley below. . . . Thus is Missouri's redemption to be made sure, and thus is she to be made the Empire State of the Mississippi Valley.[1]

Even as the constitutional convention met in St. Louis during the early months of 1865 and planned the state's future, emigrant wagons were rolling westward, bringing the first great wave of migration that was to flow into Missouri. A

177

few days after expressing the sentiments above, the editor of
the *Morning Herald* had fifteen farmers from Illinois stop by
his office and seek information on available lands. Greatly
impressed by the country, they wanted to settle there; they
expected to be joined by some twenty or thirty of their friends
from an adjoining Illinois county.[2] A few weeks later fifteen
wagons passed through St. Joseph, bringing six Indiana families to settle in the old Platte Purchase area. They carried
with them a large supply of stock and farming implements.
Soon it seemed that every train was disgorging strangers from
the East looking for homesteads. With great anticipation the
Morning Herald predicted that thousands of acres would
change hands in northwest Missouri that spring.[3] Other areas
reported similar movement. As the war came to a close, the
pace increased. By fall as many as twenty wagons a day were
crossing the Mississippi River at Quincy, carrying Missouri-
bound immigrants. One enthusiastic reporter estimated that
migrants had brought no less than five million dollars into
the state during the previous six months. The editor of the
Missouri Democrat exulted: "If the rush of immigration to
the State keeps on at the rate which is now witnessed for
two or three seasons, the wild places of Missouri will soon
blossom as the rose, and our population assume some fair
proportion with the extent of our boundaries and agricultural
resources."[4]

This sudden influx of population was no accidental phe-
nomenon. Responsible Missouri leaders and outsiders interested in the state's development had been planning for it
in a serious fashion since 1863. Large amounts of Missouri
land, much of it good farming acreage, remained sparsely
settled, especially in the western portion. Men of both political faiths realized early the desirability of attracting new
population to the state. Some estimated that nearly one-third
of Missouri's population had been lost because of war conditions; many doubted that they would return. With the South

fighting a losing cause, the state's future, of necessity, must be linked to Eastern capital and immigration. A westward movement was inevitable at the end of the war, and those with a stake in the state's future prosperity determined to channel as much of it to Missouri as possible.

From the outset of their campaign the Missouri Radicals had seen the importance of emancipation in economic as well as moral terms: Free the slaves, and Northern capital and population will flow into the state; maintain that deplorable institution, and the river of advance will bypass Missouri, and economic stagnation and decay will result. Many a budding Radical, in the political sense of that term, was also an entrepreneur who saw unparalleled opportunity and wealth stretching before him. The Radicals also hoped that Eastern immigrants would furnish votes for the Radical machine and would help offset the old Southern conservative influence of prewar days.[5]

When the New York delegation to the Chicago Ship Canal Convention visited St. Louis in early June, 1863, Radical merchants arranged a large reception in their honor. Both the Conservative Governor Gamble and the Radical Mayor Chauncey I. Filley gave assurances that emancipation would soon be a reality in Missouri and expressed the hope that such an event would make the state more attractive to Eastern capital. They stressed that Missouri's great abundance of iron and coal was just waiting for development.[6] Later that fall, Radical St. Louis businessmen who felt that the Chamber of Commerce was too conservative broke away and formed a new Union Merchants Exchange, which quickly became the city's dominant commercial organization.[7]

During that same year Governor Gamble appointed an immigration agent to promote Missouri's interests in Europe. This agent received payment for his expenses from several Missouri railroads and at least one St. Louis manufacturer, who hoped to import contract labor for his foundry. Little

resulted, however, from this early mission. To further encourage immigration from Europe, the Governor recommended to the legislature in December, 1863, that a state
immigration agency be created, but the Assembly failed to
take any action.[8] Meanwhile, private organizations worked
toward the same ends. The Methodist Church issued a circular in July, 1863, calling for the emigration of 100,000 additional members of that faith to Missouri. It gave a glowing
prospectus of what awaited them.[9] St. Louis Radicals organized the National Land Transfer Association and secured its
incorporation by the General Assembly. At the same time a
group of Conservatives incorporated the Missouri Emigration,
Land and Mining Company. Both of these organizations offered strong inducements to capital as well as labor and
worked to have the more stringent sections of Missouri law
regulating corporations removed.[10]

New Englanders became quite interested in Missouri and
its future prosperity. Amos A. Lawrence of Boston, who had
played a prominent role in sending emigrants to Kansas before the war, had purchased 85,000 acres in land-grant college
scrip at a cost of eighty cents an acre. He privately expressed
the intention of locating all of this land in Missouri for colonization by a "respectable class of people" whom he would
send from the East. Eli Thayer, a close friend and associate
of Lawrence, announced that with proper co-operation he
would place 50,000 immigrants in Missouri in one year.
Boston papers in 1863 contained glowing accounts of Missouri, and one predicted: "Freedom, with her immense resources, will soon make her [Missouri] the Empire State of
the West."

The interest of the New Englanders was attracted in part
by the agricultural and mineral potential of Missouri for
profitable development and in part by the capital investments
that had been put into the state before the war, such as the
Hannibal and St. Joseph Railroad, completed in February,

1859. This line had been built by a New England syndicate under the able leadership of John Murray Forbes, who was also constructing the Burlington Route with which it ultimately was to become linked. At the outbreak of war the Hannibal and St. Joseph was Missouri's only completed railroad. Constructed in part with federal land grants, it had begun a broad program to encourage immigration to and settlement along its right of way even before the war. In July, 1863, as conditions in north Missouri seemed to be settling down, the line advertised in a Boston paper that it had 500,-000 acres for sale in "one of the richest and healthiest agricultural and pastoral regions on this continent." During the next six years, under the efficient management of George S. Harris, this road's land department was to dispose of most of this acreage and add some 100,000 people to Missouri's population.[11]

Acting upon the recommendation of Governor Fletcher, the General Assembly created the State Board of Immigration on February 16, 1865, which would publish and distribute materials outlining the advantages Missouri offered potential residents. The board also had the authority to send agents to the East and to Europe to attract immigrants. The legislature appropriated four thousand dollars for operating expenses and authorized the board to solicit contributions from private interests that would benefit by its activities. To emphasize the importance of this agency, the Assembly provided that the Governor and the Secretary of State should be among its five members; the others would be appointed by the chief executive.[12] The board immediately went to work. It appointed the Reverend H. O. Sheldon as its traveling agent in the East. By the middle of April Sheldon had succeeded in procuring liberal dispensations for immigrants from the principal railroads serving the state from the East and from hotels along the routes. The board also dispatched an agent to Europe to attract immigrants from that quarter.

Particular emphasis was placed on encouraging further German immigration. Indeed, two of the three appointed members of the board were Germans: Isidor Bush and State Senator Frederic Muench, both of whom had engaged in immigration promotion before the war. Muench prepared educational material in the German language for use by the board's overseas agent.[13]

Early in June the board issued a general appeal for aid, which was decidedly Radical in tone:

> We ask the people of every county, every township and every neighborhood to organize auxiliary boards, or adopt such means as will put us in possession of all the facts pertaining to their respective localities which may be calculated to invite immigration. We will thus be enabled to aid them in filling up their vacant lands, or in sending them good, law-abiding, loyal and energetic residents, to purchase the farms and take the places of the disloyal, the dangerous or the useless portion of the population, and to help improve the country, contribute to the payment of our taxes, and augment the general prosperity.[14]

In August, Bush, who served as secretary of the board, followed this appeal with another one. He reported that he daily received many letters of inquiry from persons interested in moving to Missouri, and he asked that more information about the various counties be sent him so that he could answer the letters adequately. "By acting liberally and giving some inducements," Bush predicted, "many counties could double within less than two years their population, and every inhabitant could more than double the value of the balance of his property."[15]

By the end of September rapid progress was being made toward setting up auxiliary boards. Throughout 1865, letters describing the beauties, virtues, and specific economic attractions of different areas of Missouri appeared in newspapers and pamphlets, which were widely circulated by the state board and its agents. The North Missouri and the Hannibal and St. Joseph railroads made monetary contributions. These and other lines agreed to charge only half fare for immigrants who intended to settle in Missouri.[16] Private agencies and individuals continued to issue their own circulars and thereby supplemented the state's efforts. On February 20, 1865, Allen P. Richardson, a prominent Conservative, announced the establishment of the Missouri Emigrant Aid and Real Estate Office at Jefferson City, with branches in each county where business warranted it. There would be an initial fee of ten dollars for those wishing to place lands in his hands. Other terms might be effected at the time of sale.[17] Richardson's agency was but one of several. In the summer of 1865 former Congressman James S. Rollins of Columbia scattered circulars advertising Boone County lands among his Eastern friends and requested that they post them where they might do the most good. One friend replied: "Were I young I would go out but I am too old to emigrate. Missouri is to be a great state and is rich in latent fortunes for enterprising Yankees."[18]

Land sales were booming in western Missouri. "We have satisfactory authority," one paper reported, "for the statement that not less than 40,000 acres of public lands" were sold during the first three months of 1865 at the Boonville land office. In addition, private transactions were moving strongly. One private agent at Independence reported $50,000 in sales during the first two weeks in July.[19] And this was just the beginning. In May, 1866, the Commissioner of the General Land Office, in reply to a request by Congressman Henry T. Blow, reported that during the first four months of that year 247,249 acres of public land had passed into private hands in Missouri. Of this, 132,713 acres had been claimed under the Homestead Act; 25,238 acres bought for cash; 7,560 acres located with warrants of various kinds; and 81,738 acres located with land-grant college scrip. Blow, in forward-

ing this report to the *Missouri Democrat,* noted: "Nothing like
the immense extent of these sales has occurred in any State
in the Union excepting Minnesota, where something of the
same spirit is manifested by the emigration."[20] Comparative
land office statistics tend to bear him out.

Various national immigrant groups organized special societies to encourage their fellow countrymen to join them in
Missouri and to provide aid for their traveling expenses. The
German Emigrant Aid Society had long been active. A typical
German colony was the one that settled near Utica in Liv-
ingston County. Its leaders were men of considerable means
and education. Some eighty or ninety families settled there
in 1866 and directed their efforts to stock raising and wool
growing. Irish and Hebrew groups in St. Louis also organized
associations to attract and assist new arrivals.[21]

An interesting private agency was the Bryan Mullanphy
Emigrant Relief Fund, which had been established by a
former St. Louis mayor in his will. This fund had accumulated $633,899 by 1867 and during the next few years aided
over 22,000 travelers coming through St. Louis on their way
to the West. In May of 1868 the Fund's directors opened a
three-story home where emigrants could find temporary
lodging while looking for work or making arrangements to
continue their journey.[22]

As chairman of the State Immigration Board, Governor
Fletcher took an active interest in making Missouri attractive
to prospective immigrants and easy for them to reach. During
his term of office he traveled extensively for this purpose. A
typical trip in the spring of 1868 took him to New York to
secure the co-operation of the Citizens Association in chan-
neling emigrants to Missouri, and from there he went to
other cities to make similar arrangements.[23]

By 1868 immigrants had claimed most of the desirable land
in north Missouri, although there were still 300,000 acres
available along the right of way of the Hannibal and St.

Joseph Railroad and 25,000 acres along the North Missouri Railroad. Most of the remaining government tracts lay in southwest Missouri and were less desirable than the rolling acres north of the river. Some of this land sold for as little as two dollars an acre. The Southwest Pacific Railroad, seeking settlers for its proposed right of way from Rolla to Springfield and beyond, experimented for a time with paying passage for Scandinavian immigrants to the area, but lost $40,000 initially on the scheme. Ultimately, it adopted the policy of deducting the cost of railroad fare to Missouri from the price of the land if an immigrant made a purchase along its right of way within forty days after his arrival and inspection of the property.

Also interested in southwest Missouri was the Susquehanna Valley Emigrating Association of Oswego, New York. Typical of many such groups operating in the East, it had made arrangements to help the prospective settler obtain cheap railroad fare and reasonable prices for food and lodging en route to Missouri, where it had official ties with certain promoters. In describing the region, the company boasted: "The climate is the golden mean of the temperate zone. Its salubrity is proverbial. The elevation of the country above the ocean produces all the vitality of a more northern latitude, while none of the southern advantages are lost. Consumption and asthmatic complaints never originate here, and are often cured by the climate."[24] Who could resist such a promising area if he were planning to migrate?

With the extensive promotion of all these groups and agents, immigrants poured into Missouri in ever-increasing numbers. In his final message to the legislature in January, 1869, Governor Fletcher estimated that Missouri had enjoyed a 50 per cent population growth over the past four years, and he looked forward to a bright future for the state.[25] Official census figures show Missouri's population in 1870 as 1,721,295, which marked a gain of 539,283 persons or 45.6

per cent over 1860.[26] When one considers the loss of population during the Civil War, Governor Fletcher's estimate is
probably not far from being right. St. Louis in 1870 showed
a remarkable 93.4 per cent gain in population over 1860 and
stood as the nation's fourth largest city with an official count
of 310,825 persons. Kansas City, with 32,254 inhabitants,
ranked far behind in second place among Missouri's towns.
Undoubtedly, the St. Louis area retained many of the foreign
immigrants coming to Missouri. The 1870 census revealed
that about one-half of the state's foreign-born population was
living in St. Louis County. Missouri had witnessed a gain
of 61,726 in this group during the decade, which marked a
38 per cent increase. The state now had a total foreign-born
population of 222,267, more than half of whom were German.[27]

In analyzing the above figures, it becomes obvious that
many of the new immigrants settled in rural Missouri. Thirty-
six outstate counties enjoyed population gains of better than
50 per cent over 1860. Another thirty-eight experienced a
growth of 25 to 50 per cent. By 1870 the state had a total
farm acreage of 21,707,220, with 9,130,615 acres under cultivation. This represented 148,328 farms averaging 146 acres.
Implements and farm machinery had a value of $15,596,426—
a marked increase over the $9,000,000 figure ten years earlier.
In 1870 Missouri ranked seventh among the states in the
value of its agricultural products with $103,035,759. An active
state board of agriculture, created by the Radicals in 1865,
promoted the advantages of new techniques and machinery,
and Norman J. Colman broadcast the doctrines of scientific
agriculture through the columns of his widely distributed
Rural World, established at St. Louis the same year.[28]

Before the Civil War, Missouri had depended in a large
measure upon its river systems to convey its commerce and
to supply its people. Centering as it did on two mighty waterways at the crossroads of the nation, the state seemed to hold
an unrivaled geographic position. Although its political capi-

tal was Jefferson City, the economic focal point of the state
was St. Louis, and the emblem of the steamboat dominated
that city's great seal. War dealt a heavy blow to St. Louis and
Missouri trade. The natural outlet for the state's commerce
was New Orleans at the mouth of the Mississippi, but the
secession of the lower South closed that channel. In attempting to redirect commerce to the East, several disadvantages
to St. Louis arose. For one thing, the city stood on the wrong
bank of the Mississippi River, with no bridge to connect it
with the eastern shore. The railroads through East St. Louis
that did serve the city were poor and inadequate compared
with the connections that could be had via Chicago. Although
Missouri had made a significant start in the direction of railroad construction, only one line, the Hannibal and St. Joseph,
had been completed. This road proved detrimental to the
interests of St. Louis; through its connections with the Burlington, the Hannibal and St. Joseph provided a cutoff for
Missouri River traffic across northern Missouri into the
arms of the river city's great rival Chicago. With the Missouri
River not always dependable as a trade route because of ice
in winter and shallows at other times of the year, this short-
circuit route received much trade that heretofore had naturally
flowed into St. Louis. Actually, the wartime situation merely
accentuated what had been a slowly developing trend. Beyond
these difficulties, the periodic guerrilla warfare disrupted river
traffic, destroyed railroads, and constantly endangered commerce as well as lives.

After the Mississippi River began to be opened through the
South by Union arms, St. Louis merchants still found themselves handicapped. Because the city stood at the edge of the
theater of war, trade regulations imposed by the Treasury
Department required a permit for every shipment of goods
out of the city. Also, a 5 per cent tax was levied on all down-
river traffic from St. Louis. None of these restrictions ham-
pered Chicago, which made significant commercial gains over

her river rival at this time in vying for supremacy in the Mississippi Valley. St. Louis merchants protested strongly and succeeded in having the tax on the down-river traffic removed in November, 1863. Other restrictions, however, continued until the end of the war.[29]

By the summer of 1865, St. Louis had high hopes that the river traffic that had long made it the dominant city of the Mississippi Valley would revive to prewar levels. With gold-mining operations in full swing at the head of the Missouri River, the city anticipated that a real boom would soon be under way.[30] But as rail operations continued to tap such vital points as Omaha, St. Joseph, and Kansas City, the river was drained of much of its commerce long before it reached St. Louis. Residents and businesses of the upper Missouri Valley much preferred the certainty of rail traffic via Chicago to the frustrations and delays attendant upon the use of the river, particularly in the winter. Then, too, Chicago merchants outhustled their St. Louis rivals. A revealing editorial appeared in the *St. Joseph Morning Herald* toward the close of the war:

> This road [the Hannibal and St. Joseph] has ever been an eye sore to the people of St. Louis, who profess to believe, and doubtless are honest in the belief, that the whole trade of the Northwest is, through the management of this corporation, diverted from St. Louis and poured into the lap of Chicago. We believe that the trade of this section of country is taken to Chicago simply and solely for the reason that the business men of Chicago exhibit an energy and enterprise that is entirely unknown to St. Louis merchants. The Chicagoans have their runners constantly here and at other prominent points, and as our columns will attest, they do a liberal amount of advertising. Were our St. Louis friends to exhibit an equal amount of tact and spirit, we are sure that our commerce would flow through its natural channel straight to their doors.[31]

The sensitivity of St. Louis merchants to the diversion of river traffic by rail was well illustrated by a story appearing in the *Missouri Democrat* during the winter of 1867. According to the writer, a St. Louis businessman who had purchased a quantity of wheat from a grain dealer in Omaha was preparing to return the sacks under terms of his agreement. He found the river channel choked with ice and wrote the Omahan that a delay would result. Thereupon he received instructions to transmit the sacks by rail via Chicago. This proved too great a demand for the St. Louisan's pride. He consequently undertook the extra expense of returning them by the Merchants Union Express in stages along the dirt roads of the Missouri Valley.[32]

The war had greatly stimulated grain production in the West and Northwest. These sections had generally found Chicago a better outlet for their crops than St. Louis. In the postwar era, however, a wave of discontent arose against the lake city because of malpractices on the grain and livestock exchanges. The continuation of unduly high wartime charges by the railroad accentuated this situation. St. Louis, determined to take advantage of this unrest, opened its first grain elevator in the fall of 1865. This project immediately proved its utility, and plans for expansion were soon under way. At the same time steps were taken to establish direct trade facilities with South America and Europe through New Orleans.

To attract more trade, St. Louis sought to improve its attractiveness as a river port by revitalizing traffic along the Mississippi. The several natural obstructions to navigation along the upper river, particularly the Des Moines and the Rock Island rapids, presented a major problem. During the period of shallow water, which lasted over half the shipping season, these rapids made it impossible for a steamer to carry a profitable load without lighterage, which often caused as much as a five-day delay. Since no transfer elevators existed

at either of the rapids, grain had to be carried in sacks. The
dangers involved affected insurance rates adversely, and at
times no underwriter would cover the risks. If these impedi-
ments to navigation could be removed, grain shipments could
be made in bulk, which would greatly facilitate shipping in
general and reduce costs and risks. To this end and for the
general improvement of river trade, several conventions met
in St. Louis during the late 1860's. The most important meeting occurred on February 12 and 13, 1867, with a large attendance from a wide area. The *Missouri Democrat* reported
the proceedings "exceedingly harmonious" as they closed with
a large banquet at the Lindell Hotel. The chief purpose of
the meeting had been to work out a scheme for securing
federal aid for the improvement of western waterways so
they would be safer and cheaper as avenues of commerce.
All sorts of statistics were presented to show the unfair advantages given the hated railroads that allowed them to
siphon off trade that could flow more naturally and profitably
by water. Comparative figures on transportation, relative to
the cost of shipping a bushel of wheat from Dubuque to New
York via Chicago and the Great Lakes as against via St. Louis
and New Orleans, showed the Chicago cost at sixty-eight
cents as opposed to thirty-eight by the St. Louis route. Yet,
because of the problems on the waterways most upriver
farmers preferred to ship via Chicago. The convention estimated that this preference resulted in the annual diversion of
almost $100,000,000 in commerce from the Mississippi.

Progress toward attaining favorable congressional action
was slow in this era of railroad expansion. The builders of
the iron horse worked energetically in the lobbies of Congress. With that body under Radical control, little interest
existed for building up St. Louis-New Orleans trade at the
expense of Chicago and New York. Thus, while the railroads
grabbed the lion's share of land grants and subsidies, those
interested in river improvement had to be content with

crumbs from the table. Nevertheless, as more and more pressure built up and the political complexion of Congress changed, appropriations did increase during the 1870's. An extensive program for bettering navigation on the Mississippi River from its source to its mouth got under way. This work met numerous obstacles as the "Father of Waters" continued to resist improvement and defy control. Ultimately, Congress channeled $25,000,000 into the improvement of navigation on the Ohio, Mississippi, Missouri, and Arkansas rivers between 1866 and 1882. Meanwhile, the railroads refused any kind of co-operation and drove resolutely toward an absolute mastery of the nation's transportation.[33]

Although deeply involved with the problem of the improvement of the waterways, Missouri and St. Louis did not totally ignore the question of railroad construction, nor did they fail to realize the importance of developing an adequate rail network. Initially, however, they tended to look upon railroads merely as commercial feeders to the river system and as a means of regularizing commerce when river transportation was handicapped by shallows or ice.[34] Nevertheless, Missouri had embarked on a systematic policy of generosity in providing state aid for the promotion and development of a rail system during the 1850's. On the eve of the Civil War 810 miles of track had been constructed at an approximate cost of $50,000 per mile. The state had authorized the issue of bonds totaling $24,950,000, taking a first mortgage lien. County and city governments responded with subscriptions of $7,624,075 and, in the case of the Cairo and Fulton Railroad, with 514,500 acres in land grants. Of this, the city and county of St. Louis furnished $5,450,000. Congressional land grants added 1,823,699 acres.[35]

In spite of this aid, Missouri failed to realize her hopes fully. The Pacific Railroad, designed to link St. Louis and the western border, had made an auspicious start in 1851, backed by an initial $2,000,000 in state aid and $1,000,000 from the city and county of St. Louis. Ten years later, however, it had reached no farther than Sedalia, ninety-five miles from its ultimate destination. In spite of all the government aid received, the Pacific failed to attract adequate private capital within or outside Missouri. Inexperienced and inefficient management raised costs and resulted in poor construction and faulty equipment, which, in turn, increased the expenses of operation. The North Missouri Railroad was planned as St. Louis' major link with the Northwest. Crossing the Hannibal and St. Joseph at Macon, it was to extend to the Iowa line and connect there with a road being built in that state. The City of St. Louis subscribed $1,250,000 to the stock of the company. Inability to secure a land grant and many of the same difficulties that plagued the Pacific hampered its development. The line reached Macon early in 1859. There construction halted until after the war. Two lines were projected south from St. Louis. One—the St. Louis and Iron Mountain Railroad—was to link the metropolis and the mineral region to the southeast, with a possible projection to some point on the Mississippi River. The other—the southwest branch of the Pacific Railroad—was to extend from Pacific Junction on the main line of its parent through the Gasconade Valley to Springfield and beyond. Both roads were hindered by the usual difficulties. The former reached Pilot Knob, eighty-six miles from St. Louis, in 1858 and stopped; the latter finally reached Rolla, seventy-six miles from the junction, by the end of 1860.

Two other roads received state aid in the 1850's. The Platte County Railroad was to run between Kansas City and St. Joseph, with the option of continuing to the northern boundary of the state. Work on this line did not get under way until 1859. By the eve of the war forty-four miles had been completed in the center portion of the proposed road between Savannah and Weston. Some 122 miles had to be finished before Kansas City would have through rail service to the

Iowa line. In the opposite corner of the state, the Cairo and
Fulton Railroad had been projected westward from a point
on the Mississippi River opposite the mouth of the Ohio to
the Arkansas line, where it was to connect with a road of the
same name in that state. Hopefully, it would effect a junction
with the St. Louis and Iron Mountain somewhere in the region. This road also got a late start and was plagued by a
multitude of problems, so that only twenty-six and a half
miles had been completed by the end of 1860.[36]

By the eve of the Civil War all of Missouri's railroads, except the Hannibal and St. Joseph, were in serious financial
straits. The North Missouri and the St. Louis and Iron Mountain were unable to meet the semiannual payments on their
state bonds when they became due on January 1, 1859. All
of the other roads defaulted in 1860. Only the Hannibal and
St. Joseph continued its payments; it maintained an unbroken
record until it completed repayment of Missouri's initial investment of three million dollars in its building in 1881.[37]
Under these circumstances railroad construction came to a
halt, and the unsettled condition of Missouri during the war
did little to improve the situation. All of the state's railroads
suffered considerably as organized armies and guerrillas moved
across the state between 1861 and 1864. It is difficult to ascertain the extent to which the federal government helped
finance needed repairs. State officials, working through Attorney General Edward Bates at Washington, urged the federal
authorities to complete the Southwest Branch of the Pacific
from Rolla to Springfield on the ground of military necessity,
but to no avail.[38]

Wartime realities and a look into the future brought Missouri's leaders to a new awareness of the importance of completing the main line of the Pacific to Kansas City. Seven
miles of track had been laid in 1863 from Sedalia to Dresden,
with roadbed grading continuing toward Warrensburg. Half
of this work had been paid for with cash, the other half by

Johnson County bonds. In order to complete the road, the General Assembly in February, 1864, passed legislation enabling the Pacific to issue first mortgage bonds on the Dresden-Kansas City portion, with the earnings of the entire route being pledged to pay the principal and interest. The state was to take a second lien on this section while retaining its first lien on the rest of the road. With this help, construction during 1864 progressed another twenty-three miles to Warrensburg and crept the ten miles from Kansas City to Independence at the other end of the line. Before the legislature acted in 1864, the company's stock moved up to twenty cents and promised to keep climbing. The directors hoped to have the entire road completed by March, 1865, but the project suffered a severe setback in the fall of 1864. During his invasion of the state General Sterling Price destroyed all the major bridges along the western end of the road. With the treasury exhausted, a new source of funds had to be found; it came from the city of St. Louis in the form of $700,000 in bonds. Work now began on the last fifty-five miles from Warrensburg to Independence. Because conditions in the area remained unsettled by the bushwhacking activities of returning Confederates and outlaw groups, military protection was needed to ensure steady progress. The final rail went down at two o'clock on the afternoon of September 20, 1865. The first passenger train left Kansas City the following morning at five o'clock and completed the run to St. Louis in exactly fourteen hours.[39]

The North Missouri Railroad also received aid from the same 1864 legislation that started the Pacific on its road to completion. This act authorized the company to issue $2,000,-000 in first mortgage bonds, with the state taking a second lien. Half of the money was to be used to complete the Iowa connection; $700,000 was to pay for an extension from Moberly to the western border; $300,000 was to cover the cost of erecting a bridge over the Missouri River at St. Charles.

Two short lines that had partially been constructed without state aid were to be incorporated as part of the western branch.[40] The North Missouri, however, found it impossible to negotiate at par any of its first mortgage bonds, and Governor Willard P. Hall refused to allow their sale at a lesser rate. When a new General Assembly convened in 1865, the company petitioned for authority to cancel the first issue and to draw up a newer and larger one that could be discounted. It contended that the area, both north and west, which it proposed to serve needed a railroad badly, and it held that the anticipated trade would more than justify the outlay. Schuyler and Adair counties, through which the Iowa extension would run, had each subscribed $35,000 and were "ready to pay" when construction began. These funds were all the railroad had readily available. The Assembly acceded to the request and gave the company authority to issue $6,000,000 of first mortgage bonds, with the state taking a second lien.[41]

In spite of the efforts of Governor Fletcher and leading St. Louis businessmen to promote the new bond issue, the North Missouri found the market difficult. Early in December the Governor received word from John F. Hume, the fund commissioner for the road, that he had been able to arrange a contract with a New York banking house. This company represented a large amount of European capital and agreed to place the entire $6,000,000 issue at a highly favorable price.[42] Construction contracts were finally let in May, 1866, and work was begun in July with appropriate ceremonies. Slowly the rails inched west and north. By the spring of 1867 the slow movement of the bond sales in New York hindered progress as funds became scarce. One thing that kept construction going was an agreement with the contractors to take company bonds at eighty-five. In October a syndicate of Eastern and St. Louis capitalists, headed by James B. Eads, agreed to take the remaining $3,700,000 in unsold first mort-

gage bonds and to furnish the necessary means to quickly
finish the road.[43] With the new arrangements a shake-up in
the company management ensued, after which the work
moved forward more rapidly. When the next General Assembly met in January, 1868, the new directors sought a total
release from their obligation to the state. Interest on the second lien of $6,960,000 had been suspended over the past two
years, and a payment of $360,000 would soon be forthcoming.
The company argued that it could better use the money to
further the extension of the road. Two choices seemed to face
the legislators: They could force payment that might mean
default and the necessity of taking over and disposing of the
railroad, or they could release the lien in the hope of quickly
securing two hundred additional miles of badly needed road.
The Assembly decided on the latter course.

This same legislature also moved to completely liquidate
all of the state's railroad holdings. In at least one transaction
involved therein, substantial proof of bribery exists.[44] Whether
the final disposition of the North Missouri was based on
"boodle" is impossible to tell. Nevertheless, the state released
its lien of better than $6,000,000 for the nominal sum of
$200,000, which was the amount the company itself had pro-
posed as a settlement. In so doing, the Assembly added the
difference to the state debt to be absorbed by the taxpayers
of Missouri. It must be pointed out in all fairness to the legislators that they did attach several conditions to the bargain:
The main line of the road must be completed to the northern
boundary of the state within nine months; the western branch
must be finished within eighteen months; and the St. Charles
bridge must be constructed within three years of the date of
the release. To effect these guarantees, the directors were
required to post bond with the State Treasurer.[45] Now, having secured their release, the directors swiftly pushed the
completion of the road. The main line reached Kirksville in
the middle of July and covered the remaining thirty miles

to the Iowa line by the end of November. The following month the western branch of the line met the Kansas City and Cameron Railroad just across the Missouri River from Kansas City. Excursion trains bearing Governor Fletcher and various state and railroad officials toured the lines early in December, and celebrations were held at numerous points. Meanwhile, work continued on the St. Charles bridge. Although the Missouri River presented many problems, the structure was opened to traffic almost on schedule in May, 1871.[46]

The 1868 session of the General Assembly also liquidated the debt of the Pacific Railroad. Such action had been rumored during the previous session as nonpayment of interest and taxes mounted. Fearful that the line would be foreclosed and sold out from under them to foreign capital, the directors organized an energetic lobby in the winter of 1868, which they sent to Jefferson City with a carte blanche to secure release of the state's lien in their favor. The emissaries accomplished the assignment through the judicious disposition of $193,648.60 to the proper persons. In reporting their course to the directors, they admitted: "It was terribly costly for an ordinary job, but as we were going for the millions and every one off counted well, we determined, after serious consultation with discreet friends, not to fail—leaving the morality of such proceedings to those who have inaugurated the system and divided its gains." The company was indeed playing for high stakes. It owed the state some $11,000,000. If the Assembly should authorize seizure and sale to outside interests, it might be able to realize that amount. The lobbyists argued the wisdom of keeping the road under the control of local management and pointed out that the company would soon have to replace its entire track with standard gauge at considerable cost. They also presented opinions from such diverse political figures as Charles D. Drake and Samuel T. Glover that the state had no authority to seize the line until 1871 when the Dresden bonds of 1864 became due. In the end the "boodle," paid and promised, seemed the decisive factor. By act of March 31, 1868, the state released its lien to the directors for $5,000,000 payable in two installments within 180 days.[47]

The other four railroads in which the state had a financial stake were in such hopeless shape by the end of the war that there seemed little prospect of Missouri ever receiving full value for its investment, let alone seeing their completion. Utterly dismayed by the state's reckless adventures in the 1850's and by its seeming inability to recoup at any time in the near future, the convention of 1865 moved to tighten the drawstrings on state and local credit. Hopefully, this action would force private capital to take up the slack. Article XI of the new constitution forbade the use of the state's credit to aid "any person, association, or corporation"; nor could the state become a stockholder in any corporation or association unless it was for the purpose of securing loans already extended. Local governmental units were placed under similar restrictions unless they received the approval of two-thirds of their voters to the contrary. The General Assembly was also forbidden to release the state's lien upon any railroad; the 1868 legislature, however, conveniently ignored this stipulation without any serious challenge. In addition, the convention submitted a special ordinance requiring each railroad then under obligation to the state to establish a sinking fund for the retirement of its debt. Failure to comply might lead to foreclosure of the road and its sale at public auction. The voters approved these provisions at the same time they ratified the constitution.[48]

The first session of the General Assembly under the new constitution passed legislation on February 19, 1866, foreclosing the state's liens against the Southwest Pacific, the St. Louis and Iron Mountain, the Cairo and Fulton, and the Platte Country railroads. It authorized the Governor to appoint a board of three commissioners for each road to secure its sale at public auction. If it proved impossible to recover the state's debt by this means, the commissioners could purchase the road for the state and then sell it privately under the best terms available. In each case the purchasers must specifically agree to extend the line to its completion on a given schedule. Governor Fletcher went east shortly thereafter to try to interest investors in Missouri's railroads.[49] Although sales were effected for each road by one means or another during 1866, continued difficulties prevented final disposition until the 1868 session of the General Assembly when all of the state's railroad entanglements were abruptly severed.

John C. Frémont of New York purchased the Southwest Pacific initially for $1,300,000. Although he obtained a federal land grant of 17,000,000 acres, he found it necessary to resell. The new owners defaulted on the second annual payment due the state, and Governor Fletcher once again took over the road. During these exchanges only twelve new miles of track were laid. The people of the southwest corner of the state clamored for completion of the road, for the expanding region needed the line badly. Consequently, the Assembly agreed to dispose of the road and its assets in fee simple to a syndicate composed of the various competing interests that had shown a desire to take over the line. This group represented a combination of Eastern and St. Louis capital. Reconstituted as the South Pacific Railroad Company, it agreed to expend $500,000 within one year for the extension of the road and to deposit with the State Treasurer $1,500,000 in either United States or Missouri bonds. This latter sum could be withdrawn in $100,000 blocks, but only for the line's construction. Of the total, $250,000 had to be retained for the extension beyond Springfield. The road had to be completed to Lebanon within two years and to Springfield within three and one half, and had to reach the western border by June

10, 1872. To assure compliance, the company was required
to post a bond of $1,000,000 that could be forfeited. The only
direct and tangible return to the state would be three annual
payments of $300,000 each to the state's interest fund begin-
ning June 1, 1874. To aid in financing the extension, the
South Pacific could issue $7,250,000 in bonds and sell any of
the lands already granted it. Once these arrangements had
been made, work moved forward rapidly. The line reached
Springfield in May, 1870, and pushed on to the western
border by the following October. The citizens of Springfield
held a giant celebration on May 3, and a special excursion
train bearing Governor McClurg and other dignitaries arrived from St. Louis. Nonpartisanship marked the proceedings as prominent Radicals and Democrats spoke on the
occasion.[50]

The St. Louis and Iron Mountain and the Cairo and Fulton
railroads went to the same syndicate, which bid low for the
former and high for the latter. The state received a total
price of $900,000 for the package. Three days later the roads
were resold to Thomas Allen of St. Louis for $1,275,000.
Charges of collusion had already been raised against the
commissioners in the first sale; now they mushroomed. In-
vestigations were held, the Attorney General sought an injunction, the Governor seized the lines early in 1868, and
further inquiries followed. On March 17, 1868, the General
Assembly acted by confirming Allen in his title. It appropriated $664,300, the amount remaining due on both railroads
for their completion. This money was to be released by the
State Treasurer at the rate of $15,000 for every mile of new
track built. Allen proved to be one of the most able and efficient of Missouri's railroad entrepreneurs. By the middle of
August, 1869, he had completed the St. Louis and Iron Mountain to Belmont on the Mississippi River, 119 miles beyond
Pilot Knob. Ultimately, connections were established with

Texas roads, which helped to bring much of the trade of the Southwest to St. Louis.[51]

The final road to be disposed of by the 1868 legislative session was the Missouri Valley Railroad, formerly the Platte Country, which was designed to link Kansas City with St. Joseph and the Iowa border. Many considered it an essential link in the initial program of bringing the trade of northwest Missouri to St. Louis. Now the reorganized company made two proposals to the legislature: It would pay its indebtedness of about $994,000, or it would complete its road. It could not do both. Following the familiar pattern, the Assembly agreed to release its lien, on the condition that the company pay into the State Treasury $334,000 in state bonds, $334,000 in company bonds, and $100,000 in stock certificates to guarantee completion. The monies would be returned at the rate of $12,000 for every mile completed. When the road had been finished to the Iowa line, the state would cancel the $100,000 of stock. The legislators set December 1, 1869, as the deadline for completion. The company barely managed to meet it. In May, 1870, the line consolidated with the St. Joseph and Council Bluffs Railroad to give a continuous trackage from Kansas City to a point opposite Omaha.[52]

With all this flurry of activity, charges and reports concerning bribery and corruption floated freely at the capital during the closing weeks of the 1868 session. From the account already given of the disposal of the Pacific Railroad obvious justification existed for these accusations. Although there is no direct evidence of the use of "boodle" in connection with the final disposition of the other roads, it is logical to assume that the Pacific transaction set a pattern for the others to a greater or lesser extent. As the rumors spread, the legislators decided they had better quell them. Consequently, both houses passed resolutions establishing a joint investigating committee. Appointed on March 23, the committee had instructions to report its findings within twenty-four hours. One of the Senate members was John G. Woerner of St. Louis, whom the Pacific lobbyists specifically mentioned in their reports as one of the group to whom they were indebted for "valuable assistance." The committee held afternoon and evening hearings. Under the circumstances, it is not surprising that they did not obtain "one word of evidence" that any legislator had "received or indicated a willingness to receive, directly or indirectly, a single dollar, or any valuable consideration as an inducement to support or oppose any railroad bill" or that any person had "used or been authorized to use any money to secure the vote of any Senator or member of the House."[53]

So Missouri not only relinquished its claims to the railroads it had begun in the 1850's but also provided for their completion. The total railroad debt of the state stood at $31,735,840 in bonds and interest due on January 1, 1868. The total amount realized in their disposition was $6,131,496, which left $25,604,344 for the taxpayers of Missouri to retire. In 1868 the lines that received such generous consideration had completed only 914 miles of track, and very little of this had been finished during the previous two years. By the end of 1870 an additional 626 miles had been laid as the roads reached completion. Missouri had secured 1,540 miles of railroad at a cost of $16,626 per mile.

John W. Million in his thorough study of these intricate proceedings concluded that the uncompleted roads could have been finished without the legislature taking the action it did. This procedure, however, would probably have meant that the state itself would have had to undertake the work or wait until it could lure private capital at more favorable terms. If the state accepted the responsibility, this would have further increased the state's debt, which had already reached its constitutional limit for such purposes; on the other hand, seeking private capital had the disadvantage of indefiniteness at a time when the people were clamoring for the completion of the roads and the interest on the state's debt was mounting. Still, it would seem that the railroad giveaway of 1868 could have been accomplished at a more beneficial price for the people of Missouri.[54]

By the end of the war most St. Louis businessmen realized the need for bridging the Mississippi River if they were to retain their competitive position with Chicago. The Rock Island Railroad had bridged the river at Davenport, Iowa, as early as 1856 in spite of strong opposition from St. Louis commercial interests. While discussion dragged on in St. Louis regarding the financing of a bridge project, the Burlington Railroad completed the first Mississippi River bridge to touch Missouri in November, 1868, at Quincy. This bridge further strengthened the Hannibal and St. Joseph connection with Chicago.[55]

Before construction on the bridge at St. Louis could begin, many preliminary steps had to be taken in Congress and in the respective legislatures of Missouri and Illinois. Surveys were finally undertaken in March, 1867. The actual work of construction began that summer, with James B. Eads as chief engineer. From the outset he dominated the project. The estimated cost of $5,000,000 was to be raised by bond issues on the bridge corporation. The same 1868 legislature that resolved the railroad burden agreed to allow the City of St. Louis to guarantee these bonds, subject to voters' approval. Because many engineering problems still had to be solved and threats of a rival bridge company and several financial crises arose, work moved slowly. Continuing with great persistence, even at the risk of his health, Eads completed the bridge that bears his name, in the summer of 1874. It was formally opened on July 4 with a gigantic celebration. The first important bridge to use steel in truss construction instead of wrought iron, it had a central span of 520 feet and two side arches of 502 feet each. As a two-level affair, it could accommodate both rail and vehicular traffic.[56]

Although it was a major step in the right direction, the Eads Bridge did not solve all of St. Louis' difficulties. It had come too late to recover the trade lost to Chicago. Furthermore, it proved inadequate to handle all of Missouri's east-west traffic needs. The United States Bureau of Statistics report for 1878 on the nation's internal commerce revealed that Chicago had received three and a half times as much grain as St. Louis, two and a half times as many cattle, four times as many hogs, five times as much butter, and six times as much lumber. St. Louis had become a milling center and manufactured six times as much flour as Chicago, yet the latter city handled about 100,000 more barrels in shipment.[57]

At the opposite end of the state, on the giant bend of the Missouri River, a new metropolis was rising—Kansas City. As had St. Louis, it realized that its future depended on the development of a rail network and the construction of a bridge. The Census of 1860 revealed a population of 4,418 for the city, which marked a gain of 4,000 inhabitants over the previous five years. With the organization of Kansas Territory, it had stood in a highly favorable position to profit from the development of that region. Fortunately, Kansas City was blessed early in its history with forward-looking civic leaders who saw the importance of the railroad as the key to the future greatness of their city. Several formidable upriver rivals—St. Joseph on the Missouri side and Atchison and Leavenworth in Kansas—vied with this city for the connections that could make one of the towns the major junction, and potentially a booming terminal, on the way to the West. At first, the decisive factor in Kansas City's future seemed to be the Pacific Railroad, slowly edging westward from St. Louis. This line's western terminus could serve as the junction for other routes to the West and Southwest. As the directors of the Pacific vacillated about its ultimate destination, apparently in the hope of competitive bidding, construction crawled at a snail's pace. Kansas City business leaders talked

increasingly of a connection with the recently completed
Hannibal and St. Joseph to the north. In 1860 they negoti-
ated a contract with that company, whereby it would equip
and operate trains between Cameron and Kansas City if a
local group constructed the line. As the clouds of disunion
appeared, the town voted $200,000 in bonds to exchange for
stock in the projected road. Across the river, Clay County
followed suit with $150,000.[58] Then came the war.

From 1861 to 1865 Kansas City was a beleaguered town.
The old border hostility of the mid-1850's flared anew as
Kansas troops, detailed to keep the area out of the hands of
Sterling Price, mistakenly assumed that all Missourians were
ardently proslavery and staunchly in favor of the Confederacy. Their indiscriminate foraging into the midst of a population that largely desired neutrality touched off severe guerrilla
warfare, which remained unremitting for four years in spite
of strong federal and state efforts to stamp it out.[59] Yet, despite these difficulties the structure of the business power
elite in Kansas City remained surprisingly intact. As the end
of the war approached, they stood in a good position to re-
institute the promotional schemes suspended in 1861. The
Pacific Railroad was building again, and its western terminus
was no longer in doubt; the Kansas City push toward the
Hannibal and St. Joseph in 1860 had pretty well determined
that issue. With the decision of Congress to proceed with the
transcontinental railroad at the end of the war, the rivalry
among the towns of the western border received further impetus. Energetically, the leading businessmen went to work
to secure the future of Kansas City. They still saw the connection with the Hannibal and St. Joseph and its Burlington
entree into Chicago as their most advantageous move. Their
contract of 1860, however, had lapsed, and the roadbed that
had been started had badly deteriorated. Late in 1864 the
Chamber of Commerce appointed a committee to set the
program in motion once again. Robert T. Van Horn, their

state senator and a rising figure on the Radical horizon, secured a charter through the legislature for a bridge company that would span the Missouri River. That fall Van Horn's friends promoted and secured his election to Congress where he could keep an eye on their interests. Slowly, their plans developed.[60]

By the end of the war it became increasingly clear that Leavenworth would be Kansas City's chief rival. This Kansas town had also organized to promote a railroad to Cameron. Although it appeared that the Kansans might have the initial advantage, the power elite of Kansas City managed to interest James F. Joy, the Burlington's western agent, in local real estate. Things now brightened considerably. In Washington, Van Horn discreetly pushed legislation authorizing the construction of a bridge over the Missouri at Kansas City as part of an omnibus bill. At the same time he labored successfully to secure a land grant for the Missouri River, Fort Scott and Gulf Railroad, which the Kansas Citians had recently established as a potential connection with the Southwest. In both these projects he had the vigorous support of the Burlington lobby.

By 1867 the Burlington directors had largely taken over the completion of the Kansas City-Cameron route. They had been looking for an outlet to the Southwest. The Kansas City group offered this route with the added geographical advantage over Leavenworth that their line would require only one bridge, which was already being constructed, while the other would require additional structures over Kansas rivers.[61] The directors accepted the proposal. As the work on the bridge steadily progressed, Kansas City looked eagerly toward the future. "The bridge will be the making of the city," predicted the 1867–1868 town directory. Hopes became reality on July 3, 1869, as a gaily decorated train leading a two-mile procession made the first official trip over the bridge. What followed, according to a reporter for the St. Joseph Gazette, "was without parallel in Western celebrations." During the first eight months of its operation 4,131 trains crossed the bridge, which was also designed to accommodate teams and wagons. Thus, the promotional efforts of the Kansas Citians were paying off handsomely.[62]

An important adjunct to the settlement of the rail question at Kansas City was the initial development of the town as a regional livestock center. Although there had been some meat-packing companies in Kansas City before the war, only one such firm survived the years of difficulty. At the end of the war it appeared that St. Joseph, because of its eastern rail connections, would become the key center for the livestock trade. Several factors, however, altered this picture in the late 1860's. The Missouri legislature banned the entry of Texas longhorns into the state because of a disease they carried. Although immune themselves to its effects, the long-horns spread the disease to other cattle with disastrous consequences. As the Kansas Pacific Railroad edged across the prairie west of Kansas City, it became more convenient for cattle drives to stop at the end of this line. With her new bridge and direct connections to Chicago, Kansas City soon became the transfer point for the trade. St. Joseph did not complete her bridge until 1873, by which time Kansas City's head start proved a considerable handicap to the ambitions of the upriver town.

Interestingly enough, one of the first major cattle buyers, Joseph G. McCoy, had originally tried to make an arrangement for transshipment with the Pacific Railroad into St. Louis. Its directors scorned his business, whereupon he turned to the Hannibal and St. Joseph, which made him a good offer. McCoy was soon busy developing Abilene, Kansas, and using the Kansas City-Cameron branch to ship his cattle into Chicago.

In 1870 L. V. Morse, general superintendent of the Hanni-bal and St. Joseph, and James F. Joy purchased five acres in Kansas City, on which they constructed eleven cattle pens, fifteen unloading chutes, and a scale. Business boomed so rapidly that these facilities quickly became inadequate. Three million dollars annually in livestock trade money was soon passing through the Kansas City banks, and the first major industry of the town became well established. In the spring of 1871 the forerunner of the Kansas City Union Stockyards was organized, and expansion continued apace.[63] The Census of 1870 revealed that Kansas City had a population of 32,268 persons, an eightfold increase over ten years earlier, with most of the newcomers having arrived after the war. The city's latest biographer claims that this figure is too high and that 20,000 to 25,000 would be a more reasonable guess.[64] Whatever the case, Kansas City was on its way.

St. Louis and Kansas City were not the only Missouri communities concerned with railroad development. Although St. Louis subscribed more than half of the $7,624,075 that the county and city governments contributed to railroad development before the war, this amount also represented the hopes of many localities throughout the state that recognized the importance of a rail connection to their area. As already mentioned, the constitutional convention became so alarmed at growth of local indebtedness that it stipulated that, henceforth, two-thirds of the voters must approve any such subscription by their county or township government. This action, however, did little to stop the trend, for during the years following the Civil War there arose a seeming mass hysteria in communities throughout Missouri to get on the railroad bandwagon. Every locality realized that the coming of a railroad might make or break their community economically. The larger companies played off area against area in the race for subscriptions. But a great deal of the fever involved local schemes for feeder lines that would tie a community to one or several of the already established main roads. From 1866 on, the Missouri press continually reported railroad conven-

tions designed to project this or that line through an immediate area. Large-scale subscriptions, often in the hundreds
of thousands of dollars, found favor with an overwhelming
majority of the voters in county after county. In many of
these elections the disfranchised, who frequently paid a
large percentage of the taxes, were allowed to vote, in an
effort to promote county solidarity. Only seldom did strong opposition develop. The "railroad mania" had truly hit Missouri.

Edwin L. Lopata, who has made an exhaustive study of
local aid to Missouri's railroads, indicates that the counties
and cities of the state subscribed $17,219,850 to instate rail-
roads and another $1,100,000 to lines outside Missouri during
the period 1867–1872. Of this, a total of $17,199,950 was ac-
tually paid, including all of the outstate subscriptions that
came primarily from St. Louis and Kansas City. How much
of this amount went originally to main-line roads and how
much to feeders is difficult to tell because the breakdown of
Lopata's table is on a post-consolidation basis. Some $3,080,-
000 was subscribed to railroads that, for a variety of reasons,
were never built. Of this, the counties finally paid off $2,333,-
100. In the disillusioning 1870's, when hard times hit the
country and the Granger movement spread over the Middle
West, much defaulting occurred on these local railroad debts
and considerable litigation ensued. Most local governments
eventually reached some kind of compromise with their creditors, but some continued paying off their obligations into
the twentieth century.[65]

Although the process of railroad building had been a costly
one for the state and local governments in Missouri, it had
its good results. A definite correlation exists between the
coming of the railroad and the population growth and economic development of many counties and towns. The thirty-
two counties most directly affected by the railroad in the
1860's accounted for 56 per cent of Missouri's total population
gain in the decade. Regionally, the Ozarks, which remained

the last area to enjoy extensive rail development, grew more slowly than the other sections of the state. Population density by 1870 is also revealing. The southern tier of counties had fewer than 5 persons per square mile, while the area between that region and the Missouri River averaged between 5 and 15 persons. The rest of the state had a density of 15 to 40 inhabitants per square mile, but some counties along the Mississippi averaged as many as 40 to 75. In St. Louis County the density reached 125 persons.[66] The development of rail transportation also greatly aided immigration and the influx of settlers to Missouri and thereby increased the state's economy. Under the influence of railroads many towns received their initial start or grew into thriving communities. Isolated areas came into more immediate touch with the rest of the state and nation. As new ideas, new commodities, and better access to wider markets came within the reach of every corner of the state, Missourians of all sections and backgrounds took an increased pride in the growth and development of their state.

CHAPTER IX

MINING, LABOR, AND MANUFACTURING

PREWAR MISSOURI had been dominated by agricultural and trading interests deeply imbued with a conservative philosophy that placed great stress on the sanctity of property rights and the soundness of the dollar. In 1860 the state had only 3,157 manufacturing establishments, employing 19,681 persons. These companies represented a capital investment of some $20,000,000, with a total production of almost $42,000,-000. St. Louis produced slightly more than half of this amount; the rest came from a budding mining industry (lead, iron ore, stone, coal, and copper) and small manufactories scattered across the state and serving primarily local needs. The state still gave strong allegiance to the self-sufficient homestead. It ranked fourth among the states in the value of home manufactures, valued at $1,984,262.[1] As might be expected in a rapidly expanding state, Missouri enjoyed tremendous economic expansion in the postwar era. In accordance with the new constitution the General Assembly, on March

211

19, 1866, passed a comprehensive general incorporation law that did away with the prewar practice of granting individual charters through the legislature and thereby greatly facilitated corporate growth.[2]

Mining was Missouri's first industry. The discovery of lead ore had brought the first permanent French settlers to southeast Missouri early in the eighteenth century. In the decade prior to the Civil War lead mining operations had expanded into the southwestern portion of the state. Because lead was in considerable demand during the war, the mines were worked rather heavily when military conditions permitted, and some 3,500 tons found their way into the mills. The ore was obtained from open cuts or shallow drafts. By means of the "dd jigging" process it was first crushed and then placed in a sieve on the end of a long pole. This apparatus was so balanced that several men could "jig" the sieve up and down in water, the lead sinking to the bottom and the residue remaining on top. Smelting of the crude lead then followed in reverberatory furnaces. Here a six-man crew, working one shift, could usually turn out thirty-two pigs, each seventy-two pounds in weight, in twenty-four hours.[3]

The demands of the postwar industrial expansion led to stepped-up production. By the winter of 1866–1867 the Mine LaMotte, the oldest company in Missouri, was producing 320 pigs a day. That same winter the Equitable Mining Company erected a large smelter on the Harrington Mine Tract in south Franklin County about sixty-five miles from St. Louis and advertised for miners to work on the "permit system." According to a trade union paper, there was no smelter in the state of Missouri superior to this one. It made a 75 per cent yield of the best soft lead from ore at the rate of 6,000 pounds per day. Most of the sixty miners worked on shares, receiving boards, tools, powder, fuses, and other necessary equipment and keeping half the lead ore raised by them as payment. Others prospected at their own expense; when they made a discovery, they received lots two hundred feet square and paid one tenth of their ore as rent.[4] One of the most extensive operations was that of the Granby Mining and Smelting Company in Newton County, which employed 300 miners in 1870. Headed by Henry T. Blow, a prominent Radical politician, it pioneered the opening of many of the lead tracts in the southwestern part of the state.[5]

The coming of the railroad in the 1870's led to a tremendous boom in both lead and zinc mining in southwest Missouri. Lead miners there had known of the existence of zinc ore at the site of their operations almost from the beginning. They called it "jack" or "blackjack" and considered it useless. Thrown aside in the process of digging lead ore, zinc ore was not recognized as valuable until about 1870. In that same year large lead deposits were discovered near the recently established town of Joplin, and a tremendous boom hit the area as mining speculators rushed to the region to develop both minerals. By 1874 zinc production had reached 23,500 tons, with a value of better than $200,000. At the same time nearly 30,000 tons of lead were being extracted from Missouri soil.[6]

Ironmaking had its inception in Missouri some five years before statehood and played a major role in the state's industrial progress throughout most of the nineteenth century. By 1870, Missouri was producing slightly more than 300,000 tons of iron ore. Forges and furnaces became established near the ore deposits in the Ozark hill region and greatly aided that area's economic development. These early enterprises were usually organized as iron plantations, with the ironmaster, who owned the works, exerting a paternalistic sway over his workmen and their families. Readily available timber on the nearby hills provided all the materials necessary for ironmaking, and narrow arable valleys close to the settlement furnished food for men and draft animals. All belonged to the ironmaster, who exercised absolute control. This type of arrangement prevailed into the period immediately after the Civil War, but during the 1870's this situation changed. These pioneer ironworks needed transportation facilities; consequently, they served as focal points for roads and later for railroads. With the coming of the railroad and the subsequent settlement of the surrounding countryside by immigrants, isolation and self-sufficiency broke down. As company towns emerged and the ironworks passed into corporate control, paternalism decreased accordingly.[7]

In the three decades before the Civil War, St. Louis and the surrounding area on both sides of the Mississippi developed a large iron manufacturing complex. By 1856 annual production exceeded $5,000,000. During the war the ironmasters were kept busy turning out armor for James B. Eads's gunboats and other implements of combat. The discovery of coke and bituminous coal in the area in the 1860's brought an even heavier concentration of furnaces in south St. Louis and adjacent Illinois to allow the industry to be near its source of supply. By 1870 total iron production in Missouri had reached a value of nearly $9,000,000 on a capital investment of $6,130,000.[8] Better than 2,300 workers found employment in this area. Apparently, wages in the iron foundries were never high. In May, 1870, the ironmakers at Carondolet in south St. Louis cut wages from $1.75 to $1.50 a day because Congress had refused to approve a higher tariff on pig iron, which then stood at $9 a ton. A strike resulted, and the workers gained the sympathy of the editor of the *Missouri Democrat*. He claimed that the ironmakers were still making a good profit of at least $10 a ton and they had done nothing to reduce prices which would attract manufacturing to St. Louis at a time when the cost of iron stood higher there than in many other localities in the West and South.[9] As so many strikes of this period, the revolt of the iron workers had negligible results.

Large amounts of gravel, sand, and stone are found in Missouri. Aside from the large-scale quarrying of limestone in St. Louis County, little mining in stone occurred prior to 1870. The census of that year revealed a few scattered individual operations on a small scale. In St. Louis County, however, 433 men were engaged in 32 limestone quarries, extracting an annual product worth $750,950. Wages averaged $675 annually, somewhat above the St. Louis average of $596. Most of this stone found its way into the county's burgeoning building industry.[10]

Missouri has coal deposits underlying more than one-third of its area. Yet commercial production did not really get under way until about 1840. Within the next ten years the annual output climbed to almost 100,000 tons, and during the following quarter of a century it averaged 1,000,000 tons annually. Until 1874, when Iowa surpassed it, Missouri was the leading coal producer among the trans-Mississippi states. Bituminous mining centered primarily in two districts: the west central and the northeast. By the end of the Civil War the simpler methods of drifting and surface mining had given way to slope and shaft methods.[11] Operations were often precarious, working conditions dangerous, and the life of the miner exceedingly hard. With unskilled labor plentiful, the mine operators easily had the upper hand most of the time. It is not surprising, then, that militant unionism first made its appearance among the coal miners at Gravois, several miles south of St. Louis, in the fall of 1863. A riotous strike over the hiring of nonunion labor ended in the crushing of unionism temporarily, and a trial of the strike leaders ensued.[12] The movement revived, however, and spread in the postwar era under the organizing drive of John Hinchcliffe, who had been active among Illinois miners.[13]

A somewhat typical case involved the mines at Bevier in Macon County. Unionization had occurred there among the miners during the war, and a wage increase had been secured in 1864. At the end of the war the following year, the mine owners called in troops, ostensibly to search for rebels. On this pretext the company seized the union hall, broke up the organization, and re-established its arbitrary authority. Most of the 150 miners thereafter bided their time looking for an opportune moment to rebuild their union.

Early in January, 1867, one of the miners at Bevier wrote Hinchcliffe: "Politicians may grow eloquent, armies may be raised to fight, and philanthropists may wail over 'the poor African,' but let me tell you, and through you the whole world, that never were the negroes in slavery, in so degraded and abject a condition as the miners here are, and for a long time have been."[14] In his letter the writer, "Junius," also included a detailed description of the hiring procedure at the mine. When one miner went, hat in hand, to seek a job at the manager's office, the first condition laid down for employment was his promise not to join a union. Then, as the superintendent also dabbled in local real estate, he informed the prospective employee that he could have the job if he would agree to purchase two lots at $100 each. These could be paid for in eight monthly installments of $25 each at an interest of 10 per cent. Having agreed to all this, the miner went to work at a set wage of $50. When payday rolled around, he found that deductions had bitten heavily into his check; by the time he had paid the installment on his lots, his bill at the company store, and his board, only $4 remained. He continued thus for six months, when he lost his job, and he subsequently left town. The lots, on which he had paid $150 plus interest, reverted to the superintendent.[15]

Another miner, William Thomas, reported another twist to the same basic situation. He completed payments on his lot and built a comfortable cottage on it for his family. Soon afterwards he lost his job and had to leave the community to find work. When he tried to sell the house, prospective buyers proved scarce. Investigation showed that the mine superintendent had passed the word around that a purchaser would find no work with his company. In the end Thomas was forced to sell the property back to the management at a fraction of what he had invested.[16]

Hinchcliffe responded with a visit to Bevier. An attempt to organize a union followed, and a strike ensued. When "scabs" were hired, the wives of the miners sought to assist their husbands' cause by assailing their tormentors with tongues, pans, and rotten eggs. The women then drove all the nonunion miners into the engine house, which brought the intervention of the authorities. The sheriff took the women to Macon and jailed them over the weekend. This situation forced the capitulation of the union and broke the strike.[17] Other attempts at unionization among the miners were similarly unsuccessful.

The postwar years saw considerable union activity among the various craftsmen, particularly in the St. Louis area. Most of the earlier attempts at an active unionism had died out around 1850. Failure of several strikes disclosed a lack of public sympathy for the workman's cause, and abundance of labor made this kind of action disastrous for the workers. In the decade before the Civil War most organizational efforts centered on the establishment of protective and benevolent societies. A number of workingmen's savings institutions also sprang up in an effort to encourage thrift among the laboring class.[18] With the coming of the war the situation changed; wartime brought a labor shortage, and wages rose accordingly. By 1864 mechanics were receiving $3.50 to $4.00 per day as compared with $1.50 three years earlier.[19] A more militant unionism began to appear toward the close of the war as the various crafts sought to consolidate their gains. Older organizations became more active, and several new ones, led by men in the building trades, sprang up. In February, 1864, a call went out to organize all house carpenters, and an association was quickly effected. By the fall it had become strong enough to resolve that after Monday, September 12, wages would be increased from $3.25 to $3.75 per day.[20] The plasterers, stonemasons, bricklayers, moulders, and other crafts followed suit that summer. Invariably, demands for wage hikes ensued. The nonbuilding crafts were also active, as illustrated by the demands of the tailors and shoemakers that spring.[21] To encourage the latter two groups in their efforts, the printers, who claimed to have a highly efficient and cohesive organization, established a trade boycott against nonunion products in clothing and shoes.[22] Strike funds also made their appearance; the Journeymen Horseshoers' Society announced that it could aid its members during the time of stress should a strike prove necessary that summer.[23]

By the fall of 1864 a trade union league known as the Workingmen's Union of Missouri had been organized to coordinate the mutual interests of the various laboring groups. It also encouraged social activity through sponsorship of such activities as the first annual workingmen's ball at the end of October.[24] During the winter following the end of the war, resistance to the workers' demands gradually hardened. In January, 1866, the Mechanics and Manufacturers Exchange, a prewar organization that had joined together the employing mechanics, or foremen, and the suppliers of building materials, was revived. One of its most immediate concerns was the "unjust combination of journeymen" plasterers and painters who had banded together to promote their mutual interest. The Exchange argued that since the ability of men varied, their pay scale should also fluctuate and the foremen should have the right to pay each man according to his work without being forced into a uniform wage. By the end of March this counter movement became strong enough that fourteen boss plasterers announced their resolve not to employ any workman who belonged to the Journeymen Plasterers' Association. The journeymen countered with a demand for a straight wage of $4.50 a day. A protracted strike followed; apparently it had unified support, for the bosses eventually capitulated.[25]

The Workingmen's Union of Missouri began publication of a weekly eight-page paper in the fall of 1866 to focus attention on the need for labor unity. Its editor was John Hinchcliffe, a journeyman tailor and lawyer who had been connected with the American Miners Association since 1863. He had edited their paper, the *Weekly Miner*, from Belleville, Illinois, until 1865 when a libel suit forced its removal to St. Louis. There it continued publication for another year as the *Miner and Artisan*. In reality, the new paper was an outgrowth of this mineworkers' weekly. It bore the name *Industrial Advocate* and proclaimed on its masthead: "Our aim is the Social Elevation and Mental Improvement of the Working Classes, by the Gradual Adoption of all Practical Measures of Labor Reform." The first issue carried meeting notices for the following: the Ship Carpenters and Calkers Protective Union, the Laborers and Helpers Protective and Benevolent Union, the St. Louis Stove and Hollow-Ware Moulders Union, Lodges #1 and #4 of the Railroad Men's Protective Union, the Carpenters and Joiners Association, the Workingmen's Labor Union, the Journeymen Harness Makers Trade Society, the Journeymen Tobacconists Union, and the Eight Hour League. By the following week the list of notices had grown to twenty-six.[26]

An early editorial in the *Advocate* asserted: "It is the sheerest folly to suppose, for one moment, that the trades' unions of the present day are established as a means of conducting strikes, or that the more intelligent workmen favor the striking system, except as a means to be used, like war, only as a last resort, to effect objects that cannot be otherwise obtained."[27] Apparently, the "last resort" frequently became necessary. During the brief six and one-half months' span for which copies of the paper are available, its columns contained news of numerous strikes. In August, 1866, the waiters at the Lindell Hotel, St. Louis' largest hostelry, walked off the job when their wages were reduced from $30–$40 to $25–$28 monthly (the second figures being those for married men). The hotel promptly filled their places with others who presumably accepted the lower scale. The *Advocate* condemned the steward at the Lindell for the reduction and asked if he could support his family on $28 a month. As Hinchcliffe saw it, the situation pointed up two things: St. Louis had an oversupply of waiters, and many of them failed to see the value of co-operation through an effective union.[28]

A few weeks later the stonecutters went on strike, demanding a wage increase from $4.00 to $4.50 a day. Hinchcliffe did not think that this amount was unreasonable, as the bricklayers were receiving $5 to $7 a day. Although he had heard rumors that the companies were getting their stone cut at Chicago, he doubted the truth of these, since stonecutters there made $4.00 to $5.50 a day, and transportation costs added to the labor charges would make such a scheme unprofitable. He encouraged the local stonecutters with a reminder that the plasterers had gone on strike in April on a demand for $4.50 and had eventually obtained it. And more recently, the bricklayers at St. Joseph had struck successfully for higher wages. In the meantime, many of the stonecutters found employment with the city or with the federal government at Jefferson Barracks. Most of the employers had already broken ranks, some bosses having agreed to pay the higher wages.[29] In October it was the turn of the tobacconists to strike. They represented a considerable group employed by about forty-three tobacco manufactories in St. Louis. They were paid on a volume production basis, with differing wages for the various products they turned out. Their employers, in an effort to cut costs, had reduced some of the wages, whereupon the tobacconists claimed that the reduction was too much in some cases to allow them to support their families adequately. Within a week after the initial report of the strike the *Advocate* announced that a number of employers had given in and agreed to retain the original wage rates. The following week brought the news that the strike continued at only four or five factories. One of these had begun to hire Negroes, however, in preference to giving in to the white tobacconists. At another, a few outsiders and weak-kneed union men had capitulated and gone to work at the new rates. Several renegades had been expelled from the union ranks, and further purges were expected.[30]

The winter of 1866–1867 continued to be a difficult one for labor. When the ship carpenters and calkers refused a wage cut of fifty cents a day, a partial lockout followed. Moulders and machinists had recently been given wage cuts of 10 to 12 per cent, whereupon the moulders went on strike against Bridge, Beach and Company, who, in turn, promptly advertised for "scabs." Unrest also existed in the mines, and Hinchcliffe made several organizational visits to different areas. In Hannibal the railroad shops cut back from a ten- to an eight-hour day because of a slackening of work, and wages received a corresponding reduction. By early February, 1867, the *Advocate* reported about one-half the carpenters in St. Louis presently out of work. Of those employed, many received no more than $2.75 a day.[31] Still organizational activity went forward. Richard Trevalick of Detroit and Jonathan Fincher of Philadelphia, both prominent labor organizers, visited St. Louis. They spoke to rallies and worked with various groups, but the results apparently proved meager. Several local unions presented regular lectures, weekly or biweekly, for their members on a variety of topics. That fall and winter two unions held their national conventions in St. Louis: the Machinists and Blacksmiths of America in October and the Iron Moulders International in January. There was also social activity, with the third annual ball of the Workingmen's Association of Missouri being held at the end of October and similar affairs sponsored by the painters and the marble cutters in January.[32]

The major concern of organized labor in Missouri that winter, however, was the movement for the eight-hour day. Although there had been some sporadic and isolated demands before the war, the drive for a shorter workday did not really gain momentum until the early 1860's when Ira Steward, a Boston machinist, produced a "philosophy" to justify such a reform. In essence, Steward argued that a uniform working day would eliminate competition between skilled and low-standard labor and at the same time would increase productivity, raise wages, step up consumer demand, and create leisure for the workingman to enjoy a higher standard of living.[33] Several years later Eight Hour Leagues sprang up in several industrial states. In November, 1865, fifteen labor societies in St. Louis called a mass meeting to endorse the movement and promote the organization of a league there. Missouri labor agreed on the necessity of combined action to push legislation in Congress in order to accomplish the desired end. It was hoped that speakers could be secured to carry the message to the general public in anticipation that the people of the state would see the over-all advantages of such a program. Shunning an independent workingmen's political party, the League's proponents planned to question every candidate for Congress and the General Assembly to ascertain his opinion on the issue. Only those favoring the eight-hour day would receive labor's support.[34]

The Missouri workingman found a ready sympathizer in Senator B. Gratz Brown. When Congress convened that December, he introduced a resolution instructing the judiciary committee to inquire into the "expediency and rightfulness" of securing legislation for the establishment of an eight-hour day on all government work. The Senate seems to have taken no action at this time, although a similar resolution passed the House early in January, 1866.[35] On March 5, Senator Brown went one step further by introducing legislation that provided:

> In all cases in which any labourers, mechanics, or arti-
> sans shall or may be employed by or on behalf of the
> Government of the United States, or in any place which
> is within the exclusive jurisdiction of Congress, eight
> hours' labour shall be taken and construed to be a day's
> work, any law, regulation or usage to the contrary not-
> withstanding.

Congressman Andrew J. Rogers of New Jersey introduced similar legislation in the House.[36] The conception of broad interpretations of the interstate commerce clause in the Constitution was still in the future.

A week later the workingmen of St. Louis held a huge parade and rally to endorse Brown's proposal and promote the eight-hour day generally. "Eight hours for work, eight hours for rest, eight hours for recreation and mental improvement," proclaimed one banner. In an obvious appeal for the press's support, another urged: "We call on the press to advocate the system that will give us time to read their columns." A third warned aspiring politicians: "We will vote for no man who does not sustain the eight-hour law." Foreshadowing modern times was the argument that workers displaced by mechanization could find work under a reduced-hour system.[37]

The Eight Hour League kept up its agitation in St. Louis and elsewhere. The Missouri leaders received a letter in the middle of April from Congressman John Hogan that expressed his sympathy with the movement while declining with regret an invitation to return and address one of their rallies. Meanwhile, partisans were being urged to *"pour in your memorials"* to Congress if they wanted positive action on the legislative proposals. In the end, however, both bills died in committee.[38]

Late that summer seventy-seven delegates from thirteen states and the District of Columbia gathered in Baltimore to organize an informal national labor union. John Hinchcliffe, James Ashworth, and Andrew Schroeder, all of St. Louis,

represented Missouri labor. The convention chose Hinchcliffe
as both its temporary and permanent chairman. After much
discussion it adopted a platform of principles for American
labor and resolved to hold annual congresses in which "every
Trades' Union, Workingmen's Association and Eight Hour
League" could have representation. After adjournment Hinchcliffe led a delegation composed of one representative from
each state to Washington to meet with President Johnson.
The Missouri labor leader outlined the interests of the American workingman on a variety of topics, including the eight-
hour day, in a prepared address to which the President
replied in perfunctory manner.[39] Upon his return to St. Louis,
Hinchcliffe reported on the national convention to various
local union meetings in an effort to arouse enthusiasm. At
the end of September a mass meeting of workingmen endorsed the Baltimore platform and placed particular emphasis
on the eight-hour day. The Workingmen's Union of Missouri
appointed a committee to question all candidates in the forthcoming election on their stands regarding the issues proposed
at Baltimore. The Missouri leaders seemed most concerned
about four of these: the eight-hour day, public land for settlers only, the waste of public lands by giveaways to railroads
and other private interests, and the unfair competition of
convict labor. The *Industrial Advocate* printed the replies of
each candidate. All of them took a positive stand for the
eight-hour day except William A. Pile, the Radical opponent
of John Hogan in the First Congressional District.[40]

Although Hogan failed to be re-elected in the Radical land-
slide of 1866, the labor forces did secure the election of Conservative James J. McBride and a number of Radicals who
had announced their support of the eight-hour day, to the
Missouri House of Representatives. McBride introduced a bill
to accomplish the desired reform in January, 1867. As finally
reported out of the committee on manufactures, it proved
somewhat equivocal. While declaring eight hours to be the

standard unit of a day's work, the bill provided that longer hours could prevail if the labor-management contracts so stipulated. Furthermore, agricultural workers and those employed by the month would not be affected by the new legislation. In reality, the bill simply provided that the eight-hour day might prevail when agreed upon by both management and labor—nothing more. In this form it passed both the House and the Senate by large majorities.[41]

The new legislation proved a somewhat hollow victory for Missouri labor, for it really changed very little. In the fall of 1867 a committee of the National Labor Union reported to the second annual congress that six states, including Missouri, had enacted eight-hour legislation. After pointing out the broad loopholes and exceptions in each law, the committee took a dim view of the situation: "For all practical intents and purposes they might as well have never been placed on the statute books, and can only be described as frauds on the laboring class."[42] Continued turbulence lay ahead for the union movement in Missouri as elsewhere.

By 1870 Missouri had 11,871 manufacturing establishments with a work force of 65,354 persons. This marked a threefold increase over ten years earlier. Capital investment had quadrupled to $80,257,244, with a total production of $206,213,429, a fivefold increase.[43] Approximately 75 per cent of investment and total production centered in St. Louis County where a wide variety of manufactories existed. Although Chicago was making rapid strides in commerce that would carry it past its down-river neighbor within the next decade, St. Louis in 1870 could still boast an edge in many economic areas. The river city had nearly doubled its population in the 1860's and now stood fourth in the nation with 310,825 residents. To accommodate this growth, it had experienced a tremendous building boom that helped to make possible some of the successful maneuvers for wage hikes mentioned earlier. In 1870 alone, more than $2,000,000 in building materials were consumed in the city.[44] The area's geographic position made it natural for an industrial complex to develop there. The example of iron manufacturing has already been cited. Thirty-one flour mills had grown up since the first one made its appearance at the end of the war. These companies employed 684 hands and represented a capital investment of $3,850,000. As it became known that wheat raised in certain counties along the Mississippi River in Missouri and Illinois possessed milling advantages over that grown farther east, St. Louis flour became increasingly popular over the nation. A large brewing industry had developed in south St. Louis, principally under the aegis of German capital. It absorbed the labor of 761 in some 50 establishments valued at $5,000,-000. The manufacture of clothing kept 3,900 workers busy in nearly 500 manufactories whose products found wide distribution throughout Missouri. A thriving furniture industry also claimed a large market outstate. At least 19 industries in the St. Louis area claimed a capital investment in excess of $1,000,000 each. The county's industrial work force numbered 40,856 persons with an average annual wage of almost $600. As the rail network stretched its ribbons from St. Louis to every corner of the state by the late 1860's, cheap transportation brought an even greater demand on St. Louis industries.[45]

No city outstate could begin to match St. Louis. Second-ranked Kansas City had only one-tenth the population. Yet, as already seen, it had an ambitious, intelligent business elite that pushed it along the road to greater things. In addition to its growing meat-packing industry, the area had 14 flour mills with a capital investment of $248,500, ready to take advantage of the rolling wheat fields to the west. A modest complex of metalware shops, brick plants, carriage shops, clothing manufactories, and other small industry had also begun to develop. Farther up the Missouri River, St. Joseph was also undergoing a small economic boom. Located in the heart of a rich agricultural area with a rapidly expanding population, it was also dominated by meat packing and flour milling. Two furniture plants employed 78 hands and represented a capital of $100,150. In addition, the Hannibal and St. Joseph Railroad maintained a small repair shop there. At the other end of its line, the Hannibal and St. Joseph maintained a car manufacturing shop as well as a repair center. Both of these employed a total of 395 men. Two iron castings manufactories, which helped supply these shops, maintained an additional work force of 60 men. Hannibal was also a center for planed lumber, and during the postwar era many Negroes from the surrounding area found employment in the town's 11 lumber establishments. Besides these businesses, a small milling complex developed in Hannibal.

Indeed, milling dominated the outstate industry of Missouri, after mining. Twenty-two counties in 1870 reported a capital investment exceeding $50,000 each in this type of enterprise. With the production of corn and wheat on Missouri's farms doubling during this period, both grist and flour mills sprang up in every area.[46] But aside from the industrial operations and the mining interests previously mentioned, little industry existed elsewhere in the state except that which served the needs of the immediate vicinity. Outstate Missouri remained predominantly rural. Yet, as the state made tremendous steps forward in mining and manufacturing, its agricultural production also climbed.[47] Thus, Missouri in 1870 seemed to stand at the threshold of a bright future in all phases of economic development.

CHAPTER X

THE COMING OF CARL SCHURZ

T HE STRONG Radical triumph in the election of 1866 left the party in firm political control of Missouri. A confident mood pervaded the legislative atmosphere at Jefferson City that winter as the Radicals dominated the scene. Although some dissatisfaction appeared within their ranks over the election of Charles D. Drake to the United States Senate and over the question of amending the constitution to provide for Negro suffrage, the party leadership patched up most differences behind the scenes and maintained a fairly united front.

Assured of their strength, the Radicals launched an attack on several maverick members of the state judiciary. Their first victim was Judge James C. Moodey of the St. Louis circuit court. Moodey had been a target of Radical abuse from the moment he had declared the Ouster Ordinance unconstitutional and had interfered in the Supreme Court imbroglio of 1865. Further fault could be found in his laxity in admitting lawyers to his court who had not taken the test

oath. In early February, 1867, he empanelled a jury without
requiring its members to take the prescribed oath. In Radical
eyes he added insult to injury when, in addressing the jury,
he launched into a lengthy and caustic attack on the oath
in view of the recent Cummings decision. The House lost
little time in bringing impeachment proceedings against him,
and the Senate rushed through a conviction. Moodey claimed
he had inadequate time to prepare a defense and refused to
do so. It is doubtful if a different verdict would have been
reached if he had.[1] Rumors spread that Moodey's conviction
was only the beginning of the Radicals' revenge. The House,
however, initiated only one other proceeding—the impeachment of Judge Walter King of the Fifth Judicial Circuit in
northwest Missouri—just before the conclusion of the regular
legislative session. King, like Moodey, had been quite out-
spoken against the test oath provisions and lax in their enforcement. In June the Senate returned in special session to
hear his case, which lasted for nearly a month. Conviction
was a foregone conclusion; by mid-summer Judge King had
joined Moodey on the sidelines.[2]

The municipal spring elections of 1867 went quite well for
the Radicals, as local party leaders made strong efforts to
recoup some of the losses of a year earlier. With the Conservatives demoralized in many areas after the setbacks of
the previous fall, the Radicals had little difficulty. They re-
elected James S. Thomas as mayor of St. Louis and carried
a large majority of the aldermanic vacancies and board of
education posts in that city. They also recorded triumphs at
Jefferson City, Boonville, Sedalia, Kansas City, Warrensburg,
and other outstate towns.[3]

On April 16, 1867, a new figure arrived in St. Louis. During
the next two years he was to move rapidly to the forefront
of the Missouri political scene; indeed, few men have risen
to prominence and high office within the state as quickly as
Carl Schurz. He had arrived in this country in the early

1850's as a German *émigré* in the wake of the revolutions of 1848. From the outset he had assumed a position of leadership among his fellow German-Americans in Wisconsin and within the fledgling Republican party. During the Civil War he performed notable service in rallying the Germans to the Union cause. After serving for a time as brigadier general of a troop of volunteers, Schurz accepted an editorial position with the *Detroit Post.* He continued traveling on the lecture circuit, where he had been quite successful before the war. Equally adept at addressing audiences in English or German, he found ready acceptance before Radical groups across the country.[4]

During one such tour in March, 1867, Schurz visited Jefferson City and St. Louis. Emil Pretorius, the proprietor of the *Westliche Post,* one of the largest German-language papers in the country, approached him with a proposal of partnership. The offer seemed very attractive to Schurz, who was seeking a more lasting arrangement than the one he had in Detroit. He told Pretorius that he would seriously consider the proposal. His obvious enthusiasm, as reflected in a letter to his wife, left little doubt as to his final decision.[5] When Schurz returned to St. Louis in the middle of April, he quickly reached an agreement with Pretorius and his other partners. After expressing satisfaction that the paper was in good shape and promised to be an expanding enterprise, he commented that it would bring him "an abundant living . . . and a few years will suffice to make me wholly independent in my finances." In outlining the organization of responsibility, Schurz made certain that he had "a surplus of free time" to devote to his various outside activities, such as lecturing.[6]

Schurz and Pretorius quickly became good friends as well as partners. Since both their families were traveling abroad that summer, the two men set up bachelor quarters at Pretorius' home. He made certain that Schurz became acquainted with the German communities in and around St. Louis. Each Sunday they would visit some new locality. Frequently, some festival or celebration would be in progress, and the two men would be asked to speak. Soon Schurz became a familiar figure among the German element. His writing for the *Westliche Post* enhanced the favorable impression created by his excursions.[7] It was, for the most part, a quiet, leisurely summer. "Life goes forward with peaceful uniformity," Schurz wrote his wife in the middle of July. "Moreover, journalistic work at present is in no way interesting. The great fight is over; our opponents are powerless, and momentarily there is nothing left to do except to consolidate the results gained."[8]

Pretorius also introduced Schurz into the broader Radical circle, where the new editor's national reputation and connections helped greatly to pave the way for the Radicals' acceptance of him. Shortly after his arrival Schurz became district commander of the Missouri Department of the Grand Army of the Republic. When General Philip Sheridan visited St. Louis in September on his way to a new command in the West, Schurz was in his element. Because of his close friendship with Sheridan during the war he served as chairman of the reception committee. Sheridan was one of the "darlings" of the Radicals because of his stern military governance of Louisiana, and they went to great lengths to welcome him. Schurz handled most of the preparations personally and made certain that he was the General's constant escort. After he met Sheridan at the station, the two rode together in an open carriage to the Southern Hotel and were followed by 4,200 veterans in a torchlight procession "never surpassed in St. Louis." The whole demonstration had strong Radical overtones, with the marchers' banners carrying such inscriptions as "The Phil of Radicalism a tough cure for rebels." Before a crowd standing "shoulder to shoulder for almost three blocks" in front of the hotel, Sheridan and Schurz emerged on a balcony from which the latter delivered his formal address of welcome. It rang with Radical sentiments and praised the General for his zealous course in Southern reconstruction. Schurz wrote his wife that the speech received thunderous applause. The *Westliche Post* printed it in pamphlet form for wide distribution. After these ceremonies Schurz took Sheridan to the German summer theater for a performance of *Der Freischutz*. Again, a tremendous ovation greeted them, and "a brilliant illumination" was displayed in honor of the General. When they emerged, a large division of the Grand Army of the Republic escorted their carriage back to the hotel with torches and music. All told, it was quite a day.[9]

By the time Schurz departed around Christmas for a winter holiday with his family in Germany, he had definitely secured a firm hold on the German and the more liberal elements of the Radical party in Missouri. Upon his return he was to move increasingly into a position to challenge the more reactionary forces of the party on their home ground in the legislature. In many respects Schurz had arrived in Missouri at an opportune moment politically. Charles D. Drake had departed for Washington in March, 1867, and there became embroiled in the Radical quarrels with the Johnson administration over reconstruction policy. At this time Drake seemed solidly entrenched in power at home behind the test-oath façade. He had also beaten down the efforts of the Planters House group to move the party along the path of reconciliation through his firm control of the Radical caucus in the legislature. This success, however, strengthened Drake's tendencies toward inflexibility and arrogance. With old ties being resumed by Radicals and Conservatives outside of the political sphere, Missourians were becoming less concerned with raising old wartime animosities and more interested in working together for the state's economic progress. In the future Drake was to find it increasingly difficult to adjust to new issues and changing times.[10]

Since the early days of the Radical movement there had

been a strong anti-Drake minority centered around the German element within the party. Senator B. Gratz Brown had tried to furnish some leadership to this wing but had little success, at least in terms of expanding his influence beyond their confines. Brown was not too well known outside the St. Louis area, and his ultra liberalism did not attract many adherents from the hard-core element of the Radical party. Following his voluntary retirement from the Senate in 1867, he became politically inactive for two years, nursing ill health and a feeling of political frustration.[11]

Senator John B. Henderson might have filled the void left in the liberal leadership by Brown's retirement if he had not, in too many instances, followed an independent course in Washington. A prewar Democrat, Henderson had moved into the Radical ranks in 1864 when it became politically expedient for his re-election to the Senate. Although he realized that the Conservatives were fighting a losing cause in the closing years of the war, he never moved too far away from their philosophy. Apparently, he was one of the few Radical leaders willing to make patronage deals with them after the war, and he seemed to enjoy some favor with President Johnson at the White House. When patronage was at stake, he seldom conferred with his Radical counterparts in the House from Missouri. When the showdown came in the spring of 1868 over the tremendously emotional issue of President Johnson's impeachment, Henderson was tried in the Radical balance and found wanting. His conscience got the better of him, and he joined the courageous phalanx of seven Republicans who voted against the President's conviction. From that moment he became anathema to the Radical party in Missouri including the liberals. This action ruined his chances for re-election, and the Radicals now had to find someone to replace him in March, 1869.[12]

Governor Fletcher, who might have been expected to exert some positive leadership within the liberal ranks, remains something of an enigma. A popular speaker and an able executive, he had many friends and supporters among the Germans. He seldom found himself moving with the mainstream of his party, and many of the more ardent Radicals never forgave his opposition to the ratification of the constitution. As Missouri's first Radical governor, Fletcher soon discovered himself plagued by patronage problems in the midst of various partisans interested in the spoils of office. To please everyone under these circumstances was virtually impossible. More and more the Governor left patronage largely in the hands of subordinates and department heads. Nepotism became a prominent feature in the statehouse, and rumors of corruption were sometimes whispered, although they never came to the surface.[13] That the Governor felt the pangs of harassment and frustration seems evident from his anguished cry in a letter to William M. Grosvenor: "Once out of this I will be a Free Man and remain free."[14] Fletcher's refusal to actively fight Drake for the senatorship and his seeming desire to be done with political office made his "lame-duck" status during the last two years of his administration an increasing liability.

So Carl Schurz stepped into a seeming vacuum in the leadership of an element of the Radical party that was becoming increasingly restless with Drake's heavy partisanship. As a newcomer, Schurz had not been embroiled in the party battles of the past, which placed him in a good position to serve as reconciler. He was thoroughly Radical on national issues while recognizing the need to move Missouri in a more liberal direction. His return from Europe on the eve of a national election campaign was to give him ample opportunity to display his skills as orator, organizer, and political genius.

The defeat of the Conservative Union party in the fall of 1866 had all but destroyed it as an organized political faction. Many of its leaders looked increasingly to their own political interests, which meant securing whatever crumbs of federal patronage that might still be forthcoming from the Johnson administration. This was not an easy path. The President remained willing to aid his Conservative friends in Missouri; to get the appointments confirmed by a Radical Senate was something else, for Henderson and Drake constantly exercised their senatorial privileges to block matters. Twice Johnson nominated Frank Blair to serve as minister to Austria only to have the appointment meet the same fate as earlier attempts to help the fiery Missourian. The appointment of Lewis V. Bogy as director of the Bureau of Indian Affairs met a kinder fate; he continued in the post for nearly a year. On local patronage Senator Henderson finally forced a compromise whereby he would be given a number of appointments in return for letting certain Conservative nominations go through, but this arrangement did not prove completely satisfactory. Apparently, some Conservatives felt that Henderson had no sooner made his bargain than he began to try to grab the lion's share.[15] Perhaps former Congressman John Hogan, who had just been defeated for re-election from the First District, had the best strategy. President Johnson had asked him to write "if any position presented itself in which I might be usefully employed." Hogan noted the great difficulty in filling the position of surveyor of the port of St. Louis. He expressed interest, but suggested that Johnson wait and give him the post after Congress adjourned. With an interim appointment Hogan thought he could probably secure enough support for approval when Congress reconvened the next winter, whereas confirmation might not be possible at the present.[16] The Missouri patronage remained in an unsatisfactory muddle for some time.

With the Conservative collapse and the need for some focus of opposition in the spring municipal elections, what remained of the Democratic organization in St. Louis began to flex its feeble muscles. A consultative meeting on February 22, 1867, sounded the call for the revival of the party's flagging organization in every ward and township across the state. Results were meager. Many still hoped to avoid coalescence of the opposition within a resurgent Democracy; they feared it would be too difficult to overcome the old antagonisms that the Democratic party had aroused by past actions.[17] Yet, it became increasingly clear that a rejuvenated Democracy offered the best hope for success. It could unify a national opposition most effectively and could give the various state groups a common sense of identity. The Blairs reached this conclusion in the spring of 1867 and began to draft their plans for control of its machinery. They wished to keep up constant agitation against the Republicans as a build-up for the canvass of 1868. When James S. Rollins sought to tone down partisanship in the General Assembly as a means of securing Radical support for the university bills, Frank Blair condemned him: "Instead of placating the damned Radicals . . . you should be giving them hell from every stump in the state. . . . I know I am right in this, & hope you will give heed to what I say."[18] Rollins and others obviously had their doubts as to the efficacy of such a policy, at least at this time. Indeed, Rollins seemed anxious to retire from active politics and to devote more time to his own and the university's interests. One partisan from northeast Missouri admonished the veteran Conservative leader: "And it will not do for you and such as you to say that you have withdrawn from the arena of politics. The young men will reasonably look to you for advice, and it is your plain duty to give it cheerfully, and when called upon to serve them and your country faithfully."[19]

In the middle of March, 1867, the Supreme Court of Missouri handed down its decision in Frank Blair's test case against the iron-clad oath for voting. As Blair had expected, it went against him. Those Conservatives who had anticipated the opposite, in view of the recent Cummings decision, found the high tribunal still a faithful embodiment of Radical doctrine. The Court declared unanimously that the state had the right to confer voting rights on whatever ground it deemed best. Suffrage did not derive from natural law, nor could the present oath be considered ex post facto or a bill of attainder, as the voting privilege remained within the power of the people's representatives to extend or retract from time to time as circumstances demanded.[20] In a corresponding decision the same day the Court also upheld the test oath for candidates for office. The state's power to determine eligibility for officeholding was as plain and unchallengeable as its authority to set voting standards.[21] Blair immediately filed notice of appeal to the United States Supreme Court, hopeful that that body might reach a contrary decision in time to affect Democratic chances in the election of 1868.[22]

Conservative political activity was on the rise by late summer. Increasingly, it found its manifestations within the circle of the Democratic party. The circulation of the *St. Louis Times,* a militant Democratic newspaper, grew considerably, which indicated a resurgence of interest among the rank and file.[23] By the middle of October plans were going forward for the reorganization of the party under the banner of the State Democratic Association of Missouri. Its executive committee issued a call to all "Democratic voters of Missouri" on November 1 and urged the formation of county associations and township clubs to pave the way for the campaign of 1868.[24]

An unexpected opportunity to assert themselves came to the Democrats of southeast Missouri's Third Congressional District. Conservative Congressman Thomas E. Noell died suddenly in early October, whereupon Governor Fletcher called a special election to fill the vacancy. The Democrats nominated Dr. James R. McCormick, a popular state senator from Arcadia, and elected him by a slim margin over Radical James H. Chase. The *Missouri Democrat* urged Secretary of State Rodman to check the returns and see if fraud could be

found to reverse the results. Rodman decided first to seek an
opinion from Attorney General Wingate as to his power in
such matters. Wingate declared that the Secretary of State
had no authority beyond accepting and certifying the voting
records presented to him by the county clerks. Rodman acquiesced in this opinion, and McCormick hastened to Washington to take his seat.[25]

With the display of strength being shown by the national
Democracy in off-year elections in New York and elsewhere,
most Conservatives came to see that united support for the
Missouri Democratic party was their best hope for over-
throwing Radical rule. In sending their congratulations to the
Democracy of the city and state of New York that November,
the Missouri Democrats bemoaned their own condition. They
had been "downtrodden and oppressed for a period of six
years, hunted and hounded like wild beasts and [were] still
bound to the iron hoofs of Radicalism by every species of test
oaths and unconstitutional enactments that the brain of man
could conceive and ultra Radical legislatures pass to deprive
honest free-born men from the exercise of their rights." Yet,
they took courage from the triumph of their fellows and
pledged anew their determination to fight for success in Missouri.[26] "We are going to make a mighty effort to break the
shackles on our limbs," Lewis Bogy wrote President Johnson
early in the new year, "so as to enfranchise our people who
are now anything but free men."[27]

The organization of county and township Democratic groups
proceeded well that winter. State headquarters circulated a
printed constitution to be used by the local clubs. All of the
elements of opposition coalesced in the Democracy on the advice of one veteran leader that "names are nothing, principles
are everything." Even where Radicalism existed in strength,
the Democrats made inroads with their drive for a more formal
establishment. By the end of February, 1868, the party had
established organizations in sixty-five or seventy counties; the

push continued.[28] Two topics dominated most of the Democratic meetings: the proposed constitutional amendment for Negro suffrage and the struggle between the President and Congress over the removal of Secretary of War Stanton. The amendment received firm opprobrium from Democratic orators; they deplored its enactment at a time when thousands of whites were still unable to vote and participate in political affairs. Johnson's courageous course in removing Stanton a second time after the Senate had reinstated him in office drew their warm admiration and strong resolutions of support.[29]

The struggle in Washington aroused heated passions on both sides of the political fence in Missouri. The St. Louis Democrats had again sought unsuccessfully to promote the interests of Frank Blair as Secretary of War when they heard of the first removal of Stanton the previous fall. Now, as the President found himself impeached, they invited him to visit St. Louis and participate in their birthday banquet in honor of Washington. No doubt they hoped to compare their martyred image with Johnson's but the President could not travel that far at such a crucial moment. The same group recommended Samuel T. Glover as one of Johnson's legal counsel in his defense before the Senate. They argued that Glover had gained invaluable experience over the past three years in his own contests with "the lawless extra-constitutional power that now assails the head of the government." These cases had given him "a minute philosophical and legal familiarity with the spirit and letter of the Federal Constitution, which few men possess." When rumors reached St. Louis that some of the President's remarks made there during his 1866 "swing around the circle" might be used against him at the trial, the Democrats urged that the proprietor of the *Missouri Republican* be subpoenaed to set the record straight. Beyond this, they also gave Johnson open support in their press and forwarded their resolutions of approval.[30]

The Radical press heaped its abuse on Johnson and strongly

urged his conviction and removal from office. The Grand Vice-Commander of the Grand Army of the Republic, John S. Cavender of Missouri, offered fifty thousand of the state's veterans "to carry out the action of Congress" against the President in the event it proved necessary. The editor of the *Missouri Republican* mocked this announcement, but professed his dilemma as to whether the country should prepare for bloody revolution or should treat the whole affair as the ludicrous and absurd gesture of a few comic-opera generals. The Missouri G. A. R., however, was deadly serious; a meeting of representatives of the various local posts unanimously adopted resolutions pledging their unconditional support to Congress should an open breach develop with the President.[31]

Many Radical leaders looked to Johnson's removal as an opportunity to seize complete control of federal patronage in the state. Congressman Joseph McClurg wrote a St. Louis party leader: "Your views as to removal of officials in case impeachment succeeds (and it will) are correct, and I think every radical representative here will work, when proper time comes, to carry them out."[32] As already mentioned, Senator Henderson found himself caught in the crossfire. When it began to appear that he might vote to uphold the President, the state's Radical congressmen served warning that to do so would be considered a betrayal of his constituents. Henderson declined to heed their veiled threats of political retribution and voted his conscience. By his vote the President escaped conviction.[33]

The Radical party organization in Missouri was far from idle that winter. With the governorship and other state offices to be filled in the next election, political jockeying for the various nominations began early. Since most Radicals were convinced of the triumph of their party, the state and district nominating conventions became the important targets. The Radicals also needed to come to some agreement regarding the Negro suffrage amendment. Although this proposal aroused little enthusiasm among the rank and file of the party, the leadership believed that it was necessary to give a formal endorsement, inasmuch as the Radical legislature had set in motion the drive for its adoption. Drake urged such a policy through a letter to one of the Radical legislators, which the *Missouri Democrat* published early in January, 1868. When the Radicals met in convention at Jefferson City the following month to select delegates to the Republican national conclave at Chicago, the leaders secured adoption of a resolution placing the party officially behind the amendment.[34]

At the same time the Radicals in the legislature moved to assure their continued dominance of the election machinery by enacting a new registry law. To the dismay of the hopelessly outnumbered Democrats and Conservatives, the Radical majority ruthlessly engineered the bill's passage through a special committee in each house. Frank Blair urged Rollins "to oppose it, oppose it, denounce it with all the power & ability of which you are the master." Yet, the Radicals throttled most of the discussion and beat down all attempts at modification.[35] The new registry act revised its predecessor in a number of important ways. The old measure had provided that the county supervisors of registration would be subject to popular election for the 1868 canvass. This requirement raised the problem of their "reliability" in those counties with Conservative majorities. The new law drastically curtailed their authority through the creation of a new class of officials appointed by the Governor: the superintendents of registration. There would be thirty-four of these, one for each senatorial district. They would have general control of registration within the counties of their respective areas. To assist the elected county supervisors, the superintendent would appoint three-man boards of registration in each county. These would actually oversee the administration of the program. To further assure "incorruptible" officials at the polls, the new act transferred the power to appoint election judges from the county courts to these boards. Each board, with the county supervisor, served as a general review body to hear protests arising out of local registration. In this capacity it had virtually unlimited powers in making up the final lists. To prevent possible obstruction of the board's activities through the normal channels of the circuit courts, the new law forbade those judicial bodies to issue writs of mandamus or any other instruments that would compel a board to add or remove any name from its list of qualified voters.[36] It is no wonder that the passage of this measure is often considered the high tide of Radicalism in Missouri; it gave its sponsors a virtual strangle hold over the electorate.

The partisan press both praised and condemned the measure, depending upon the viewpoint of each individual paper. Because its passage came too late to affect the spring municipal elections, the hard work and organizational activity of the Democrats over the past winter paid off. In St. Louis they elected six of the eleven aldermanic candidates, a street railway commissioner, and a majority of the members of the school board. Similar triumphs occurred outstate in Kansas City, St. Joseph, Mexico, and elsewhere.[37]

That spring some of Missouri's Democratic leaders began making plans on a somewhat larger scale as they looked to the forthcoming state and national conventions of their party. Rollins wrote Frank Blair early in March that George Pendleton of Ohio seemed to be the western favorite for the Democratic presidential nomination and that he had the support of the "rebel element" in Missouri. Nevertheless, Rollins reported, "I still think with good management, your chances for the nomination will be good." Blair needed little urging to throw his hat in the ring. He had been seriously considering it all winter. Rollins and many other Missouri Democrats feared Pendleton because of his "soft money" stand. To them, Blair seemed a natural counterbalance, and

Rollins believed that with sufficient spadework his nomination could be accomplished.

It was essential, of course, to win effective support of the Missouri Democracy. Rollins feared that Blair had lost favor with many of them because of his inability to obtain effective patronage. The editors of both the *Missouri Republican* and the *Times,* the party's two St. Louis newspapers, had proved skeptical when approached. Still, time and circumstances might change their attitudes. Rollins thought he could secure an endorsement from the Conservatives in the legislature if Blair thought this wise. Subsequent letters from Rollins showed that cultivation was increasing Blair's strength in the state.[38] The Missouri Democrats in Washington had also come to much the same conclusion as Rollins. William F. Switzler, who was in the capital trying to secure the congressional seat denied him by Secretary of State Rodman in 1866, wrote Blair that they had agreed "without any question" that he was "the man to run for the Presidency." Switzler promised a strong effort by all of them to accomplish that end.[39]

Blair sought to help his own cause by bringing himself prominently before Missourians and the nation in a nonpolitical way. A former military aide, James Peckham, had recently produced a highly laudatory study of General Nathaniel Lyon and the beginning of the Civil War in Missouri. In this book, Blair ranked equally with Lyon as being responsible for saving the state to the Union. Certainly, no one could doubt after reading Peckham's account that Blair had acted wisely and magnificently in the hour of crisis. The Blairs saw to it that the book received wide distribution where it would do the most good. Arrangements were also made for Blair to deliver the memorial address at the dedication of a statue of Thomas Hart Benton in St. Louis. This was only fitting, as Blair had been Benton's closest political aide in the declining years of the great Senator's life. But here was another chance to dredge up memories of past greatness and service to the

Democratic party. Rollins urged Blair to dwell at length on Benton's character and patriotism with an eye to making it plain that "Old Bullion" would have had little sympathy with postwar Radicalism. Many prominent Missourians attended the ceremonies to pay homage to one of the state's most imposing figures. Yet, Blair's high hopes for extensive publicity from the occasion failed to materialize, as the press outside St. Louis gave only minor coverage to the event.[40]

On May 28, the day following the Benton dedication, the Missouri Democracy met for their state convention in St. Louis. Delegates from nearly every county attended, and everyone appeared to be enthusiastic over the party's prospects in spite of the registry law. Two matters dominated this meeting: the consolidation of organization and the selection of delegates to the national Democratic convention in New York. Another conclave was to be held later in the summer to select a slate of nominees for state offices. For the present, the Democrats elected a new state central committee with general powers to manage the campaign. They also sent an uninstructed delegation to New York with the implicit understanding that eighteen of the twenty-two men chosen would support Blair at the right moment. This arrangement, it was hoped, would leave them freer to work against Pendleton.[41]

The Republicans had held their national convention at Chicago earlier in May. Carl Schurz had returned from Germany just in time to be elected delegate-at-large by the Radical state convention in February. The Missouri delegation requested he serve as their chairman. Further recognition came his way when the Republican national committee appointed him temporary chairman of the Chicago convention, which meant that he would deliver the keynote address.[42] This honor did not go unnoticed in Missouri. The Republicans at Chicago united behind the standard of General Grant in a grand showing of harmony.

Immediately after the national meeting the state Radical executive committee issued the call for the state nominating convention to be held on July 16 in the Hall of Representatives at Jefferson City. With the Drake adherents in firm control of the committee, representation was fixed at one delegate from each county for every 100 Radical votes or fraction thereof cast in the congressional election of 1866.[43] To secure funds for the coming campaign, the committee unanimously agreed on a levy of twenty-five cents for every Radical vote cast for members of Congress in 1866. The state group called on the county committees to collect this money and forward it to headquarters. It gave no specific directions for raising the assessment, since each local group would "best understand how to approach its own constituency for the desired end." It cared not "whether each voter gives his share, or few all"; only the amount was the essential thing, for "the money is sorely needed." The importance of solid financial support from the local organizations was further underscored by this plea:

> Would you have your county flooded with sound Republican documents? Do you desire at your service the best speakers of the State & nation? . . . Have you at heart the interests of the Republican cause? Then know that your wishes can be realized only through money & plenty of it placed at the disposal of the State Committee. . . . Shall yours be the banner county?[44]

Since Radical organizations at the local level had been girding themselves for action throughout the spring, the money undoubtedly poured in. Radical editors met twice in St. Louis in May to better co-ordinate their propaganda efforts. A "full and frank" discussion took place on how to best get the party's message before the electorate. The editors returned from these sessions ready to fight for their principles of "loyalty and progress."[45]

As the time for the state convention neared, behind-the-scenes maneuvering for the various nominations continued. Fully realizing the importance of cementing the veterans' support for the Radical cause, certain party leaders organized a "soldiers' convention" for the day preceding the regular state meeting. Here, too, the interests of the various candidates could be promoted on the eve of the important decision. The idea of this preliminary meeting engendered great enthusiasm. Many veterans saw it as an opportunity to push the candidacy of some of their own number. One wrote: "So let us appear en masse at the capital on the day designated and show the politicians that we have the material and the numbers to elect, and if we push out our strongest men and secure four out of the eight offices we have made a good commencement."[46] This veteran little realized that the affair was the brain child of the managers of one of the gubernatorial candidates whose military record would thereby be enhanced when reflected against his major opponent's lack of one.[47]

The two conventions proved a rousing success, although a large number of St. Louis delegates experienced considerable inconvenience in getting to the closing evening session of the veterans' meeting on July 15. They had planned to come down to Jefferson City on the Pacific express leaving St. Louis at 4:15, which would get them there in plenty of time. They fretted impatiently at the Seventh Street station as the hour of six approached, but the train still did not move. General Sherman was also on board, and General Grant was waiting at the Webster station. The two men were bound for Fort Hays, Kansas, to confer with General Sheridan on Indian disturbances. Finally, the express pulled out at six. When it arrived at the suburban station of Cheltenham, however, another two-hour delay occurred. Word spread through the coaches that the company had had a dispute with its passenger train engineers and had discharged them all. Although the company had arranged for some of the freight engineers to take their places and had hired others, the trains could not leave because the passenger men blocked the yards and refused to allow the running of the trains. The whole dispute had grown out of the railroad's order to withdraw one engine from the Jefferson City run, which meant that the remaining engineers had to make more trips at no increase in pay. A strike ensued, with the engineers using their current tactics to draw attention to their plight. At eight o'clock, when the St. Louis yards began to clog and reasoning failed to sway the strikers, the company finally called in the police. They cleared the tracks, and the express got under way. A grumbling group of delegates arrived in Jefferson City too late for any of the evening session; they immediately went to their hotels to catch up on what they had missed and to get ready for the regular convention the next day.[48]

Over seven hundred men crowded into Jefferson City in the sweltering July heat. Many served as delegates at both conventions. The regular party conclave virtually ignored Governor Fletcher and his subordinates. Since Congress was still in session, Drake remained in Washington; his followers, nevertheless, had firm control. The moderates found themselves constantly outmaneuvered. A well-managed preconvention campaign paid off for Congressman Joseph W. McClurg of Camden County when he received the party's gubernatorial nomination over Lieutenant Governor George Smith of Caldwell County. It was McClurg's lieutenants who had played the major role in organizing the soldiers' convention. A colonel in the state militia during the war, McClurg had also served in the wartime state convention. Although trained in the law, he had spent most of his life as a merchant and trader in southwestern Missouri. He was now completing his third term in Congress, where he had served the Radical interests of Missouri well. One paper of the opposition characterized McClurg as "the embodiment of all that is narrow, bigoted, revengeful, and ignorant in the Radical party."[49] The convention renominated only one of the incumbent state

officeholders—Secretary of State Rodman. Rumor had it that
Rodman won support because of his threat to reveal the "real
means" by which the constitution had been adopted. The
remainder of the offices were distributed in a way that would
secure the greatest possible party unity.[50]

The party managers had worked well behind the scenes,
for harmony marked the proceedings both in the nominations
and the adoption of the platform. The convention reaffirmed
the stand taken in February in favor of the Negro suffrage
amendment and justified the continued disfranchisement of
Southern sympathizers as the only means of protecting the
"loyal" citizenry from abuse and depredation. "We stand
ready to restore every political privilege at the earliest moment consistent with state and national safety," read the
platform, thus consigning this issue to a vague future.[51]

The Democrats met again at St. Louis in August to nominate their candidates and draft their platform. According to
William F. Switzler, the delegates were mainly native Missourians, not johnny-come-latelies. They were "the men of
character, intelligence and wealth, representative citizens of
their respective counties—in short, the governing men of Missouri."[52] It might better be said they wanted to govern Missouri! Rollins had written Glover and Broadhead from Omaha
a week earlier to warn against the danger of letting anyone
"who was not thoroughly identified with the Government
during the rebellion" on the ticket. At least one of the Democratic presidential electors had been in the Confederate army,
which boded ill for the party in Rollins' eyes. To counteract
this, he recommended designating "at least 50 of the best
speakers in the State" to carry the Democratic message of
sane conservatism to every corner of Missouri. "Let us in this
way speak Radicalism to death," he urged.[53]

The convention accomplished what Rollins sought, although
he had some misgivings about the party's nominee for governor. He had encouraged Glover or Broadhead to seek the

nomination, but the convention united behind John S. Phelps of Springfield. Phelps was a wise choice in many respects. A native of New England, he had practiced law in Springfield for the past thirty years. For better than half of that time he had served as southwest Missouri's representative in Congress. In 1863 President Lincoln had appointed him military governor of Arkansas, where he served well under trying circumstances. Since he was a staunch Union Democrat, there could be no aspersions cast on his loyalty. Furthermore, he had a large personal following in southwest Missouri, which had become a Radical stronghold. Rollins respected Phelps, but feared that "on account of his health & his utter destitution of speaking talent he is not the man for the crisis."[54] Most of the Democracy thought differently. The rest of the ticket was composed of equally staunch Union men with the popular agriculturalist Norman J. Colman running for lieutenant governor and Bernard Poepping of Carondolet, who might attract the German element, for secretary of state.[55] In their subsequent district conventions the Democrats nominated seven of nine congressional candidates who had active war records in the Union cause. Nominees for the General Assembly were also well screened, for the new Democracy was earnestly seeking to get away from a "Copperhead" image.[56]

In view of the national ticket and campaign this policy was exceedingly wise. The national Democracy had chosen Horatio Seymour, former Governor of New York, as its presidential nominee. Republican orators had little difficulty in painting him in "Copperhead" hues in the light of his activity against conscription during the war. Although Missouri's favorite son Frank Blair secured second place on the ticket, he proved as controversial as Seymour. Republicans labeled him as revolutionary and dangerous because of a preconvention letter he had written James O. Broadhead. In this, Blair had sought to make the reconstruction acts of Congress the key issue of the campaign. He maintained that if a Democratic President should be elected, it would be his obligation to ignore and nullify by personal action those measures and to restore the rule of the Bourbon whites in the South.[57]

Carl Schurz launched the Radicals' national campaign in Missouri. Sponsored by the Young Men's Republican Club, he spoke at a rally in St. Louis' Mercantile Library hall on Friday evening, June 19. He staunchly upheld congressional reconstruction and asserted the necessity of Negro suffrage in order "to place the governments of the late rebel States upon an enlarged democratic basis."[58] The fiery German editor spent much of the late summer and early fall speaking for the national Republican ticket throughout the Middle West. By the middle of August he found himself being prominently mentioned as a possible congressional candidate in the faction-torn First District of Missouri. He dispatched a letter to William M. Grosvenor, the editor of the *Missouri Democrat*, disclaiming any desire for a seat in Congress or for any other office.[59]

In reality, however, Schurz had his eye on higher stakes than a House seat. Since John B. Henderson was obviously anathematized by the Radicals in view of his stand on the impeachment of President Johnson, the party, if victorious, would send a new senator to Washington. Schurz secretly coveted the honor. For this reason, among others, he deliberately reserved the final five or six weeks of the campaign for a speaking tour of Missouri on behalf of the state and national tickets. On August 9 Schurz wrote his wife that the main deterrent to his selection was the practice of dividing the state's Senate seats between the St. Louis and outstate areas. Because Drake was from St. Louis, the choice of Henderson's successor would normally fall to an outstate man. Several names from rural Missouri had been mentioned by the press, but Schurz hoped that they would "neutralize one another in influence." The Radical caucus would then have to turn to a compromise candidate, and Schurz would be waiting in the wings. It was essential that he "make a strong impression throughout the state" during his speaking tour, but at the same time he had to play a coy game publicly. When Pretorius wrote, seeking advice regarding moves by various newspapers to put Schurz forward for the Senate, his partner replied from Indiana, "Nothing at all."[60]

By the first of September the Missouri campaign was in full swing. When McClurg made an early St. Louis appearance, the Young Men's Republican Club marched to his hotel for a serenade and rally. As the gubernatorial nominee addressed the crowd gathered before the porch, hecklers of a more conservative hue constantly interrupted. A few firecrackers added their noise to the confusion, and then a Seymour flag suddenly appeared in one of the windows on the top floor. After the banner was removed, the crowd quieted down and the meeting was able to continue. But when General Pile, the Radicals' congressional candidate, rose to speak, another outbreak occurred. Police arrived and made several arrests. Nevertheless, the Democratic supporters had achieved their purpose; the Radical rally had been far from a success.[61]

As Radical and Democratic speakers crisscrossed the state, rally followed rally until it seemed that no one had an interest in anything but politics. One prominent St. Louis businessman wrote a friend that there existed an "almost total stagnation in the movement of real estate, and general prostration in business," with no hope of improvement until after the election. He reported the canvass being waged "with unexampled spirit, almost to the neglect of general business."[62] William B. Napton noted in his diary that almost every night of the week there were torchlight processions by one group or another through the streets of St. Louis. In amused fashion he commented:

> It would seem that men are after all but "children of a larger growth." Hundreds and thousands of dollars are

expended on these fantastic shows—the members of each club being attired in some showy garb of bright colors, sparkling with tinsel, and looking for all the world like a parade on the stage in some spectacular play. Of course they have music and a crowd of urchins and loafers on all sides cheering them with their huzzas. It must be supposed by the knowing ones that these things make votes, or they would not go to such expense—and if they do, we see "with how much wisdom the world is governed."[63]

Two major issues dominated the Missouri political scene that fall. One was the continuing question of Negro suffrage. Radical leaders felt committed to the attainment of a positive referendum on the amendment they had pushed through the legislature. How deep their convictions ran on the actual issue itself remains uncertain. It became increasingly obvious as the campaign moved forward that many in the rank and file of the party held strong reservations. In their hesitancy the Missouri Radicals were not alone, for constitutional amendments seeking to enfranchise Negroes had been rejected by popular referendums in Kansas, Michigan, Minnesota, and Ohio in 1867. Nevertheless, Radical editors and orators evoked strong moral and practical arguments to support the Missouri proposal. They pointed out that suffrage would elevate the Negro and help him to assume a more responsible position in society. It would also complete the work of emancipation begun in 1865. Beyond this, they subtly hinted, it would ensure the votes of the Negroes to the Radical party in future days when they might be badly needed. As provided in the constitution, the General Assembly, by absolute majority vote in each house, could drop the disqualifications for voters after January 1, 1871. If this should occur, an estimated fifty thousand more votes would be added to the Democratic column. The need for ballots to counteract such an avalanche was obvious.[64]

The Democrats strongly opposed the amendment. From

their conservative viewpoint it was too early to commit the
ballot to a group less than four years out of slavery. Then,
too, they vehemently denounced a scheme designed to enfranchise Negroes untrained for citizenship while large numbers of whites still remained outside the circle of this political
privilege.[65]

The major concern of the Democrats, however, was the
highhanded system of registration that the Radicals sought
to impose on the electorate. As the time to institute the plan
approached, the Radical superintendents of registration gathered in St. Louis for an informal session to discuss ways of
ensuring uniform implementation. Democratic leaders condemned this closed-door meeting as a scheme to promote
further political skulduggery. The *Missouri Democrat*, in turn,
denounced the registrars' detractors and praised the Radical
officials for their conscientiousness.[66] The Democratic state
convention had appointed a committee to devise a workable
plan of opposition. In late August this group issued an address that called for the establishment of local watchdog
committees to keep an eye on the registration process in their
areas. Every Democrat should attempt to take the test oath
and qualify to vote, as the United States Supreme Court
might still rescue rejected voters through a favorable decision
in Blair's case. Whatever the tactics of the Radicals might be,
the Democratic leaders urged nonviolence and compliance
with the law, even if it meant total rejection in the end.[67]

The Radicals did not deem it necessary to announce a systematic policy on registration, but they did warn local registrars to keep a sharp eye out for "traitors" who would seek
to evade the law. Their orators "waved the bloody shirt,"
with Charles D. Drake being particularly effective in this
kind of demonstration. He stumped the state in September,
proclaiming:

> This then is the one solitary and vivid issue: *Shall the
> people that saved the country rule it, or shall rebels and*

traitors? . . . Patriotism smothers Democracy, as Democracy smothers Patriotism. The question then is, whether we shall have patriotism without Democracy, or Democracy without patriotism? Take the former with Grant, Colfax, the old Flag, and the Boys in Blue; take the latter with Seymour, Blair, Jeff Davis, Wade Hampton, Napoleon Butcher Forrest, Pirate Semmes, and the whole army of graybacks, with the New York gang of rioters, Seymour's "friends," as he called them, thrown in, to tip the music of the brogue for the Democracy's grand dance over the graves of 300,000 dead.[68]

Carl Schurz took a somewhat calmer view of the problem. He talked of the necessity for congressional reconstruction in order to assure a new South. The justice of Negro suffrage received a prominent place in every speech. The harmony of progress pervaded his thoughts more than the specter of the past.[69]

Another, somewhat pathetic, figure touring the state that September was Senator John B. Henderson, who refused to be counted out for re-election. While stumping for the national Republican ticket, he also sought to vindicate his stand on President Johnson's impeachment. Henderson obviously hoped to make himself available to the moderates of both parties. He not only called for the enfranchisement of the Negro but also demanded the repeal of the test oath for voters and predicted its ultimate overthrow by the Supreme Court. In a challenging letter to his colleague Drake, he urged: "The enslavement of the white race is not likely to bring about the liberty and happiness of the negro; let us try the amendment, and if defeated, let us enfranchise our own race and try it again. . . . I propose to secure the negro rights by an appeal to reason and not by the permanent enslavement of a large body of our own race." For the most part Henderson appeared to be wandering in a no man's land. Although some Radical moderates agreed with him, they did not consider the moment right for saying so. Furthermore,

Henderson's stand on the impeachment question still loomed too large to be ignored.[70]

When the process of registration actually got under way, violence inevitably broke out in scattered areas. In central and northwestern Missouri, where conservative Democratic strength was threatened by rigid enforcement and seemingly underhanded tactics, Radical registrars found themselves frequently threatened by irate "rejects." At Martinsburg in Audrain County, for instance, registration was proceeding without difficulty until a Radical farmer named Reedy handed the registering board a list of his neighbors whom he thought should be rejected. The acceptance of this list brought a vehement protest from Democrat Sam Fletcher, whom the registrars ordered arrested for disturbing the peace. In the ensuing scuffle shots were exchanged, with both sides blaming the other for the first one. Before the fray ended, three Democrats, including Fletcher, lay dead and one of the registrars was wounded.[71]

The *Missouri Statesman*, in discussing registration in conservative Boone County, reported that the registrars accepted only 21 out of 49 persons who presented themselves in Columbia the first day. "Among the rejected are some of the most loyal men in Boone County, . . . all of whom took appeals to the board of review." They had little success in appealing, as the final list showed only 410 qualified voters out of an eligible white male population of 4,290.[72] Similar ratios prevailed for most deep-dyed conservative counties. John A. Hockaday of Fulton wrote James S. Rollins after the election that Rollins' Radical opponent for the Missouri Senate seat had accompanied the registrars in Callaway County to a number of precincts. He was also "closeted with the Board of Review day and night for several days." As a result, some 400 or 500 names disappeared from the list. In spite of this, Callaway gave Rollins and the other Democrats a comfortable margin.[73]

There were undoubtedly areas that produced opposite results in registration, although testimony was usually partisan
and confusing. Apparently, in the Fourteenth Senatorial District of western Missouri, Superintendent Thomas Phelan,
although appointed as a Radical, acted in collusion with the
Democrats. His policy led to a laxness in the administration
of the registry law, and many were enrolled who, strictly
speaking, should have been rejected. In Jackson County, a
part of this district, 5,186 persons registered in 1868 as opposed to 2,284 in 1866. This had been one of the most notorious bushwhacker-infested regions during the war.[74] At the
other end of the state, in St. Louis County, the registrars
rejected only 697 applicants, while enrolling 31,938, which
was probably a fair ratio. Total registration across the state
stood at 154,080 persons, as opposed to 125,000 in 1866. This
difference can probably be accounted for by increased immigration from northern states, a rise in the number of men who
had come of age, and, in many areas, a moderating atmosphere brought about by the passage of time.[75]

While registration moved forward, the campaign rolled on
toward an inevitable climax. State and local candidates
stumped back and forth from rally to rally, with Drake,
Schurz, Blair, and others joining the fray. Torchlight parades continually fired the streets of the cities and villages,
but during the final week of the campaign the *Missouri
Democrat* reported that crowds were falling off because "the
boys are tired of marching."[76] Since there was little doubt
that the Radicals would carry Missouri for Grant and elect
their state-wide ticket by a comfortable margin, attention
focused on the congressional races, control of the legislature,
and the fate of the Negro suffrage amendment. For a time
it appeared that local factional quarrels among the Radicals
would hinder their chance for a sizable margin in the General Assembly, but these difficulties were smoothed over with
the help of Drake's and Schurz's canvasses. As election day

neared, the Radicals were bursting with well-founded confidence.[77]

Joseph W. McClurg and the entire state Radical ticket were victorious by an approximate 20,000-vote margin. Grant received the state's electoral vote by a similar majority. The new General Assembly would have a Senate composed of twenty-five Radicals and nine Democrats and a House containing ninety-two Radicals, thirty-five Democrats, and two Independents. The Democrats made their greatest gains in the congressional races; they re-elected McCormick in the Third District and picked up seats in the First, Sixth, and Ninth districts.[78] The *Missouri Democrat* immediately cried "fraudulent" in regard to the returns in the Sixth and Ninth districts and called on the Radicals' "hatchet-man," Secretary of State Rodman, to throw out the vote of certain counties as he had done in 1866. Although the Secretary had been warned by the Attorney General that he had no powers to do so when the question arose in the special Third District race a year earlier, he now ignored that opinion. He refused to open and certify the votes of Monroe, Jackson, Platte, Dunklin, Wayne, Oregon, Shannon, and Ripley counties on the ground of illegal registration. In an adroit bit of "buck-passing" Rodman announced that he would leave the question of counting these votes to the General Assembly. That body certified the votes as Rodman presented them and ordered new elections for local offices and the legislature in the counties in question.

In the meantime, Rodman had proceeded to issue certificates of election on the basis of the remaining "official" vote. In the process William F. Switzler of Columbia again found himself victimized out of an apparent victory in the Ninth District. Failure to include the ballots of Monroe County changed his 681-vote majority into a 460-vote deficit in favor of David P. Dyer of Pike County. During the campaign Dyer had stated that he would never accept a verdict of this type, but he now grasped Rodman's certificate readily and proceeded to Washington. In the Sixth District the exclusion of the returns from Jackson and Platte counties transformed a majority of 1,032 votes for Democrat James Shields, former United States senator from Illinois and Minnesota, into an 879-vote margin for Radical incumbent Robert T. Van Horn of Kansas City. Both Switzler and Shields brought contests for the seats before the national House of Representatives. That body's committee on elections reported Switzler's cause favorably, but again the Republican House refused to seat him.[79]

The election of 1868 brought the Radicals to the zenith of their political power in Missouri. Only one disappointment marred the results for their leaders: the decisive defeat of the amendment that would have given the Negro the franchise. A strong defection of Radical voters, combined with almost solid opposition by the Democrats, produced a negative result of a 74,053-to-55,236 vote. St. Louis County voted against it by a better than two-to-one margin.[80] Prejudice among the Radical rank and file overcame all moral and political arguments advanced by their leaders. Many obviously feared an inundation of Negro immigration should Missouri prove more liberal than her northern sister states. Radical leadership sought to pin the blame for the amendment's defeat squarely on the shoulders of the Democrats. William M. Grosvenor, speaking through the editorial columns of the *Missouri Democrat*, expressed the opinion that most Radicals would support the removal of all restrictions if the Democrats would go along with impartial suffrage. It quickly became obvious, however, that this sentiment did not meet the general approval of the party hierarchy, for Charles D. Drake promptly dispatched a letter from Washington demanding Negro suffrage *first* and restoration of the franchise to "rebels" later.[81] Herein lay the seeds for the eventual dissolution of the Radical party.

On the eve of the election Carl Schurz wrote his wife: "Our papers have been full of my doings, and the demand for me to become Senator grows daily. The matter begins to trend toward a higher probability." Although Schurz in his *Reminiscences* was to lead his readers to believe that the idea of putting him forward for the Senate took him by surprise, his letters to his wife and to Pretorius indicate that a carefully calculated program had been devised to make himself "available" once Senator Henderson's re-election became questionable.[82] The only announced candidate for the senatorial post was Congressman Benjamin F. Loan of St. Joseph, a faithful party hack and the personal choice of Drake. Loan had played a prominent role in the Missouri militia during the war. That conflict had converted him from a Whig into an intense Radical. His three terms in Congress had been distinguished by partisan zeal, but little else. Loan's announcement at an early stage of the campaign met with little enthusiasm outside his home area, but until Schurz made his impressive tour of the state in October, there seemed no formidable challenger.[83]

Although the earliest apparent mention of Schurz as a senatorial possibility appeared in the *LaGrange National American* at the end of July, the real impetus for his candidacy came from St. Louis under the aegis of the *Missouri Democrat*. Shortly after the election Schurz had brought together a group of German and American friends for a Saturday luncheon to discuss politics and current events. The men readily agreed to make this meeting a weekly affair and adopted the name, Twentieth Century Club. Pretorius, Grosvenor, Brown, and other liberals participated. From their discussions came the planning and strategy for Schurz's candidacy. Grosvenor agreed to put out a feeler through the pages of the *Democrat* for support elsewhere. The response from outstate proved immediate and enthusiastic; its extent even surprised Schurz somewhat.[84] Grosvenor now undertook the direct management of the campaign. Nearly every issue of the *Democrat* during December played up Schurz's capabilities and achievements. Excerpts from the pro-Schurz press outstate abounded in its pages. By the middle of December Grosvenor counted twenty-eight papers favoring the German editor and only twelve for Loan. The bandwagon had begun to move.[85]

Loan suddenly bestirred himself to win friends, but with little success. His press began a vituperative attack upon Schurz by maligning his German origins and his moral character. The papers also accused him of playing a major role in the defeat of the Negro suffrage amendment and of wishing to immediately enfranchise the "rebel" element. One of their major weapons was the expected charge that because Missouri already had one senator from St. Louis, Henderson's successor should come from outstate.[86]

As the heated contest flamed, Senator Henderson took heart. If the Radical caucus deadlocked, he might still retain his seat as the most attractive compromise choice. He wrote Rollins from Washington on Christmas Eve: "Loan's friends will go for me if Loan cannot succeed, and a majority of Schurz's friends are for me in preference to Loan. So stands the fight. I think I hold the balance of power between them, and if the caucus is broken, I know I hold it in joint session." Henderson claimed Grant's covert support; the President-elect supposedly agreed with his position on suffrage for both the Negro and the disfranchised white.[87]

Henderson was seemingly not whistling in the dark when he expressed these hopes. Schurz, still unannounced as a candidate, had written Congressman Elihu B. Washburne of Illinois, a close friend of Grant, a few weeks earlier and had expressed his concern. He explained:

> Two or three weeks ago Henderson seemed to be still a dead man politically. Now he gathers strength in an unexpected quarter: among Drake's friends, the extreme proscriptive wing of the Radicals. The combination seems unnatural, but there is some bottom to it. Drake is dead against me, for the reason that my election would throw

him out four years hence, he being also a St. Louis man.
He will do anything to defeat me and combine with
anybody.

Schurz was particularly annoyed by Henderson's contentions
that he had the confidence of Grant and would be "likely to
dispose of the patronage in this state" if returned to the Senate. Schurz hoped that he, too, might have some influence
with the incoming national administration and "*should like
to have that understood* so as to counteract the impression
which Henderson and his allies are bound upon creating."
Could Washburne help him?[88] The Illinois congressman replied that he felt sure that Schurz enjoyed the esteem of
General Grant, who appreciated the efforts made by the editor to enlist German-American support behind his election,
but he could produce no direct statement of support.[89]

With the convening of the legislature early in January, 1869,
the struggle for the senatorship moved to Jefferson City.
Thrust and parry began in earnest. Schurz wrote his wife
that he was "going to the theatre of war" in "splendid fighting trim." He thought his chances generally favorable, but
he took nothing for granted. And neither did his opposition.
Senator Drake returned from Washington to personally lead
the attack. Obviously concerned by the Schurz "boom," Drake
saw his dominant position within the party hierarchy threatened by this formidable new rival from his own St. Louis
bailiwick. After a week of confrontation Schurz quite accurately summed up the situation for his wife: "The battle in
which I am engaged does not turn solely on the senatorship.
It involves the leadership of one or the other element, the
narrowly despotic or the liberal people in Missouri."[90]

Drake became particularly disturbed by threatened defec-
tions of some of the legislators from southwestern Missouri,
which had always been one of his strongholds. During a private caucus he apparently gave them positive assurances of
federal aid for the extension of the South Pacific Railroad to

Springfield and beyond. At the same time he berated Schurz as a foreign intruder, an immoral atheist, and a revolutionist. It became increasingly obvious that Drake was more concerned with stopping Schurz than with electing Loan.[91] Although the Senator saw the contest as a key to his political future as leader of Missouri's Radicals, many of his followers in the outstate area saw no basis for his concern. The rural press had not considered their endorsement of Schurz as a repudiation of Drake's previous leadership. Some even resented his direct interference and believed that he was placing his own welfare above that of the party. Typical was the comment of the *Missouri Weekly Patriot* at Springfield: "Senator Drake has been the recipient of high favors from the Radical party of this State, but in leaving his post of duty at Washington to interpose his selfish interests in opposition to those of the whole people, he is deserving of the severest censure, and has placed his past prestige in deadly peril."[92]

The Schurz-Grosvenor strategy involved bringing their opponents out into open debate where they could grapple with the personal attacks being circulated against the German editor. Some of Schurz's supporters in the legislature made arrangements for the principal senatorial antagonists to appear in an open forum at the Radical caucus on Thursday evening, January 7, to present their views. To emphasize the importance of the occasion, Schurz sent Loan a direct challenge that same morning. He accused the St. Joseph congressman of allowing his friends to circulate "statements concerning my political principles and opinions calculated to prejudice the minds of members of the Radical party against me." When Loan feigned innocence and sought to misconstrue Schurz's letter, the fiery German shot back: "The misrepresentations, the echo of which I find in your letter have gone far enough." He warned that he would address the meeting that evening whether Loan appeared or not.[93]

The forum turned out to be a rather one-sided affair.

Schurz made a brief and fairly moderate talk in which he defended his own record while implying, unfairly, that Drake had been the chief roadblock to Negro suffrage. He pledged his wholehearted support not only to a new attempt in this direction but also to the adoption of a federal constitutional amendment guaranteeing Negroes the right to vote. In regard to the re-enfranchisement of disloyal whites, Schurz denied his opponent's accusations that he favored this in the immediate future. He stood by the national and state party platforms of 1868, which vaguely promised the removal of restrictions "as may be consistent with the safety of the loyal people." As to when this situation would exist, he made no prediction. Pleading ill health, Loan did not make an appearance. The correspondent for the *Missouri Republican* described the malady as "neuralgia of the jaw." Senator Drake attended but did not speak. He stated that he was not prepared to reply at this time, but would do so after seeing a published version of Schurz's remarks. The group then called for Senator Henderson, who spoke for nearly an hour in a rather humorous vein, assuring the legislators that he "was still alive and kicking."[94]

The Radicals now made arrangements to hold a debate on the following Monday evening to give the three principal candidates—Schurz, Loan, and Henderson—another opportunity to discuss their views. Concerned about the effect of the election on his own position, Drake announced that he would also speak. In the interim Schurz and Loan met with a group of southwestern legislators on Saturday evening to discuss the railway interests of the state. Schurz, according to his own account, "swept Loan so absolutely from the field that his friends were ashamed of him."[95] It was but the prelude to the final triumph.

With the inauguration of Governor McClurg scheduled for Tuesday, Radical partisans from across the state came to Jefferson City a day early to witness the senatorial showdown.

The Hall of Representatives was packed on Monday evening, January 11, as Loan rose to speak first. His remarks were brief and certainly unspectacular. After making the expected attack on his opponents, he defended his own record in hackneyed phrases and sat down. A scattered, polite applause came from the audience.[96] Loan was not their principal reason for being there; they had come to hear Drake debate Schurz. With a contemptuous, defiant air, Missouri's "Mr. Radical" rose to launch his attack. An excited hush settled over the crowded hall. Drake began by reiterating his stand on Negro suffrage and his antagonism toward any concessions to the "rebel" element. He then delivered a bitter attack on his political enemies within the party. With scarcely a mention of Loan, Drake charged: "The whole contest . . . is a war upon me. It will place in the Senate one who represents a body of men hostile to me; antagonistic to my views and principles." He vilified Schurz as the "frontman" for the old Planters House group of 1866, which sought to take over the party and wrench the control of federal patronage from him.

At this point Schurz began to interject questions about Drake's conduct at the constitutional convention, which somewhat unnerved the Senator. Drake finally called for adjournment with the promise that he would finish his remarks the following evening. When the group reconvened, Drake gave a caustic two-hour diatribe against his old protagonists, the German wing of the party. No longer able to suppress his rancorous hatreds of the past, he attacked the Germans for their opposition to the constitution and blamed them for the recent defeat of Negro suffrage. Drake's speech dragged on, and when the Senator launched into an impassioned eulogy of Loan and himself his audience interrupted with catcalls and cries for Schurz. Finally, Drake sat down.

Schurz now rose to give his final defense. The editor likened himself to "a young David, who, single-handed and without any weapon except his sling and a few pebbles in his pouch, had to meet in combat two heavily-armed Goliaths at once." His listeners roared; Schurz knew they were with him. Passing quickly over Loan's speech, he concentrated on Drake. With ruthless candor he asked: Where was the Senator when the Germans were taking Camp Jackson and saving Missouri for the Union? With profound disdain, Schurz answered his own question: Drake was sitting quietly in his office; a proslavery Democrat in prewar days, he was meditating on when it might be safe for him to change his colors while the Germans spilled their blood for the Union. This remark brought Drake to his feet in rejoinder that friends had advised that he could do far more for the cause at home than at the front. One of these men was in the room and quickly replied: "Yes, but that was long after the beginning of the war." Drake returned to his seat, chagrined, amid the laughter of the audience. Several other exchanges followed before Schurz moved to a final dissection of Drake's career as leader of the Radical party. He painted a picture of a man who could brook no opposition to or criticism of his program or his control. By his narrowness and vindictive proscription, Schurz contended, Drake would continue to alienate the very people whose support he needed until eventually he would stand "lonesome and forlorn, surrounded by an immensity of solitude, in desolate self-appreciation." Having thus stripped his opponent before a howling throng, Schurz closed with a plea for unity so that the party could move on to the great tasks before it.[97]

A tremendous round of applause followed as many rushed to the platform to shake Schurz's hand and congratulate him. Only with great difficulty was he able to make his way back to his hotel through the push of well-wishers. Henderson's brief closing remarks were strictly anticlimactic. Drake, thoroughly whipped and with scarcely a friend to console him, hastened back to his hotel alone. He quietly checked out and caught the night train back to St. Louis.[98] In writing to a St. Louis ward leader a few days later, Congressman-elect Samuel S. Burdett of Osceola summed up the feelings of many Radicals:

> It has been for a long time patent to us all that we stood sadly in need of an injection of brains into our party leadership not merely of brains, working within the narrow sphere of self interest and glorification such as our Drake possesses, but brains loving and laboring for the great humanity such as the world's Schurz controls. I never had any abiding faith in Drake, there is too much of the gall of bitterness in his nature to be consistent with real statesmanship or true catholicity of spirit.[99]

Although their true leader had apparently abandoned the fight, as evinced by his hasty departure, the Loan forces did not go down in the Radical caucus without a struggle. On Wednesday evening all but one of the 115 Radicals from both houses gathered to make their decision. The Loan adherents moved for a secret ballot; such a procedure might give courage to some of their would-be supporters, wavering under the momentary enthusiasm for Schurz. After this proposal met defeat by a tie vote of 57 to 57, the caucus agreed, 59 to 55, to proceed by open balloting. The legislators also approved another hotly contested motion to invite certain Radical leaders from outside their ranks to attend the meeting in order that due publicity could be given to their decisions. These preliminary victories paved the way for Schurz's nomination on the first ballot, although he received a bare majority of 59 votes to Loan's 40. The remaining votes were scattered among three other nominees. A Loan man immediately moved to make the decision unanimous, and the motion carried. As soon as the party closed ranks, many of the Radicals rushed over to Schurz's hotel to congratulate the victor. About one o'clock in the morning an impromptu musical organization gathered to serenade the candidate. Open house continued in Schurz's rooms until three.[100]

The election that followed, on January 19, was a mere formality. The Democrats cast their minority ballot for John S. Phelps, their recent gubernatorial nominee, while Schurz received the unanimous vote of the Radicals. The Senator-elect appeared before a joint session the following day to announce his acceptance of the long-sought prize. He saw his victory as "evidence of the liberal and progressive spirit moving the people of Missouri." After commending the Assembly for having "broken through all those prejudices and set aside all those traditional considerations" formerly governing such elections, he urged the co-operation of all parties and factions in an "endeavor to close up the distracting agitations which have sprung from our civil conflict." Schurz reiterated his plea for Negro suffrage and seemed to hold out an olive branch to the disfranchised whites to prove themselves worthy of regaining their political privileges. "Let us make them understand that they have only to do full justice to all the friends of the Union, and they may count upon full mercy to themselves; that they have only to come to us as men sincerely loyal to the new order of things and we shall meet them with the open hand of welcome."[101]

The new Radical senator thus began the campaign for reconciliation that would split his party within two years and bring its eventual downfall. Schurz's victory in 1869 was far from a clear-cut triumph in terms of his assertion of leadership over all of the party. This had been amply shown in the division of the Radical caucus on its first ballot. Yet, it did mark the definite rise of the liberal element to a position of strength and power that it had not enjoyed before, and it indicated that the tired old clichés would have to give way to the consideration of new issues.

CHAPTER XI

THE BIRTH OF LIBERAL
REPUBLICANISM

Wʀɪᴛɪɴɢ to his friend William K. Patrick, a prominent St. Lous Radical, on January 18, 1869, Congressman-elect Samuel S. Burdett of Osceola remarked:

> I was (to be quite frank) not at all favorably impressed with our new Governor, he seemed to me to be a very ordinary and rather narrow man; but I hope that my impressions are incorrect. I have great confidence however in his integrity of purpose, and thorough loyalty and believe he will make a safe and trustworthy executive officer, but not an ornamental one.[1]

This observation came from a partisan Radical who had been active in securing McClurg's nomination and election. It gives a rather clear indication of the nature of and the limitations to party leadership during the postwar era. The Radical leaders were, for the most part, average men with narrow outlooks of a highly partisan bent. Few had had any important political responsibility before the war. That conflict had opened the door of opportunity for them. They had rushed through the aperture and seized power with the determination to hold on to it by any and every means at their disposal. The principal method they used was proscription of the enemy as practiced under the test oath and the registry act. When this procedure did not prove equal to the situation, they called on their faithful Secretary of State, Francis Rodman, to ignore enough ballots to allow their purpose to be carried out. If a judge became too obnoxious, impeachment proved an effective weapon, as in the cases of Moodey and King. Under the leadership of Charles D. Drake and his constant "waving of the bloody shirt," the Radicals had managed to secure an iron grip on Missouri. Their control had not been all for the bad, however, as noted in the chapters on education and economic progress.

Within the party a certain element began to look more and more beyond the narrow bounds of partisan politics. Desirous of healing the scars of war and concentrating on the development of Missouri's future potential, they became increasingly dissatisfied with a leadership that seemingly failed to see the necessity of building a stronger party foundation than the present one based on the continued proscription of the enemy. The glimmerings of liberalism had first been seen at the Planters House conference of 1866. The influence of this group had been stifled at that time by the election of Drake to the Senate. Although the movement for Negro suffrage had gained sufficient momentum to carry the issue before the voters in 1868, revolt by many of the Radical rank and file, together with solid Democratic opposition, had killed that proposal.

Out of the ashes of this defeat there arose in the ranks of the moderates a new and growing conviction that Negro suffrage must now be coupled with the removal of all proscriptions, even as B. Gratz Brown had proposed at the Planters House. Senator Henderson had preached this doctrine during the campaign of 1868, but his cries seemed like a "voice in the wilderness" at that time. Also, the sincerity of his conversion to liberalism remained open to question in view of his personal political circumstances.[2] Drake and Henderson engaged in a heated exchange of letters over this issue immediately following the election, with the former adamant in resisting all attempts at re-enfranchisement of "rebels" until "the ballot had been secured to the negro."[3]

The opening salvo in the moderates' drive to end proscription was fired by Governor Fletcher, who had nothing to lose thereby. In his final message to the General Assembly four days before leaving office Fletcher attacked the test oath in no uncertain terms. He called for a constitutional amendment to remove virtually all restrictions on the suffrage. The Governor could see no necessity for continuing a policy that had long ceased to serve its initial purpose. Furthermore, he believed that the United States Supreme Court would soon perform the task for Missouri through an unfavorable decision in the Blair case. It would be far better for the Radicals to assume responsibility for voluntary relinquishment of the program they themselves had inaugurated.[4]

The dominant party sentiment found reiteration four days later when Governor McClurg delivered his inaugural address. He called for the resubmission of the Negro suffrage amendment in 1870 and emphasized the responsibility of the Radical party, in fulfilling its God-given mission, to bring the colored man into full citizenship. With regard to the "unrepentant rebels," McClurg maintained that they would probably regard any attempt to couple their re-enfranchisement with that of the Negro as degrading and would therefore oppose it. The stronger implication of the message lay in the fear, shared by many Radicals, that removal of restrictions would restore too many voters to the Democratic ranks.[5] One of the chief accusations circulated against Schurz by the Drake-Loan camp was that the German editor favored the immediate cessation of restrictions. Schurz had vehemently denied this charge in his correspondence with Loan prior to their debates. In his initial speech before the Radical caucus the fiery German made it specifically clear that he agreed with Drake that Negro suffrage must come first.[6] Although his thinking might be moving toward full amnesty, Schurz fully realized that advocacy of any such policy at this crucial moment could quickly dash his senatorial hopes to the ground. Such a program could not be delayed much longer, but opportunity must first be given to educational endeavor on its behalf by a favorable press.

The majority of the Radicals in the legislature showed little inclination to tackle the suffrage question in any form during the 1869 session. Some moderates had held high hopes that the election of Schurz marked the beginning of a significant break-through, but such was not the case. Although the Radicals were continually prodded by Grosvenor through the editorial columns of the *Missouri Democrat* and were urged by House Speaker John C. Orrick of St. Charles and other leaders to submit a combination amendment, they remained lethargic. Both the Senate and the House referred all such proposals to special committees, where they were conveniently bottled up and left to die. Attempts to modify the registry act met a similar fate.[7]

As it became evident that little direct action could be expected from the legislature because of the basic disagreement over policy, agitation began to appear for a new constitutional convention that might consider a more thorough revision in view of changing times. Grosvenor raised the issue editorially on January 29 and reported considerable press support from outstate ten days later. After lengthy debate the Radical caucus rejected the idea, and attempts to push the proposal through the legislature without official party approval also met defeat. Sensing the mood of his party, Governor McClurg made no effort to force a decision. Rather, he used his influence against any proposition that would go beyond his inaugural message.[8]

Several factors account for the reticence of the Radical majority. There still remained the adjourned session of the legislature a year hence. If action needed to be taken in regard to the election of 1870, it could be done then. By that time the legislators would have a better idea of popular sentiment. Then, too, two events that were taking shape in Washington might resolve the suffrage questions without the need for further action at Jefferson City. The first of these involved the drafting of the Fifteenth Amendment by their Radical counterparts in Congress to secure Negro suffrage on a nationwide scale. The other concerned the contest of Frank Blair before the United States Supreme Court over the validity of the test oath for voters.

Congress passed the Fifteenth Amendment on February 26, 1869, and sent it to the states for ratification. This forbade the abridgement of any citizen's right to vote "on account of race, color or previous condition of servitude" and empowered Congress to enforce this provision with appropriate legislation. When word of this action flashed over the telegraph wires, the Radicals at Jefferson City, without waiting for official confirmation from the Secretary of State, rushed through both houses a resolution of ratification, which Governor McClurg gladly signed. Those members whose Radical constituencies had shown their disapproval of such a step only a few months earlier justified their support by pointing out that Negro suffrage on a national scale would alleviate local fears that Missouri might attract a large colored immigration if it acted alone. The Democratic opposition remained true to its previous contentions that the freedmen were not yet ready for suffrage and certainly should not be admitted to the ranks of voters while large numbers of whites still remained disfranchised.[9] The Assembly adjourned three days after acting on this fateful issue; most of the members hoped

The Birth of Liberal Republicanism

that by the time they reconvened enough states would have followed suit to incorporate the Fifteenth Amendment into the Constitution.

In the middle of March the Supreme Court heard arguments in the case of *Blair v. Ridgely* et al. William M. Evarts and Montgomery Blair represented the appellant. Vehemently attacking Radicalism and its manifestations in Missouri, Blair argued that the oath was being used to proscribe Democrats generally rather than to disfranchise "rebels." Such action set a dangerous political precedent. Although straying somewhat from the legal aspects of the case, this line of argument had been determined upon after Samuel Glover, who had represented Frank earlier, had talked with Justice David Davis. This jurist had seemed to indicate that such reasoning would find favor with Chief Justice Chase, whom the Blairs considered the key man in the decision. Charles D. Drake appeared for the defendants as he had in Missouri. His argument rested upon the sovereign power of any people, in framing their constitution, to prescribe conditions of suffrage. He included a vivid description of the turmoil in Missouri during the war that had led to the necessity for proscriptive measures. After Drake completed his defense, Evarts concluded with a tight summation of the plaintiff's legal and constitutional arguments based on the familiar bill of attainder and ex post facto contentions.[10]

The Blairs anticipated a quick and favorable decision. Frank wrote Rollins on April 13 that he had "some reasons of a private nature for believing that the Court will in this case give a just decision." Glover, "who always looks to the gloomy side of every question," and his brother Montgomery were equally optimistic.[11] The optimism faded as the weeks passed with no announcement being issued; apprehension and misgivings set in. After the Supreme Court twice postponed its decision, it finally announced it would carry the case over to the October term. The *Missouri Republican*

pessimistically prophesied that if the Blair case should be decided in favor of the Radicals there could be "very little hope
in regard to the result of future elections."[12]

Glover expressed the dismay of many Democrats in the
middle of November as delay followed delay: "When will it
be decided? That it is impossible to answer. There is a painful
mystery about it. . . . Once justice was done in our country
without this cruel delay. Once a suitor had a right to reasonably prompt administration of the law. It is not so now."
Nevertheless, the St. Louis attorney continued to have no
doubt as to what the ultimate decision would be in view of
such past precedents as the Cummings case.[13] At the same
time Frank Blair wrote his brother from St. Louis: "Is it
possible to hurry the Supreme Court in my case? Our people
are getting into a great fever about it."[14] The Court would
not be hurried; its work load was heavy, and with only eight
justices it had fallen behind in its schedule.[15]

In all the agitation over the suffrage another group raised
its voice in a demand to be heard and to be given favorable
consideration. This was the Women's Suffrage Association of
Missouri. The wartime activities of women through the Western Sanitary Commission and other such organizations had
begun to crystallize sentiment for granting the fairer sex a
larger voice in the management of governmental affairs. Miss
Phoebe Couzins, one of the Missouri movement's most important leaders, had worked with the Commission during
the conflict. Her experiences had led her to the conclusion
that women, if they possessed political power, could prevent
war. She directed most of her efforts to this end. Admitted
to the Washington University Law School, she received the
Bachelor of Laws degree in two years and thereby became
the first professional woman lawyer in the United States. One
newspaper deridingly dubbed her "a female bachelor," but
she continued her course undaunted.[16]

Apparently, B. Gratz Brown was the first prominent political figure in the state to give definite public expression to the idea of women's suffrage. In Senate debate over the suffrage question in the District of Columbia in December, 1866, Senator Brown declared that he was in favor of the universal exercise of franchise regardless of "race, color or sex." Upon reading this, Mrs. Virginia Minor of St. Louis sent Brown a letter of commendation with a number of signatures affixed.[17] That same winter, 355 ladies of St. Louis forwarded a petition to the General Assembly asking for the franchise. Noting the agitation over the question of Negro suffrage, the ladies gave their approval to such a proposal, but added that it did not go far enough. One half of the population of Missouri remained ballotless, although they were "subject to the law and taxed to support the Government." The House referred the petition to the committee on constitutional amendments, which never reported it back. Undismayed, the women called a meeting in the directors' room of the Mercantile Library on May 8, 1867, and organized their association with Mrs. Minor as president.[18]

Early newspaper comments indicated that there existed some skepticism concerning the movement, but no great ill will. The *Missouri Republican* observed: "The social position and the respectability of many of the women concerned in this movement are such that even if they do not conciliate favor to the proposed political reform, they will command deferential treatment from its opponents." The editor of the *Missouri Democrat* noted that Kansas voters had the issue under consideration in their fall election. If the ladies proved successful there, he presumed that Missouri women could not long be denied. He saw the movement as an outgrowth of the agitation over Negro suffrage and believed that the same principles were involved in both.[19]

The Women's Suffrage Association forwarded another petition to the legislature in 1868. To encourage support, several national leaders visited St. Louis. The organization continued to recruit adherents quietly and to plan its strategy. By the beginning of 1869 the movement seemed to be making much headway. Regular meetings, held twice each month, were well attended by both men and women. The St. Louis press gave full coverage to these gatherings while maintaining a somewhat neutral attitude editorially. Several prominent businessmen and political leaders gave the movement their support and encouragement.[20] Early in February the Association sent a delegation of ten women with the annual petition to Jefferson City in the hope of impressing the legislators with the earnestness of their appeal. Speaker Orrick and Lieutenant Governor Stanard met their train and showed the ladies every courtesy. The following morning the delegation called on Governor McClurg at the mansion and secured his signature on one of their petitions. An informal meeting of both houses convened that afternoon in the Hall of Representatives with the Speaker presiding. Miss Phoebe Couzins and Mrs. John S. Phelps, wife of the recent Democratic gubernatorial nominee, spoke for the women. They presented a strong plea for equal rights, and several members of the legislature followed with supporting speeches. The *Democrat's* correspondent at the capital gave a favorable assessment: "It is evident that the mission of the ladies has not been in vain. A serious attention was paid to all that was advanced, not as a matter of etiquette or show of gallantry to them alone, but as a matter of great moment and deep concern to the commonwealth."[21] Others did not look so benignly upon the delegates' mission. One member of the House asserted disparagingly that the women had "unsexed themselves by coming here with their demands." On the morning following the meeting the House tabled an equal suffrage resolution by a vote of 64 to 50 on the ground that it was premature, since the delegates' petition had not yet been formally presented. That afternoon friends of the movement held a caucus with the women, which representatives of both political parties attended. Strategy was laid; but, similar to other attempts to settle the suffrage question at this session of the legislature, the petition died aborning in committee.[22]

When the women returned from Jefferson City, they felt that they had made some progress. At the next meeting of the Association they reported that they had found more support in the Senate than in the House. Yet, much work still needed to be done. A petition to the St. Louis City Council met an unfavorable reception at the end of February. Meetings continued, with the press usually reporting average attendance. The vociferousness of the Association's leaders began to wear on William M. Grosvenor, who complained editorially in the *Democrat*: "Those who believe that the enfranchisement of women is desirable will wisely seek to convince the present voters of that position, by adopting a practical and sensible course. Unlimited orating to no practical purpose is not at all calculated to advance the object of the Association."[23] But the women had been doing more than just talking. That spring they had periodically held "working women's" meetings. In July, they organized the Working Women's Protective Association, its purpose being "to promote the general welfare of each other, by lending our assistance in obtaining employment and ample remuneration therefor." The group promised to be nonsectarian and nonpolitical in all matters not affecting the interests of women.[24]

The high point of the year's activities came in October when the annual national convention met at the Mercantile Library Hall in St. Louis. Susan B. Anthony and Julia Ward Howe headed the group of leaders present for the occasion, and several of the St. Louis women played prominent roles in the proceedings. Speech followed speech as the cause of equal rights received eloquent treatment at the hands of its advocates. As a climax to its deliberations the convention adopted resolutions framed by Mrs. Minor that expressed the revolutionary idea that in denying women the right to vote the states had violated the letter and spirit of the Constitution. Although the Constitution left voting qualifications to the individual states, Mrs. Minor contended that it did not give them the privilege to deny the elective franchise to any adult citizen.[25]

While the Democrats waited hopefully for a favorable decision in the Blair case and the women of St. Louis agitated for equal rights, the Radical press began debate over enfranchisement. When the legislature adjourned early in March without having taken any stand on removing the restrictions, Grosvenor admonished through the editorial columns of the *Missouri Democrat*: "Sooner or later that policy must prevail which seeks to remove the distinctions created by a state of war, and justified by the necessities of war. We can wait. How long the party can afford to wait is a matter for it to decide."[26] In a strong editorial on June 5, Grosvenor called for submission by the next session of the legislature of a dual amendment giving both Negroes and disfranchised whites the suffrage. Although some Radicals might favor continued proscription because they felt it was necessary to maintain party supremacy, the editor of the *Democrat* could see no statistical evidence for such precaution. Schurz gave editorial support to this proposal in the *Westliche Post*. In the middle of June Grosvenor claimed that his recommendations represented "the actual position of the Radical party today on the franchise question."[27] Drake quickly retorted in an open letter to the Radical party on June 21. Pontifical as always, he insisted, "I demand justice for the loyal Negro, without any complication with questions about the rebel." The *Missouri State Times* of Jefferson City asserted in mid-July that most out-state Radical papers supported Drake's position and produced numerous citations as evidence.[28] The debate continued, with a number of papers decrying the agitation and contending that the dispute served no good purpose pending the outcome of events elsewhere.[29]

The debate was still rampant when the General Assembly reconvened in January, 1870. Few had changed their minds. Governor McClurg evinced some disposition to find middle ground. In his annual message he declared: "There is no county in the State where organized resistance to the law exists, and where the sheriff cannot procure a posse to aid in the enforcement of the laws. The rights of person and property are as secure as in any State of the Union." In view of these conditions, McClurg implied that the time might not be far distant when the suffrage could be restored with safety to the disfranchised. He favored a thorough discussion of the question in the forthcoming election campaign and suggested that particular emphasis be placed on the constitutional provision that would allow the General Assembly to remove restrictions by a simple majority vote after January 1, 1871. Such action would avoid the necessity of submitting an amendment to the voters and might better preserve Radical harmony. Inasmuch as ratification of the Fifteenth Amendment had not yet been completed, the Governor urged the resubmission of a state proviso for Negro suffrage.[30]

Far from expressing any willingness to compromise on this seemingly moderate position, the more liberal element pushed ahead with its own program. When criticized by the *Missouri State Times* for its continued agitation of the issue, the *Missouri Democrat* declared that it would continue to express its own opinions while respecting those of others. It accused the *Times* of trying to stir up the outstate Radicals against their city brethren and repeated its assertion that submission of the entire franchise question in the form of amendments would be the best way to avoid a party rupture.[31]

The Radicals in the legislature caucused twice in January for a thorough discussion. A good spirit prevailed, with little or no acrimony. Speaker Orrick, generally considered the leader of the liberal cause, offered a resolution stating that expediency dictated the submission of an amendment enfranchising all adult males. He did not force the issue, however. The *Democrat's* correspondent at the capital reported that no policy seemed to be emerging and that a showdown would probably have to be forced on the floor of the legislature. In spite of this note of caution, Grosvenor remained editorially optimistic that the liberal policy would prevail.[32]

At this moment of impasse the two outside events that Missouri Radicals had been watching expectantly reached their culmination. The United States Supreme Court handed down its decision in the Blair case at the end of January. In a rare occurrence it divided evenly, 4 to 4, thereby affirming the decision of the Supreme Court of Missouri through lack of a majority against it. This outcome left Democrats despondent and Radicals with mixed feelings. Most of the Radicals saw the result as a justification for their postwar policy. The liberals considered it all the more imperative that what had once been a justifiable policy must now be ended by the group that had imposed it.[33] By February 7 the Fifteenth Amendment had been ratified by the requisite twenty-eight states to make it a part of the Constitution. With this hurdle passed and the Negro now entitled to vote, many Radicals became more receptive to the liberal proposals. Even Drake, in response to an inquiry, agreed to the submission of the disfranchisement question.[34]

The Radical caucus had assembled on February 2 with approximately three-fourths of the members present. Orrick resubmitted his resolution on enfranchisement. After a full and constructive debate the caucus approved it by a vote of 51 to 22. An analysis of the opposition reveals that most of it came from the border counties where Radical extremism still held its tenacious grip. Many of the twenty-six absentees shared the minority's opinion.[35] Grosvenor, rejoicing at this triumph of liberal principle, urged that the action of the caucus be taken as party policy. The liberals immediately introduced the resolution in the House and in the Senate. Although some

Democrats preferred to remain aloof from the proceedings, the more sagacious argued that they could not ignore a proposal for which they had been fighting so ardently in past sessions. The Democratic caucus consequently endorsed the resolution by unanimous vote on February 7. Most liberals were indifferent to this support; they believed that they had a sufficient majority without the help of the opposition. Although attempts were later made by some Democratic members to rescind the caucus action, these failed. On final passage most Democrats voted "aye."[36]

Approval of the proposals by the Senate came late in February, with only five negative votes. The House followed suit a few weeks later with large majorities. Most of the scattered opposition came from the staunchly Radical legislators from southwest Missouri. In their final form the proposals embodied three amendments: one would modify the constitutional provisions concerning the test oath for voting by eliminating the iron-clad features and substituting a simple declaration of support for state and national constitutions; the second would rescind the test oath for jurors, something that had seldom been practiced anyway; the third would repeal the test oath as a requirement for officeholding and for corporate or educational activity and would remove racial barriers to officeholding.[37]

Throughout the proceedings Grosvenor continued to assure his readers that the new policy would in no way endanger the hold of the Radical party upon the state. If the amendments passed, the disfranchised would not have their first opportunity to vote in a state-wide election until 1872. The liberal editor estimated that by then the Radical strength would stand at some 141,000 votes with augmentations from Negro suffrage and continued immigration. The Democrats would be able to muster only 83,700 votes, exclusive of the disfranchised. Grosvenor estimated the disfranchised at 25,000, which was undoubtedly a conservative count. He contended that many of them would not vote the Democratic ticket. As old animosities died out, new issues would arise to divide the people; under such circumstances no one could predict how the disfranchised would line up by 1872. The Radical party had just as good a chance of drawing their votes as the Democrats.[38]

Many Democrats expressed dissatisfaction with the liberal program because they feared it did not go far enough. Its failure to embrace drastic modification or the total elimination of the notorious registry system caused them to have qualms for the future.[39] During the previous fall some relief had appeared on the horizon when the Supreme Court of Missouri decided that registrars were liable in civil actions for their decisions. Abraham M. Pike had brought suit for damages against the registering officials of Ralls County because of their refusal to enroll him in 1868. The high tribunal sent the case back to the circuit court to be tried on its merits.[40] This decision opened the floodgates for similar litigation in other cases. Such an involved process, however, did nothing to upset the law itself.

Early in the legislative session the Democratic minority had introduced measures in both houses to modify the registry act primarily through administrative decentralization. The Assembly established a joint committee on registration to which it sent all such proposals. Here moderation prevailed. Early in March the committee reported a bill to the House that would change the existing law in some important particulars. Registrars would virtually be required to accept anyone who presented himself as willing to take the oath. Specifically, they could no longer exclude an applicant on their own knowledge or suspicion of disloyalty. Concrete evidence would have to be produced to justify a rejection, and even then it would be necessary to have a hearing before a properly constituted judicial body.[41] These provisions were too much for the Radical majority. Interestingly enough, even

Grosvenor rejected the idea of major changes in the registry act for fear that perjured "rebels" would be admitted to the rolls. The party caucus rejected the proposals and voted to back only those changes that seemed necessary: the authorization of Negro registration and a prohibition on registrars seeking elective offices.[42]

With the session nearly over, the Radicals rushed legislation through both houses that effected these minor modifications in the registry law. Democratic attempts for more drastic changes in the Senate were in vain.[43] The Missouri election of 1870 would be governed by the same notorious machinery that had controlled the last two for the Radicals. Grosvenor editorially approved with the wry comment:

> A change of the registry laws, just at this time, might possibly enable Democrats to give the result [election of 1870] the appearance of a Radical defeat. . . . It might put it in the power of Democrats to elect members of the next Legislature in undue number. We do not propose to run any such risk to give a beaten foe any such chance.[44]

He was to change his tune when the actual registration process got under way and when he found liberal partisans suffering discrimination with Democrats.[45]

This legislative action by the Radicals tended to confirm for several Democratic leaders a decision toward which they had been moving since January. They looked upon the statewide prospects of their party with increasing despair. In spite of strong efforts put forth in 1866 and 1868, the Conservatives and the Democrats had found themselves battering against a stone wall made impenetrable by the proscriptive policies of the ruling Radicals. It had been a demoralizing experience, and these Democratic leaders questioned the advisability of repeating the performance. Momentum began to build for the adoption of a program of "masterful inactivity" on the state

level in 1870. Its sponsors advocated that the Democrats refrain from putting up a state ticket and concentrate instead
on the election of local and congressional candidates. This
strategy became popularly known as the "possum policy."

Apparently, its original mover had been William Hyde, the
editor of the *Missouri Republican,* the party's chief newspaper in St. Louis. He received the full backing of the paper's
owners, John and George Knapp. Realizing the backlash that
could come from an uninformed rank and file, Hyde and his
associates began quietly sounding out state party leaders in
the hope of enlisting their adherence. Ere long they prevailed
on Aylett H. Buckner, state party chairman, to call a secret
meeting of his central committee in St. Louis to push the idea.
When this group convened late in January, the "possum"
advocates were prepared with resolutions, which they forced
through the meeting without debate. The skeptics acquiesced
but counseled that time and subtle planning would be needed
to convince the rank and file.[46] Shortly thereafter the *Republican* and other leading party journals began an adroit campaign to convince the Democratic faithful of the wisdom of
Hyde's policy. Typical was the comment of the *Peoples'
Weekly Tribune* at Jefferson City: "Unless the registration
laws are amended, so far as we are concerned, an election is
something worse than a disgraceful farce. Why, then, should
we engage in it, so long as the farce is played at our expense,
and for our chagrin and humiliation."[47]

The annual gathering of St. Louis Democrats on Washington's birthday drew only a meager attendance. Many outstate
leaders who normally attended stayed away. Significantly,
those present adopted a resolution that declared it inexpedient to hold a state party convention that summer.[48] The
state central committee used this action as a natural spring-
board for seeking the advice of the Democrats in the General
Assembly. Their response came quickly. Caucusing on March
18, less than a week after their futile last-ditch effort to water

down the registry act, the legislators supported the "possum policy" by advising against any activity on the state level that fall. At the same time, their debate, as reported in the partisan press, clearly indicated that they did not intend to be quiescent in local or legislative races. Of the two, it was the legislative offices that held the greater importance for the Democrats. Should the proposed amendments fail to pass in the fall election, the next General Assembly would still have the power to remove the restrictions under the constitution.[49]

Although the "possum" movement seemed to be making satisfactory progress, some prominent Democratic spokesmen doubted its wisdom. William F. Switzler questioned this "temporary surrender to the enemy" and warned: "It will encourage that faction to believe, we hope without good reason, that they can revel unrestrained and unopposed in wrongs and usurpations even more flagrant than those which have hitherto disgraced its reign."[50] Others, including the new state chairman, David H. Armstrong, denied the authority of either the legislative caucus or the state central committee to make the final decision. They contended that a state convention should be called for that purpose. Apparently, Armstrong won over Hyde and the others, for the *Missouri Republican* came out in favor of such a move in the middle of April.[51]

In view of these considerations, Armstrong called another special meeting of the state central committee at St. Louis for April 30. The general lethargy of the party leadership was revealed when only two of nine members appeared. Five others sent letters outlining their views, all of which indicated strong opposition to a convention. Those present quickly fell in line and issued a brief, informal statement to this effect.[52] As the summer months passed and Radical quarrels became more incessant, Democratic leaders came to have a profound appreciation for the wisdom of the possum policy. In the absence of a state Democratic ticket the Radicals had no one

to fight but themselves. If they should split, the Democrats
would be in a particularly enviable bargaining position.[53]

The Democratic state central committee issued its final communiqué in late July. Outlining the problems facing the party
and their possible solutions, the notice officially endorsed the
possum policy. Going one step further it foresaw no possibility of alliance with either faction of the Radical party
should that group split before the fall campaign. With regard
to local elections, each branch of the party was to decide its
own action, depending upon the immediate circumstances.
The committee did urge, however, that the major criterion
for the support of legislative candidates be their readiness to
vote for the removal of all restrictions if the issue should come
up in the next legislature.[54]

The Radical party of Missouri stood less than three weeks
from its convention when the Democrats officially adopted
the possum policy. Over the spring and summer the regular
and liberal wings of the party in power had been finding
more and more differences. Although both acknowledged the
wisdom of submitting the amendments, they did not agree on
whether the party should officially endorse them. Since many
of the rank and file, especially in the border areas, were
strongly opposed to the relaxation of restrictions, it seemed
to the regulars to be the better part of wisdom to let every
man vote his own conscience without concern for an official
policy. Grosvenor and the liberals, on the other hand, argued
that the party must commit itself to the passage of the amendments in order to fulfill its just obligation to remove what it
had initiated. For the regulars who feared that re-enfranchisement would open the doors to Democratic control by 1872,
Grosvenor produced reams of statistics to prove the contrary.
Yet, this did little to allay local fears where the end of proscription might mean loss of the courthouse.[55]

A second question that Grosvenor thrust into the campaign
was the problem of the tariff. Ardently committed to the

principle of a revenue tariff, he and Schurz maintained that protection increased the tax burden of the average citizen and bloated further the already extensive profits of the manufacturers. Few issues of the *Missouri Democrat* passed without an editorial on the tariff. Grosvenor debated the issue before the St. Louis Board of Trade and elsewhere. In his spare time he worked on a book embracing his ideas, which Schurz thought would be of great help to him in Congress where he was fighting the battle for reduction.[56] Most of the regular Radical leadership in Missouri, however, favored the protective principle. Some were rising entrepreneurs with vested economic interests at stake. Others supported it because such a platform tended to be the policy of the national party. Many wished to play it down as a political issue on the ground that it had more national than state importance.[57]

As factional battle lines became more clearly drawn in the weeks following the legislature's adjournment, various names began to be put forward as possibilities for the party's gubernatorial nominee. A list of potential candidates, all of whom had been mentioned by one or more Radical journals, appeared in the *Missouri Democrat* in the middle of March. Of this group, the paper looked most favorably upon either former Senator B. Gratz Brown or Lieutenant Governor Edwin O. Stanard as the best man to carry the liberal banner.[58] In the closing days of the legislative session the liberals had caucused informally. They drew up a tentative slate of candidates, which was headed by Brown for governor. When word of this leaked out, the regulars strongly condemned the action as an attempt at dictation by the Grosvenor element in St. Louis.[59]

Although refraining from any endorsement of a specific candidate, Grosvenor did begin a campaign in the middle of April against the renomination of Governor McClurg. In the eyes of the editor of the *Democrat*, McClurg's selection "would be absurd, because he is not competent to advocate the liberal policy, and could only make it ridiculous." Grosvenor continued to belabor this theme until the convention met four and one-half months later.[60] Other liberal papers joined the chorus. Much of the liberal opposition to McClurg was based on his general antipathy toward the amendments as a means of resolving the issue of re-enfranchisement. Having long been associated with the Drake regulars, he showed little inclination to move very far from dead center. McClurg supported protective tariffs, which was enough to make him anathema to Grosvenor even if he had no other faults. The Germans suspected him because he was a prohibitionist who refused to serve liquor at receptions in the Governor's Mansion; they feared he might attempt to broaden this type of proscription throughout the entire state or at least to rigidly control the liquor traffic. Beyond all this, leaders of all shades of political opinion saw McClurg as a mediocre figure with little real potential for dynamic leadership.[61]

B. Gratz Brown launched his campaign for the governorship with a Memorial Day speech at Jefferson City. In calling for reconciliation and an end to the spirit of animosity, he reminded his audience, "[An] insidious spirit of revenge is the surest and speediest road to a violent reaction." Grosvenor was full of praise for the speech and declared that it well suited the new mood of the people. Three weeks later the *Missouri Democrat* formally endorsed Brown's candidacy and again excoriated McClurg. By carefully tracing Brown's political background over the past two decades, Grosvenor had no difficulty in establishing him as a consistent liberal.[62] As a Free-Soil Democrat and one of the founders of the Missouri Republican party, Brown had long been in the forefront of the struggle for emancipation and Negro rights. He had been the guiding spirit of the Planters House conference of 1866, where he first proposed most of the liberal program. His enforced retirement since that time had been in part because of ill health, but it also reflected his serious disagreement with the regular wing of his party. He now took up the liberal cudgel once more in what he hoped would be a more favorable atmosphere.

The regular Radical press quickly came to McClurg's support and indicated its bitterness at what it considered Grosvenor's attempts to dictate to the party. When the Editors' and Publishers' Association of Missouri held its annual meeting at Kansas City, a number of Radical editors informally got together to discuss the forthcoming campaign and platform issues. They deliberately ignored the editor of the *Missouri Democrat,* who deeply resented being excluded. Although Grosvenor denied any intention of dictating to the party in regard to Brown or any particular issue, others viewed it differently. Many moderates began seeking a middle ground of compromise. They generally looked to Edwin O. Stanard as the candidate who could unite both factions. As lieutenant governor, he had co-operated with the liberals in the legislature; yet, as a manufacturer, he shared the regulars' views on the tariff and in general opposed agitation of that subject.[63]

In the midst of this rising turmoil, the Radical state executive committee met at St. Louis early in May to make plans for the party convention. By unanimous vote they selected Jefferson City as the site for the convention beginning August 31. Following precedent, they agreed that each county should be entitled to a delegate for every 150 votes or fractional part thereof cast for Grant in 1868. With the passage of the Fifteenth Amendment a new problem faced them in determining Negro representation. J. Milton Turner, probably the most ardent spokesman for the colored people, was present. He contended that the Negroes would vote as a bloc for the Radical ticket only if they were given a fair share in its selection. Accordingly, the committee decided that each county should be additionally represented by one delegate for every 150 male Negroes of voting age or fraction thereof. Although this system would provide the convention with more than 700 delegates, the *Missouri Democrat* professed satisfaction with it. Grosvenor declared: "The larger the convention, the more fully will the Radical masses be represented, and the less opportunity there will be for any clique or combination to thwart the will of the people."[64]

It soon became evident that not everyone agreed with the apportionment decision. Many on the committee, including the liberals, had considered that "fraction thereof" meant a minimum of 50 votes, as this had always been the arrangement in the past. The secretary of the state central committee interpreted the agreement literally, which meant that a county casting 151 votes for Grant in 1868 would have two delegates, as would a county casting 299 votes. Inequities became even more evident in view of the fact that many counties had an exceedingly small number of eligible Negro voters. In some instances, less than half a dozen colored men were on the census rolls; yet, that county would be entitled to one delegate, thereby equaling a county with 150 Negro voters. Particularly objectionable was the plan to keep the 1868 voting and the eligible Negro voter potential as separate entities rather than placing them together and apportioning representation on the total.[65]

In view of this new source of irritation, State Chairman E. W. Fox called another meeting of the state central committee to study the matter. Homer H. Winchell of Hannibal, who had made the original motion at the first meeting, wrote the *Missouri Democrat* that he had intended to keep the minimum requirement of 50 votes, although favoring separation of white and Negro representation. Grosvenor agreed that adoption of such an interpretation would make the system acceptable.[66] When the committee met on August 2, it quickly agreed on the fifty minimum formula for white voter representation. On the question of apportioning Negro delegates the committee was opposed by J. Milton Turner who demanded representation for the colored of each county regardless of whether they numbered fifty or not. In the end he prevailed, to the dismay of the liberals. Turner was close to Governor McClurg in his viewpoint and had already announced his opposition to the amendments. Supposedly, he could control the Negro delegates for the antiliberal program. Under the plan adopted, there would be 180 Negro delegates out of a total of 797. Almost half of these would come from counties with less than fifty eligible Negro voters. In a close convention contest the Negroes would hold the balance of power.[67] Thus another item joined the list of divisive elements threatening Radical harmony.

With the decision on apportionment reached, the struggle turned to the county conventions where the delegates would be chosen and instructed. These meetings were held over a two-week period during the middle of August, with bitter acrimony arising in many instances. Results varied. Both sides made the usual claims regarding delegate strength. There appeared to be more interest in the gubernatorial nominees than in the amendments. Grosvenor claimed that Brown and McClurg stood even with about three hundred delegates each. His analysis pictured two hundred delegates holding the balance. Some had been committed to Stanard or other candidates. A more impartial source saw McClurg with nearly two-thirds of the delegates in his favor. At best, the liberals might force a deadlock and hope for agreement on a compromise candidate.[68]

As the preconvention campaign neared its end, the regulars leveled a barrage of accusations at Brown. Depicting him as a disruptive force, they held that he would bolt the party if he failed to get his own way at the convention. The *Missouri Republican* informed its readers, on supposedly good authority, that the liberals would be satisfied with no one but Brown. Should he fail to receive the Radical nomination, he would undoubtedly head an independent liberal ticket.[69] Liberal leaders remained noncommittal, but with the bitterness that any contest of personalities engenders, the possibility of compromise appeared increasingly difficult. Moderates hoped for conciliation through some backstage meeting of responsible leaders, yet no one could be sure what would happen. Under the circumstances, delegates and observers flocked into Jefferson City in unprecedented numbers at the end of August in anticipation of the most crucial convention in the short history of the party.

State Chairman E. W. Fox opened the sessions in this tense atmosphere with a defense of the state central committee and a plea for party unity. Jockeying for position quickly got under way with the election of a temporary chairman. The liberals backed moderate John F. Benjamin of Shelby County, who won a close contest over regular A. J. Harlan of Andrew County. They suffered their first setback that afternoon when a motion by former Governor Fletcher to revamp the basis of representation in their favor met violent opposition and was defeated by a vote of 539 to 242. Still, at the end of the day Grosvenor optimistically reported, "All looks lovely for the nomination of B. Gratz Brown."[70]

The following morning the liberals renewed their attack on the system for apportioning delegates with a resolution condemning the method used by the state central committee. They coupled to this proposal another that sought to bind the convention and its nominees to support publicly the amendments. Heated debate followed before the sponsor withdrew both of the proposals. Almost immediately, liberal Congressman David P. Dyer of Pike County put forth a unique new scheme for redetermining representation. This system would allow each county to cast as many votes as the combined total of its vote for Grant in 1868 and its population of adult male Negroes. Fully aware that such an arrangement would throw the control of the convention from the rural border areas to populous St. Louis and her allies, the regulars attacked it bitterly. The liberals, in turn, gave heated replies. Finally, a motion to table the proposal carried by a vote of 416½ to 366½. Cheers went through the ranks of the regulars, while dark scowls flitted across the faces of the liberals. Apparently, some of the latter thought that the time had come to bolt. Schurz and others held back, pending the final disposition of the report of the resolutions committee. Just before adjournment the convention agreed that the report of this group would be the first order of business the next day. Grosvenor found less cause for optimism in his dispatch that evening; but, in spite of all the setbacks suffered by the liberals, he closed on a cautiously hopeful note, "Our faith, however, is still strong in Brown's success."[71]

In the intervening period before the next day's sessions some of the moderate delegates tried to effect a compromise that would save the party. They first held a caucus of the regulars in the hope of securing some kind of agreement on re-enfranchisement. This group, dominated largely by Mc-Clurg men, enthusiastically agreed to a platform so liberal that a bolt by the Brown men would have no adequate base. This, however, marked the extent of their willingness to sacrifice for harmony. Few showed any inclination to abandon McClurg, who, if anything, had become a symbol of regular intransigence.[72] A conference of party leaders from all factions followed in an attempt to reach a definite agreement. McClurg's representatives announced their willingness to support the so-called Carroll County resolutions that went far toward meeting the liberal demands for the platform, but the Brown men balked. The resolutions committee, with Schurz as chairman, was meeting at the same moment. Because this group contained a liberal majority, Grosvenor confidently believed it would report a liberal platform. He and Schurz would brook no compromise; if necessary, the liberals would present a minority stand.

Failing to reach an agreement on the platform, the leaders

discussed a compromise gubernatorial nominee. The moderates proposed Benjamin, a former congressman with liberal leanings. The other state offices could be equally divided between the two factions. To appease the liberals, the moderates even expressed a willingness to accept a specific platform endorsement of the amendments. This proposition was too great a sacrifice for the regulars; convinced that they had enough votes to nominate their candidate the following day, they now stood firmly behind McClurg, though willing to compromise on the platform. The Brown men, on the other hand, supported only their version of the platform, but were ready to abandon their candidate for a moderate. So compromise failed. The conferees returned to their rooms to catch a few hours of sleep before the explosive final day of the convention.[73]

The third day of deliberations opened in an atmosphere of hostility and distrust. The regulars immediately made their move by introducing a resolution that would bind the delegates and the party nominees to support the platform about to be adopted. This proposal aroused mixed feelings among the liberals, but were mitigated by Schurz's motion, which carried, to refer it without debate to the resolutions committee. Schurz then rose to report for his nine-man resolutions committee. They stood in unanimous agreement on all planks of the platform except the one concerning re-enfranchisement. On this issue three reports were submitted. The majority resolution, endorsed by Schurz and four others, declared:

> That the Republican party stands pledged to remove all disqualifications and restrictions imposed upon the late rebels in the same measure as the spirit of disloyalty may die out and as may be consistent with the safety of a loyal people; that we consider the time to have come, and we cordially indorse the action of the legislature of Missouri in submitting to the qualified voters of the State the amendments removing all disqualifi-

cations from the disfranchised people of Missouri and conferring equal political rights on all classes, and we earnestly recommend them to the people for their approval and adoption.

Harrison E. Havens, veteran regular from Springfield, presented the minority report. It reflected the opinions expressed at many county conventions and by several party leaders over the past few months:

> That we are in favor of re-enfranchising those justly disfranchised for participating in the late rebellion, as soon as it can be done with safety to the State; and that we concur in the propriety of the legislature having submitted to the whole people of the State the question whether such time has now arrived, upon which question we recognize the right of any member of the party to vote his honest convictions.

One other member submitted his own statement that sought to evade the issue and preserve harmony through deliberate vagueness, but he received no consideration or support.

The debate now centered on which of the first two reports to accept and opened with Schurz boldly challenging his opponents. In unequivocal terms, he declared:

> We are resolved to have that which is declared in this platform and nothing else. . . . Some such platform will go before the people of this State at the next election, and a candidate will go before the people for their suffrages who does not by his known opinions, by his associations, and by his record give the lie to that which is declared in the platform upon which he is nominated.

Havens quickly took up the challenge. Strongly opposed to the amendments himself, he warned that there were thousands like himself in the Radical ranks. They should not be pushed too far by the liberals if the party was to hope for any success that fall.

After this exchange the convention agreed to allow each faction to present five speakers for ten minutes each. None of them put forward any new arguments. At last the voting began. As the liberal leaders huddled around Schurz on the convention floor, William McKee, owner of the *Missouri Democrat*, kept a watchful eye on the proceedings from the lobby. He, as much as anyone, was responsible for the adamant stand of the liberals on both platform and candidate. His viewpoint was actuated far less by the honorable motivations of Schurz and Grosvenor than by disappointment over failure to receive a sinecure for his brother from Grant's administration.[74] Of such strange bedfellows are all movements made.

With the tallies completed, the clerks announced that the convention had adopted the minority resolution by almost a 100-vote margin. Most of the opposition had come from St. Louis and the river counties with their strong German influence. The moment had arrived! All eyes turned to the liberal leaders, who reacted quickly. General John McNeil jumped to his feet and announced: "I desire to say to the friends of the majority report . . . and to the friends of enfranchisement to the white man, that they will withdraw from this convention to the Senate chamber." He then turned and strode from the Hall of Representatives with some eighty other delegates from thirty-five counties following closely behind him.[75]

The liberals now resolved themselves into another convention. A number of bogus delegations that had not been a part of the regular convention joined the proceedings. The combined forces elected McNeil temporary chairman before adjourning until afternoon. The regulars also adjourned until later.[76]

Fully anticipating the ultimate break in the Radical ranks, St. Louis newspapers had sent two sets of reporters to Jefferson City and a double relay of telegraph operators to handle the emergency. Thus, continued coverage of both meetings was possible.[77]

During the adjournments the Stanard moderates sought to effect a last-minute compromise based on their man's candidacy. Although they made little headway, they did not give up. As soon as the regulars reconvened, they proposed the selection of a conference committee to effect a reconciliation with the bolters. After considerable debate the McClurg men managed to defeat the motion by a vote of 365 to 342. The die was cast! Some one hundred Stanard men now withdrew to join the liberals across the way. An "enthusiastic and exciting scene" took place as the Lieutenant Governor led his followers into the Senate chamber. Stanard explained their coming in an indignant tone: "We have worked with a determination to create harmony, but we have failed; there was a party of men who had such a greed for office, such a determination to have the spoils, that they would not listen to reason."[78]

With Schurz now presiding as permanent chairman, the liberals moved to select candidates and adopt a platform. Brown received the gubernatorial nomination by a unanimous vote, and the other places on the ticket were generally allocated according to geographic consideration. Grosvenor reported a platform that included all of his cherished ideas: re-enfranchisement, a revenue tariff, civil service reform, tax reduction, and opposition to the alienation of government land to private corporations.[79] To climax the proceedings, Brown accepted his nomination with a ringing speech in which he denounced the regulars for their shortsighted obstinance and condemned their methods of trying to secure the support of the Negroes. He concluded with a strong positive statement of the liberal position. As the session drew to a close, someone spotted James S. Rollins among the spectators. The Democratic leader was promptly "called out by the crowd." In a gesture indicative of what was to come, Rollins pledged his support to the Brown ticket. He further predicted that many who had "hitherto acted with him in politics" would follow the same course.[80]

In the meantime, the regulars, unhampered by the liberal dissenters, quickly renominated McClurg and approved a platform whose plank on re-enfranchisement repeated the vague statement of 1868. Ignoring the bolters, the regulars pledged a continuation of the present programs, which they claimed had brought Missouri unprecedented growth and prosperity during the past five years. They included within their platform a complimentary endorsement of Grant's administration, which the liberals deliberately omitted from theirs.[81]

And so the various elements of the Radical party came to a parting of the ways. From the very beginning their union had been tenuous. They had bickered among themselves since the constitutional convention of 1865 about the dimensions of the new order they wished to impose upon Missouri. At first, unable to find a strong leader to cope with the magic of Charles D. Drake, the moderates had contented themselves with being a vocal minority within the party and had been able to secure a fair share of spoils because of their affinity to Governor Fletcher. With the coming of Carl Schurz they had found a spokesman with broad appeal and political shrewdness. Drake's failure to modernize his image and his personal panic and ineptness before Schurz's challenge in 1869 had opened the door to the moderates' hopes for a more forward-looking party policy under their control. The breakdown of Drake's power, however, made both wings of the party increasingly adamant against compromise, fearing that any concession might result in a diminution of their own political influence. In their refusal to negotiate a settlement they destroyed the Radical party. The campaign of 1870 between these warring antagonists was to be crucial to the future of

Missouri. The possum policy of the Democrats seemed to be paying off; the next eight weeks would reveal whether they could bring it to a successful finish.

CHAPTER XII

THE END OF THE RADICAL ERA

SINCE THERE were only two months before the election, both the Radicals and the Liberals had to move quickly to complete their plans of strategy and begin their campaigns. Grosvenor, who became the Liberals' state chairman, called for a thorough organization. He issued stern marching orders: "Republicans! . . . Waste no time in personal issues with the Proscriptives. Let them abuse you as much as they like. Present your principles to the people with the calmness, kindness and sure confidence of men who know that truth will conquer."[1] On September 10, Schurz, Stanard, Orrick, and two other legislators issued a manifesto outlining the action taken by the Liberals and explaining the reasons for it. Schurz and Brown had formally launched the Liberal campaign the previous day at a St. Louis rally, where they portrayed the significance of their cause and defended their actions in bolting the regular party. From there they quickly hit the campaign trail and were joined by other Liberal spokesmen in the days that followed. During the next six weeks they visited every corner of the state, with large demonstrative crowds flocking to every rally.[2]

The Radicals seemed confused in the beginning. As the full implication of their dilemma dawned upon them during the first few weeks after the the conventions, they began to fumble for the right formula. With a good record of economic and social progress they still could not come to grips with its presentation to the people. Into this climate of uncertainty stepped Charles D. Drake. Returning from Washington in the middle of September, he assumed more-or-less active control of the Radical campaign. He was determined to use every means available in this desperate struggle for the retention of the power of his party. Soon stumping the state with his old vituperativeness, he charged that the Liberals, in bolting the party, had sold their souls to the "rebels" in return for support in future elections. It marked but the beginning, as he saw it, of an amalgamation with the Democrats in a move to control the next presidential election. Hitting hard at the revenue tariff stand taken by Grosvenor and Schurz, Drake asserted: "General Schurz is a German, perhaps he might not be expected to have quite as warm sympathies for the industries of America as for the industries of his Fatherland." As for the amendments, Drake refused to be committed to their support; each voter must decide for himself what to do about them. When Schurz challenged Drake to open debate in St. Louis, Drake refused on the ground that he was too busy outstate. Grosvenor praised Drake's "good judgment" in thus avoiding his previous detractor and commented, "A burnt child dreads the fire." Schurz finally caught up with the elusive Radical leader at Rolla on October 31, but their debate proved largely indecisive, as Drake steered clear of the personality clash that had hurt him at their previous meeting.[3]

Both groups went after the votes of the newly enfranchised

Negroes. The Fifteenth Amendment had been ratified just in time to allow the colored men to vote in the municipal spring elections. Great rejoicing had occurred among the Negro population. In many of the larger towns they had marked the event with parades and celebrations. Some twenty thousand Negroes turned out for a grand jubilee in St. Louis. A two-mile-long procession with four thousand men in the ranks wound through the city's streets to Yeager's Garden for festivities and speech-making. Two young ladies presided as the Goddess of Liberty and the Queen of Honor. J. Milton Turner delivered the principal address and exhorted his audience to use their new privilege wisely, which for him meant voting the Radical ticket.[4] Other Negroes also expressed concern over the use that might be made of the new gift by their fellows. James D. Bowser of Kansas City wrote Frederick Douglass' *New Era*, a national Negro weekly, that not all of the colored men were reliable in terms of voting for their best interests. Democrats had been active with food and drink to woo the colored voters, and many of the Negroes were in danger of succumbing. Bowser pleaded with the *New Era* to help inform the Negro of the issues before the spring election took place.[5]

Negroes in Morgan County had their first opportunity to vote at a railroad election early in March. The issue involved granting aid to a projected line, to which the conservative property owners were opposed. Democratic leaders tried to persuade the Negroes that a railroad would bring in Irish laborers who would take their jobs away from them, but a Radical meeting at the courthouse the night before the election persuaded them of the economic importance of the road. The Negroes helped to carry the issue, and Democratic wrath was unabated.[6]

That fall, Negro speakers appeared at practically every rally and urged their people to support one or another of the candidates. In gaining the support of the Negroes, the Radicals were far more successful than their opponents. J. Milton Turner served as their chief spokesman. Having toured the state extensively on behalf of Lincoln Institute and Negro suffrage, he was a well-known figure among Missouri's colored population and commanded their trust. Now that his people had secured the right to vote, Turner opposed re-enfranchisement for the "rebel" whites, which earned him the enmity of the Liberals. Having been a dominant figure in the councils of the Radical state central committee in the pre-convention planning, he now assured McClurg and other Radical leaders that he could deliver the Negro vote almost intact. Hitting the campaign trail, he worked diligently in attempting to fulfill his promise.[7]

While most Negroes followed Turner in supporting the Radical ticket, many questioned his stand on re-enfranchisement. Bowser again wrote Douglass and sought his advice. The great Negro leader replied in the columns of his paper that the colored men of Missouri should support the amendments. "This is not less the dictate of sound political wisdom than of genuine magnanimity." He pointed out that the disfranchised class was less dangerous with than without the ballot, especially if the Democrats could trace defeat to the Negro voters. At the same time Douglass advised Negro support of the Radical ticket. "In that party the colored voter is a power," he reminded his readers. "There is no safety outside the ship."[8] C. H. Tandy and George B. Wedley, both of St. Louis, were Turner's counterparts in the Liberal ranks. They decried his opposition to the amendments as an attempt to rouse needless antagonisms between the races and called for harmony through an acceptance of re-enfranchisement. Disputing Turner's claim that he had the Negro vote sewed up for McClurg, they also toured the state in an effort to enlist their people behind Brown.[9]

The Democrats in Clay County seemingly worked out the most persuasive program for securing the Negro vote for the

Brown ticket. They entertained the colored people at the courthouse every night for a week before the election with speeches, refreshments, and dancing. From a meager attendance the first two nights the crowds grew until most of the Negroes of Clay County were to be found at the outings. The Democratic orators informed their hearers that McClurg's administration planned a levy of fifty dollars on each Negro over eighteen years of age if its officials were returned to office and that failure to pay would bring a two-year prison term. In such an underhanded way they deceived the Negroes to their side and carried the county.[10] The Clay County success, however, proved the exception. Most Missouri Negroes stayed with Turner and the Radicals to the end.[11]

One of the major questions facing the separate wings of the Republican party was their attitude toward the Democracy. Both sides accused the other of plotting for Democratic support. According to Drake, the Liberals had schemed with Democratic leaders long before the Radical convention. Within two weeks after the momentous split, Grosvenor was talking of a Radical sellout to the Democrats. Consultations had taken place, Grosvenor contended, between the Radical and the Democratic leaders, at which time McClurg had agreed to announce support for the amendments in return for Democratic endorsement. If the amendments failed, he was to sign an enfranchisement bill from the next legislature. It was also thought that arrangements had been made for splitting the legislative and congressional tickets yet to be nominated.[12]

In reality, there is no evidence of any direct collusion by the Democrats with either of the rival groups. Democratic leaders and the rank and file of the party came quickly to see that the principles of the Liberals embraced much of what they had been fighting for over the past few years. The smoldering animosity between Democrats and Radicals that had grown up in the postwar era could not be overcome by the regular Republicans no matter how much shifting they did.[13] Democrat William Hyde formally announced support of the Brown ticket in the *Missouri Republican* on September 29. Other Democratic leaders, such as Rollins, Broadhead, Phelps, and Glover, had already written letters to the same effect. None of these endorsements had the sanction of official party policy; indeed, they were considered to be only a matter of expediency. The Democrats realized that the Liberals constituted a minority group that would need support to accomplish its program. William F. Switzler and others, however, indicated clearly that Democratic aid would be temporary. "The Democratic party does not think at all of abdicating," Switzler wrote at the end of September. "It hopes, on the contrary, to welcome the Liberals into its own camp in 1872."[14] Democrats agreed to support Liberal candidates for Congress in the Second, Fourth, Seventh, and Eighth districts, while the Liberals backed the Democratic nominee in the Sixth. All such arrangements were local, and no attempt was made to work out a state-wide pattern. In areas where either party thought it had a chance to elect its own candidate it did not hesitate to enter into competition with the other as well as with the Radicals. This situation was particularly true of the legislative contests; here the Democrats saw their real opportunity to seize power for the future.[15]

This bargaining between the Democrats and the Liberals did not mean that the Radicals wrote off any hope of Democratic support. As more and more Democratic leaders endorsed the Brown ticket, the McClurg men fully realized the danger. In an attempt to attract some Democratic votes they now reversed themselves in several important ways. Governor McClurg made it known through a series of letters to superintendents of registration and to the Radicals' state chairman that he favored a liberal interpretation of the registry law. Any man who presented himself as a qualified voter should be registered unless the registrar had direct and open evidence to the contrary.[16] Realizing that their position regarding the amendments was probably the crucial factor alienating Democratic support, McClurg and other Radical leaders announced that they personally favored re-enfranchisement, although they could not commit their party. Grosvenor denounced this about-face as a false front on the part of "those bread-and-butter heroes who follow McClurg solely for office or the control of office." Nevertheless, McClurg formally endorsed the amendments near the close of the campaign. Even J. Milton Turner began to urge his Negro followers to vote "yes" for re-enfranchisement.[17]

During the week before the election, M. A. Rosenblatt, secretary of the Radical state central committee, issued a confidential circular to county committees and "all true Republicans." It asked that all other interests be subjugated to McClurg's re-election. Local Democratic candidates should be supported if the Democrats would in turn swing behind the Governor. To accomplish this end, Rosenblatt suggested printing ballots with McClurg's name at the top followed by the local Democratic ticket. When one of these circulars fell into the hands of the Liberal press, Rosenblatt denied that he had acted in an official capacity. The final returns were to indicate that this policy, even if tried, met with little success.[18]

The registration process got under way in September. Democrats expressed general amazement at the liberal policy of most of the registrars. McClurg's letter of September 15 to the Radicals' state chairman explained this new attitude in part. But in some local instances the old tactics remained. A notable case occurred in Ralls County in northeast Missouri, where Grosvenor complained of heavy proscription against Democrats, Brown men, and Negroes. This particular incident of severity concerned Thomas R. Dodge, editor of the local *Ralls County Record* and a Union veteran of three and one-half years of service. Dodge had been proscribed in 1868 and now found himself rejected again. This time he decided to take action. In the preceding year Congress had passed the Enforcement Act that provided for interference by federal commissioners in state elections in order to assure Negroes their voting rights. The law was broadly worded, however, and Dodge brought suit against the registrars on the ground that they had willfully and illegally deprived him of his right to vote even though he had offered to take the oath. The registrars were arrested and brought before a commissioner for hearing. They gave Dodge's rejection in 1868 as the reason for their action. In view of his good service record with the Union army, this line of argument was an ineffective defense. The commissioner ordered that Dodge was to be registered, but took no further action. The knowledge of this new weapon in Democratic hands probably kept other registrars from being too partisan.[19]

When the final registration figures were released, it became clear that proscription had been much less rigorous than on previous occasions. Officially, 199,297 voters had registered, as compared with 154,080 in 1868. New Negro voters accounted for 18,000 to 20,000 of this increase. The continuing flow of immigrants also contributed. A notable difference in the figures appeared in Democratic counties where the registrars had been unduly severe in previous contests. For instance, the three counties of Boone, Callaway, and Audrain in the heart of "Little Dixie" showed a striking increase of 4,000 registrants over 1868.[20] It was soon to become apparent that a considerable number of the voters of 1868 did not register. Throughout the final three weeks of the campaign the *Missouri Democrat* constantly complained of the lackadaisical attitude of many potential voters, particularly in the St. Louis area. It urged those eligible to make every effort to register. Final figures for St. Louis County showed 30,671 registered voters on the books, 2,395 of whom were colored and 1,500 new registrants. The *Democrat* calculated that this indicated a loss of almost 3,000 voters who had registered in 1868 but failed to do so in 1870.[21]

As the Radicals began to weigh seriously the difficulties facing them in the campaign, they determined to employ every trick they knew in their efforts to win. Their ultimate weapon was a policy of reprisal against recalcitrant Republican officeholders through a broad use of the federal and state patronage. Securing the attention of President Grant, Drake persuaded him that the bolt in Missouri was the beginning of a general rebellion against the administration and that it must be stamped out immediately. To remove this threat, Grant gave the Senator complete control over the Missouri patronage. Heads soon began to roll. Those federal officeholders who had indicated support of Brown found themselves removed from their posts, and faithful Radical partisans took their places. In a letter to the Collector of Internal Revenue at St. Louis, the President emphasized his displeasure with the Liberals and implied that he expected all federal officials in the state to support the regular ticket inasmuch as the Liberals had betrayed the party.[22]

At the same time Governor McClurg moved to purge the ranks of the state employees. A notice from the Radical state central committee went out to all state, district, and county officials at the beginning of the campaign, directing them to contribute the equivalent of 5 per cent of their annual salaries to the party's war chest. Those who failed to respond promptly found themselves out of their jobs. In the heart of the enemy's country McClurg removed three Liberal members of the St. Louis police board on the basis of the secret information that they had offered protection to certain gambling houses. The *Missouri Democrat* denounced the move for its obvious political implications and claimed that the charges had already been disproved by a board of inquiry.[23] To climax this policy, a "confidential and important" communiqué went out of the Radical state headquarters on Oc-

tober 24, which asserted that the state committee had "great
and imperative needs for funds." To relieve this condition,
it had been agreed in consultation with "our friends at Washington" that an assessment of 1 per cent would be levied on
the gross receipts of all federal offices. These funds were
payable "without delay." The notice concluded ominously:
"The exigencies are great, and delay or neglect will rightly
be construed into unfriendliness to the Administration."[24]

Undoubtedly, this policy backfired on the Radicals in terms
of votes, for Missourians naturally resented this heavy-handed
outside interference. The Liberals denounced it vehemently
and asserted that it pointed up the need for civil service reform as advocated in their platform. Grosvenor noted with
pleasure near the end of the campaign that Hyde and the
Missouri Republican were saying that Grant's interference
made it absolutely necessary for honest Democrats to support
Brown.[25]

Election day passed without any major disturbance. Better
than 160,000 voters went to the polls. By overwhelming majorities they approved all of the amendments—an indication of
their desire to forget the past and proceed with the work of
building a strong Missouri for the future. "The fetters which
were forged in 1865 by the DRAKE Convention have fallen
from the wrists of seventy-five thousand white men, and the
ballot is free," exulted William F. Switzler. "Infamous registry laws, odious test oaths, and venal and villainous registry
officers will be known to our State no more forever."[26] Although exaggerating the number of re-enfranchised, Switzler
did reflect the general rejoicing of Democrats long "held in
bondage." His newspaper reported jubilee celebrations across
the state as the disfranchised regained the suffrage.[27]

The entire Liberal ticket swept to a smashing victory. B.
Gratz Brown swamped McClurg by 40,000 votes. In St. Louis
he had a 13,000-vote margin. He also made a strong showing
outstate, carrying seventy-eight counties to McClurg's thirty-

six. The Governor's vote came largely from the border areas, which remained true to the Radical cause to the bitter end. The Springfield *Missouri Weekly Patriot* claimed that bad weather had held down the Radical vote in the southwest, but this made little difference in the total figures. The Democrats, with considerable justification, contended that the victory of Brown was largely attributable to their support.[28]

The Democrats also triumphed in the elections. They won four of the five congressional races in which they had candidates. In three of these the Democratic nominee outpolled the total vote cast for both of his Republican rivals. In the four districts where the Democrats did not have a candidate, the Liberals and the Radicals came off with an even split. Radical Samuel S. Burdett carried the remaining district over his two opponents.[29] Most Democrats were more concerned with the results in the legislative contests than in the congressional races. In the lower house they carried 77 of the 138 seats, while the Radicals secured only 27 seats and the Liberals 21. In many counties the Liberals had failed to nominate an independent ticket and threw their strength to the Democratic slate. Thirteen seats went to fusion candidates who could be counted on to generally support any liberal policy the others agreed upon. One of the more prominent members of the House to fall by the wayside was Speaker John C. Orrick of St. Charles. A prominent Liberal, he apparently fell victim to the hostility of his German constituency toward his somewhat prominent advocacy of female suffrage. In the Senate races, 6 Democrats and 6 Liberals secured election, with 3 seats going to fusionists and 2 to the Radicals. Holdover senators numbered 10 Radicals and 7 Democrats.[30] The Democrats thus held an absolute majority in the House and could control the Senate through coalition with the Liberals and fusionists. The Democracy also fared well in the local elections. Nearly three-fourths of the new county officers were acknowledged Democrats, which augured well for the political rebuilding of the party.[31]

A great deal of national interest had centered on the Missouri election. The prominence of Schurz in the Republican party had been enhanced during his two years in the Senate. His leadership in bolting the regular organization raised many questions in the minds of his friends and the party leaders, particularly when President Grant raised his hand in support of Drake's group. To Senator Matthew H. Carpenter of Wisconsin, Schurz explained:

> You do not seem to be aware that Grant has read me out of the Republican party and is vigorously at work chopping off the official heads of those who are suspected of sympathizing with me. . . . Had not Grant given himself in Drake's keeping and interfered in our affairs, we "bolters" would have swept almost the whole Republican party with us. . . . Oh, there is much wisdom in high places.[32]

Henry Adams wrote Schurz on October 28 and asked him to prepare an article on political conditions in Missouri and the West for the *North American Review*. "I do this," Adams confided, "not because I am an editor, but because I would like to support your course, and make known to the eastern people the true nature of the contest you are engaged in."[33]

Schurz chose to make his explanation in Washington on the Senate floor. On December 15, 1870, in connection with his resolution calling for the removal of all national restrictions on "persons lately in rebellion," he proceeded to give a detailed analysis of the campaign in Missouri and his hopes for the future in view of the Liberal victory. Explaining his move from support of disfranchisement after the war to the removal of restrictions now, Schurz declared: "It has always been my opinion that, although the new order of things had to be established under a pressure of force and restriction, other agencies than a continued protection by force and restriction—a system uncongenial to our principles of government—had to be relied upon for its development and perpetuation." Since there was little reason remaining for disfranchisement in Missouri, he elucidated the position of those Republicans "who were not willing to sacrifice every consideration of honor and decency to party advantage." Schurz then attacked the Radical organization in Missouri and pictured the battle just won as a struggle of "inveterate prejudice and unscrupulous greed for office arrayed against fidelity to sacred pledges and sound statesmanship." Looking to the future, he sought to answer questions raised by many as a result of the Missouri campaign: "Is Schurz walking into the arms of the Democrats? Does he want a new party?" Denying that he wished to unite with the Democrats, the fiery German asserted the need for a new political party. He maintained that this could be the Republican party if it would concern itself less with spoils and more with principles. To the accomplishment of that end he pledged himself and his fellow Liberals.[34]

Events were moving forward in Missouri that were to somewhat diminish Schurz's hope. Democratic leaders saw no need for a new party of principle, especially if it was to be called Republican. Whether Schurz and the Liberals realized it or not, the triumph of Brown in 1870 was largely a Democratic victory, and the Democrats intended to treat it as such. Switzler observed:

> This bolt is planned on the verdant expectation that the Democratic party will join it and make it a majority! Or as a recent telegram [from Schurz] expresses it, that the Republican bolters will furnish the candidates and the Democratic party the voters! But the Democrats feel no such dissatisfaction with their party as leads many Republicans to seek new political connections.[35]

On the evening of November 14 the Democrats of St. Louis serenaded Governor-elect Brown, as the Liberals had not yet gotten around to it. Led by State Chairman David H. Armstrong, the party faithful turned out in large numbers. In his introductory remarks Armstrong extolled Democratic virtues. Brown then responded by praising the Democrats for their diligence to newly found principles. With regard to their role in his victory, he spoke quite candidly: "I can say to you, frankly, my fellow-citizens, that I am the last man in this nation to disregard the obligations under which I stand, and that in this election I recognize that my obligations are in the largest measure due to the Democratic party of the State of Missouri."[36]

Schurz expressed dismay at these remarks. He wrote Grosvenor from Washington: "Here they quite generally put him down as having gone over to the Democrats—in consequence of his first serenade speech." Brown denied the charge and agreed to attempt to redress the damage through another such talk "to our Republican friends." A serenade was quickly arranged for the evening of November 29. In spite of inclement weather, a large group of Liberals turned out to hear the Governor-elect praise them for the singleness of their devotion to the principles that had triumphed in the recent election.[37]

While the Liberals concerned themselves with principles, the Radicals continued to press for spoils. Removals from federal offices did not cease with the election; instead, many from the ranks of the discredited Radical party sought increased intervention by the administration to assure them some position in the future. Postmasters and other federal agents who had sympathized with the Liberal movement and had managed to avoid the first onslaught now found themselves required to surrender their offices to the Radical stalwarts. The scramble for office extended to the upper ranks of the party as well. As a reward for his services in bringing the Negro vote into the Radical fold, J. Milton Turner received appointment as Minister Resident and Consul General to Liberia, thereby becoming the first Negro to enter the diplomatic corps.[38]

On December 8 Grosvenor wrote disparagingly: "It is still reported that the President means to pension his faithful servant, Mr. Drake, by giving him a place for life as one of the Judges of the Court of Claims."[39] The wheels to effect this appointment had long since been set in motion. When Chief Justice Casey had resigned at the beginning of November, rumors immediately spread around Washington that Grant would appoint Drake to the post. Some doubt arose after the Democratic triumph in the Missouri legislative election; if Drake should resign his Senate seat, a member of the opposition party would likely replace him. Yet, that election made it all the more imperative to the Senator that he secure the judgeship. On November 18 he was closeted with the President for two hours, and that evening he dined at the White House. Apparently, the conference clinched the appointment. Shortly after Congress reconvened at the beginning of December, Grant sent Drake's appointment to the Senate, which quickly confirmed it.[40]

Only one task remained to the "father" of Missouri Radicalism before he took his leave of the Senate. On December 16 Drake took the Senate floor to reply to Carl Schurz's remarks on the Liberal movement. He gave a lengthy defense of the course of the Radical party in Missouri, from its inception to the present. Casting aside attempts of Schurz to interrupt, Drake pressed home his charges of betrayal by the Liberals, which had resulted in what he saw as a Democratic triumph. He recalled his father's words about those "who of old would rend the oak, but dreamed not of the rebound." So would it be with the Liberals, he prophesied accurately. Drake's last presentation was a forceful performance that drew involuntary applause from the Senate floor and galleries.[41]

The resignation of Drake increased the excitement and

speculation of the Democrats as they looked forward to the convening of the new General Assembly. Since the election their leaders and press had been hard at work formulating a party program for the coming session, where they would dominate proceedings for the first time in ten years. Party thinking primarily centered on two issues: the desire for a new constitutional convention to revise drastically the hated document of 1865 and the demand for the complete repeal, or at least drastic alteration, of the equally despised registry system. It was hoped that Brown and the Liberals would lend their support to both these ends.[42] Numerous names cropped up with regard to the senatorship. With a Democratic majority seemingly assured on any joint ballot, attention focused largely on the aspirants of that party. Blair, Phelps, Glover, Broadhead, Rollins, and even Brown received mention in various quarters. It soon became clear that Frank Blair was the front runner.[43] He had hoped for a seat in the Senate from the moment he had returned to Missouri after his heroic role in the Civil War. He confided to Rollins that Drake had been elected "or rather declared to be elected" senator in 1867 "by the grossest fraud & outrage on the rights of the people of this State." As the Democratic candidate at that time, Blair claimed he had really represented two-thirds of Missouri's citizens, but with the aid of disfranchisement the Radical "minority" had carried the day. Now Blair considered himself entitled to Drake's vacant seat.[44]

A man of great magnetism and driving ambition, Frank Blair worked assiduously in his bid for the coveted place. While Drake's promotion was still in the early rumor stage, Frank wrote his brother Montgomery for a confirmation of it. "It is very important for me to know if this appointment of Drake is a probable thing," he stressed, "for if it is likely to be made I can be working for it while others may be thinking that nothing of the kind will happen." Not desirous of taking any chances, he even urged: "If you can find any

way to strengthen him [Drake] you must by all means help
him *out of my way*."⁴⁵

With the definite announcement of Drake's retirement from
the Senate it immediately became evident that Blair had
strong support throughout the state. Having just been elected
to the lower house of the Assembly from one of the St. Louis
districts, Blair would have the added advantage of sitting in
the body that would make the selection. When speculation
centered on him as a possible candidate for speaker, he wrote
Rollins quite candidly that he had his eye on higher things.⁴⁶

The General Assembly convened in January, 1871. The
Democrats had little difficulty in organizing both houses. Although they had to share some offices with the Liberals and
the fusionists in the Senate, the early roll calls showed that
many of the latter could be included rather permanently
within their ranks. Pressing their advantage, the Democrats
caucused to select a senatorial candidate. Rollins, who was
directing the Blair campaign, invited the Liberals to participate, but only four did so. A spirited session ensued, with
Blair, Glover, Phelps, and Silas Woodson being put forward
for consideration. When the caucus balloted, Blair emerged
as the nominee by a substantial margin.⁴⁷

A short time later the Liberals held their caucus, with
twenty-three in attendance. They first tendered their nomination to former Senator John B. Henderson in the hope that
he would attract the votes of the Democratic moderates.
When Henderson declined, they turned to Supreme Court
Judge David Wagner, whom the *Missouri Democrat* had been
pushing for some time. Although Wagner, who had been on
the bench since 1865, had participated in all of the test oath
decisions, he had taken in recent years increasingly liberal
stands in cases coming before the Court. However, he also
declined, which left the Liberals only a choice of which of
the other camps to enter.⁴⁸

Forty-six legislators from both wings attended the Radical

caucus. Earlier efforts at reconciliation had met with moderate success. Active on the scene was Grosvenor, who communicated Schurz's hope that the Republican party would unify, forget past differences, and work for the election of an acceptable moderate. Brown was nowhere to be seen. He remained deliberately aloof, which brought the private condemnation of many Liberals. In the end the Republicans turned to Henderson, with the pessimistic outlook that theirs was a lost cause from the beginning. The former senator accepted his party's call with reluctance. Those who had hoped that he would make a strong enough showing on the joint ballot to at least force a deadlock were disappointed by his lethargy. Grosvenor complained: "Had Henderson worked one tenth as hard as he did in 1869 he would have won. As it was, we came very close, & then he went off to St. Louis & stayed until it was too late."[49]

The joint session of the legislature elected Blair with no difficulty. He received 102 votes on the first ballot, as compared with 59 for Henderson. This gave him 18 votes more than a majority and 12 more than the total strength of his party. Grosvenor wrote Schurz somewhat philosophically that he thought Blair would not be too harmful in Washington. "He went, I know, with an idea of cooperating as far as he possibly could with liberal Republicans like yourself; and I believe, if you encourage instead of fighting him you can do much to keep him straight or straighter."[50] Blair did indeed desire co-operation but strictly with an eye to his own promotion in the presidential sweepstakes of 1872.[51]

Blair's easy victory greatly pleased the Democrats. To many of them he symbolized the resistance to Radical domination they had carried on over the past five years. Heady with success, they turned their attention to the other concerns that made up their legislative program: the question of a constitutional convention and the revamping of the registry law.

Both of these had received endorsement from Governor Brown in his inaugural address.[52]

The eight Democrats and Liberals on the House committee on constitutional amendments had little difficulty in agreeing to a resolution to submit the convention question to a popular referendum in May, 1871. The four Republicans on the committee demurred. They argued, with some insight, that such action "would arouse all the slumbering passions of the past ten years" at a time when the recent adoption of the amendments made it necessary. The House debated the issue at length before passing the resolution on March 1 by a vote of 71 to 43.[53] A similar proposal in the Senate met determined opposition. There the Liberals had been drawing closer to their Radical brethren. Near the close of the session the Senate committee on constitutional amendments reported the House resolution adversely, with only the two Democratic members dissenting. With the Liberals and Radicals standing firmly behind the committee, all Democratic efforts to push the measure through came to nought.[54]

Success attended the Democratic drive for the revision of the registry act. Although the thoughts of most Democrats during the campaign had been of total repeal, Governor Brown took a more moderate stand in his inaugural address. Brown wanted to retain voter registration, but he thought that its procedure should be simplified and its control localized. When the Attorney General ruled that much of the old law remained in force even though the test oath had been vanquished, Brown sent a special message to the Assembly that urged prompt consideration of revision.[55] Although some talk of total repeal continued in the Democratic ranks, the party's leaders in the legislature took their cue from the Governor and pushed a moderate bill through both houses with little opposition. The product of much consultation and conciliation, it basically provided for a simplified process of registration that would be under the direct control of locally elected administrative and judicial officials. There would be no boards of review, nor could the Secretary of State exercise any arbitrary functions.[56] The passage of this measure stood as the most important single accomplishment of this legislative session. With its enactment the last of the proscriptive features of Radical rule was eliminated. The Radical reconstruction of Missouri could be considered officially at an end.

In reality, the old spirit of vindictiveness had been slowly ebbing in the minds and hearts of many Missourians for some time. As the postwar years had lengthened, Missourians of both political faiths and of differing wartime loyalties found common economic, cultural, and social ties. In so doing, old animosities frequently proved a hindrance to communication and a needless burden. The churches of Missouri, which flourished during this time, proved to be major forces in reconciliation, particularly after the overthrow of the test oath for the clergy. In 1866 the Missouri Sunday School Association, an interdenominational group, organized to promote the exchange of ideas and techniques. The annual meetings attracted large groups and some excellent speakers. County associations carried on the work at the local level.[57]

This was also an era of protracted revivals in which concern for "lost souls" outweighed political considerations. One meeting held by the St. Louis Conference of the Methodist Episcopal Church, South, at its campgrounds lasted for over two weeks. A large tent was erected at the center of the grounds; in it the preaching services were held, while around it were clustered smaller tents to accommodate the throngs that attended the meeting. Many adherents came for only a few days and brought their own tents and cooking equipment. Some fifteen ministers led the meeting, and more than one hundred professions of faith resulted. The church's official historian reported: "The ministers seemed baptized with the spirit of the Master, and labored with unabated zeal for the conversion of sinners. Indeed, the whole Church seemed

alive to her responsibilities and privileges, and on every side
might be heard the voice of prayer and praise."[58] Similar
meetings on a smaller scale, but frequently for a more extended time, were a regular part of the life of nearly every
church. The Census of 1870 revealed 3,229 churches in Missouri, with property valued at $9,709,358. The Methodists
were the largest denomination, followed by the Baptists and
the Presbyterians. After these three, in order of membership,
came the Christians (Disciples of Christ), the Roman Catholics, and the Lutherans.[59]

Missourians in the late 1860's were "joiners." They were
attracted to a wide variety of organizations, old and new.
The enthusiasm of the various military groups has been discussed. Interestingly enough, as rabid partisanship died out,
around 1870, these organizations, too, went into eclipse.[60] Fraternal organizations enjoyed considerable growth. Nearly
every town with a population over six hundred persons had
a fraternal lodge—in most cases either Masonic or Odd Fellow.
Most of these had suffered attrition during the war years, but
with the return of peace their leadership took strong moves
toward reconciliation and rehabilitation. The Missouri Grand
Lodge, A.F.&A.M., grew steadily from a low of 175 lodges in
1865 (many of them inactive) and less than 10,000 members
to 368 lodges and 18,443 members in October, 1870.[61] Similarly, the Missouri Grand Lodge, I.O.O.F., more than doubled
its membership between the end of the war and 1870, growing from 4,052 members in 1866 to 8,897 by the end of the
decade. The first official reference to Rebekah lodges appeared in 1870, several being chartered that year. The Knights
of Pythias also made their appearance that year with lodges
being established at Kansas City and St. Louis. A grand lodge
was organized the following year.

Several organizations with exclusive membership based on
national origins could also be found. The Fenian movement
was quite active in St. Louis in the years immediately fol-

lowing the war. James Stephens, the organization's national commander, was entertained with a grand ball during a visit to the city in 1866. Apparently, there was some Fenian activity outstate also, for mention can be found of a meeting in Jefferson City that year at which Irish Republic bonds were sold at 6 per cent. The Germans formed a secret society called the Sons of Hermann, and another group, known as the Sons of Malta, organized. Several other fraternal organizations, unknown today, had flourishing memberships.[62] The Germans also had their *Turnvereins*, which originally were physical culture clubs but more recently had become the center of family social activity. Both Kansas City and St. Louis had Y.M.C.A. and Y.W.C.A. groups.[63]

Considerable discussion has already centered on labor unions, chambers of commerce, and the Missouri State Teachers Association. Various professional groups also organized on a state-wide basis. The Missouri State Dental Association was founded in 1865. Two years later, medical doctors followed suit with the organization of the state's allopaths and homeopaths into separate associations.[64] Another of the more important groups helping to heal the breach of misunderstanding was the Editors' and Publishers' Association of Missouri, founded in 1867. It embraced both Conservative and Radical newspapermen and elected William F. Switzler, the highly respected editor of the *Missouri Statesman* at Columbia, as its first president. It accomplished a number of benefits for the betterment of the press, including agreement for a set standard of printing rates to be used on a state-wide basis. The annual meetings came to be more social as the years went by. After the 1869 convention in St. Louis, Switzler wrote that he agreed with the editor of the *Richmond Conservator* in his remark: "Take it all in all, it was a big thing, a grand commingling of good drinkers, good thinkers, heavy feeders, a few blow hards, and a sprinkling of hard facts."[65]

By 1870, Missouri had 279 newspapers, with a circulation

of 522,866. The bulk of these, 225 papers, were weeklies; but 21 dailies existed, with 86,555 circulation.[66] When the newspaper plant of the *Missouri Republican* burned in May, 1870, at a loss of $150,000, the editor of the rival *Missouri Democrat* extended his deepest regrets. Although the two papers might be bitter political opponents, Grosvenor acknowledged that the brotherhood of the working press united them, and he expressed his hope that the *Republican* would speedily return to the newsstands.[67]

A short-lived but important organization was the Missouri Southern Relief Association, established in the winter of 1866 to help "relieve the suffering and indigent of the South." The group sponsored a Southern relief concert in St. Louis in April that was so "crushingly attended" that it had to be repeated. In October the ladies of the association held a great fair in St. Louis, which netted $130,000. As part of the proceedings, a grand tournament took place in which the jousts of chivalric days were re-enacted. The "successful knight" received a prize and had the honor of choosing the queen of the tournament. This event, too, proved so popular that another was held a few weeks later. Similar affairs took place elsewhere across the state, and by the end of the year about $150,000 had been collected and distributed. Having accomplished its purpose, the association dissolved soon afterwards.[68]

Fairs of all sorts became increasingly popular. By 1870 forty-four agricultural and mechanical expositions were being held by counties and cities throughout Missouri. Most of them occurred in September or October and showed a wide variety of exhibits to which Conservative and Radical alike submitted entries. Trotting and racing frequently accompanied the proceedings. The St. Louis fair, which had achieved considerable recognition before the war, resumed operations in 1866 and was highly successful. Within two years it had as many as ninety thousand visitors in a single day, and exhibits had come from all over the country.[69]

All of these groups and activities, plus many more like them, encouraged Missourians to bury wartime animosities and to think of themselves less frequently as Unionists or Confederates. Although plagued by Jesse James and others of his ilk, Missouri after 1870 settled down to a steady growth economically and culturally. Population continued to flow into the state, in the 1870's showing an increase of 26 per cent.[70]

After much debate and discussion, Missourians called a new constitutional convention in 1875. The majority on the referendum was only 283 votes, which indicated that many Missourians had learned to live quite well under what remained of the 1865 document. The personnel of the new convention reflected the steadily growing trend toward reconciliation. Eighteen of the sixty-eight delegates had seen service, either civil or military, with the Confederacy, while fifteen had served in the Union army. The president of the convention was former Senator Waldo P. Johnson of Osceola, who had been expelled from the United States Senate in 1862 for desertion to the Confederacy and had then served as a lieutenant colonel under Sterling Price before being chosen a senator from Missouri in the Confederate Congress. The document produced by the convention represented moderate reforms of a somewhat conservative nature, and it remained the state's organic law for the next seventy years. Its predominant note was the restriction of state and local governmental units in the areas of finance and taxation, a reflection of conservative discontent with some of the excesses of the preceding ten years.[71]

Politically, Missouri returned to the permanent security of the Democratic fold. Although the Liberal Republican-Democratic coalition continued in effect in 1872, it was on Democratic terms, and a Democratic governor was elected. This election showed in concrete terms the effect of the removal of voter restrictions. Based on the gubernatorial vote, 111,287 more ballots were cast in 1872 than two years earlier. Many counties nearly doubled their voting strength. At this time a large number of Liberals returned to the regular Republican fold, and after 1872 the Liberal movement completely collapsed, its members seeking the particular party that best suited their individual needs. Once in the saddle, the Democrats controlled Missouri for thirty-five uninterrupted years.[72]

When Carl Schurz reached the end of his Senate term in 1875, the Democrats replaced him with Francis M. Cockrell, an ex-Confederate general who had been practicing law in Warrensburg. Cockrell served for the next thirty years. That same year Jefferson Davis, former President of the Confederacy, made a tour of the state and received a warm welcome. Four years later George G. Vest, who had represented Missouri in both houses of the Confederate Congress, joined Cockrell in the United States Senate, where he remained for four terms.[73] During this long period of exile from the state offices, Republican strength remained concentrated in the southwestern and border regions and in the German-dominated counties along the Missouri River. Particularly in the southwest the memories of a war-torn Missouri died hard.

Following his failure to secure re-election in 1875, Carl Schurz concentrated on national politics and the reform of his party at that level. Named Secretary of the Interior by President Rutherford B. Hayes in 1877, he departed from Missouri for Washington and never returned except for an occasional visit. Charles D. Drake continued as Chief Justice of the Court of Claims in Washington until his retirement in 1885. In this capacity he was far removed from the Missouri political scene. Joseph W. McClurg retired to his mercantile business at Linn Creek in Camden County. His predecessor in the governor's chair, Thomas C. Fletcher, pursued a successful legal practice in St. Louis and Washington. In 1872 B. Gratz Brown unsuccessfully sought the Vice-Presidency on the Liberal Republican ticket, after which he retired from active politics and settled down to the practice of law in St. Louis. John B. Henderson upheld the Republican standard as its gubernatorial candidate in 1872 as the party went down in a crushing defeat. Most of the other men who had served Missouri under Radical rule dropped back into political obscurity, although some enjoyed occasional patronage positions from the national Republican administrations in the remaining years of the nineteenth century. In Missouri nothing remained of the brief political empire of the Radicals except control of a few courthouses in those areas where they had been able to consolidate their strength.[74]

The Radical Union party of Missouri had ridden into power on the whirlwind of emotion generated by four long years of internecine strife. Led by men with many progressive ideas, it had set Missouri on the road to a postwar future brightened by prosperity and social advance. To accomplish the better tomorrow, its leaders, especially Charles D. Drake, had considered it necessary to completely overhaul the state's basic constitutional framework. Yet, in carrying out their program, they went to vindictive extremes. Few would deny the necessity for some control over the returning "rebels" and the disloyal who remained at home to feed the fires of guerrilla warfare. The example of Kentucky, where Conservatives entrenched themselves in power at the end of the war only to succumb to infiltration from ex-Confederates, contrasts markedly with Missouri. In Kentucky, economic and social stagnation characterized the five years after the war, and the state was long in recovering.[75] Yet, a group that could secure a 40,000-vote mandate in 1864 did not need such ultraproscriptive measures to maintain itself in power. The Radicals stretched such a wide net that they needlessly antagonized many groups and individuals, as evinced by the controversies that arose over the test oath required of lawyers and clergy. The illegal methods used by Secretary of State Rodman to secure elections where legal means had failed accomplished little of permanent value but aroused tremendous ill will.

More emphasis on the positive aspects of their program and less concern with extreme vindictiveness might have allowed the Radicals to build a strong progressive party of long-standing duration. As it was, they laid a good foundation for Missouri in the areas of education, Negro rights, and economic growth. With less political antagonism they could have accomplished much more. Even in view of their extreme measures of 1865 and 1866 the Radicals might still have salvaged the future of their party had they been willing to move in the direction of the Planters House proposals of B. Gratz Brown when these were first suggested. The memory of war was still fresh, however, and partisans with newly won fruits of office feared lest these be lost. Succumbing to that fear proved their ultimate downfall and brought total eclipse except in a few scattered strongholds. Fortunately for Missouri, the Liberal wing of the Radical party infused the Democratic ranks with much of its progressive spirit during the 1870's. As a consequence, the good beginnings of the postwar era were consolidated and advanced in the following decade.

NOTES

CHAPTER I

1. St. Louis *Missouri Republican,* January 9, 1865.
2. *The War of the Rebellion: Official Records of the Union and Confederate Armies,* Ser. I, Vol. XLVIII, Part 1, 458-59. Hereafter cited as *O. R.*
3. *St. Joseph Morning Herald,* January 31, 1865; James O. Broadhead Papers, T. T. Eales to Broadhead, June 27, 1865; Jefferson City *Missouri State Times,* July 14, 1865; Columbia *Missouri Statesman,* July 28, 1865.
4. William E. Parrish, *Turbulent Partnership: Missouri and the Union, 1861-1865,* 1-47.
5. *Ibid.,* 123-35.
6. Ida M. Nowells, "A Study of the Radical Party Movement in Missouri, 1860-1870," unpublished Master's thesis, University of Missouri, 93-105; Raymond D. Thomas, "A Study in Missouri Politics, 1840-1870," *Missouri Historical Review,* XXI, 576; George W. Smith, "New England Business Interests in Missouri During the Civil War," *Missouri Historical Review,* XLI, 12-18.
7. Parrish, *Turbulent Partnership,* 135-39.
8. *Ibid.,* 139-48.
9. Allen Johnson and Dumas Malone, eds., *Dictionary of American Biography,* V, 425-26. Hereafter cited as *D. A. B.*
10. David D. March, "The Life and Times of Charles Daniel Drake," unpublished doctoral dissertation, University of Missouri, 212-14, 222-24; Parrish, *Turbulent Partnership,* 155-60.
11. St. Louis *Missouri Democrat,* September 2 and 4, 1863; Charles D. Drake, *Union and Anti-Slavery Speeches Delivered*

During the Rebellion, 271-307; Charles D. Drake, "Autobiography" (manuscript), 911-13.

12. John G. Nicolay and John Hay, *Abraham Lincoln, A History*, VIII, 214-20; Roy P. Basler, ed., *The Collected Works of Abraham Lincoln*, VI, 499-504.

13. *Missouri Democrat*, October 23, 1863; *Missouri State Times*, October 24, 1863.

14. *Missouri Democrat*, October 21 and 30 and November 2, 1863.

15. *Missouri Republican*, October 9 and November 1, 1863; *Missouri Statesman*, October 16, 1863; *Morning Herald*, October 29, 1863; *O. R.*, Ser. I, Vol. XXII, Part 2, 547.

16. *Missouri Republican*, November 9 and 11 and December 2, 1863; *Missouri Democrat*, November 9 and 27, 1863; Robert Todd Lincoln Collection of the Papers of Abraham Lincoln, John M. Schofield to Lincoln, November 9, 1863.

17. Nowells, "Study of the Radical Party Movement," 35.

18. *Missouri Republican*, November 18 and 20, 1863.

19. *Laws of the State of Missouri, 22nd General Assembly, Adjourned Session, 1863–1864*, 24-26.

20. *Journal of the House of Representatives of the State of Missouri, 22nd General Assembly, Adjourned Session*, 564-65.

21. Allan Nevins, *Fremont, Pathmarker of the West*, 573-74; *Missouri Democrat*, May 30, 1864; *Missouri Republican*, June 6, 1864; Drake, "Autobiography," 951-52.

22. *Missouri Statesman*, May 27, 1864.

23. Parrish, *Turbulent Partnership*, 186-87; James S. Rollins Papers, Peter Foy to Rollins, February 7, 1865.

24. *Missouri Democrat*, May 30, 1864.

25. Floyd C. Shoemaker, *Missouri and Missourians: Land of Contrasts and People of Achievements*, I, 936-37.

26. Parrish, *Turbulent Partnership*, 193-95.

27. Shoemaker, *Missouri and Missourians*, I, 934-36; March, "Charles Daniel Drake," 324-26, 330-31.

28. Nowells, "Study of the Radical Party Movement," 35-36, 93-95. The counties were Audrain, Boone, Callaway, Cass (the one exception in later elections), Clay, Clinton, Jackson, Lafayette, Maries, Mississippi, Monroe, Platte, Ray, Reynolds, and Scott. A dozen other counties that were consistently in the conservative Democratic column during the Reconstruction period also broke over in this election for reasons that are difficult to surmise.

29. Grace G. Avery and Floyd C. Shoemaker, eds., *The Messages and Proclamations of the Governors of the State of Missouri*, IV, 54.

CHAPTER II

1. *Journal of the Missouri State Convention Held at St. Louis, 1865,* 3-4. Hereafter cited as *Convention Journal.* Galusha Anderson, *A Border City During the Civil War,* 343.
2. Drake, "Autobiography," 1054-56.
3. March, "Charles Daniel Drake," 349-50.
4. *Convention Journal,* 6, 8-9, 15, 17, 19, 224, 244; St. Louis *Missouri Republican,* January 11, 1865; Columbia *Missouri Statesman,* January 13, 1865; Rollins Papers, William F. Switzler to Rollins, January 15, 1865.
5. *Laws of Missouri, 1863–1864,* 25-26; *Convention Journal,* 14; Drake, "Autobiography," 1061.
6. St. Louis *Missouri Democrat,* January 11, 1865.
7. *Convention Journal,* 16-17, 25-27; *Missouri Republican,* January 13, 1865; *Missouri Democrat,* January 13, 1865.
8. *Ibid.,* January 13, 1865; *Convention Journal,* 27.
9. Jefferson City *Missouri State Times,* January 14, 1865; Avery and Shoemaker, *Messages and Proclamations,* IV, 256.
10. *Missouri Democrat,* January 16, 1865.
11. *Convention Journal,* 30; Rollins Papers, Switzler to Rollins, January 15, 1865.
12. Shoemaker, *Missouri and Missourians,* I, 578, 941.
13. *Missouri Republican,* February 3, 1865; *Journal of the Senate of the State of Missouri, 23rd General Assembly, Regular Session,* 209.
14. No church could own any property other than that on which its house of worship or its parsonage was located; even the amount of the land was limited to five acres in rural areas and to one acre in urban communities. Also, gifts of land could be given to a religious group only if a church or parsonage was to be built on it. *Constitution of the State of Missouri, 1865,* Art. I, Secs. 13 and 14. These restrictions were an outgrowth of Drake's strong anti-Catholic bias, which many of the delegates shared.
15. *Missouri Democrat,* January 18–February 8, 1865; *Missouri Statesman,* January 20, 1865; *Missouri Republican,* January 23–February 6, 1865.
16. March, "Charles Daniel Drake," 367-68.
17. *Missouri Republican,* February 6, 1865.
18. Drake, "Autobiography," 1061a-1061c.
19. *Convention Journal,* 89-90.
20. *Missouri Democrat,* February 17 and March 1, 1865; Drake, "Autobiography," 1062-65.
21. *Missouri Democrat,* February 20 and 22, 1865; *Convention Journal,* 102-3, 131.
22. *Ibid.,* 96, 102, 109, 124, 129, 142-43, 146.

23. *Missouri Democrat,* February 22, 1865.

24. *Ibid.,* February 24, 1865.

25. *Ibid.*

26. *Convention Journal,* 203.

27. *Missouri Republican,* March 31, 1865.

28. *Missouri Democrat,* January 20, 1865.

29. *Missouri Constitution, 1865,* Art. IV, Secs. 23-25.

30. *Ibid.,* Art. IV, Sec. 27; Art. VIII, Secs. 4 and 5.

31. *Ibid.,* Art. XII, Secs. 2 and 3.

32. *Convention Journal,* 35; *Missouri Constitution, 1865,* Art. II, Sec. 3. Drake supposedly wrote this entire section.

33. Dr. Linton's remark had reference to the first codification of laws in ancient Greece in the seventh century, B. C., by a man named Dracon. Although Dracon did not establish any new laws, his work of systematizing the existing practices of the courts brought the harshness of society into bold relief. Upon their realization of the extremity of the law, especially as it applied to homicide, the common people are said to have cried out: "The laws of Dracon are written in blood. These are not the laws of Dracon, but of dracon (dragon)." Herbert N. Couch and Russel M. Geer, *Classical Civilization: Greece,* 109.

34. *Missouri Republican,* January 30 and February 3, 1865; Drake, "Autobiography," 1076.

35. *Missouri Democrat,* January 27, February 8, and April 3, 1865; *Convention Journal,* 40, 49, 211. The Germans strongly opposed the inclusion of the professions within the range of the iron-clad oath.

36. *Missouri Constitution, 1865,* Art. II, Secs. 4 and 5.

37. See Chapter VI.

38. *Missouri Republican,* March 29, 1865.

39. *Convention Journal,* 201-2.

40. *Missouri Republican,* February 20 and 22, 1865.

41. *Missouri Democrat,* February 13, 1865; *Missouri Constitution, 1865,* Art. IV, Sec. 2.

42. *Convention Journal,* 22.

43. *Missouri Democrat,* January 16, 1865; *Convention Journal,* 28.

44. *Ibid.,* 101.

45. See above, page 23.

46. *Missouri Democrat,* February 22 and 24, 1865; *Convention Journal,* 109.

47. *Missouri Democrat,* March 8, 1865; Lincoln Papers, Lincoln to Fletcher, February 20, 1865, Fletcher to Lincoln, February 27, 1865, Pope to Lincoln, March 8, 1865.

48. *Convention Journal*, 155-59. For the results of the enforcement of the ordinance, see pp. 50-55.

49. Drake, "Autobiography," 1077.

50. *Convention Journal*, 247; *Missouri Democrat*, April 10, 1865.

51. Drake, "Autobiography," 1086. One member of the convention, Thomas B. Harris of Callaway County, had had his seat declared vacant because of alleged disloyal acts committed in 1861. Another delegate never appeared to take his seat.

52. Drake, "Autobiography," 1078-79.

53. *Convention Journal*, 249-51.

CHAPTER III

1. Drake, "Autobiography," 1065; *Convention Journal*, 174.

2. *Ibid.*, 246.

3. *Missouri Constitution, 1865*, Art. XIII, Sec. 6.

4. *Convention Journal*, 283; Civil War Papers, Francis Rodman to Albert Sigel, May 4, 1865.

5. St. Louis *Missouri Democrat*, April 10, 1865.

6. *Ibid.*, April 24, 1865.

7. Columbia *Missouri Statesman*, April 24, 1865; *Missouri Democrat*, April 26 and 28, 1865.

8. *Ibid.*, April 28, 1865; *St. Joseph Morning Herald*, May 6, 1865. Cf. *St. Louis Dispatch*, April 29, 1865.

9. *Missouri Democrat*, May 1 and 3, 1865.

10. Drake, "Autobiography," 1095½-1096; *Missouri Democrat*, June 2, 1865.

11. Jefferson City *Missouri State Times*, May 6, 1865.

12. *Missouri Democrat*, June 2, 1865.

13. *Ibid.*, April 28, 1865.

14. St. Louis *Missouri Republican*, May 3, 1865.

15. *Ibid.*, March 15, 1865; Drake, "Autobiography," 1078.

16. *Dispatch*, April 26, 1865; *Missouri Democrat*, April 28, 1865; Drake, "Autobiography," 1115-18.

17. March, "Charles Daniel Drake," 403.

18. Shakespeare's *A Midsummer Night's Dream*.

19. *Missouri Republican*, May 3, 1865.

20. *Dispatch*, April 15 and May 2, 1865.

21. Howard K. Beale, ed., *The Diary of Edward Bates, 1859–1866*, 470-85, 571-612.

22. *Missouri Statesman*, April 17–June 2, 1865.

23. Thomas S. Barclay, "The Liberal Republican Movement in Missouri," *Missouri Historical Review*, XX, 38n.

24. Frederick W. Lehmann, "Edward Bates and the Test Oath," *Missouri Historical Society Collections*, IV, 394-95.

25. *Missouri Republican,* May 31, 1865.

26. *Missouri State Times,* April 22, 1865.

27. *Missouri Democrat,* April 19, 1865.

28. Andrew Johnson Papers, B. Gratz Brown to Johnson, April 22, 1865.

29. *Ibid.,* Charles D. Drake to Johnson, April 17, 24, and 27, 1865.

30. Beale, *Bates Diary,* 486.

31. *Missouri Democrat,* July 3, 1865.

32. *Ibid.,* June 9 and 16, 1865.

33. *Ibid.,* July 3, 1865.

34. *Missouri Republican,* June 13, 1865; Broadhead Papers, James Brown to Broadhead, June 23, 1865, Robert C. Fulkerson to Broadhead, June 26, 1865.

35. Springfield *Missouri Weekly Patriot,* April 19, 1866.

36. Barclay, "The Liberal Republican Movement," 44n.

37. *Missouri Statesman,* June 9 and 16, 1865; *Missouri Democrat,* June 12 and July 3, 1865.

38. *Missouri Republican,* June 26, 1865; *Missouri Democrat,* June 30, 1865; *Missouri State Times,* July 7, 1865; Drake, "Autobiography," 1144-48.

39. *Ibid.,* 1148-49.

40. *Missouri Democrat,* July 3, 1865; Avery and Shoemaker, *Messages and Proclamations,* IV, 262-64.

41. *Missouri Statesman,* September 15 and October 20, 1865; *Missouri State Times,* December 8 and 15, 1865; Gist Blair Papers, Thomas Gantt to Montgomery Blair, October 6, 1865. That winter the Conservatives also sought to secure an official investigation of the constitutional referendum in the General Assembly. Their proposal failed by the tie-breaking vote of the presiding officer in the Senate. *Senate Journal, 23rd General Assembly, Adjourned Session,* 129-30.

CHAPTER IV

1. Howard L. Conard, ed., *Encyclopedia of the History of Missouri,* V, 169. The complete list of new officeholders can be found in the Jefferson City *Missouri State Times,* May 20, 1865.

2. St. Louis *Missouri Democrat,* May 26 and 31, 1865.

3. *Ibid.,* May 19 and October 11, 1865; Columbia *Missouri Statesman,* May 26, 1865; Drake, "Autobiography," 1127-30.

4. Beale, *Bates Diary,* 481; Drake, "Autobiography," 1130.

5. *Ibid.,* 1130-32; Beale, *Bates Diary,* 481.

6. Drake, "Autobiography," 1133-37; St. Louis *Missouri Republican,* June 15, 1865; *Missouri Democrat,* June 16, 1865.

7. *Ibid.*, June 19, 1865. Cf. *An Address to the People of Missouri*, a pamphlet written by Conservative lawyers.

8. *Missouri Democrat*, June 30, 1865.

9. Thomas v. Mead and Moodey (1865), 36 Mo. 232-49.

10. State v. Bernoudy (1865), 36 Mo. 279-81.

11. Advisory Opinion upon Election of Circuit Attorneys (1866), 38 Mo. 419.

12. State *ex rel.* Conrad v. Bernoudy (1868), 40 Mo. 192-93; State v. Neal (1868), 42 Mo. 119.

13. *Missouri Statesman*, July 14 and October 6, 1865; *Missouri Democrat*, April 13 and 18, 1866.

14. Rollins Papers, Foy to Rollins, February 7, 1865; John F. Hume, *The Abolitionists*, 161-62, 171; *Missouri Democrat*, June 7, 1865.

15. Johnson Papers, John Hogan to Johnson, June 19, 1865, Joseph W. McClurg to Johnson, June 23, 1865, Samuel T. Glover *et al.* to Johnson, June 26, 1865, Truman Woodruff to Johnson, July 20, 1865, Henry T. Blow to Johnson, August 10, 1865, James S. Rollins to Johnson, September 2, 1865.

16. Parrish, *Turbulent Partnership*, 15-18, 27-30; *Missouri Democrat*, June 26, 1865; *Missouri Statesman*, June 30, 1865.

17. William E. Smith, *The Francis Preston Blair Family in Politics*, II, 328-30, 339.

18. Johnson Papers, James S. Rollins to Johnson, June 7, 1865, Glover *et al.* to Johnson, June 26, 1865.

19. *Ibid.*, McClurg to Johnson, June 23, 1865, Woodruff to Johnson, July 20, 1865, Blow to Johnson, August 10, 1865.

20. Blair Papers, Gantt to Montgomery Blair, October 6, 1865; *Missouri Statesman*, October 13, 20, and 27, 1865; Springfield *Missouri Weekly Patriot*, October 26, 1865.

21. *Missouri Democrat*, October 23, 1865.

22. *Missouri Statesman*, November 3, 1865.

23. Blair Papers, Frank Blair to Francis P. Blair, November 2, 1865; *Missouri Statesman*, November 17, 1865.

24. Blair Papers, Frank Blair to Montgomery Blair, November 4, 1865; *Missouri Republican*, November 10, 1865.

25. *Ibid.*, November 8, 1865; *Missouri Democrat*, January 5, 1866.

26. *Ibid.*, April 20, 1866.

27. *Ibid.*, June 27, 1866; Drake, "Autobiography," 1178-79.

28. *St. Louis Dispatch*, August 9, 1865; *Missouri Democrat*, September 1, 1865.

29. *Ibid.*, September 13 and 22, 1865; *Dispatch*, September 21, 1865.

30. *Missouri Statesman*, September 29, October 27, and Novem-

ber 10, 1865; Blair Papers, Gantt to Montgomery Blair, October 14, 1865; *Dispatch*, October 24, 1865; Charles P. Johnson, *Personal Recollections of Some of Missouri's Eminent Statesmen and Lawyers*, 25-30. Glover's stand had little effect on his immense legal business. Henry D. Bacon Papers, Samuel P. Gaty to Bacon, April 10, 1866.

31. *Missouri Democrat*, October 2 and 20, 1865; William B. Napton, "Diary" (manuscript), 312; State v. Garesche (1865), 36 Mo. 256-62. The United States Supreme Court refused to consider Garesche's petition. Harold M. Hyman, *Era of the Oath: Northern Loyalty Tests During the Civil War and Reconstruction*, 98-99.

32. Napton, "Diary," 313, 318.

33. *Missouri Democrat*, September 13 and 15 and November 8, 1865; *Missouri Statesman*, October 6, 1865. The same laxity existed in regard to the taking of the oath by jurors in many areas. *The American Annual Cyclopedia and Register of Important Events for the Year 1865*, 591.

34. Broadhead Papers, M. M. Modisett to Broadhead, August 8, 1865.

35. *Dispatch*, August 1, 1865.

36. *Missouri Democrat*, August 28, 1865.

37. *Ibid.*, August 30, 1865.

38. William M. Leftwich, *Martyrdom in Missouri*, II, 321-22; Robert S. Duncan, *A History of the Baptists in Missouri*, 919; Robert S. Douglass, *History of Missouri Baptists*, 231-36.

39. *Missouri Democrat*, October 6, 1865; Douglass, *Missouri Baptists*, 238-40.

40. *Missouri Democrat*, August 28, 1865.

41. *Dispatch*, September 2, 1865.

42. *Missouri Democrat*, September 1, 1865.

43. *Ibid.*, September 6, 1865.

44. *Missouri Statesman*, October 6, 1865.

45. *Dispatch*, September 2, 1865; *Missouri Democrat*, September 4, 1865; *Missouri Statesman*, September 15, 1865.

46. *Missouri Democrat*, September 20, 1865.

47. *Ibid.*, September 25 and 27, 1865; Leftwich, *Martyrdom in Missouri*, II, 341; St. Louis *Christian Advocate*, November 9, 1865, and March 15, 1866.

48. *Missouri Republican*, September 16, 21, and 24, 1865; *Missouri Democrat*, September 20, 1865. Judge Fagg was later promoted to the Supreme Court of Missouri.

49. *Missouri Republican*, September 21, 1865; John J. O'Shea, *The Two Kenricks*, 296-97.

50. *Dispatch*, September 24, 1865; *Missouri Democrat*, October 11, 1865.

51. *Ibid.*, November 3 and 8, 1865; *Missouri State Times*, December 22, 1865.

52. *Missouri Democrat*, September 25 and 27 and October 4, 1865; *Missouri Statesman*, October 20, November 24, and December 15, 1865.

53. Leftwich, *Martyrdom in Missouri*, II, 341; *Christian Advocate*, March 1, 1866.

54. Thomas S. Barclay, "The Test Oath for Clergy in Missouri," *Missouri Historical Review*, XVIII, 365, 371-72.

55. Missouri v. Cummings (1865), 36 Mo. 264-68.

56. *Missouri Republican*, October 19 and 26, 1865; *Dispatch*, October 20, 1865.

57. Missouri v. Cummings (1865), 36 Mo. 271-74.

58. Blair Papers, Frank Blair to Montgomery Blair, November 4, 1865.

59. Smith, *Blair Family*, II, 352.

60. Avery and Shoemaker, *Messages and Proclamations*, IV, 77-79.

61. Barclay, "Test Oath for Clergy," 362-64.

62. Cummings v. Missouri (1866), 4 Wallace 277-306.

63. *Missouri Democrat*, June 4, 1866; *Missouri Statesman*, June 8, 1866; *St. Joseph Morning Herald*, September 21, 1866; Theodore C. Pease and James G. Randall, eds., *The Diary of Orville Hickman Browning*, II, 67-69.

64. *Morning Herald*, May 5, June 9, and September 21, 1866; *Dispatch*, May 5, 1866; *Missouri Democrat*, June 4, 1866; *Missouri Statesman*, June 8, 1866.

65. Salmon P. Chase Papers, Joel F. Asper to Chase, June 18, 1866.

66. *Chillicothe Spectator*, June-August, 1866.

67. Chase Papers, Samuel F. Miller to Chase, June 5, 1866; cf. Pease and Randall, *Browning Diary*, II, 69.

68. Chase Papers, Stephen J. Field to Chase, June 30, 1866.

69. *Missouri Democrat*, June 14, 1866; *St. Louis Evening News*, June 25, 1866.

70. *Missouri Democrat*, June 27, 1866.

71. Quoted in Willard L. King, *Lincoln's Manager: David Davis*, 261-62.

72. Avery and Shoemaker, *Messages and Proclamations*, IV, 83-84.

73. Cummings v. Missouri (1866), 4 Wallace 318-28.

74. *Ibid.*, 382-92.

75. *Missouri Democrat*, January 23, 1867.

76. *Ibid.*, February 18, 1867.

77. *Ibid.*, January 16, 1867.

78. Barclay, "Test Oath for Clergy," 378; State v. Murphy (1867), 41 Mo. 339-88. This decision in no way affected the test oath for voting.

79. Harold C. Bradley, "In Defense of John Cummings," *Missouri Historical Review*, LVII, 13-14.

CHAPTER V

1. St. Louis *Missouri Democrat*, November 3 and 5, 1865; Columbia *Missouri Statesman*, November 3 and 24, 1865; St. Louis *Missouri Republican*, January 8, 1866.

2. *Missouri Democrat*, November 13, December 6 and 15, 1865; Jefferson City *Missouri State Times*, December 8 and 15, 1865; *House Journal, 23rd General Assembly, Adjourned Session*, 167-77; *Senate Journal, 23rd General Assembly, Adjourned Session*, 161-66; Drake, "Autobiography," 1209.

3. *Laws of Missouri, Adjourned Session, 23rd General Assembly, 1865-1866*, 117-24.

4. *Missouri State Times*, December 15 and 22, 1865; *Missouri Democrat*, December 19 and 25, 1865; Springfield *Missouri Weekly Patriot*, December 21, 1865.

5. Johnson Papers, Henry Myers to Johnson, August 30, 1865.

6. *Missouri Republican*, February 26, 1866; *Missouri Democrat*, February 26, 1866; Rollins Papers, Lewis V. Bogy to Rollins, May 21, 1866, John M. Richardson to Rollins, July 13, 1866; Johnson Papers, Abner L. Gilstrap to Johnson, May 26, 1866.

7. *Missouri Republican*, February 19 and 23, 1866.

8. Rollins Papers, Frank Blair to Rollins, May 23, 1866; *Missouri Statesman*, June 1, 1866; *Missouri Republican*, June 6, 1866.

9. Johnson Papers, *passim*, February–April, 1866; *Missouri Statesman*, *passim*, March, 1866.

10. *Missouri Democrat*, February 26, 1866; Johnson Papers, Henry T. Blow to Johnson, October 26, 1865, and March 19, 1866; *Missouri Weekly Patriot*, March 8, 22, and 29, 1866; *Missouri Statesman*, March 9, 1866; *Chillicothe Spectator*, April 12, 1866.

11. Johnson Papers, Arden R. Smith to Johnson, February 27, 1866.

12. *Ibid.*, Edwin M. Stanton to Johnson, March 10, 1866.

13. Chase Papers, Isaac H. Sturgeon to Chase, January 20, 1865; Rollins Papers, Foy to Rollins, February 7, 1865; Johnson Papers, Blow to Johnson, August 10, 1865, Rollins to Johnson, September 2, 1865, Frank Blair to Francis P. Blair, May 2, 1866; *Missouri Democrat*, August 21, 1865, February 2 and May 14, 1866; Blair Papers, Thomas E. Noell to Frank Blair, January 8, 1866, Frank Blair to Montgomery Blair, January 10, 14, and 23, 1866; *Missouri State Times*, March 23, 1866.

14. Johnson Papers, Edward Bates to Johnson, July 12, 1866, O. D. Filley to Montgomery Blair, July 30, 1866, Samuel T. Glover to Johnson, August 1, 1866, George Knapp to Montgomery Blair, August 3, 1866; *Richmond Conservator,* July 21, 1866; *Missouri Statesman,* August 3, 1866; Rollins Papers, Orville H. Browning to Rollins, September 24 and 28, 1866, Browning to Clark H. Green, September 29, 1866.

15. *Missouri Democrat,* April 4, 1866; *Missouri Statesman,* April 13, 1866.

16. Johnson Papers, Frank Blair to Francis P. Blair, May 2, 1866; *Missouri Statesman,* May 4, 1866; Blair Papers, Frank Blair to Francis P. Blair, May 6, 1866.

17. *Missouri Democrat,* May 21 and June 6 and 11, 1866; *Missouri Statesman,* May 25, 1866; *Spectator,* June 14, 1866; Rollins Papers, Frank Blair to Rollins, May 23, 1866.

18. Huston Crittenden, "The Warrensburg Speech of Frank P. Blair," *Missouri Historical Review,* XX, 101-4.

19. *Missouri Statesman,* April 25 and June 29, 1866.

20. Blair Papers, Frank Blair to Francis P. Blair, June 17, 1866; Rollins Papers, Bogy to Rollins, May 21, 1866.

21. *Missouri Statesman,* May 11 and June 29, 1866.

22. *Missouri Democrat,* April 16 and May 16, 1866.

23. *Ibid.,* May 11, 1866.

24. *Ibid.,* May 16 and 18, 1866.

25. Rollins Papers, Bogy to Rollins, May 21, 1866; *Spectator,* June 7 and 14, 1866; *Missouri Statesman,* June 15, 1866; *Missouri Democrat,* June 8, 13, and 18, 1866.

26. *Ibid.,* June 13, July 4, 14, 18, 20, and 25, August 17, September 10, October 8, 29, and 31, 1866; *Missouri Weekly Patriot,* July 5 and 12, 1866; Drake, "Autobiography," 1180-81.

27. *Ibid.,* 1192-95; Blair Papers, Evans Casselberry to Montgomery Blair, May 19 and 27, 1866; *Missouri Democrat,* July 2 and November 23, 1866.

28. *Ibid.,* July 13, 1866.

29. *Ibid.,* July 16, 1866.

30. *Ibid.,* August 13, 1866.

31. *Missouri Republican,* August 8 and 11, 1866.

32. Johnson Papers, Bates to Johnson, July 12, 1866.

33. *St. Louis Evening News,* July 5, 1866.

34. *Missouri Statesman,* July 6 and 13, 1866.

35. Johnson Papers, Thomas Gantt to John Hogan, July 28, 1866.

36. *Ibid.,* Thomas C. Ready to Johnson, July 24, 1866, William Douglass to Gantt, July 26, 1866, Gantt to Hogan, July 27 and 28, 1866, Roger Jones to R. M. Sawyer, August 15, 1866.

37. Records of the Department of the Missouri, Letters Sent,

Vol. 532, p. 661, John Pope to Thomas C. Fletcher, February 5, 1866.

38. *Missouri State Times*, February 16, 1866; *Missouri Statesman*, February 23, 1866; Shoemaker, *Missouri and Missourians*, I, 1017.

39. *Missouri Democrat*, November 17, 1865.

40. Shoemaker, *Missouri and Missourians*, I, 1015-16; *History of Greene County, Missouri*, 497-503; Ewing Cockrell, *History of Johnson County, Missouri*, 120-27; *Missouri Weekly Patriot*, May 31, 1866.

41. Johnson Papers, Ready to Johnson, July 24, 1866, Douglass to Gantt, July 26, 1866, William T. Sherman to Johnson, August 9, 1866, Gantt to Hogan, August 10, 1866.

42. *Ibid.*, Gantt to Hogan, July 27 and 28, 1866.

43. *Ibid.*, Sherman to Johnson, August 9, 1866, Gantt to Hogan, August 10, 1866.

44. *Ibid.*, Edward McCabe *et al.* to Johnson, n. d. (August 13, 1866, penciled in above manuscript); *Missouri Democrat*, August 22, 1866.

45. *Ibid.*

46. *Ibid.*, August 17, 1866.

47. Edwin M. Stanton Papers, Winfield S. Hancock to Stanton, August 28, 1866.

48. Avery and Shoemaker, *Messages and Proclamations*, IV, 288-91.

49. *Missouri Democrat*, September 7, 1866.

50. William T. Sherman Papers, Thomas Gantt to Sherman, September 3, 1866.

51. Records of the Department of Missouri, Letters Sent, Vol. 532, pp. 958-61, 1010, Winfield S. Hancock to William T. Sherman, September 12 and 16 and October 2, 1866.

52. *Ibid.*, Letters Received, Register 525, Entry 70, Thomas C. Fletcher to Winfield S. Hancock, September 15, 1866.

53. *Ibid.*, Letters Received, Registers 525 and 526, Letters Sent, Vol. 532, *passim*, September–November, 1866.

54. *Ibid.*; Blair Papers, Winfield S. Hancock to Frank Blair, November 2, 1866; *Conservator*, November 10, 1866.

55. *Missouri Statesman*, October 5 and 26, 1866.

56. Drake, "Autobiography," 1212-15.

57. Records of the Department of Missouri, Letters Received, Register 526, entries 59, 61, and 551, James R. Kelly to Chauncey McKeever, October 20, 1866, Austin A. King *et al.* to Winfield S. Hancock, October 22, 1866, William A. Marshall to Hancock, October 8, 1866; *Missouri Statesman*, February 15, 1867.

58. *Missouri Democrat*, October 29, 1866.

59. Drake, "Autobiography," 1196; Bacon Papers, Samuel P. Gaty to Bacon, August 16 and 27, 1866; Blair Papers, Thomas Gantt to Montgomery Blair, August 18, 1866, Casselberry to Montgomery Blair, August 22, 1866; *Missouri Democrat*, September 10 and October 15, 1866.

60. *Ibid.*, October 29 and 31, 1866.

61. *Conservator*, November 10, 1866.

62. *Missouri Statesman*, January 4, 1867.

63. *Missouri Democrat*, December 7 and 12, 1866; *Missouri Statesman*, January 4, 1867.

64. Chester H. Rowell, ed., *A Historical and Legal Digest of All the Contested Election Cases in the House of Representatives of the United States from the First to the Fifty-sixth Congress, 1789–1901*, 219; *Missouri Statesman*, February 15, 1867.

65. *Ibid.*, January 4, 1867; Rowell, *Contested Election Cases*, 219-20; Johnson Papers, Rollins to Johnson, November 22, 1867; Blair Papers, William F. Switzler to Frank Blair, March 16, 1868; William K. Patrick Papers, Joseph W. McClurg to Patrick, May 2, 1868.

66. *Missouri Democrat, passim*, November, 1866–February, 1867.

67. Drake, "Autobiography," 1216-19; *Evening News*, November 23 and 28 and December 1 and 10, 1866; *Missouri Democrat*, December 1, 1866; *Missouri Republican*, December 1, 1866.

68. Drake, "Autobiography," 1219; Barclay, "The Liberal Republican Movement," 277-78.

69. *Evening News*, November 29 and 30, 1866; Drake, "Autobiography," 1219. For a private reaction, see Blow Family Papers, Henry T. Blow to Minerva Blow, December 1, 1866.

70. *Ibid.; Missouri Democrat*, December 1, 1866.

71. See above, pp. 73-74.

72. Quoted in Barclay, "The Liberal Republican Movement," 297.

73. Drake, "Autobiography," 1221-23; *Missouri Weekly Patriot*, January 3, 1867.

74. *Missouri Democrat*, November 23, 24 and 26, December 3 and 24, 1866; *Evening News*, November 23 and 27, 1866; John F. Darby Papers, R. H. Cooper to C. H. Branscomb, January 1, 1867.

75. *Missouri Democrat*, January 7, 1867; *Missouri Statesman*, January 11, 1867; Drake, "Autobiography," 1223-24.

76. Rollins Papers, Samuel M. Breckinridge to Rollins, January 9 and 12, 1867; *Missouri Statesman*, January 18, 1867.

77. *Missouri Democrat*, January 9, 1867; *Missouri Statesman*, January 25, 1867.

78. Quoted in Barclay, "The Liberal Republican Movement," 303n.

79. *Missouri Democrat*, January 9, 1867; *Missouri Statesman*, January 18, 1867.

80. *Missouri Democrat*, January 17, 1867.

CHAPTER VI

1. Columbia *Missouri Statesman*, February 24, March 10 and 31, and April 14, 1865; *O. R.*, Ser. I, Vol. XLVIII, Part 1, 1078.

2. *Ibid.*, 1257.

3. *Missouri Statesman*, June 23 and 30, 1865. Jim Jackson and one of his men were captured in Pike County as they were leaving Missouri after being granted parole under President Johnson's amnesty. Although they had not violated their parole, too many held grudges against them for past deeds. One man claimed that Jackson had robbed him and murdered his friend. A quick trial followed; Jackson was found guilty and executed by a squad of militia.

4. St. Louis *Missouri Democrat*, May 22, 1865.

5. *O. R.*, Ser. I, Vol. XLVIII, Part 2, 295.

6. Records of the Bureau of Refugees, Freedmen and Abandoned Lands, Missouri-Arkansas District, L. M. Tuttle to John W. Sprague, August 16, 1865; E. O'Brien to Sprague, August 4, 1865; Sprague to O. O. Howard, August 7, 1865; Charles H. Lovejoy to Sprague, August 28, 1865; Jefferson City *Missouri State Times*, August 4, 1865; *Missouri Democrat*, October 4, 1865.

7. Freedmen's Bureau Records, Missouri-Arkansas District, Chaplain A. Wright to Sprague, August 2, 1865. The counties visited were Audrain, Boone, Buchanan, Cooper, Howard, and Macon.

8. *Ibid.*, R. B. Taylor to Sprague, September 25, 1865; *Missouri Democrat*, October 4, 13, and 27, 1865.

9. *Ibid.*, October 27, 1865.

10. *Ibid.*, October 2, 1865.

11. Esque Douglas, "The History of the Negro in Northeast Missouri, 1820–1870," unpublished Master's thesis, Lincoln University, 74-75, 134-35; *New York Tribune*, July 6, 1871.

12. Paul S. Peirce, *The Freedmen's Bureau: A Chapter in the History of Reconstruction*, 131.

13. *New York Tribune*, July 6, 1871; Washington D. C., *New National Era*, December 7, 1871.

14. *Ibid.*, July 28, 1870. The National Freedmen's Savings and Trust Company closed its doors nationwide on June 28, 1874, because of insolvency. The St. Louis branch had had $58,397.00 on

deposit as of January 24, 1874. Creditors ultimately received back $28,355.88 of this amount. Walter L. Fleming, *The Freedmen's Savings Bank*, 97, 99, 143.

15. Darby Papers, Isaac H. Sturgeon to C. H. Branscomb, January 19, 1867; *Missouri Democrat*, February 25, 1867.

16. *Ibid.*, June 4 and 5, 1867; *Missouri Statesman*, May 8, 1868.

17. Washington, D. C., *New Era*, June 2, 1870. This paper became the *New National Era* with the issue of September 8, 1870.

18. Douglas, "Negro in Northeast Missouri," 115-20.

19. *A Compendium of the Ninth Census (June 1, 1870)*, 66-69.

20. *Convention Journal*, 25.

21. *Ibid.*, 26.

22. *Missouri Democrat*, January 20, 1865.

23. *St. Joseph Morning Herald*, January 6, 1865.

24. *Missouri Democrat*, February 6 and 8, 1865.

25. *Missouri Constitution*, 1865, Art. II, Sec. 18; Art. IV, Secs. 3 and 5; Art. V, Sec. 2.

26. *Missouri Democrat*, January 20, 1865; St. Louis *Missouri Republican*, February 27, 1865; *Convention Journal*, 196-99, 222; *Missouri Constitution, 1865*, Art. IX, Sec. 2.

27. *New York Tribune*, July 6, 1871. Additionally, some attempts at prewar education may have been accomplished through Sunday schools in some of the Negro churches, especially in St. Louis. Shoemaker, *Missouri and Missourians*, I, 523; John M. Peck, *Forty Years of Pioneer Life*, 210.

28. Douglas, "Negro in Northeast Missouri," 98.

29. Henry C. Bruce, *The New Man: 29 Years a Slave*, 76-77.

30. J. G. Forman, *The Western Sanitary Commission: A Sketch*, 95.

31. *Missouri Democrat*, February 22, 1865.

32. *Final Report of the Western Sanitary Commission, May 9, 1864–December 31, 1865*, 128-29.

33. *Ibid.*; *Missouri Democrat*, September 13, 1865.

34. *Ibid.*, December 1, 1865, December 17, 1866, and January 29, 1869; Charlotte C. Eliot, *William Greenleaf Eliot: Minister, Educator, Philanthropist*, 270.

35. *Laws of Missouri, 23rd General Assembly, Regular Session, 1864–1865*, 125-26.

36. *Missouri State Times*, March 18 and October 4, 1865.

37. *Report of the Superintendent of Public Schools of the State of Missouri to the General Assembly, 1865*, 111.

38. *Laws of Missouri, 1865–1866*, 173, 177.

39. See below, pp. 139-40.

40. *Report of the Superintendent of Public Schools, 1867*, 9-11, 44-152.

41. "Colored Schools," *Journal of Education*, II, 5, citing St. Louis *Westliche Post;* Henry S. Williams, "The Development of the Negro Public School System in Missouri," *Journal of Negro History*, V, 144; *Ninth Census Compendium*, 452-53.

42. *Missouri Statesman*, November 27, 1868, and November 12, 1869; *History of Boone County, Missouri*, 818.

43. *Missouri Democrat*, September 19 and November 13, 1867, June 24, 1868; *New York Tribune*, July 6, 1871.

44. *Chillicothe Spectator*, January 3 and February 28, 1867.

45. *Missouri Democrat*, December 30, 1867, and March 4, 1868; *Missouri State Times*, March 6, 1868; *New York Tribune*, July 6, 1871.

46. *Report of the Superintendent of Public Schools, 1869*, 35.

47. *Laws of Missouri, 24th General Assembly, Adjourned Session, 1868*, 170; *Report of the Superintendent of Public Schools, 1872*, 44; *Report of the Superintendent of Public Schools, 1874*, 18; *Laws of Missouri, 27th General Assembly, Adjourned Session, 1874*, 168; Williams, "Negro Public School System," 140; Robert I. Brigham, "The Education of the Negro in Missouri," unpublished doctoral dissertation, University of Missouri, 86.

48. *Laws of Missouri, 1868*, 170; *Laws of Missouri, 25th General Assembly, Regular Session, 1869*, 86-87; *Laws of Missouri, 1874*, 164.

49. *Report of the Superintendent of Public Schools, 1871*, 257; *Report of the Superintendent of Public Schools, 1872*, 246; *Report of the Superintendent of Public Schools, 1873*, 38; Williams, "Negro Public School System," 146-47.

50. *Thirteenth Annual Report of the Board of Directors of the St. Louis Public Schools, 1866–1867*, 32, 39; *Laws of Missouri, 1869*, 86-87; *Laws of Missouri, 1874*, 164.

51. *Report of the Superintendent of Public Schools, 1869*, 34.

52. *Report of the Superintendent of Public Schools, 1873*, 216-17, 223-327; *Report of the Superintendent of Public Schools, 1875*, 12.

53. *Report of the Superintendent of Public Schools, 1869*, 36-37.

54. W. Sherman Savage, *The History of Lincoln University*, 1-3.

55. *Ibid.*, 3-4; *Missouri State Times*, February 15, 1867.

56. Savage, *Lincoln University*, 7.

57. *Ibid.*, 10.

58. *Ibid.*, 8, 12; *New National Era*, September 15, 1870.

59. Savage, *Lincoln University*, 13-14; Frank F. Stephens, *A History of the University of Missouri*, 207-8.

60. *Missouri Democrat*, January 24, 1870; *Journal of Education*, II, 113; *Laws of Missouri, 25th General Assembly, Adjourned Session, 1870*, 136-37. For a general discussion of higher education in Missouri, see Chapter VII.

61. *Missouri Democrat*, March 12, 1870.

62. Savage, *Lincoln University*, 17-18; *New York Tribune*, July 6, 1871; Shoemaker, *Missouri and Missourians*, II, 672.

63. *Missouri Democrat*, April 19, 1865; *Missouri Statesman*, June 30 and September 15, 1865.

64. *Missouri Democrat*, October 4, 1865.

65. *Ibid.*, October 16, 1865.

66. *D. A. B.*, X, 597-98; *Missouri Democrat*, February 20, 1865.

67. *Ibid.*, November 29, 1865.

68. *Ibid.*, January 12, 1866, and January 15, 1867; *Missouri Statesman*, January 19, 1866.

69. *Missouri Democrat*, January 12, 1866, and January 11, 1867.

70. *Ibid.*, December 13, 1865, and January 15, 1867; Irving Dilliard, "James Milton Turner: A Little Known Benefactor of His People," *Journal of Negro History*, XIX, 374-81.

71. *House Journal, 23rd General Assembly, Adjourned Session*, 753, Appendix, 842; *Missouri Democrat*, March 14, 1866.

72. See above, p. 100.

73. *Missouri Democrat*, January 18, 1867.

74. *Ibid.*, January 11 and 15, 1867.

75. *D. A. B.*, V, 406-7; *Missouri Democrat*, February 8, 1867.

76. *Morning Herald*, January 31, 1867; *Missouri Democrat*, February 8, 1867; *Senate Journal, 24th General Assembly, Regular Session*, 280-81; *Missouri Statesman*, March 15, 1867; *House Journal, 24th General Assembly, Regular Session*, 410-11, 504, 525, 556.

CHAPTER VII

1. St. Louis *Missouri Democrat*, January 4, 1867.

2. Maynard G. Redfield, "Some Social and Intellectual Influences in the Development of Public Education in Missouri, 1865 to 1900," unpublished doctoral dissertation, Washington University, 72-73; Shoemaker, *Missouri and Missourians*, I, 806.

3. *Ibid.*, I, 807, 994.

4. David P. Dyer, *Autobiography and Reminiscences*, 48-49. Permission to quote granted by George C. Dyer.

5. Shoemaker, *Missouri and Missourians*, I, 807; Dela Lange, "A Century of Achievement in the St. Louis Public High Schools, 1853-1953," *St. Louis Public School Journal*, VI, 3; Redfield, "Public Education in Missouri," 58.

6. Shoemaker, *Missouri and Missourians*, I, 806-7.

7. Parrish, *Turbulent Partnership*, 24-25, 78; Shoemaker, *Missouri and Missourians*, I, 994, 996.

8. *Missouri Constitution, 1865*, Art. IX; *Convention Journal*, 213-14.

9. *Report of the Superintendent of Public Schools, 1865*, 106-11.

10. Kurt F. Leidecker, *Yankee Teacher: The Life of William Torrey Harris*, 173.

11. *Laws of Missouri, 1865–1866*, 183-84; "County Superintendents," *Journal of Education*, I, 25-26.

12. *Laws of Missouri, 1865–1866*, 189-90.

13. *Ibid.*, 171-76; *Report of the Superintendent of Public Schools, 1870*, vi-vii.

14. *Laws of Missouri, 1874*, 147-68.

15. *Laws of Missouri, 1865–1866*, 173.

16. *Report of the Superintendent of Public Schools, 1868*, 7.

17. "School Houses and School Furniture," *Journal of Education*, I, 56; "Another Warning," *Journal of Education*, II, 7; *Sedalia Times*, August 5, 1869.

18. *Report of the Superintendent of Public Schools, 1867*, 8-9; George O. Garnsey, "School Architecture," *Journal of Education*, I, 165.

19. *Laws of Missouri, 1865–1866*, 176-77.

20. *Report of the Superintendent of Public Schools, 1870*, viii.

21. Redfield, "Public Education in Missouri," 77-78, 112.

22. *Laws of Missouri, 1865–1866*, 191-94.

23. *Report of the Superintendent of Public Schools, 1870*, vi.

24. *Kansas City Daily Journal of Commerce*, June 6, 1867.

25. *Ibid.*, September 29, 1867; Norton, "Kansas City Public Schools," *Journal of Education*, I, 21; Carrie W. Whitney, *Kansas City, Missouri: Its History and Its People*, I, 305-6.

26. "St. Joseph Public Schools," *Journal of Education*, I, 131-32; *History of Buchanan County, Missouri*, 540-53.

27. Leidecker, *Yankee Teacher*, 167-79, 246-48.

28. *Missouri Democrat*, September 2, 1867.

29. Leidecker, *Yankee Teacher*, 245-48, 328-44.

30. William T. Harris, "What Shall We Study?" *Journal of Education*, II, 1-3.

31. "The Public Schools and the Polytechnic Institute," *Journal of Education*, I, 24-25; "The Public School Polytechnic Building of St. Louis," *Journal of Education*, I, 154-55; Leidecker, *Yankee Teacher*, 287-89.

32. Lange, "A Century of Achievement," 20-21; "St. Louis High School," *Journal of Education*, I, 75.

33. *Report of the Superintendent of Public Schools, 1870*, xv.

34. Leidecker, *Yankee Teacher*, 273-74; Redfield, "Public Education in Missouri," 125.

35. Joseph Schafer, ed., *The Intimate Letters of Carl Schurz, 1841–1869*, 382-83. Permission to quote granted by the State Historical Society of Wisconsin.

36. Redfield, "Public Education in Missouri," 127-31. For a typical article expressing this viewpoint, see J. H. B., "Importance of Aids to Illustration in Schools," *Journal of Education*, I, 109-11.

37. *Times*, August 5, 1869.

38. *Daily Journal of Commerce*, December 11, 1868. The paper noted that the plan had been used in the schools of Lawrence, Kansas, to good effect.

39. "The Government of Children," *Journal of Education*, I, 35.

40. *Daily Journal of Commerce*, September 27, 1867.

41. Leidecker, *Yankee Teacher*, 268.

42. "School Visiting," *Journal of Education*, III, 6-7; J. M. Olcott, "The Teachers' Institute," *Journal of Education*, III, 6.

43. "What Ought to be Done?" *Ibid.*, II, 45.

44. *Laws of Missouri, 1865–1866*, 183, 189.

45. *Report of the Superintendent of Public Schools, 1867*, 20-21.

46. *Times*, May 6, 1869.

47. Ironton *Iron County Register*, October 14, 1869.

48. *Report of the Superintendent of Public Schools, 1867*, 21; *Missouri Democrat*, September, 1867, *passim*.

49. *Ibid.*, May 30, June 6 and 22, 1866, and September 2, 1867.

50. *Report of the Superintendent of Public Schools, 1866*, 15, 17; Columbia *Missouri Statesman*, July 28, 1865; *Laws of Missouri, 24th General Assembly, Regular Session, 1867*, 9.

51. Jonas Viles, *The University of Missouri, A Centennial History*, 127-30.

52. *Report of the Superintendent of Public Schools, 1867*, 20.

53. Lucy Simmons and Paul O. Selby, "The Northeast Missouri State Teachers College and Its Founder, Joseph Baldwin," *Missouri Historical Review*, XXII, 162-66.

54. Eugene M. Violette, *History of the First District State Normal School*, 36-37; Claude A. Phillips, *A History of Education in Missouri*, 104.

55. Simmons and Selby, "The Northeast Missouri State Teachers College," 166-67.

56. Phillips, *History of Education*, 98; Mount Vernon *Spring River Fountain*, July 9, 1868; *A Reminiscent History of the Ozark Region*, 350-51; *Journal of Education*, I, 9-10, 26.

57. Phillips, *History of Education*, 98-99; *Journal of Education*, I, 213.

58. *Times,* June 24, July 8, and September 2, 1869; *Sedalia Democrat,* July 15 and 22, 1869.

59. *Times,* June 24, July 29, and September 2, 1869.

60. *Ibid.,* September 2 and October 7, 1869.

61. *Laws of Missouri, 1870,* 134-36.

62. Kirksville *North Missouri Register,* February 16, 1871; Violette, *First District State Normal School,* 49.

63. *Ibid.,* 50; *North Missouri Register,* February 16, 1871; *Democrat,* March 16, 1871.

64. *Warrensburg Weekly Standard,* January 5, 1871; *North Missouri Register,* February 16, 1871.

65. *Ibid.; Weekly Standard,* January 5, 1871; *Democrat,* March 23, 1871.

66. *Ibid.,* May 4 and 11, 1871; *Weekly Standard,* May 4 and 11, 1871; *History of Johnson County, Missouri,* 292-96.

67. *Weekly Standard,* May 11, 1871. Sedalia held its own privately operated normal school that same summer. *Democrat,* May 17, 1871. This school, however, was a short-lived project.

68. Shoemaker, *Missouri and Missourians,* I, 1000; William B. Smith, *James Sidney Rollins: A Memoir,* 41; Stephens, *A History of the University of Missouri,* 13-18, 150-87; Viles, *University of Missouri,* 109-10.

69. *Missouri Statesman,* September 1 and 29, 1865, February 9, March 16, and May 4, 1866, and November 1, 1867.

70. Jefferson City *Missouri State Times,* January 21, 1865.

71. *Missouri Constitution, 1865,* Art. IX, Sec. 4; *Convention Journal,* 207.

72. *Missouri State Times,* January 14 and 21, 1865.

73. *Missouri Statesman,* February 3, 1865.

74. Avery and Shoemaker, *Messages and Proclamations,* IV, 86-87.

75. Smith, *James Sidney Rollins,* 40-50; Stephens, *University of Missouri,* 196-97; *Missouri Democrat,* March 16, 1867.

76. Dyer, *Autobiography,* 126; Stephens, *University of Missouri,* 194-99; Rollins Papers, Daniel Read to Rollins, February 2, 1867.

77. Dyer, *Autobiography,* 126-27; Smith, *James Sidney Rollins,* 41-42; Rollins Papers, Read to Rollins, February 2, 1867.

78. *Laws of Missouri, 1867,* 9.

79. John J. Jones, "The Morrill Lands of the University of Missouri," *Missouri Historical Review,* LI, 127-28.

80. *Laws of Missouri, 22nd General Assembly, Regular Session, 1862–1863,* 34-36; *Laws of Missouri, 1865–1866,* 91.

81. *Missouri Statesman,* July 28, November 17 and 24, 1865.

82. Viles, *University of Missouri,* 117-20, 126; Rollins Papers, J. W. Hoyt to Rollins, February 20, 1867.

83. *Report of the Commissioner of the General Land Office to the Secretary of the Interior, 1867,* 186-89; *Missouri Statesman,* February 8, 1867. Cf. Carl Schurz Papers, J. S. Wilson to Schurz, November 29, 1869, and January 28, 1870.

84. *Report of the Commissioner of the General Land Office, 1866,* 145; *Report of the Commissioner of the General Land Office, 1867,* 186-89.

85. Rollins Papers, Frank Blair to Rollins, February 9, 1867, and March 15, 1868; *Missouri Democrat,* March 17, and April 11, 1868.

86. Rollins Papers, Read to Rollins, January 14, February 6, and March 6, 1868, and February 1, 1869; *Missouri Democrat,* July 14, 1869.

87. *Missouri Statesman,* February 11 and 18, 1870; *Laws of Missouri, 1870,* 15-21. The school of mines was located at Rolla in Phelps County the following year.

88. *Missouri Statesman,* March 4, 1870.

89. *Laws of Missouri, 1870,* 15-21.

90. Jones, "Morrill Lands," 130-38.

91. *Ninth Census Compendium,* 487-90, 499; *The American Annual Cyclopedia and Register of Important Events for the Year 1868,* 518.

92. Jefferson City *People's Weekly Tribune,* May 31, 1871; *Ninth Census Compendium,* 506-7.

93. "Public Lectures," *Journal of Education,* I, 60.

CHAPTER VIII

1. *St. Joseph Morning Herald,* January 7, 1865.

2. *Ibid.,* January 10, 1865.

3. *Ibid.,* February 5 and 9, 1865.

4. St. Louis *Missouri Democrat,* January 30, March 20 and 31, April 14, October 6, 18, and 27, November 1 and 24, 1865; Springfield *Missouri Weekly Patriot,* October 19, 1865.

5. For typical comment, see *Missouri Democrat,* October 22 and 29, 1863; *Morning Herald,* February 4 and 10, 1865.

6. *Missouri Democrat,* June 6 and 8, 1863.

7. *Ibid.,* September 25, 1863.

8. Buel Leopard and Floyd C. Shoemaker, eds., *The Messages and Proclamations of the Governors of the State of Missouri,* III, 473-74; Edwin L. Lopata, *Local Aid to Railroads in Missouri,* 68; *The American Annual Cyclopedia and Register of Important Events for the Year 1863,* 658.

9. *Missouri Democrat,* July 4, 1863.

10. *Laws of Missouri, 1863–1864,* 218-20, 225-26.

11. Smith, "New England Business Interests in Missouri," 13-16;

Wyatt W. Belcher, *The Economic Rivalry Between St. Louis and Chicago, 1850–1880*, 89-91; Richard C. Overton, *Burlington West: A Colonization History of the Burlington Railroad*, 161-62, 257-58, 290.

12. Avery and Shoemaker, *Messages and Proclamations*, IV, 60-61; *Laws of Missouri, 1864–1865*, 43-45.

13. *Missouri Democrat*, April 5 and 21, June 7, July 24, and August 4, 1865.

14. Jefferson City *Missouri State Times*, June 16, 1865.

15. *Missouri Democrat*, August 4, 1865.

16. *Ibid.*, March 15, April 14, and September 8 and 27, 1865; Lopata, *Local Aid to Railroads*, 69.

17. *Missouri Democrat*, March 1, 1865.

18. Rollins Papers, Theodore M. Pomeroy to Rollins, July 25, 1865, George W. McKee to Rollins, October 13, 1865.

19. *Missouri Democrat*, July 17, 1865.

20. *Ibid.*, May 25, 1866.

21. Norman L. Crockett, "A Study of Confusion: Missouri's Immigration Program, 1865–1916," *Missouri Historical Review*, LVII, 254-55; *Chillicothe Spectator*, May 10, 1866.

22. *Missouri Democrat*, July 17, 1868.

23. *Ibid.*, April 13, 1868.

24. *Missouri Weekly Patriot*, September 27, 1866; *Missouri Democrat*, September 19, 1866, and March 26, 1868; Lopata, *Local Aid to Railroads*, 69-70.

25. Avery and Shoemaker, *Messages and Proclamations*, IV, 145.

26. *Ninth Census Compendium*, 8.

27. *Ibid.*, 241-50, 376-77, 444-49.

28. *Ibid.*, 688-90; Shoemaker, *Missouri and Missourians*, II, 446-51.

29. Belcher, *Economic Rivalry*, 54, 90-91, 97-98, 139-57, 164-65.

30. *Missouri Democrat*, June 19, 1865.

31. *Morning Herald*, February 14, 1865.

32. *Missouri Democrat*, January 17, 1867.

33. Belcher, *Economic Rivalry*, 170-76, 193-96; *Missouri Democrat*, February 13 and 14, 1867.

34. Belcher, *Economic Rivalry*, 75-77.

35. John W. Million, *State Aid to Railways in Missouri*, 44-139, 232-43; Lopata, *Local Aid to Railroads*, 43-59.

36. Belcher, *Economic Rivalry*, 77-92.

37. Lopata, *Local Aid to Railroads*, 19-23.

38. Million, *State Aid to Railways*, 126-27; Margaret L. Fitzsimmons, "Missouri Railroads During the Civil War and Reconstruction," *Missouri Historical Review*, XXXV, 189-97; Lincoln Papers, *passim*, February, 1862–July, 1864.

39. *Laws of Missouri, 1863–1864,* 50-58; Samuel L. M. Barlow Papers, Henry D. Bacon to Barlow, April 5, 1864; *Missouri Democrat,* April 17, September 18 and 22, 1865; St. Louis *Missouri Republican,* September 21, 1865.

40. *Laws of Missouri, 1863–1864,* 50-58.

41. Million, *State Aid to Railways,* 133-37; *Laws of Missouri, 1864–1865,* 90-96.

42. *Missouri Democrat,* July 14, 1865; *Missouri State Times,* December 8, 1865.

43. *Missouri Democrat,* May 7 and July 27, 1866, April 6 and October 18, 1867. The specific terms of the Eads arrangement may be found in Rollins Papers, James B. Eads to Isaac H. Sturgeon, October 15, 1867.

44. This transaction involved the Pacific Railroad. See below, p. 197.

45. Million, *State Aid to Railroads,* 159-68; *Laws of Missouri, 1868,* 112-13; *Missouri Democrat,* March 2, 1868.

46. *Ibid.,* June 26, July 20, and December 5, 1868, and May 30, 1871; Schurz Papers, James B. Eads to Schurz, April 16, 1870; Avery and Shoemaker, *Messages and Proclamations,* IV, 355.

47. Million, *State Aid to Railroads,* 173-87; 253-56. Certain stockholders of the Pacific Railroad shortly thereafter secured an injunction in Federal District Court to prevent payment of the greater part of the promised "boodle." *Ibid.,* 244-57.

48. *Missouri Constitution, 1865,* Art. XI, Secs. 13-15; *Convention Journal,* 278-79; *Missouri State Times,* July 7, 1865.

49. *Laws of Missouri, 1865–1866,* 101-16; *Missouri Weekly Patriot,* March 29, 1866.

50. Million, *State Aid to Railroads,* 168-73; Fitzsimmons, "Missouri Railroads," 200-201; *Laws of Missouri, 1868,* 118-26; *Missouri Democrat,* June 24 and July 31, 1867, March 11, 1868, and May 4, 1870; *Missouri Weekly Patriot, passim,* January–June, 1868; Blair Papers, Gustavus V. Fox to Montgomery Blair, April 15, 1870; Thomas Allen to Montgomery Blair, May 26, 1870.

51. Million, *State Aid to Railroads,* 145-57; *Laws of Missouri, 1868,* 61-63; Belcher, *Economic Rivalry,* 119; Margaret L. Fitzsimmons, "Railroad Development in Missouri," unpublished Master's thesis, Washington University, 300-28; *Missouri Democrat,* March 13, 15, and 26, April 13, 17, and 20, May 6, August 2, October 21, and November 14, 1867; *Missouri Republican,* August 15 and 17, 1869; Logan U. Reavis, *St. Louis: The Future Great City of the World,* 267-68.

52. Million, *State Aid to Railroads,* 157-59; *Laws of Missouri, 1868,* 107-11; Fitzsimmons, "Railroad Development," 340-45.

53. *House Journal, 24th General Assembly, Adjourned Session,*

730, 755; *Senate Journal, 24th General Assembly, Adjourned Session*, 510-11, 526-27.

54. Million, *State Aid to Railroads*, 187-90, 227-28. Missouri's total state debt had stood at $36,094,908.00 in 1865. This figure included a war debt of $7,546,575.00. The Federal Government reimbursed $4,863,924.90 of this latter amount in 1866 under wartime agreements concerning the expenses of Missouri militia. By a variety of other means, including the sale of the railroads, Missouri had reduced its total indebtedness to $21,675,000.00 by January 1, 1869. This debt was not completely cleared until 1903. Shoemaker, *Missouri and Missourians*, I, 775-76.

55. Belcher, *Economic Rivalry*, 92-94, 181, 197-201; Shoemaker, *Missouri and Missourians*, I, 779; George R. Taylor and Irene D. Neu, *The American Railroad Network, 1861–1890*, 40-41; Fitzsimmons, "Railroad Development," 174-78.

56. *Missouri Democrat*, July 7, 1865, January 26, February 21, and May 9, 1866, January 18, February 6, March 27, July 16, September 27, November 25, and December 25, 1867, March 25, 1868, *passim*, 1870; *Missouri Republican*, July 5, 1874; Bacon Papers, Samuel P. Gaty to Bacon, February 24, March 13 and 26, April 6, and November 21, 1868, August 5, 25, and 30, and October 3, 1871, November 20, 1873; James B. Eads Papers, W. M. McPherson to Eads, January 12, 1869; Schurz Papers, Eads to Schurz, April 16, 1870, Isaac H. Sturgeon to Schurz, May 21, 1870; Ernest Kirschten, *Catfish and Crystal*, 236-40; Calvin M. Woodward, *A History of the St. Louis Bridge*.

57. Belcher, *Economic Rivalry*, 199-200.

58. A. Theodore Brown, *Frontier Community: Kansas City to 1870*, 115-30, 156.

59. Parrish, *Turbulent Partnership*, 84-86, 97-100, 155-60, 188-89.

60. Brown, *Frontier Community*, 190-92, 197-200, 203-13; *Laws of Missouri, 1864–1865*, 238-40.

61. Charles N. Glaab, *Kansas City and the Railroads: Community Policy in the Growth of a Regional Metropolis*, 143-67.

62. Brown, *Frontier Community*, 227-28.

63. *Ibid.*, 217-21; Glaab, *Kansas City and the Railroads*, 168-69.

64. Brown, *Frontier Community*, 228.

65. Million, *State Aid to Railways*, 232-43; Lopata, *Local Aid to Railroads*, 43-127.

66. Shoemaker, *Missouri and Missourians*, I, 782-83.

CHAPTER IX

1. Shoemaker, *Missouri and Missourians*, I, 796-98.

2. *Missouri Constitution, 1865*, Art. VIII, Sec. 4; *Laws of Missouri, 1865–1866*, 20-70.

3. Shoemaker, *Missouri and Missourians*, II, 482-84; St. Louis *Industrial Advocate*, September 8, 1866.

4. *Ibid.*, August 4 and November 10, 1866, and February 2, 1867; *The Statistics of the Wealth and Industry of the United States*, Vol. III of the Ninth Census, 778-79.

5. Reavis, *St. Louis*, 353; Springfield *Missouri Weekly Patriot*, September 28, 1865, and January 11, 1866; *Statistics of the Wealth and Industry*, 778-79; Blow Family Papers, P. E. Blow to Henry T. Blow, May 9, 1864.

6. Shoemaker, *Missouri and Missourians*, II, 484-85; Arrell M. Gibson, "Lead Mining in Southwest Missouri after 1865," *Missouri Historical Review*, LIII, 319-26.

7. Arthur B. Cozzens, "The Iron Industry of Missouri," *Missouri Historical Review*, XXXV, 509, 518-20.

8. *Ibid.*, 511-15; St. Louis *Missouri Democrat*, May 6, 1868, and May 19, 1870; *Statistics of the Wealth and Industry*, 686-90; *Ninth Census Compendium*, 873-74.

9. *Missouri Democrat*, May 13, 1870.

10. *Statistics of the Wealth and Industry*, 778-79.

11. Shoemaker, *Missouri and Missourians*, II, 495-97.

12. St. Louis *Missouri Republican*, September 2, 4, and 23, 1863, and February 13, 1864.

13. *Missouri Democrat*, December 25, 1865; *Industrial Advocate*, August 4 and November 10, 1866.

14. *General History of Macon County, Missouri*, 103-4; *Industrial Advocate*, January 12, 1867.

15. *Ibid.*

16. *Ibid.*, February 9, 1867.

17. *History of Macon County*, 103-4.

18. Walter R. Houf, "Fifty Years of Missouri Labor, 1820–1870," unpublished Master's thesis, University of Missouri, 65-84.

19. *Ibid.*, 85-89.

20. *Missouri Republican*, February 17, April 11, and September 12, 1864.

21. *Ibid.*, February 15, March 9, 11, 16, and 30, April 11, 15, and 18, May 6, July 11 and 13, 1864.

22. *Ibid.*, April 6, 1864.

23. *Ibid.*, April 15, 1864.

24. *Ibid.*, September 21, 1864. In all, nine unions were known to be in existence by the end of 1864. John R. Commons and others, *History of Labour in the United States*, II, 17-19.

25. *Missouri Democrat*, January 8, March 21 and 28, 1866; *Industrial Advocate*, September 22, 1866.

26. Commons, *History of Labour*, II, 17; *Missouri Republican*, April 15, 1864; *Missouri Democrat*, December 25, 1865; *Industrial Advocate*, August 4 and 11, 1866.

27. *Ibid.*, August 18, 1866.

28. *Ibid.*, August 11, 1866.

29. *Ibid.*, September 22, 1866.

30. *Ibid.*, October 6, 13, and 20, 1866.

31. *Ibid.*, October 20 and 27, and November 10, 1866, February 9, 1867.

32. *Ibid.*, September 8 and October 13, 1866, January 5, 12, and 26, and February 2, 1867.

33. Commons, *History of Labour*, II, 87-91.

34. *Ibid.*, II, 91-96; *Missouri Democrat*, November 6, 1865.

35. *Congressional Globe*, 39th Cong., 1st Sess., 50.

36. *Ibid.*, 1178.

37. *Missouri Democrat*, March 26, 1866.

38. *Industrial Advocate*, August 11, 1866; Commons, *History of Labour*, II, 104.

39. *Industrial Advocate*, August 25 and September 1, 1866; John R. Commons and others, eds., *A Documentary History of American Industrial Society*, IX, 127-41.

40. *Industrial Advocate*, September 8 and 29, October 27 and November 3, 1866.

41. *House Journal, 24th General Assembly, Regular Session*, 21, 61, 599-600; *Senate Journal, 24th General Assembly, Regular Session*, 448; *Laws of Missouri, 1867*, 132.

42. Commons, *History of Labour*, II, 109.

43. *Ninth Census Compendium*, 796-97.

44. *Ibid.*, 830-31; *Missouri Democrat*, December 10, 1870

45. *Statistics of the Wealth and Industry*, 686-90.

46. *Ibid.*

47. See above, p. 186.

CHAPTER X

1. St. Louis *Missouri Democrat*, March 6, 1867; Drake, "Autobiography," 1153-55.

2. Jefferson City *Missouri State Times*, May 31 and June 7, 1867.

3. Patrick Papers, William A. Pile to Patrick, April 1, 1867, J. H. Clendening to Patrick, May 6, 1867; *Missouri Democrat*, April 3, 1867; *Missouri State Times*, April 5 and 12, 1867.

4. *D. A. B.*, XVI, 466-68.

5. Schafer, *Intimate Letters of Carl Schurz*, 373-74.

6. *Ibid.*, 374, 376-77.

7. *Ibid.*, 377-83, 387, 395-97.

8. *Ibid.*, 383-84.

9. Robert B. Beath, *History of the Grand Army of the Republic,* 547; Schafer, *Intimate Letters of Carl Schurz,* 391-95; *Missouri Democrat,* September 11, 1867.

10. March, "Charles Daniel Drake," 426.

11. Norma L. Peterson, "The Political Fluctuations of B. Gratz Brown, 1850–1870," *Missouri Historical Review,* LI, 28-29.

12. Parrish, *Turbulent Partnership,* 172-73; Johnson Papers, Allen P. Richardson to Johnson, April 9, 1867; Patrick Papers, Pile to Patrick, April 1, 1867, J. H. Clendening to Patrick, May 12, 1868; *Missouri Democrat,* May 13, 1868; Springfield *Missouri Weekly Patriot,* May 23, 1868; Schafer, *Intimate Letters of Carl Schurz,* 441-43; David M. DeWitt, *The Impeachment and Trial of Andrew Johnson, Seventeenth President of the United States,* 522-29, 552.

13. Columbia *Missouri Statesman,* January 27, 1865; Cyrus Thompson, "Reminiscences of Official Life in Jefferson City, 1865–1875," *Missouri Historical Review,* XXIII, 551-53; Patrick Papers, Samuel Bonner to Patrick, March 13, 1866, Joseph W McClurg to Patrick, March 14, 1868.

14. Quoted in Barclay, "The Liberal Republican Movement," 303n.

15. Johnson Papers, Frank Blair to Johnson, March 3, 1867, Richardson to Johnson, March 29 and April 9, 1867, John B. Henderson and Thomas E. Noell Memos, April, 1867; Patrick Papers, Pile to Patrick, April 1, 1867; Rollins Papers, Lewis V. Bogy to Rollins, December 3, 1866, Orville H. Browning to Rollins, February 20, April 11, and May 18, 1867; *Missouri Statesman,* March 15, 1867; Reavis, *St. Louis,* 234-35; *History of Greene County, Missouri,* 506.

16. Johnson Papers, John Hogan to Johnson, April 4, 1867.

17. *Missouri Democrat,* February 23, 1867; Rollins Papers, H. J. Drummond to Rollins, April 22, 1867.

18. *Ibid.*, Frank Blair to Rollins, February 9, 1867; Smith, *Blair Family,* II, 383-90.

19. Rollins Papers, Drummond to Rollins, April 22, 1867.

20. Blair v. Ridgely *et al.* (1867), 41 Mo. 63-184.

21. State v. Woodson (1867), 41 Mo. 227-38.

22. *Missouri Statesman,* March 29, 1867.

23. *Ibid.*, August 2, 1867.

24. *Ibid.*, October 11, 1867. The Johnson Papers contain a copy of the printed circular of the State Democratic Association.

25. Ironton *Iron County Register,* October 10, 17, and 24, 1867; *Missouri Democrat,* November 20, 1867; *Missouri Statesman,* November 22 and December 27, 1867.

26. Johnson Papers, Democratic State Association of Missouri to the Democracy of the State and City of New York, November 7, 1867; *Missouri Statesman*, October 18 and November 15, 1867.

27. Johnson Papers, Lewis V. Bogy to Johnson, February 19, 1868.

28. *Missouri Statesman, passim*, January–February, 1868.

29. *Ibid.*, February 7, 1868. Resolutions of these Democratic meetings in Johnson Papers, February, 1868.

30. Johnson Papers, Bogy to Johnson, September 7, 1867, August W. Alexander to Johnson, September 8, 1867, Barton Able to Johnson, September 10, 1867, James O. Broadhead *et al.* to Johnson, February 13 and March 30, 1868, E. B. Brown to Ed Cooper, March 31, 1868, L. Hutchins to Johnson, April 14, 1868; *Missouri Republican*, February 22, March 14 and 23, 1868; *Missouri Statesman*, March 20 and April 10, 1868.

31. *Missouri Republican*, March 2, 1868; *Missouri State Times*, March 6, 1868; Beath, *Grand Army of the Republic*, 547; Carl Schurz, *The Reminiscences of Carl Schurz*, III, 282-83, 293; *Missouri Democrat*, March 27, 1868.

32. Patrick Papers, McClurg to Patrick, March 28, 1868.

33. DeWitt, *Impeachment and Trial*, 522-29, 552; *Missouri Democrat*, May 13, 1868.

34. Patrick Papers, J. H. Clendening to Patrick, August 26 and December 6, 1867, and February 25, 1868, McClurg to Patrick, February 25, 1868; Darby Papers, C. I. Filley to C. H. Branscomb, January 8, 1868; *Missouri Democrat*, October 16, 1867, and January 9, 1868; *Missouri Statesman*, February 28, 1868.

35. Blair Papers, James S. Rollins to Frank Blair, March 14, 1868; Rollins Papers, Frank Blair to Rollins, March 15, 1868; *Missouri Statesman*, April 3, 1868; *Senate Journal, 24th General Assembly, Adjourned Session*, 324, 379-89, 490; *House Journal, 24th General Assembly, Adjourned Session*, 271, 403, 407, 591, 619-22.

36. *Laws of Missouri, 1868*, 131-41.

37. *Missouri Statesman*, April 10 and 17, 1868.

38. Blair Papers, Rollins to Frank Blair, March 6, April 27, and May 8, 1868.

39. *Ibid.*, William F. Switzler to Frank Blair, March 16, 1868.

40. Smith, *Blair Family*, II, 394-97.

41. *Missouri Statesman*, June 5, 1868; Blair Papers, Frank Blair to Montgomery Blair, May 29, 1868.

42. Schurz, *Reminiscences*, III, 283-84.

43. *Missouri Democrat*, June 3, 1868; Patrick Papers, McClurg to Patrick, May 2, 1868.

44. *Ibid.*, M. Hilton to Patrick, May 26, 1868.

45. *Missouri Democrat*, May 2 and 25, 1868.

46. *Ibid.*, June 29 and July 3, 1868; Patrick Papers, W. E. Peck to Patrick, June 9, 1868.

47. *Ibid., passim,* April–July, 1868.

48. *Missouri Democrat,* July 17, 1868. The labor dispute was resolved a few days later when the engineers agreed to return to work on the railroad's terms.

49. *Ibid.,* July 17, 1868; Patrick Papers, *passim;* Shoemaker, *Missouri and Missourians,* I, 973; *Dispatch,* quoted in Barclay, "The Liberal Republican Movement," 320n.

50. *Missouri Democrat,* July 20, 1868; *Missouri Statesman,* July 24, 1868.

51. *Missouri Democrat,* July 20, 1868.

52. *Missouri Statesman,* August 14, 1868.

53. Broadhead Papers, James S. Rollins to Glover and Broadhead, July 28, 1868.

54. *Ibid.; Missouri Statesman,* August 14, 1868; Shoemaker, *Missouri and Missourians,* I, 641-42.

55. *Missouri Statesman,* August 14, 1868.

56. *Ibid.,* August 28 and September 4, 1868; Napton, "Diary," 444.

57. Smith, *Blair Family,* II, 405-29.

58. *Missouri Democrat,* June 17 and 20, 1868.

59. *Ibid.,* August 18, 1868.

60. Schafer, *Intimate Letters of Carl Schurz,* 441-44.

61. *Missouri Democrat,* August 14, 1868.

62. Bacon Papers, Samuel P. Gaty to Bacon, October 6, 1868.

63. Napton, "Diary," 449-50.

64. *Missouri Statesman,* May 29, 1868; *Missouri Democrat,* July 2 and September 12, 1868; *Missouri Weekly Patriot,* October 8, 1868.

65. *Missouri Statesman,* August 14, 1868.

66. *Missouri Democrat,* August 14, 1868.

67. *Missouri Statesman,* August 28, 1868.

68. *Missouri Democrat,* September 11 and 16, 1868.

69. *Missouri Weekly Patriot,* October 1, 1868; *Warrensburg Weekly Standard,* October 22, 1868.

70. *Missouri Democrat,* September 1, 1868; *Missouri Statesman,* September 18, 1868; Schurz, *Reminiscences,* III, 292-93; Rollins Papers, John B. Henderson to Rollins, December 24, 1868.

71. *Missouri Statesman,* October 2 and 9, 1868. For other accounts, see *Missouri Statesman* and *Missouri Democrat, passim,* September–October, 1868.

72. *Missouri Statesman,* September 4 and October 31, 1868.

73. Rollins Papers, John A. Hockaday to Rollins, December 14, 1868.

74. *Missouri Democrat*, September 4 and October 27, 1868; Rowell, *Contested Election Cases*, 259.

75. *Missouri Republican*, November 2, 1866; *Missouri Statesman*, October 23, 1868; *Missouri Democrat*, October 27 and November 15, 1868.

76. Napton, "Diary," 451-52, 454; Thompson, "Reminiscences," 556; *Weekly Standard*, September 17 and October 8, 1868; *Missouri Democrat*, November 2, 1868.

77. *Weekly Standard*, October 1, 1868; *Missouri Democrat*, October 14 and 26, 1868.

78. *Missouri Statesman*, November 13 and 20, 1868.

79. *Ibid.*, *passim*, November, 1868–February, 1869; Rowell, *Contested Election Cases*, 250-52, 259. In July, 1869, Switzler filed a $2,000 damage suit against Secretary of State Rodman on the ground that Rodman illegally denied him his congressional seat. Three years later the Columbia editor received a judgment of $1,000. Because Rodman had declared bankruptcy and left Missouri by that time, Switzler received only the satisfaction, as he stated it, of receiving a court decision in his favor. *Missouri Statesman*, July 2, 1869, and December 27, 1872.

80. *Missouri Democrat*, December 25, 1868.

81. *Missouri Weekly Patriot*, November 5 and 26, 1868; *Missouri Democrat*, November 17 and December 14, 1868.

82. Schafer, *Intimate Letters of Carl Schurz*, 447-49; Schurz, *Reminiscences*, III, 294-95.

83. *New York Times*, April 24, 1872.

84. *Missouri Democrat*, December 8, 1868; Schafer, *Intimate Letters of Carl Schurz*, 449-56; Schurz, *Reminiscences*, III, 294-95.

85. *Missouri Democrat*, *passim*, December, 1868.

86. *Ibid.*, December 21 and 23, 1868; Schafer, *Intimate Letters of Carl Schurz*, 460-62.

87. Rollins Papers, Henderson to Rollins, December 24, 1868.

88. Elihu B. Washburne Papers, Carl Schurz to Washburne, December 10, 1868. Cf. Schafer, *Intimate Letters of Carl Schurz*, 460-62.

89. Schurz Papers, Elihu B. Washburne to Schurz, December 29, 1868.

90. Schafer, *Intimate Letters of Carl Schurz*, 460-63; Cf. Schurz, *Reminiscences*, III, 294-96.

91. *Missouri Democrat*, January 20 and 25, 1869; Schurz, *Reminiscences*, III, 295-96.

92. *Missouri Weekly Patriot*, January 21, 1869.

93. Schurz Papers, Schurz–Loan exchange, January 7, 1869.

94. *Missouri Democrat*, January 8, 1869; *Missouri Republican*, January 9, 1869.

95. Schafer, *Intimate Letters of Carl Schurz,* 462-63; *Missouri Republican,* January 9, 1869; *Missouri Democrat,* January 11, 1869.
96. *Ibid.,* January 13, 1869; Schurz, *Reminiscences,* III, 297-98.
97. *Missouri Democrat,* January 14 and 18, 1869; Schurz, *Reminiscences,* III, 298-300; Schafer, *Intimate Letters of Carl Schurz,* 464-67.
98. Schurz, *Reminiscences,* III, 300-301; Schafer, *Intimate Letters of Carl Schurz,* 464-67.
99. Patrick Papers, Samuel S. Burdett to Patrick, January 18, 1869.
100. *Missouri Republican,* January 15, 1869; *Missouri Democrat,* January 20, 1869; Rollins Papers, Thomas E. Tutt to Rollins, January 18, 1869; Schafer, *Intimate Letters of Carl Schurz,* 464-67. Schurz's support came from the areas of German rural strength, most of the St. Louis districts, and counties in central Missouri. Loan carried most of the districts in the south and southwest and received almost unanimous backing from those in the northwest and the northern tier of counties. Henderson failed to receive a single vote; he followed Drake in a quick and quiet retreat to Washington.
101. *Missouri Democrat,* January 20 and 21, 1869; Frederic Bancroft, ed., *The Writings of Carl Schurz,* I, 474-80.

CHAPTER XI

1. Patrick Papers, Burdett to Patrick, January 18, 1869.
2. See above, p. 254.
3. St. Louis *Missouri Democrat,* November 27, 1868. Drake reemphasized his position a short time later in another letter to one of his St. Louis followers. *Ibid.,* December 14, 1868.
4. Avery and Shoemaker, *Messages and Proclamations,* IV, 137-44.
5. *Ibid.,* 395-406.
6. Schurz Papers, Schurz to Benjamin F. Loan, January 7, 1869; *Missouri Democrat,* January 8, 1869.
7. *Ibid.,* February 1, 4, 8, and 15, 1869; *Senate Journal, 25th General Assembly, Regular Session,* 75, 95, 112, 173, 185, 284-85; *House Journal, 25th General Assembly, Regular Session,* 145, 148, 162, 199, 209, 211, 274, 363, 393, 406, 484.
8. *Missouri Democrat,* January 28 and 29, February 8 and 13, 1869; *House Journal, 25th General Assembly, Regular Session,* 345-46, 710; *The American Annual Cyclopedia and Register of Important Events of the Year 1869,* 467.
9. *House Journal, 25th General Assembly, Regular Session,* 605-6, 621; *Senate Journal, 25th General Assembly, Regular Session,* 432-

33; St. Louis *Missouri Republican,* March 3, 1869; Columbia *Missouri Statesman,* March 5, 1869.

10. Blair Papers, Frank Blair to Montgomery Blair, February 26, 1869; *Missouri Democrat,* March 22, 1869; *Missouri Statesman,* April 9, 1869.

11. Rollins Papers, Frank Blair to Rollins, April 13, 1869.

12. *Missouri Republican,* June 9, 1869.

13. *Missouri Statesman,* November 19, 1869.

14. Blair Papers, Frank Blair to Montgomery Blair, November 12, 1869.

15. Charles Warren, *The Supreme Court in United States History,* III, 232n.

16. Floyd C. Shoemaker, ed., *Missouri, Day by Day,* II, 163-64.

17. *Congressional Globe,* 39th Cong., 2nd Sess., 76-77; *St. Louis Evening News,* December 19, 1866.

18. *House Journal, 24th General Assembly, Regular Session,* 482, Appendix, 121; *Missouri Republican,* May 19, 1867.

19. *Ibid.; Missouri Democrat,* June 10, 1867.

20. Monia C. Morris, "The History of Woman's Suffrage in Missouri, 1867–1901," *Missouri Historical Review,* XXV, 69; *Missouri Republican,* January 5 and 18, 1869; *Missouri Democrat,* January 18 and 29 and February 1, 1869.

21. *Missouri Republican,* February 4 and 5, 1869; *Missouri Democrat,* February 5, 1869.

22. *Ibid.,* February 6, 8, and 12, 1869.

23. *Ibid.,* February 15 and 24 and May 25, 1869.

24. *Ibid.,* July 9, 1869.

25. *Ibid.,* October 7, 1869; *Missouri Republican,* October 7, 8, and 9, 1869.

26. *Missouri Democrat,* March 1, 1869.

27. *Ibid.,* June 5 and 19, 1869.

28. Jefferson City *Missouri State Times,* July 2 and 16, August 6, 1869.

29. *Ibid.,* July 16, 1869; *Warrensburg Weekly Standard,* July 22, 1869.

30. Avery and Shoemaker, *Messages and Proclamations,* IV, 408-9.

31. *Missouri Democrat,* January 12, 1870.

32. *Missouri Republican,* January 20, 1870; *Missouri Democrat,* January 28, 1870.

33. *Ibid.,* February 2, 1870; *Missouri Statesman,* February 4, 1870.

34. *Missouri Democrat,* February 7 and 26, 1870; Jefferson City *People's Weekly Tribune,* March 2, 1870.

35. *Missouri Democrat*, February 4 and 7, 1870; *Missouri Republican*, February 3 and 23, 1870.

36. *Missouri Democrat*, February 4, 5, and 9, 1870; *Missouri Republican*, March 4, 1870.

37. *Senate Journal, 25th General Assembly, Adjourned Session*, 368, 378-79; *House Journal, 25th General Assembly, Adjourned Session*, 801-2, 817-20; *Laws of Missouri, 1870*, 502-4. Once again the women invaded Jefferson City in an effort to win suffrage rights, but with no more success than in 1869. *Missouri Democrat*, February 8 and 26, 1870.

38. *Ibid.*, February 17, 1870.

39. *Missouri Republican*, February 14, 1870.

40. Pike v. Megoun *et al.* (1869), 44 Mo. 491-500.

41. *Senate Journal, 25th General Assembly, Adjourned Session*, 59, 520; *House Journal, 25th General Assembly, Adjourned Session*, 50-51; *Missouri Statesman*, March 11 and 25, 1870.

42. *Missouri Democrat*, March 9 and 23, 1870; *Missouri Republican*, March 22, 1870.

43. *House Journal, 25th General Assembly, Adjourned Session*, 1078-81; *Senate Journal, 25th General Assembly, Adjourned Session*, 691-92.

44. *Missouri Democrat*, March 25, 1870.

45. *Ibid.*, September 29 and October 27, 1870.

46. Walter B. Stevens, *Centennial History of Missouri (The Center State), One Hundred Years in the Union, 1820–1921*, I, 643.

47. *Missouri Republican*, February 9, 1870; *Peoples' Weekly Tribune*, February 23, 1870.

48. *Missouri Democrat*, February 23, 1870.

49. *Missouri Republican*, March 21, 1870; *Missouri Statesman*, March 25, 1870.

50. *Ibid.*

51. *Sedalia Democrat*, April 14, 1870; *Missouri Republican*, April 16, 1870.

52. *Missouri Democrat*, April 18 and May 10, 1870.

53. *Missouri Statesman*, August 12, 1870.

54. *Ibid.*, August 19, 1870.

55. *Missouri Democrat*, June 1, 1870; *Missouri State Times*, June 3, 1870; Bancroft, *Schurz Writings*, II, 11-12.

56. *Missouri Democrat*, January 17 and 19, 1870; Schurz Papers, Schurz to William M. Grosvenor, November 30, 1869, and December 13, 1870. For typical editorial, see *Missouri Democrat*, June 11, 1870.

57. *Ibid.*, February 9 and 14 and August 5, 1870; Schurz Papers, A. C. George to Schurz, May 28, 1870; *Missouri State Times*, June 17 and 24, 1870.

58. *Missouri Democrat*, March 17, 1870.

59. *Missouri Republican*, March 15, 1870; *Peoples' Weekly Tribune*, March 16, 1870; *Missouri Statesman*, March 25, 1870.

60. *Missouri Democrat*, April 13, 1870.

61. *Ibid.*, February 24, 1869, February 14 and April 13, 1870; Patrick Papers, Burdett to Patrick, January 18, 1869. For McClurg's position on liquor control, see Avery and Shoemaker, *Messages and Proclamations*, IV, 459-60.

62. *Missouri Democrat*, June 1, 2, and 27, 1870. Schurz's St. Louis *Westliche Post* endorsed Brown early in July. Conard, *History of Missouri*, V, 173.

63. *Missouri Democrat*, June 1 and August 3, 1870; Springfield *Missouri Weekly Patriot*, June 2 and 16, 1870; Schurz Papers, George to Schurz, May 28, 1870; *Missouri State Times*, June 24 and August 19, 1870.

64. *Missouri Democrat*, May 13, 1870; *Missouri State Times*, May 27, 1870.

65. *Missouri Democrat*, July 27 and 29 and August 2, 1870.

66. *Ibid.*, July 26 and 30, 1870.

67. *Ibid.*, August 3 and 4, 1870; Bancroft, *Schurz Writings*, II, 13-15. To alleviate the threat of rural domination, each of the twelve counties, with the exception of St. Louis County, that had more than one representative in the House received an additional delegate. For Turner's friendship with Governor McClurg, see *Missouri Democrat*, July 26, 1870.

68. *Ibid.*, August 27, 1870; *Missouri Republican*, August 28, 1870. For a more detailed analysis, see Barclay, "The Liberal Republican Movement," 557-61.

69. *Missouri Republican*, August 28, 1870.

70. *Ibid.*, September 1, 1870; *Missouri Democrat*, September 1, 1870.

71. *Ibid.*, September 2, 1870; *Peoples' Weekly Tribune*, September 7, 1870.

72. Barclay, "The Liberal Republican Movement," *Missouri Historical Review*, XXI, 65.

73. *Peoples' Weekly Tribune*, September 7, 1870; *Missouri Democrat*, September 7, 1870; *New York Times*, April 24, 1872.

74. *Missouri Democrat*, September 3, 1870; Schurz Papers, William M. Grosvenor to Schurz, February 16, 1871; Barclay, "The Liberal Republican Movement," XXI, 72n.

75. The figure eighty used here is based on the difference between the total vote cast for the platform substitute and the total vote cast for the reconciliation resolution later that afternoon in the regular convention.

76. Estimates of the exact size of the Liberal convention vary.

The *Missouri Weekly Patriot,* published by Havens at Springfield, remarked: "The bolters' convention was a slim and gloomy affair, and most of those who participated in it looked very sick over the part they were playing." *Missouri Weekly Patriot,* September 8, 1870. Grosvenor, on the other hand, placed delegate strength at 400 and emphasized the enthusiasm of the group. *Missouri Democrat,* September 6, 1870. The convention probably attracted about 250 delegates, including the original bolters, the bogus delegations, and the Stanard men. Cf. Barclay, "The Liberal Republican Movement," XXI, 72n.

77. Conard, *History of Missouri,* V, 173.

78. *Missouri Democrat,* September 3, 1870; Bancroft, *Schurz Writings,* I, 515.

79. *Missouri Democrat,* September 3, 5, and 6, 1870.

80. *Ibid.,* September 5, 1870.

81. *Ibid.,* September 3, 1870; *Missouri Republican,* September 4, 1870.

CHAPTER XII

1. St. Louis *Missouri Democrat,* September 5, 1870.

2. *Ibid., passim,* September–October, 1870; Bancroft, *Schurz Writings,* I, 510-18; Jefferson City *Missouri State Times,* October 21, 1870.

3. *Missouri Democrat,* September 22 and 30, October 4, and November 1, 1870; St. Louis *Missouri Republican,* September 23, 1870; Bancroft, *Schurz Writings,* II, 37-43. For some strange reason, Governor McClurg did not actively campaign. *Missouri State Times,* October 7 and 14, 1870.

4. *Missouri Democrat,* April 12, 1870; Washington, D. C., *New Era,* June 2 and August 25, 1870.

5. *Ibid.,* April 7, 1870.

6. *Missouri Democrat,* March 14, 1870.

7. *Ibid.,* July 26 and October 14, 1870; *Missouri State Times,* September 30 and October 14, 1870; Bancroft, *Schurz Writings,* II, 14-15.

8. *New National Era,* September 22, 1870.

9. *Missouri Democrat,* July 26, September 7, 10, and 29, and October 14, 1870.

10. William H. Woodson, *History of Clay County, Missouri,* 141-42.

11. *Missouri State Times,* November 11, 1870; *Louisiana Journal,* November 12, 1870.

12. *Missouri Democrat,* September 14 and October 4, 1870.

13. *Missouri Republican* and Columbia *Missouri Statesman, passim,* September, 1870.

14. *Missouri Republican,* September 29, 1870; Blair Papers, Charles Gibson to Montgomery Blair, September 30, 1870; *Missouri Statesman,* September 30, 1870.

15. *Missouri Democrat, passim,* September–October, 1870.

16. *Missouri Republican,* September 24, 1870; *Missouri Statesman,* September 30, 1870.

17. *Missouri Democrat,* September 8 and October 31, 1870; *Missouri Statesman,* November 4, 1870.

18. *Missouri Democrat,* November 5 and 7, 1870. One paper claimed that Turner urged Negro voters to follow this policy. *Missouri State Times,* November 11, 1870.

19. *Missouri Democrat,* September 29, October 9, and November 1, 1870; *Missouri Republican,* October 8 and 12, 1870.

20. *Missouri Democrat,* November 8, 1870.

21. *Ibid.,* October 17, 27, and 30, 1870.

22. *Ibid.,* September 22 and 24 and October 10, 1870; Schurz Papers, S. C. Hall *et al.* to Schurz, October 3, 1870, W. J. Chandler to Schurz, December 13, 1870, H. R. Keeton to Schurz, December 17, 1870, J. Munson to Schurz, December 22, 1870; Blair Papers, Frank Blair to Montgomery Blair, November 17, 1870; Bancroft, *Schurz Writings,* II, 47-50.

23. *St. Joseph Morning Herald,* September 20, 1870; *Missouri Democrat,* September 27, 1870.

24. *Ibid.,* October 28, 1870.

25. *Ibid.,* October 10, 23, and 28, and November 4, 1870.

26. *Missouri Statesman,* November 18, 1870; *Missouri Democrat,* December 14, 1870.

27. *Missouri Statesman,* December 2 and 9, 1870.

28. Springfield *Missouri Weekly Patriot,* November 17, 1870; *Missouri Democrat,* December 14, 1870; *Missouri Republican,* December 18, 1870.

29. *Missouri Statesman,* December 16, 1870.

30. *Ibid.,* December 23, 1870; *Missouri Democrat,* November 12, 1870.

31. Kirksville *North Missouri Register,* December 14, 1870.

32. Schurz Papers, Schurz to Matthew H. Carpenter, October 20, 1870.

33. *Ibid.,* Henry Adams to Schurz, October 28, 1870.

34. Bancroft, *Schurz Writings,* II, 2-70.

35. *Missouri Statesman,* December 2, 1870.

36. *Missouri Democrat,* November 15, 1870.

37. Bancroft, *Schurz Writings,* II, 2; Schurz Papers, B. Gratz Brown to Schurz, November 26, 1870; *Missouri Democrat,* November 30, 1870.

38. Schurz Papers, Keeton to Schurz, December 17, 1870,

Munson to Schurz, December 22, 1870; Dilliard, "James Milton Turner," 381.

39. *Missouri Democrat*, December 8, 1870.

40. Washington, D. C., *Evening Star*, November 10 and 18, 1870; Blair Papers, Frank Blair to Montgomery Blair, November 11, 1870; *Missouri Republican*, November 19, 1870; Ulysses S. Grant Letterbooks, Orville E. Babcock to the Attorney General of the United States, December 12, 1870; Bancroft, *Schurz Writings*, II, 1.

41. *Congressional Globe*, 41st Cong., 3rd Sess., Appendix, 1-8; *Evening Star*, December 16, 1870.

42. Barclay, "The Liberal Republican Movement," XXI, 100.

43. *Missouri Republican, passim*, November–December, 1870; Broadhead Papers, J. W. Henry to Broadhead, November 18, 1870. Governor McClurg appointed Daniel T. Jewett, a partisan Radical, to fill the vacancy in the interim. Schurz Papers, James S. Rollins to Schurz, December 25, 1870.

44. Rollins Papers, Frank Blair to Rollins, December 14, 1870.

45. Blair Papers, Frank Blair to Montgomery Blair, November 17, 1870.

46. *Ibid.*, Frank Blair to Montgomery Blair, November 27, December 2, 11, 17, 22, and 26, 1870; Rollins Papers, Frank Blair to Rollins, December 14, 18, and 28, 1870.

47. *Missouri Democrat*, January 5, 6, and 13, 1871. The caucus vote stood: 52 votes for Blair, 16 for Glover, 13 for Phelps, and 10 for Woodson. *Missouri Republican*, January 13, 1871.

48. *Missouri Democrat*, January 11, 1871; *Missouri Republican*, January 12, 1871.

49. *Missouri Democrat*, January 4 and 17, 1871; *Missouri Republican*, January 14, 15, and 17, 1871; Schurz Papers, Schurz to William M. Grosvenor, January 7, 1871, Robert L. Lindsay to Schurz, January 21, 1871, Grosvenor to Schurz, February 16, 1871, W. E. Gilmore to Schurz, February 28, 1871.

50. *House Journal, 26th General Assembly, Regular Session*, 73; Schurz Papers, Grosvenor to Schurz, February 16, 1871.

51. Smith, *Blair Family*, II, 439-40.

52. Avery and Shoemaker, *Messages and Proclamations*, V, 20-21.

53. *House Journal, 26th General Assembly, Regular Session*, 385-87, 471-72.

54. *Senate Journal, 26th General Assembly, Regular Session*, 347-48, 358, 469-70, 499-502.

55. Avery and Shoemaker, *Messages and Proclamations*. V, 21, 131-32.

56. *House Journal, 26th General Assembly, Regular Session*, 187,

206, 350, 365, 471, 492, 498; *Senate Journal, 26th General Assembly, Regular Session*, 137, 159, 252; *Laws of Missouri, 26th General Assembly, Regular Session, 1871*, 67-73.

57. *Missouri Democrat*, October 26, 1866.

58. W. H. Lewis, *The History of Methodism in Missouri*, III, 378-81.

59. *Ninth Census Compendium*, 516-27.

60. James N. Primm, "The G. A. R. in Missouri, 1866–1870," *Journal of Southern History*, XX, 373-75.

61. William F. Kuhn, *Centennial History of the Grand Lodge, Free and Accepted Ancient Masons of Missouri, 1821–1921* (n. p., n. d.), 122-136. Other branches of York Rite Masonry also existed in Missouri at this time: Grand Chapter of Royal Arch Masons, fifty-four chapters with over 2,000 members; Grand Council of Royal and Select Masters with 377 members; Grand Commandery, Knights Templar, sixteen lodges with 690 members. Shoemaker, *Missouri and Missourians*, I, 1009-10.

62. *Ibid.*, I, 1010; *Missouri Democrat*, March 28 and October 17, 1866.

63. Shoemaker, *Missouri and Missourians*, I, 1010.

64. *Missouri Democrat*, December 11 and 18, 1867, and June 2, 1869.

65. *Missouri Statesman*, June 21, 1867, and May 14, 1869.

66. *Ninth Census Compendium*, 510-11.

67. *Missouri Democrat*, May 25, 1870.

68. *Ibid.*, April 2 and 9, October 5, 12, and 29, 1866; *Chillicothe Spectator*, July 12, 1866; *Richmond Conservator*, August 11, 1866; Shoemaker, *Missouri and Missourians*, I, 1008-9; *History of Marion County, Missouri*, 557-58; *History of St. Charles, Montgomery and Warren Counties, Missouri*, 662-63.

69. *Missouri Democrat*, October 1, 1866; *Missouri Republican*, October 9, 1868; Jefferson City *Peoples' Weekly Tribune*, August 10, 1870.

70. Shoemaker, *Missouri and Missourians*, II, 586.

71. Isidor Loeb, "Constitutions and Constitutional Conventions in Missouri," *Missouri Historical Review*, XVI, 207-24.

72. Shoemaker, *Missouri and Missourians*, II, 18-22.

73. *Ibid.*, II, 45, 48, 67; William E. Parrish, "Jefferson Davis Comes to Missouri," *Missouri Historical Review*, LVII, 344-56.

74. Shoemaker, *Missouri and Missourians*, I, 940-41, 955, 985-90, II, 9, 21.

75. *Missouri Democrat*, January 29, 1866; E. Merton Coulter, *The Civil War and Readjustment in Kentucky*, 257-439.

BIBLIOGRAPHY

I. UNITED STATES PUBLIC DOCUMENTS

Bibliographical Directory of the American Congress, 1774–1961. Washington, 1962.

A Compendium of the Ninth Census (June 1, 1870). Washington, 1872.

Congressional Globe. Thirty-ninth and Forty-first Congresses. Washington, 1866–1867, 1870–1871.

A Historical and Legal Digest of All the Contested Election Cases in the House of Representatives of the United States from the First to the Fifty-sixth Congress, 1789–1901. Edited by Chester H. Rowell, Washington, 1901.

Report of the Commissioner of the General Land Office to the Secretary of the Interior, 1865–1870. Washington, 1865–1872.

The Statistics of the Wealth and Industry of the United States. Vol. III of the Ninth Census. Washington, 1872.

Wallace's Reports of Cases Argued and Determined in the Supreme Court of the United States. Vol. IV. Washington, 1867.

The War of the Rebellion: Official Records of the Union and Confederate Armies. 4 series, 70 vols. Washington, 1880–1902.

II. STATE PUBLIC DOCUMENTS

Constitution of the State of Missouri, 1865. St. Louis, 1865.

Journal of the House of Representatives of the State of Missouri. Twenty-second General Assembly, Adjourned Session, through Twenty-sixth General Assembly, Regular Session. Jefferson City, 1864–1871.

Journal of the Missouri State Convention Held at St. Louis, January 6–April 10, 1865. St. Louis, 1865.

Journal of the Senate of the State of Missouri. Twenty-second General Assembly, Adjourned Session, through Twenty-sixth General Assembly, Regular Session. Jefferson City, 1864–1871.

Laws of the State of Missouri. Twenty-second through Twenty-sixth General Assemblies. Jefferson City, 1863–1872.

The Messages and Proclamations of the Governors of the State of Missouri. Vol. III, edited by Buel Leopard and Floyd C. Shoemaker; Vols. IV and V, edited by Grace G. Avery and Floyd C. Shoemaker. Columbia, 1922, 1924.

Report of the Superintendent of Public Schools of the State of Missouri to the General Assembly, 1865–1875. Jefferson City, 1866–1876.

Reports of Cases Argued and Determined in the Supreme Court of the State of Missouri. Vols. 36-44. St. Louis, 1866–1870.

III. MANUSCRIPTS

Henry D. Bacon Papers. Huntington Library, San Marino, California.

Samuel L. M. Barlow Papers. Huntington Library, San Marino, California.

Gist Blair Papers. Library of Congress.

Blow Family Papers. Missouri Historical Society, St. Louis.

James O. Broadhead Papers. Missouri Historical Society, St. Louis.

Salmon P. Chase Papers. Library of Congress.

Civil War Papers. Missouri Historical Society, St. Louis.

John F. Darby Papers. Missouri Historical Society, St. Louis.

Charles D. Drake, "Autobiography" (manuscript). State Historical Society of Missouri, Columbia.

James B. Eads Papers. Missouri Historical Society, St. Louis.

William G. Eliot Papers. Missouri Historical Society, St. Louis.

Ulysses S. Grant Letterbooks. Library of Congress.

Andrew Johnson Papers. Library of Congress.

Robert Todd Lincoln Collection of the Papers of Abraham Lincoln. Library of Congress.

William B. Napton, "Diary" (manuscript). Missouri Historial Society, St. Louis.

William K. Patrick Papers. Missouri Historical Society, St. Louis.

Records of the Bureau of Refugees, Freedmen and Abandoned Lands, Missouri-Arkansas District. National Archives.

Records of the Department of the Missouri, 1865–1867. National Archives.

James S. Rollins Papers. State Historical Society of Missouri, Columbia.

Carl Schurz Papers. Library of Congress.
William T. Sherman Papers. Library of Congress.
Edwin M. Stanton Papers. Library of Congress.
Robert T. Van Horn Papers. State Historical Society of Missouri, Columbia.
Elihu B. Washburne Papers. Library of Congress.

IV. PUBLISHED COLLECTIONS

The American Annual Cyclopedia and Register of Important Events, 1865–1870. New York, 1866–1871.
Annual Report of the Board of Directors of the St. Louis Public Schools, 1865–1870. St. Louis, 1865–1870.
Bancroft, Frederic, ed., *The Writings of Carl Schurz.* 6 vols. New York, 1913.
Basler, Roy P., ed., *The Collected Works of Abraham Lincoln.* 9 vols. New Brunswick, New Jersey, 1953–1955.
Beale, Howard K., ed., *The Diary of Edward Bates, 1859–1866.* The Annual Report of the American Historical Association for the Year 1930. Vol. IV. Washington, 1933.
Commons, John R., and others, eds., *A Documentary History of American Industrial Society.* 10 vols. Cleveland, 1910.
Diary and Correspondence of Salmon P. Chase. The Annual Report of the American Historical Association for the Year 1902. Vol. II. Washington, 1903.
Drake, Charles D. *Union and Anti-Slavery Speeches Delivered During the Rebellion.* Cincinnati, 1864.
Final Report of the Western Sanitary Commission, May 9, 1864– December 31, 1865. St. Louis, 1866.
Johnson, Allen and Dumas Malone, eds., *Dictionary of American Biography.* 20 vols. New York, 1928–1936.
Pease, Theodore C., and James G. Randall, eds., *The Diary of Orville Hickman Browning.* 2 vols. Springfield, Illinois, 1927, 1933.
Schafer, Joseph, ed., *The Intimate Letters of Carl Schurz, 1841– 1869.* Madison, Wisconsin, 1928.

V. NEWSPAPERS

Evening Star, Washington, D. C., December, 1870. University of Missouri Library, Columbia.
New Era, Washington, D. C., 1870–1871. After September 8, 1870, this paper took the name *New National Era.* Lincoln University Library, Jefferson City.
New York Times, New York City, April 24, 1872. University of Missouri Library, Columbia.

New York Tribune, New York City, July 6, 1871. University of
Missouri Library, Columbia.

The following newspapers, published in Missouri, are in the library
of the State Historical Society of Missouri at Columbia, unless
otherwise noted:

Christian Advocate, St. Louis, 1865–1866.
Conservator, Richmond, 1865–1870.
Daily Journal of Commerce, Kansas City, 1865–1871.
Democrat, Sedalia, 1869–1871.
Dispatch, St. Louis, 1865–1866. Washington University Library,
St. Louis.
Evening News, St. Louis, 1866. Missouri Historical Society, St.
Louis.
Industrial Advocate, St. Louis, August, 1866–February, 1867.
Iron County Register, Ironton, 1867–1870.
Journal, Louisiana, 1870.
Missouri Democrat, St. Louis, 1863–1871.
Missouri Republican, St. Louis, 1863–1871.
Missouri Statesman, Columbia, 1865–1872.
Missouri State Times, Jefferson City, 1865–1870.
Missouri Weekly Patriot, Springfield, 1865–1870.
Morning Herald, St. Joseph, 1865–1870.
North Missouri Register, Kirksville, 1871.
Peoples' Weekly Tribune, Jefferson City, 1866–1871.
Spectator, Chillicothe, 1866–1867.
Spring River Fountain, Mount Vernon, 1868.
Times, Sedalia, 1866–1871.
Weekly Standard, Warrensburg, 1867–1871.

VI. UNPUBLISHED THESES AND DISSERTATIONS

Brigham, Robert I., "The Education of the Negro in Missouri."
Doctoral dissertation, University of Missouri, Columbia, 1946.
Douglas, Esque, "The History of the Negro in Northeast Missouri,
1820–1870." Master's thesis, Lincoln University, Jefferson
City, 1950.
Fitzsimmons, Margaret L., "Railroad Development in Missouri."
Master's thesis, Washington University, St. Louis, 1931.
Hall, Elizabeth D., "William F. Switzler." Master's thesis, Univer-
sity of Missouri, Columbia, 1951.
Houf, Walter R., "Fifty Years of Missouri Labor, 1820–1870."
Master's thesis, University of Missouri, Columbia, 1958.
Kidd, Florence, "Efforts to Encourage Immigration to Missouri
After the Civil War." Master's thesis, University of Missouri,
Columbia, 1933.

March, David D., "The Life and Times of Charles Daniel Drake."
Doctoral dissertation, University of Missouri, Columbia, 1949.

Nowells, Ida M., "A Study of the Radical Party Movement in
Missouri, 1860–1870." Master's thesis, University of Missouri,
Columbia, 1939.

Redfield, Maynard G., "Some Social and Intellectual Influences in
the Development of Public Education in Missouri, 1865 to
1900." Doctoral dissertation, Washington University, St. Louis,
1956.

VII. ARTICLES

"Another Warning." *Journal of Education* (St. Louis), II (September, 1869), 7.

B., J. H., "Importance of Aids to Illustration in Schools." *Journal
of Education,* I (March, 1869), 109-11.

Barclay, Thomas S., "The Liberal Republican Movement in Missouri." *Missouri Historical Review,* XX (October, 1925), 3-78;
(January, 1926), 262-332; (April, 1926), 406-37; (July,
1926), 515-64; XXI (October, 1926), 59-108.

———, "The Test Oath for the Clergy in Missouri." *Missouri Historical Review,* XVIII (April, 1924), 345-81.

Bradley, Harold C., "In Defense of John Cummings." *Missouri Historical Review,* LVII (October, 1962), 1-15.

"Colored Schools." *Journal of Education,* II (September, 1869), 5.

"County Superintendents." *Journal of Education,* I (October, 1868), 25-26.

Cozzens, Arthur B., "The Iron Industry of Missouri." *Missouri Historical Review,* XXXV (July, 1941), 509-38.

Crittenden, Huston, "The Warrensburg Speech of Frank P Blair."
Missouri Historical Review, XX (October, 1925), 101-4.

Crockett, Norman L., "A Study of Confusion: Missouri's Immigration Program, 1865–1916." *Missouri Historical Review,* LVII
(April, 1963), 248-60.

Dilliard, Irving, "James Milton Turner: A Little Known Benefactor
of His People." *Journal of Negro History,* XIX (October, 1934),
372-411.

Fitzsimmons, Margaret L., "Missouri Railroads During the Civil
War and Reconstruction." *Missouri Historical Review,* XXXV
(January, 1941), 188-206.

Fletcher, Ralph and Mildred, "Some Data on Occupations Among
Negroes in St. Louis from 1866 to 1897." *Journal of Negro
History,* XX (July, 1935), 338-41

Garnsey, George O., "School Architecture." *Journal of Education,*
I (June, 1869), 165.

Gates, Paul W., "The Railroads of Missouri, 1850–1870." *Missouri
Historical Review,* XXVI (January, 1932), 126-41.

Gibson, Arrell M., "Lead Mining in Southwest Missouri After 1865." *Missouri Historical Review*, LIII (July, 1959), 315-28.

"The Government of Children." *Journal of Education*, I (November, 1868), 35.

Harris, William T., "What Shall We Study?" *Journal of Education*, II, (September, 1869), 1-3.

Jones, John J., "The Morrill Lands of the University of Missouri." *Missouri Historical Review*, LI (January, 1957), 126-38.

Lange, Dela, "A Century of Achievement in the St. Louis Public High Schools, 1853–1953." *St. Louis Public School Journal*, VI (February, 1953), 3-129.

———, "Information Concerning One Hundred Years of Progress in the St. Louis Public Schools." *Public School Messenger*, XXXV (January 3, 1938), 3-86.

Lehmann, Frederick W., "Edward Bates and the Test Oath." *Missouri Historical Society Collections*, IV (1923), 389-401.

Loeb, Isidor, "Constitutions and Constitutional Conventions in Missouri." *Missouri Historical Review*, XVI (January, 1922), 189-246.

March, David D., "Charles D. Drake and the Constitutional Convention of 1865." *Missouri Historical Review*, XLVII (January, 1953), 110-23.

———, "The Campaign for the Ratification of the Constitution of 1865." *Missouri Historical Review*, XLVII (April, 1953), 223-32.

McDougall, H. C., "A Decade of Missouri Politics—1860 to 1870—from a Republican Viewpoint." *Missouri Historical Review*, III (January, 1909), 126-53.

Mering, John V., "The Political Transition of James S. Rollins." *Missouri Historical Review*, LIII (April, 1959), 217-26.

Morris, Monia C., "Teacher Training in Missouri Before 1871." *Missouri Historical Review*, XLIII (October, 1948), 18-37.

———, "The History of Woman's Suffrage in Missouri, 1867–1901." *Missouri Historical Review*, XXV (October, 1930), 67-82.

Nolen, Russell M., "The Labor Movement in St. Louis, 1860–1890." *Missouri Historical Review*, XXXIV (January, 1940), 157-81.

Norton, "Kansas City Public Schools." *Journal of Education*, I (October, 1868), 21.

Olcott, J. M., "The Teachers' Institute." *Journal of Education*, III (March, 1871), 6.

Parrish, William E., "Jefferson Davis Comes to Missouri." *Missouri Historical Review*, LVII (July, 1963), 344-56.

———, "Moses Lewis Linton, 'Doctor of Epigrams'." *Missouri Historical Review*, LIX (April, 1965), 293-301.

Peterson, Norma L., "The Political Fluctuations of B. Gratz Brown, 1850–1870." *Missouri Historical Review*, LI (October, 1956), 22-30.

Primm, James N., "The G. A. R. in Missouri, 1866–1870." *Journal of Southern History*, XX (August, 1954), 356-75.

"Public Lectures." *Journal of Education*, I (December, 1868), 60.

"The Public School Polytechnic Building of St. Louis." *Journal of Education*, I (May, 1869), 154-55.

"The Public Schools and the Polytechnic Institute." *Journal of Education*, I (October, 1868), 24-25.

Q., O. P., "What Ought to Be Done." *Journal of Education*, II (November, 1869), 45.

Riegel, Robert E., "The Missouri Pacific Railroad to 1879." *Missouri Historical Review*, XVIII (October, 1923), 3-26.

"St. Joseph Public Schools." *Journal of Education*, I (April, 1869), 131-32.

"St. Louis High School." *Journal of Education*, I (January, 1869), 75.

Savage, W. Sherman, "The Legal Provisions for Negro Schools in Missouri from 1865 to 1890." *Journal of Negro History*, XVI (July, 1931), 309-21.

"School Houses and School Furniture." *Journal of Education*, I (December, 1868), 56.

"School Visiting." *Journal of Education*, III (April, 1871), 6-7.

Simmons, Lucy, and Paul O. Selby, "The Northeast Missouri State Teachers College and Its Founder, Joseph Baldwin." *Missouri Historical Review*, XXII (January, 1928), 157-70.

Skinker, Thomas K., "The Removal of the Judges of the Supreme Court of Missouri in 1865." *Missouri Historical Society Collections*, IV (1914), 243-74.

Smith, George W., "New England Business Interests in Missouri During the Civil War." *Missouri Historical Review*, XLI (October, 1946), 1-18.

Switzler, William F., "Constitutional Conventions of Missouri, 1865–1875." *Missouri Historical Review*, I (January, 1907), 109-20.

Thomas, Raymond D., "A Study in Missouri Politics, 1840–1870." *Missouri Historical Review*, XXI (July, 1927), 570-80.

Thompson, Cyrus, "Reminiscences of Official Life in Jefferson City, 1865–1875." *Missouri Historical Review*, XXIII (July, 1929), 550-67.

Williams, Henry S., "The Development of the Negro Public School System in Missouri." *Journal of Negro History*, V (April, 1920), 137-65.

VIII. BOOKS

Anderson, Galusha, *A Border City During the Civil War*. Boston, 1908.

Bay, William V. N., *Reminiscences of the Bench and Bar of Missouri*. St. Louis, 1878.

Beath, Robert B., *History of the Grand Army of the Republic*. New York, 1889.

Belcher, Wyatt W., *The Economic Rivalry Between St. Louis and Chicago, 1850–1880*. New York, 1947.

Bentley, George R., *A History of the Freedmen's Bureau*. Philadelphia, 1955.

Brown, A. Theodore, *Frontier Community: Kansas City to 1870*. Columbia, 1964.

Bruce, Henry C., *The New Man: 29 Years a Slave*. York, Pennsylvania, 1895.

Cockrell, Ewing, *History of Johnson County, Missouri*. Topeka, 1918.

Commons, John R., and others, *History of Labour in the United States*. 2 vols. New York, 1918.

Conard, Howard L., ed., *Encyclopedia of the History of Missouri*. 6 vols. New York, 1901.

Coulter, E. Merton, *The Civil War and Readjustment in Kentucky*. Chapel Hill, North Carolina, 1926.

DeWitt, David M., *The Impeachment and Trial of Andrew Johnson, Seventeenth President of the United States*. New York, 1903.

Donald, Henderson H., *The Negro Freedman: Life Conditions of the American Negro in the Early Years after Emancipation*. New York, 1952.

Douglass, Robert S., *History of Missouri Baptists*. Kansas City, 1934.

Duncan, Robert S., *A History of the Baptists in Missouri*. St. Louis, 1882.

Dyer, David P., *Autobiography and Reminiscences*. St. Louis, 1922.

Eliot, Charlotte C., *William Greenleaf Eliot: Minister, Educator, Philanthropist*. Boston, 1904.

Elwang, William W., *The Negroes of Columbia, Missouri*. Columbia, 1904.

Fleming, Walter L., *The Freedmen's Savings Bank*. Chapel Hill, North Carolina, 1927.

Forman, J. G., *The Western Sanitary Commission: A Sketch*. St. Louis, 1864.

General History of Macon County, Missouri. Chicago, 1910.

Glaab, Charles N., *Kansas City and the Railroads: Community*

Policy in the Growth of a Regional Metropolis. Madison, Wisconsin, 1962.

History of Boone County, Missouri. St. Louis, 1882.

History of Buchanan County, Missouri. St. Joseph, 1881.

History of Greene County, Missouri. St. Louis, 1883.

History of Johnson County, Missouri. Kansas City, 1881.

History of Marion County, Missouri. St. Louis, 1884.

History of St. Charles, Montgomery and Warren Counties, Missouri. St. Louis, 1885.

Hume, John F., *The Abolitionists.* New York, 1905.

Hyde, William, and Howard L. Conard, eds., *Encyclopedia of the History of St. Louis.* 4 vols. New York, 1899.

Hyman, Harold, *The Era of the Oath: Northern Loyalty Tests During the Civil War and Reconstruction.* Philadelphia, 1954.

Johnson, Charles P., *Personal Recollections of Some of Missouri's Eminent Statesmen and Lawyers.* Columbia, 1903.

King, Willard L., *Lincoln's Manager: David Davis.* Cambridge, Massachusetts, 1960.

Kirschten, Ernest, *Catfish and Crystal.* New York, 1960.

Kuhn, William F., *Centennial History of the Grand Lodge, Free and Accepted Ancient Masons of Missouri, 1821–1921.* n. p., n. d.

Leftwich, William M., *Martyrdom in Missouri.* 2 vols. St. Louis, 1870.

Leidecker, Kurt F., *Yankee Teacher: The Life of William Torrey Harris.* New York, 1946.

Lewis, W. H., *The History of Methodism in Missouri.* 3 vols. Nashville, 1890.

Lopata, Edwin L., *Local Aid to Railroads in Missouri.* New York, 1937.

Miller, George, *Missouri's Memorable Decade, 1860–1870: An Historical Sketch, Personal-Political-Religious.* Columbia, 1898.

Million, John W., *State Aid to Railways in Missouri.* Chicago, 1896.

Nevins, Allan, *Frémont, Pathmarker of the West.* New York, 1955.

Nicolay, John G., and John Hay, *Abraham Lincoln, A History.* 10 vols. New York, 1890.

O'Shea, John J., *The Two Kenricks.* Philadelphia, 1904.

Overton, Richard C., *Burlington West: A Colonization History of the Burlington Railroad.* Cambridge, Massachusetts, 1941.

Park, Eleanora G., and Kate S. Morrow, *Women of the Mansion: Missouri, 1821–1836.* Jefferson City, 1936.

Parrish, William E., *Turbulent Partnership: Missouri and the Union, 1861–1865.* Columbia, 1963.

Peck, John M., *Forty Years of Pioneer Life.* Philadelphia, 1864.

Peirce, Paul S., *The Freedmen's Bureau: A Chapter in the History of Reconstruction.* Iowa City, 1904.

Peterson, Norma L., *Freedom and Franchise: The Political Career of B. Gratz Brown.* Columbia, 1965.

Phillips, Claude A., *A History of Education in Missouri.* Jefferson City, 1911.

Randall, James G., and David Donald, *The Civil War and Reconstruction.* 2nd ed. Boston, 1961.

Reavis, Logan U., *St. Louis: The Future Great City.* St. Louis, 1875.

A Reminiscent History of the Ozark Region. Chicago, 1894.

Riegel, Robert E., *The Story of the Western Railroads.* New York, 1926.

Savage, W. Sherman, *The History of Lincoln University.* Jefferson City, 1939.

Scharf, John T., *History of St. Louis City and County.* 2 vols. Philadelphia, 1883.

Schurz, Carl, *Reminiscences of Carl Schurz.* 3 vols. New York, 1908.

Shoemaker, Floyd C., *Missouri and Missourians: Land of Contrasts and People of Achievements.* 5 vols. Chicago, 1943.

―――, ed., *Missouri, Day by Day.* 2 vols. Columbia, 1942–1943.

Smith, William B., *James Sidney Rollins: A Memoir.* New York, 1891.

Smith, William E., *The Francis Preston Blair Family in Politics.* 2 vols. New York, 1933.

Stephens, Frank F., *A History of the University of Missouri.* Columbia, 1962.

Stevens, Walter B., *Centennial History of Missouri (The Center State), One Hundred Years in the Union, 1820–1921.* 3 vols. St. Louis, 1921.

Taylor, George R., and Irene D. Neu. *The American Railroad Network, 1861–1890.* Cambridge, Massachusetts, 1956.

Viles, Jonas, *The University of Missouri, A Centennial History.* Columbia, 1939.

Violette, Eugene M., *History of the First District State Normal School.* Kirksville, 1905.

Warren, Charles, *The Supreme Court in United States History.* 3 vols. Boston, 1922.

Waterhouse, Sylvester, *The Resources of Missouri.* St. Louis, 1867.

Wesley, Charles H., *Negro Labor in the United States, 1850–1925.* New York, 1927.

Whitney, Carrie W., *Kansas City, Missouri: Its History and Its People.* 3 vols. Chicago, 1908.

Williams, Walter, and Floyd C. Shoemaker. *Missouri, Mother of the West.* 5 vols. Chicago, 1930.

Woodson, William H., *History of Clay County, Missouri.* Topeka, 1920.

Woodward, Calvin M., *A History of the St. Louis Bridge.* St. Louis, 1881.

INDEX

375

378   MISSOURI UNDER RADICAL RULE

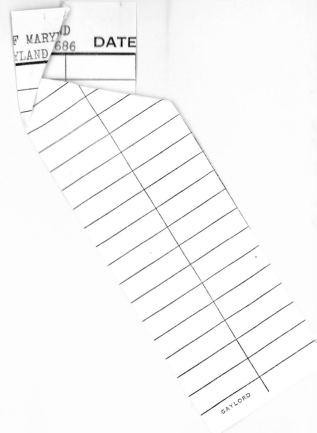

GAYLORD